Brigitta Benzing, Bernd Herrmann (Eds.)

Exploitation and Overexploitation in Societies Past and Present

IUAES-SERIES

edited for the

International Union
of Anthropological and Ethnological Sciences

by

Brunetto Chiarelli (Florence)
and Peter J. M. Nas (Leiden)

vol. 1

LIT

Brigitta Benzing, Bernd Herrmann (Eds.)

Exploitation and Overexploitation in Societies Past and Present

IUAES-Intercongress 2001 Goettingen

LIT

Bibliographic information published by Die Deutsche Bibliothek
Die Deutsche Bibliothek lists this publication in the Deutsche Nationalbibliografie; detailed bibliographic data are available in the Internet at http://dnb.ddb.de.

ISBN 3-8258-5654-2

Grevener Str./Fresnostr. 2 48159 Münster
Tel. 0251-23 50 91 Fax 0251-23 19 72
e-Mail: lit@lit-verlag.de http://www.lit-verlag.de

Distributed in North America by:

Transaction Publishers
New Brunswick (U.S.A.) and London (U.K.)

Transaction Publishers
Rutgers University
35 Berrue Circle
Piscataway, NJ 08854

Tel.: (732) 445 - 2280
Fax: (732) 445 - 3138
for orders (U. S. only):
toll free (888) 999 - 6778

Content

Introduction

Exploitation and Overexploitation in Societies Past and Present

This volume makes available to the reader Proceedings of the Intercongress of the International Union of Anthropological and Ethnological Sciences (IUAES) held in Goettingen (Germany) from July 18th to 21st, 2001.

The Intercongress which took place in Goettingen was in line with the Intercongress in Beijing in 2000 and Tokyo in 2002 – all three were meant to pave the way for the next IUAES World Conference in Florence (Italy) from July 5th to 12th, 2003

Humankind / Nature Interaction: Past, Present and Future

by centering attention on differing, but closely related topics. It is worth mentioning that an Intercongress was held for the first time in a German University town since the IUAES's founding in 1948. More than 100 full participants representing 20 nations were present, and a fluctuating attendance of scholars and students enlarged the audience of presentations related to their own specific fields of interest.

The topic "Exploitation and Overexploitation in Societies Past and Present" has been chosen as it covers a subject intensely discussed in the scientific communities of anthropology, ethnology, environmental history, archaeology, historical geography and related fields. Questions of resource economics and evaluation of the human impact on natural systems gain more and more importance in scientific and public discourse. The Goettingen Precongress aimed at bringing together researchers of the relevant, but often too distant, fields.

Consequences of human activities on landscape as well as on societal structures and activities can be conceptualized in terms of socially governed ecological systems. In the past the adaptive capacity of human cultural systems has been emphasized. Nowadays, a shift towards modified views can be recognized. Resources are discussed as prerequisites for establishing complex human societies. This implies a stronger biology based approach from the point of view of the humanities. In such a view, human societal complexes can be understood as systems that manage energy and matter. The concept of socio-metabolic regimes has developed in such a context. Cultures, as seen within this paradigm, are not merely autopoietic symbolic entities but results of an interaction of material prerequisites and emerging social structures. One might dismiss this epistemological shift as part of the play of science with itself. However, in terms of evolutionary theory, the question remains unsolved so far if, as an example, the ultimate goal of evolution is reproductive success or accessibility to and optimizing of energy and matter managing systems.

These proceedings conceptualize aspects of man's impact on earth, trying to bring together insights from a retrospection, digging deep into the prehistory of mankind, with a critical assessment of ecological changes induced by socio-economic factors historically retraceable. How far can man's impact on earth go without endangering sustainability in a given local surrounding or in global perspective? What can be learnt from societies in an "harmonious" adaptation to nature, and from the fact that the destruction of nature and marginalization of indigenous peoples – though not a new phenomenon – is progressing at accelerated speed?

The scope of the 31 contributions to the topic presented in this volume is wide-ranging. It goes beyond the still valid questions of how human groups used forests, pastures, arable soils, lakes and seas for their energy-transformations and survival, on the one side, and related methodological questions in the various fields of research, on the other. Urbanization and industrialization being irreversible evolutionary steps, population growth seeming hardly possible to stem, the concepts of space and time gain importance as aspects of man's use and overuse of nature, in small-scale as well as large-scale perspective. In the same way as we dig in the remnants of our past, including waste as a byproduct of use and overuse, the remnants of present urban and industrialized societies will reveal to future generations much about complex forms of impact on earth, but also about the weaknesses of industrial man to handle his basis for survival in a responsible way. Can we attempt to change some value judgements on nature and its use prevalent since early capitalism?

What do we learn from the exemplary studies? It becomes increasingly evident that man-nature-relationships, which are strongly expressed in exploitation strategies, are turning into the most decisive issue for our new century. The proceedings focus on urgent questions of this development and add much-needed aspects to the discourse on Global Change. We ought to refurnish the changing world with social subjects, their reasoning, their suffering and their culturally and biologically driven ability for coping with the challenges of survival.

The editors
and Scientific Organizers of the Intercongress 2001
Brigitta Benzing
Bernd Herrmann

Sponsors

Deutsche Forschungsgemeinschaft (DFG)

IWF Knowledge and Media Göttingen

The State of Lower Saxony

The Environment Foundation of Lower Saxony

University of Göttingen

Gothaer Versicherung

HUNESCO

Kleinwanzlebener Saatzucht

Perkin-Elmer-Applied Biosystems

Breuninger-Stiftung

Acknowledgements

The editors are expressing their gratitude to the Intercongress-participants who made available their presentations for publication without royalty.

They express their thanks for the patronage of the Minister of Science and Culture of the State of Lower Saxony and the sponsors of the IUAES Intercongress in Goettingen, 2001, whose list is given on the opposite page. The project management was in the hands of the "IWF Knowledge and Media"; Thanks go to Dr. Beate Engelbrecht and Dr. Rolf Husmann, Social Anthropologists in this internationally well-known Multi-Media Scientific Research and Documention-Center in Goettingen. Behind the curtain there, many helping other hands were at work.

A great deal of support came from the two University-Institutes at Goettingen involved in the project: The Institute of Historical Anthropology and the Institute of Ethnology, which both offered their facilities in the preparation and realization of the congress and the editing of the Proceedings. In many cases, much editorial work was needed, without, however, interfering in content and meaning. We also have to express our thanks to so many helpers from the above mentioned Institutes who stood, from morning till evening, behind the copy-machines, coffee-machines and computers to facilitate the scientific communication during the congress! Special thanks go to Mr. Holger Jendral, M. A., Institute of Ethnology, Goettingen University, without who's assistance this volume would not have been published in due course. He was of invaluable help in so many ways in the phase of editing and in the layout work. Thanks also go to Mr. Markus Libiseller, M. A., who assisted in the layouting of the Proceedings, – not an easy task, because of the originally different formats of graphs, maps and diagrams sent by the authors.

Brigitta Benzing
Bernd Herrmann

1. Man's Impact on Earth

Andrew S. Goudie

Global Perspective on the History of Landscape Transformation

Abstract

The history of landscape transformation by human activities over the last 3 million years is difficult to establish. It is possible, however, that prehistoric humans were far from impotent and that early use of fire and faunal overkill may have had significant impacts. In the early to mid-Holocene, deforestation, mining and smelting, domestication, ploughing and irrigation began to have impacts that may have been even greater. In the modern era, growth of human numbers, increasing use of energy, movement into new environments, higher rates of consumption of materials and new technologies have led a further crescendo of potential change, including that at a global scale. However, attributing particular landscape changes to human actions is far from simple and, for example, the role of humans in the denudation of the Mediterranean lands may have been exaggerated. Likewise studies of gully incision in Swaziland, Madagascar and the United States have demonstrated the high level of debate that there is relating to causation. Frequently we do not know the causes of non-geomorphological changes (e.g. Pleistocene extinctions, the Elm Decline, vegetation change in Australia in aboriginal times, highland podsolization and peat bog development in Europe) and therefore it is difficult to attribute the subsequent possible geomorphological responses to human actions.

Introduction

In the history of land transformation there are a series of major driving forces that determine the level of impact at a particular time. These include population growth, the concentration of population in settlements, the diffusion of population across the globe, technological developments (from the use of fire to genetic modification), the harnessing of sources of energy, and the level of resource consumption. These developments have been discussed by Simmons (1989; 1993), Meyer (1996), Goudie (1999) and McNeill (2000). In a general sense all these driving factors have become of increasing power through time, though environmental degradation does not inevitably develop with, for example, population growth and concentration (Tiffen *et al.* 1994), and using the simple formula, I = PAT, the human impact (I) is *not* a simple response to population (P), affluence (A) and technology (T). That said, we can see the history of land transformation as consisting of three main phases, which are listed in *Table 1 (see p. 13)*. Some of the major technological developments are listed in a time sequence in *Table 2 (see p. 13)*.

Prehistoric impotence?

Although modern humans have caused immense changes to the landscape, we need to ask whether prehistoric societies were impotent or important in landscape modification. It is difficult to know, and there will have been great differences between different groups in different environments and at different times. As recent studies in Australia have shown, there remains a great deal of controversy as to the impacts of aboriginal people (Kohen, 1995). Nevertheless, even in the Pleistocene, when human population levels would have been very low, one can argue that the use of fire and the hunting of mega-fauna may have had far from trivial effects. In the Holocene, major vegetation change was achieved in the Mesolithic and Neolithic, and domestication of plants and animals, the invention of the plough and the wheel, the harnessing of animal power, the adoption of irrigation and the exploitation of metals, may all have caused major change in some locations by 5 000 years ago.

One way in which prehistoric groups could have had an early effect on soil erosion (and stabilisation) is through their effect on populations of large mammals. There is considerable debate as to whether climate or humans caused spasms of mega-faunal extinctions, but in many parts of the world there is reasonably compelling evidence that early hunters caused overkill in late Pleistocene and Holocene times. By analogy with the role of large elephant populations in savanna ecosystems today it is reasonable to assume that large herds of prehistoric mega-fauna could cause extensive damage to soils by trampling and wallowing and would have opened up vegetation associations by grazing, browsing and barging. An average 1700 kg adult elephant consumes around 100 kg of biomass per day. A clan of 500 of these beasts would thus consume 50, 000 kg of biomass a day. At an annual primary production rate of 1000 kg per ha, this is equivalent to a clearance of 50 ha per day. Thus, anthropogenic mega-faunal extinction could have reduced pressures on the soil.

One of the foremost ways in which prehistoric groups could have caused land transformation is through the use of fire. We do not know precisely when humans first used fire deliberately, but it may have been as much as 1.4 million years ago. There were many reasons why fire may have been used, including defence, the need for warmth, the breaking up of stone for tool manufacture, encouragement of new shoots to attract game, game driving and many others. As Schule (1990: 289) has remarked:

"The ecological advantages of fire were immense for early man, but so was the damage to ecosystems. To give an idea of the ecological effects of man-made fires, one has to imagine a population of children or chimpanzees playing with matches in an African savanna at the end of a dry season. I think I can see everyone burning pale."

Certainly, burnt ground can be subject to accelerated soil erosion because of a variety of factors:

loss of plant cover;

loss of surface litter;

loss of organic matter in the soil;

loss of soil burrowing fauna;

movement of a water repellent layer.

There are many modern studies of the effects of fire on runoff, sediment yield and debris flow production (see Goldammer, 1990) but we have little information on how often fires were caused by prehistoric groups and uncertainties surround the dating of the institution of human fire regimes (McGlone and Wilmshurst, 1999). It is also difficult to differentiate the effects of natural fires from anthropogenic ones. Nevertheless, periods of different fire regimes as societies have evolved have had marked effects on vegetation type and the nature of sedimentation (Hope, 1999).

Man or nature?

Ever since classical times there has been concern about the role of humans in degrading environments around the Mediterranean basin, and this was something that had a great impact on the thinking of George Perkins Marsh (1864). However, in recent years some caution has been expressed as to the extent to which humans have been responsible for landscape degradation in this region. Rackham and Moody (1996: 9) have paraphrased the traditional view thus:

"The persistent theory in Mediterranean studies is that of the Ruined Landscape or Lost Eden, which runs like this. Well into historic times, the land was covered with magnificent forests. Men cut down the forests to make homes and ships, or burned them to make farmland; the trees failed to grow again, and multitudes of goats devoured the remains. Trees, unlike other vegetation, have a magic power of retaining soil. The trees gone, the soil washed away into the sea or the plains, the land became 'barren', and some say that the very climate got worse".

They then go on to question it:

"Scholars play up the landscape of the past and play down the landscape of the present: they write about ancient forests when the original text mentioned only trees; they ignore modern for-

ests or dismiss them as mere 'scrub' or 'maquis'." (ibid.: 10)
This is a view that has been developed by Roberts (1998: 191):
"...it would be wrong to assume that all Mediterranean hills are anthropogenic landscapes. A salutary lesson in this comes from the badlands of southeast Spain. Here integrated geoarchaeological studies have found in situ Bronze Age sites lying uneroded on vulnerable bare slopes. The badlands had already formed by *c.* 4500 years ago, and later agricultural clearances have done little to alter erosion rates. While giving the appearance of recent degradation, these and similar Mediterranean badlands... are ancient landscapes created by long-term geological instability rather than the ravages of the goat and the plough."

In the southwestern United States many valleys and plains became incised with gullies (arroyos) over a short period between 1865 and 1915, with the 1880s being especially important (Cooke and Reeves, 1976). This cutting had a rapid and detrimental effect on the flat, fertile and easily irrigated valley floors.

The causes of phases of incision has created a long history of debate (Bull, 1997; Elliott *et al.* 1999). Many students of this phenomenon have believed that thoughtless human actions caused the entrenchment, and the apparent coincidence of white settlement and arroyo development tended to give credence to this viewpoint. The range of actions that could have been culpable is large: timber-felling, overgrazing, cutting grass for hay in valley bottoms, compaction along well-travelled routes, channelling for runoff from trails and railways, disruption of valley-bottom sods by animals' feet, and the invasion of grasslands by miscellaneous types of scrub.

On the other hand, study of the long-term history of the valley fills shows that there have been repeated phases of aggradation and incision and that some of these took place before the influence of humans could have been a significant factor. This has prompted a debate as to whether the arrival of white communities was in fact responsible for this particularly severe phase of environmental degradation. Huntington (1914), for example, argued that valley filling would be a consequence of a climatic shift to more arid conditions. These, he believed, would cause a reduction in vegetation which in turn would promote rapid removal of soil from slopes during storms, and overload streams with sediment. With a return to humid conditions, vegetation would be reestablished, sediment yields would be reduced and entrenchment of valley fills would take place. Bryan (1928) put forward a contradictory climatic explanation. He argued that a move towards drier conditions, by depleting vegetation cover and reducing soil infiltration capacity, would produce increases in storm runoff which would erode valleys. Another climatic interpretation was advanced by Leopold (1951), involving a change in rainfall intensity rather than quantity. He indicated that a reduced frequency of low-intensity rains would weaken the vegetation cover, while an increased frequency of heavy rains at the same time would increase the incidence of erosion. More recent support for this contention comes from the work of Balling and Wells

(1990). They attributed early twentieth-century arroyo trenching to a run of years with intense and erosive rainfall characteristics that succeeded a phase of drought conditions in which the productive ability of the vegetation had declined. Certainly, in recent years there has been an increasing appreciation of the scale and frequency of climatic changes in the Holocene (McFadden and McAuliffe, 1997). For example, Waters and Haynes (2001) have argued that arroyos first appeared in the American southwest after c 8000 years ago, and that a dramatic increase in cutting and filling episodes occurred after c 4000 years ago. They believe that this intensification could be related to a change in the frequency and strength of El Niño events. It is also possible, as Schumm *et al.* (1984) have pointed out, that arroyo incision could result from neither climatic change nor human influence, but from the crossing of some natural geomorphic threshold. Under this argument, conditions of valley-floor stability decrease slowly over time until some triggering event initiates incision of the previously 'stable' reach *(see Table 3, p. 14).*

It is clear that the mechanisms that can lead to alternations of cut-and-fill of valley sediments are complex, and that any attribution of all arroyos in all areas to human activities may be a serious oversimplification. In addition, it is possible that natural environmental change, such as changes in rainfall, have operated at the same time and in the same direction as human actions.

In the Mediterranean lands there have also bee controversies surrounding the age and causes of alternating phases of aggradation and erosion. Vita-Finzi (1969) suggested that at some stage during historical times many of the streams in the area, which had hitherto been engaged primarily in down-cutting, began to build up their beds. Renewed down-cutting, still seemingly in operation today, has since incised the channels into the alluvial fill. He proposed that the reversal of the down-cutting trend in the Middle Ages was both ubiquitous and confined in time, and that some universal and time-specific agency was required to explain it. He believed that devegetation by humans was not a medieval innovation and that some other mechanism was required. A solution he gave to account for the phenomenon was precipitation change during the Little Ice Age (AD 1550-1850). This was not, however, an interpretation which found favour with Butzer (1974). He reported that his investigations showed plenty of post-classical and pre-1500 alluviation (which could not therefore be ascribed to the Little Ice Age), and he doubted whether Vita-Finzi's dating was precise enough to warrant a 1550-1850 date. Instead, he suggested that humans were responsible for multiple phases of accelerated erosion from slopes, and accelerated sedimentation in valley bottoms, from as early as the middle of the first millennium BC.

Butzer's interpretation has found favour with van Andel *et al.* (1990), who have detected an intermittent and complex record of cut and fill episodes during the late Holocene in various parts of Greece. They believe that this evidence is compatible with a model of the control of timing and intensity of landscape destabilization by local economic and political conditions.

A further location with spectacular gullies, locally called *lavaka*, is Madagascar. Here too there have been great debates about cultural versus natural causation. Proponents of cultural causes have argued that since humans arrived on the island in the last two thousand years, there has been excessive cattle grazing, removal of forest for charcoal and for slash-and-burn cultivation, devastating winter (dry season) burning of grasslands and erosion along tracks and trails. However, the situation is more complex than that and the *lavaka* are polygenetic. Tectonism and natural climatic aridification may be at least as important as human agency, and given the climatic and soil types of the island many *lavaka* are a natural part of the landscape's evolution. Some of them also clearly predate primary (i.e. uncut) rain forest. The many factors, natural and cultural, involved in *lavaka* development are well reviewed by Wells and Andriamihaja (1993).

In southern Africa there are many deep erosional trenches and scars called *dongas*. Many of them *appear* very fresh, but monitoring of some of them over two decades in Swaziland, suggests that this may be misleading. Even after the great cyclone Domoina in 1984, which deposited the equivalent of the normal mean annual rainfall in just a few days, had little effect. This suggests that they are unlikely to result from present land-use pressures. In neighbouring KwaZulu-Natal, battlefield maps from the Zulu War battlefields show large dongas were in existence by that time. There is therefore the possibility that the dongas are either the result of long-term cycles of colluvial deposition and erosion that date back to the Pleistocene (Botha 1996) or that some of them are the result of Iron Age smelting activities that led to localised deforestation. Iron Age furnaces appear to occur in close proximity to the Swaziland dongas.

Erosion and sedimentation

One of the consequences of, and part of the evidence for soil erosion, is accelerated sedimentation on floodplains and in coastal lowlands. Serious sedimentation of bays and estuaries has been caused by human activity on the eastern coast of America. As Gottschalk (1945: 219) wrote:

"Both historical and geological evidence indicates that the preagricultural rate of silting of eastern tidal estuaries was low. The history of sedimentation of ports in the Chesapeake Bay area is an epic of the effects of uncontrolled erosion since the beginning of the wholesale land clearing and cultivation more than three centuries ago."

He calculated that at the head of the Chesapeake Bay, 65 million cubic metres of sediment were deposited between 1846 and 1938. The average depth over and area of 83 square kilometres was reduced by 0.76 m. New land comprising 318 ha was added to the state of Maryland and, as Gottschalk remarked, 'the Susquehanna River is repeating the history of the Tigris and Euphrates.' Much of the material entrained by erosive processes on upper slopes as a result of agriculture in Maryland, however, was not evacuated as far as the coast. Costa (1975) has suggested, on the basis of the study of sedimentation, that only about one-third of the eroded material left the river valleys. The remainder accumulated on floodplains as alluvium and colluvium at rates of up to 1.6 cm per year. Similarly, Happ (1944), working in Wisconsin, carried out an intensive augering survey of floodplain soil and established that, since the development of agriculture, floodplain aggradation had proceeded at a rate of approximately 0.85 cm per year. He noted that channel and floodplain aggradation had caused the flooding of low alluvial terraces to be more frequent, more extensive and deeper. The rate of sedimentation has since declined (Trimble, 1976), because of less intensive land use and the institution of effective erosion control measures on farmland (see also Magilligan, 1985).

Such valley sedimentation is by no means restricted to the newly settled terrains of North America. There is increasing evidence to suggest that silty valley fills in Germany, France and Britain, many of them dating back to the Bronze and Iron Ages are the result of accelerated slope erosion produced by the activities of early farmers (Bell, 1982). Indeed, in recent years, various studies have been undertaken with a view to assessing the importance of changes in sedimentation rate caused by humans at different times in the Holocene in Britain. Among the formative events that have been identified are initial land clearance by Mesolithic and Neolithic peoples; agricultural intensification and sedentarization in the late Bronze Age; the widespread adoption of the iron plough in the early Iron Age; settlement by the Vikings; and the introduction of sheep farming *(see Table 4, p. 15)*.

A core from Llangorse Lake in the Brecon Beacons of Wales (Jones *et al.* 1985 provides excellent long-term data on changing sedimentation rates:

Period	**Sedimentation rate**
(years BP)	*(100cm/yr)*
9000-7500	3.5
7500-5000	1.0
5000-2800	13.2
2800-	14.1
c. AD 1840 - present	59.0

The thirteen-fold increase in rate after 5000 BP seems to have occurred rapidly and is attributed to initial forest clearance. The second dramatic increase of more than fourfold took place in the last 150 years and is a result of agricultural intensification.

The work of Binford *et al.* (1987) on the lakes of the Peten region of northern Guatemala, an area of tropical lowland dry forest, is also instructive with respect to early agricultural colonisation. Combining studies of archaeology and lake sediment stratigraphy, they were able to reconstruct the diverse environmental consequences of the growth of Mayan civilisation. This civilisation showed a dramatic growth after 3000 BP, but collapsed in the ninth century AD. The hypotheses put forward to explain this collapse include warfare, disease, earthquakes and soil degradation. The population has remained relatively low ever since, and after the first European contact (AD 1525) the region was virtually depopulated. The period of Mayan success saw a marked reduction in vegetation cover, an increase in lake sedimentation rates and in catchment soil erosion, and increased supply of inorganic silts and clays to the lakes, a pulse of phosphorus derived from human wastes, and a decrease in lacustrine productivity caused by high levels of turbidity.

Another good example of using long-term sedimentation rates to infer long-term rates of erosion is provided by Hughes *et al.*'s (1991) study of the Kuk Swamp in Papua New Guinea. They identify low rates of erosion until 9000 BP, when, with the onset of the first phase of forest clearance, erosion rates increased from 0.15 centimetres per thousand years to about 1.2 centimetres per thousand years. Rates remained relatively stable until the last few decades when, following European contact, the expansion of anthropogenic grasslands, subsistence gardens and coffee plantations has produced a rate that is markedly higher: 34 centimetres per thousand years. On the other hand, major vegetation changes brought about by human colonisation have not always been reflected in changed rates of sedimentation processes (see, for example, Stevenson *et al.*, 2001 on New Caledonia).

In the last two centuries rates of sedimentation in lake basins have changed in different ways according to the differing nature of economic activities in the catchments. Some data from various sources are listed for comparison in *Table 5 (see p. 16).* In the case of the Loe Pool in Cornwall (southwest England) rates of sedimentation where high while mining industry was active, but fell dramatically when mining was curtailed. In the case of Seeswood Pool in Warwickshire, a dominantly agricultural catchment area in Central England, the highest rates have occurred since 1978 in response to various land management changes, such as larger fields, continuous cropping and increased dairy herd size. In other catchments, pre-afforestation ploughing may bring about sufficient disturbance to bring about accelerated sedimentation. For example, Battarbee *et al.* (1985) looked at sediment cores in the Galloway area of south-west Scotland and found that in Loch Grannoch the introduction of ploughing in the catchment caused an increase in sedimentation from 0.2 to 2.2 centimetres per year.

The modern era and the future

Part of the history of landscape modification is that caused by rapid European colonisation of new worlds. We can see this in the context of the Antipodes. For example, Page and Trustrum (1997) found that in New Zealand rates of erosion in European times (post AD 1878) were 8 to 17 times those under indigenous forest (pre 2000 BP) and 5 to 6 times those under forest and fern in Polynesian times (post *c.* 560 BP). Likewise, Sheffield *et al.* (1995) found that in New Zealand the rate of estuarine infilling by sediment was 0.1mm p.a. in pre-Polynesian times, 0.3 mm p.a. in Poynesian times and 11mm p.a. in European times. Likewise, in their study of Whangape Harbour on the North Island, Nichol *et al.* (2000) found that sedimentation rates in the estuary increased by an order of magnitude during the period of human occupation. In Australia, the European introduction of domesticated stock in the last two centuries has had a dramatic effect on Australian soils. Sheep and cattle exert pressures of 0.65 to 1.7 kg per square cm, whereas the indigenous kangaroo exerts a pressure of 0.1 kg per square cm. Australian soils were not accustomed to such new pressures so erosion resulted.

Equally, the growth of mechanised agriculture, based on the use of the internal combustion engine, has permitted an ever greater depth of ploughing and soil disturbance. Whereas ploughing depth reached about 5 cm with a donkey and 10 cm with an ox during Roman times, and up to 18 cm with the introduction of horse yoking in the twelfth century, with modern mechanisation tillage depth reaches up to 40 cm (van Vliet-Lanoë *et al.*, 1992).

In the modern era, humans have developed the potential to cause unparalleled landscape change, and this is especially true for the last 300 years (Turner *et al.*, 1990). For example, world cement production (an indicator of the size of the construction industry) increased from 583 million tonnes in 1970 to 1154 million tonnes in 1990. Over the same period, world coal production (an indicator of power generation and of excavation) grew from 2924 to 4700 million tonnes. The number of tractors in use (a measure of the role of modern agriculture and deep ploughing) grew from 15.48 to 25.95 million.

The most important of all the developments of the last three hundred years has been the progressive increase in the harnessing of energy, primarily through the burning of fossil fuels. Increasingly energy use gives the potential for increasing environmental change, and though climate changes may result from the building up of greenhouse gases in the atmosphere there is the likelihood that soils and landforming processes will be modified to a substantial degree. In a warmer world, the depth of the active layer and the frequency of debris flows may become greater in permafrost terrains; in some arid regions dunes may be reactivated and dust storms generated with increasing frequency as soil moisture levels decline; increases in storm intensity could lead to greater erosion in hurricane-prone areas; and changes in land use in response to climate change could alter the nature of human pressures on the land.

The degree of change in the rate of operation of erosion processes that has been caused in the past and will be achieved in the future depends crucially on land management. There are many methods, some of great antiquity, that have been developed by indigenous peoples to decrease erosion and these deserve to diffuse to a greater geographical area than the one in which they have been used until now (Reij *et al.*, 1996). Likewise the erosional consequences of deforestation depend crucially on how the forest is removed (e.g. by clear felling or by selective felling), how the forest products are removed (badly designed logging roads are a major cause of erosion), and what the forest is replaced with. Well managed plantations, for example, with buffer strips along the channels, terracing on steep slopes, and with good ground cover, can have rates of soil loss that are no greater than those under virgin forest.

Conclusions

Although intuitively one can assert that the intensity of landscape transformation achieved by humans has been magnified through time, there remain many problems in trying to write a history this transformation and of particular elements of it such as soil erosion (Bell and Boardman, 1992). We can assert that the use of fire and advanced hunting technologies may have enabled Pleistocene humans to modify vegetation conditions and soil characteristics so that erosion rates were changed. We can suggest that the use of the plough and the clearing of forest in the Holocene would have accelerated rates of erosion. However, we have few reliable long-term data on anthropogenically accelerated rates of erosion, though sediment cores offer great potential. It remains fiendishly difficult to separate the roles of man and nature in causing such phenomena as gullies (Brookfield, 1999). We know that environmental changes of an entirely natural sort have been of great frequency and degree in the Quaternary at a whole range of temporal scales and that they can lead to phases of erosion and aggradation.

Table 1 Phases of land transformation and their mechanisms

Pre Holocene

Extinctions
Fire

Holocene

Clearance for agriculture and pastoralism
Ploughs
Irrigation
Settlements
Mining and smelting

Modern

Energy from fossil fuels
Ecological globalisation
Global change

Table 2 A sequence of major technological developments

HUMANS IN EAST AFRICA
2.5 million years ago

FIRE IN AFRICA
1.4 million years ago

NAVIGATION TO AUSTRALIA
40 000 years ago

DOMESTICATION
11 000 years ago

METAL WORKING
7 000 years ago

WHEEL
5 500 years ago

PLOUGHING AND IRRIGATION
5 000 years ago

Table 3 *Possible causes of arroyo incision*

INCREASE IN ERODIBILITY OF VALLEY FLOOR

Removal of vegetation as a result of wild animals, domestic animals, fire, or climatic change

Disruption of the sod by ploughing, trampling

INCREASE IN FLOW VELOCITY

Increase in discharge due to climatic change or vegetation change (interception and evapotranspiration role)

Reduction in surface roughness, embankments, puddling of surface, concentration of flow off roads and tracks (game tracks, cattle tracks, sledge tracks)

MISCELLANEOUS

Base level changes (tectonics, sea level)

Thresholds exceeded (the Schuum model)

Table 4 *Accelerated sedimentation in Britain in prehistorical and historical times*

Location	*Source*	*Evidence and date*
Howgill Fells	Harvey et al. (1981)	Debris cone production following tenth century AD introduction of sheep farming
Upper Thames basin	Robinson and Lambrick (1984)	River alluviation in Late Bronze Age and early from Age
Lake District	Pennington (1981)	Accelerated lake sedimentation at 5000 BP at Llangorse due to forest clearance
Mid-Wales	Macklin and Lewin (1986)	Floodplain sedimentation (Capel Bangor unit) on Bredol as a result of early Iron Age sedentary agriculture
Brecon Beacons	Jones et al. (1985)	Lake sedimentation increase after 5000 BP at Llangorse due to forest clearance
Weald	Burrin (1985)	Valley alluviation from Neolithic onwards until early Ice Age
Bowland Fells	Harvye and Renwick (1987)	Valley terraces at 5000-2000 BP (Bronze or Iron Age settlement) and after 1000 BP (Viking settlement)
Southern England	Bell (1982)	Fills in dry valleys Bronze Age and Iron Age
Callaly Moor (Northumberland)	Macklin et al. (1991)	Valley fill sediments of late Neolithic to Bronze Age

Table 5 *Data on rates of erosion and sedimentation in lakes in the last two centuries*

Dates	Activity	*Rates of erosion in catchment (R. Cober) as determined from lake sedimentation rates ($t\ km^{-2}\ y^{-1}$)*
(a) Loe Pool (Cornwall) (From O'Sullivan et al. 1982)		
1860-1920	Mining and agriculture	174
1930-6	Intensive mining and agriculture	421
1937-8	Intensive mining and agriculture	361
1938-81	Agriculture	12
(b) Seeswood Pool (Warwickshire) (From Foster et al. 1986)		
1765-1853		7.0
1854-80		12.2
1881-1902		8.1
1903-19		9.6
1920-5		21.6
1926-33		16.1
1935-47		12.7
1948-64		12.0
1965-72		13.9
1973-7		18.3
1978-82		36.2

References

Andel T. H. van, Zangger E. and Demitrack A. 1990 „Land use and soil erosion in prehistoric and historic Greece". *Journal of Field Archaeology* 17, 379-96.

Balling R. C. and Wells S.G. 1990 „Historical rainfall patterns and arroyo activity within the Zuni river drainage basic, New Mexico". *Annals of the Association of American Geographers* 80, 603-17.

Battarbee R. W., Appleby P. G., Odel K. and Flower R. J. 1985 „^{210}Pb dating of Scottish Lake sediments, afforestation and accelerated soil erosion". *Earth surface processes and landforms* 10, 137-42.

Bell M. and Boardman J. (eds.) 1992 *Past and present soil erosion.* Oxford: Oxbow Books.

Bell M. L. 1982 „The effect of land-use and climate on valley sedimentation". In A. F. Harding (ed.) *Climatic change in later prehistory.* Edinburgh: Edinburgh University Press.

Binford M. W., Brenner M., Whitmore T. J., Higuera-Grundy A., Deevey E. S. and Leyden B. 1987 „Ecosystems, paleoecology, and human disturbance in subtropical and tropical America". *Quaternary Science Review* 6, 115-28.

Botha G. A. 1996 „Cyclical colluvial accretion on bedrock pediments during the late Quaternary in northern KwaZulu-Natal, South Africa". *Zeitschrift für Geomorphologie Supplementband* 103, 85-102.

Brookfield H. 1999 „Environmental damage: distinguishing human from geophysical causes". *Environmental Hazards* 1, 3-11.

Bryan K. 1928 „Historic evidence of changes in the channel of Rio Puerco, a tributary of the Rio Grande in New Mexico". *Journal of geology* 36, 265-82.

Bull W.B. 1997 „Discontinuous ephemeral streams". *Geomorphology* 19, 227-276.

Burrin P. J. 1985 „Holocene alluviation in southeast England and some implications for palaeohydrological studies". *Earth surface processes and landforms* 10,257-71.

Butzer K. W. 1974 „Accelerated soil erosion a problem of man-land relationships". In I.R. Manners and M. W. Mikesell (eds.) *Perspectives on environments.* Washington DC: Association of American Geographers.

Cooke R. U. and Reeves R. W. 1976 *Arroyos and environmental change in the American south-west.* Oxford: Oxford University Press.

Costa J. E. 1975 „Effects of agriculture on erosion and sedimentation in the Piedmont province, Maryland". *Bulletin of the Geological Society of America* 86, 1281-6.

Foster I. D., Dearing J. A. and Appleby R. G. 1986 „Historical trends in catchment sediment yields a case study in reconstruction from lake-sediment records in Warwickshire. UK". *Hydrological science journal* 31, 427-43.

Elliott J.G., Gellis A. C. and Aby S. B. 1999 „Evolution of arroyos: incised channels of the southwestern United States". In S.E.Darby and A.Simon (eds.) *Incised River Channels*. Chichester: Wiley, pp. 153-185.

Goldammer J. G. (eds.) 1990 *Fire in the tropical biota*. Berlin: Springer Verlag

Gottschalk L. C. 1945 „Effects of soil erosion on navigation in Upper Chesapeake Bay". *Geographical Review* 35, 219-38.

Goudie A. S. 1999 *The human impact on the natural environment* (5th edition). Cambridge, Mass: MIT Press.

Happ S. C. 1944 „Effects of sedimentation on floods in the Kikapoo Valley, Wisconsin". *Journal of geology* 52, 53-68.

Harvey A. M. and Renwick W. H. 1987 „Holocene alluvial fan and terrace formation in the Bowland Fells, Northwest England". *Earth surface processes and landforms* 12, 249-57.

Harvey A. M., Oldfield F., Baron A. F. and Pearson G. W. 1981 „Dating of post-glacial landforms in the central Howgills". *Earth surface processes and landforms* 6, 401-12.

Hope G. 1999 „Vegetation and fire response to late Holocene human occupation in inland and mainland north west Tasmania". *Quaternary International* 59, 47-60.

Hughes R. J., Sullivan M. E. and Yok D. 1991 „Human-induced erosion in a highlands catchment in Papua New Guinea: The prehistoric and contemporary records". *Zeitschrift für Geomorphologie, Supplementband* 83, 227-39.

Huntington E. 1914 *The climatic factor as illustrated in arid America*. Carnegie Institution of Washington Publication, 192.

Jones R., Benson-Evans K. and Chambers F. M. 1985 „Human influence upon sedimentation in Llangorse Lake, Wales". *Earth surface processes and landforms*. 10, 227-35.

Kohen J. 1995 *Aboriginal Environmental Impacts*. Sydney: University of New South Wales Press.

Leopold L. B. 1951 „Rainfall frequency: An aspect of climatic variation". *Transactions of the American Geophysics Union* 32, 347-57.

Macklin M. G. and Lewin J. 1986 „Terraced fills of Pleistocene and Holocene age in the Rhiedol Valley, Wales". *Journal of Quaternary Science* 1, 21-34.

Macklin M. G. and, Passmore D. G., Stevenson A. C., Colwey A. C., Edwards D. N. and O'Brien C. F. 1991 „Holocene alluviation and land-use change on Callaly Moor, Northumberland, England". *Journal of Quaternary Science* 6, 225-32.

Magilligan F. J. 1985 „Historical floodplains sedimentation in the Galena River basin, Wisconsin and Illinois". *Annals of Association of American Geographers* 75, 583-94.

Marsh G. P. 1864 *Man and Nature*. New York: Scribner.

McFadden L.D. and McAuliffe J.R. 1997. „Lithologically influenced geomorphic responses to Holocene climatic changes in the southern Colorado Plateau, Arizona: A soil-geomorphic and ecologic perspective". *Geomorphology* 19, 303-332.

McGlone M.S. and Wilmshurst J.M. 1999. „Dating initial Maori environmental impact in New Zealand". *Quaternary International* 59, 5-15.

McNeill J. 2000 *Something new under the Sun.* London: Allen Lane.

Meyer W. B. 1996 *Human impact on the earth.* Cambridge: Cambridge University Press.

Nichol S. L., Augustinus P.C., Gregory M. R., Creese R. and Horrocks M. 2000. „Geomorphic and sedimentary evidence of human impact on the New Zealand coastal landscape". *Physical Geography* 21, 109-132.

O'Sullivan P. E., Coard M. A. and Pickering D. A. 1982 „The use of laminated lake sediments in the estimation and calibration of erosion rates". *Publication of the International Association of Hydrological Science* 137, 385-96.

Page M. J. and Trustrum N. A. 1997 „A late Holocene lake sediment record of the erosion response to land use change in steepland catchment, New Zealand". *Zeitschrift für Geomorphologie* 41, 369-92.

Pennington W. 1981 „Records of a lake's life in time: The sediments" *Hydrobiologia* 79, 197-219.

Rackham O. and Moody J. 1996 *The making of the Cretan landscape.* Manchester: Manchester University Press.

Reij C., Scoones I. and Toulmin C. 1996 *Sustaining the soil.* London: Earthscan.

Roberts N. 1998 *The Holocene* (2nd edition). Oxford: Blackwell.

Robinson M. A. and Lambrick G. H. 1984 „Holocene alluviation and hydrology in the Upper Thames Basin". *Nature* 308, 809-14.

Schule W. 1990 „Landscape and climate in prehistory: Interactions of wildlife, man and fire" In J. G. Goldammer (ed.) *Fire in the tropical biota.* Berlin: Springer Verlag, 273-318.

Schumm S. A., Harvey M. D and Watson C. C. 1984 *Incised channels: morphology, dynamics and control.* Littleton, Colorado: Water Resources Publications.

Sheffield A. T, Healy T. R. and McGlone M. S. 1995 „Infilling rates of a steepland catchment estuary, Whangamat, New Zealand". *Journal of Coastal Research* 11 (4), 1294-1308.

Simmons I. 1989 *Changing the face of the Earth.* Oxford: Blackwell.

Simmons I. 1993 *Environmental history: a concise introduction.* Oxford: Blackwell.

Stevenson J., Dodson J.R. and Prosser I.P. 2001. „A late Quaternary record of environmental change and human impact from New Caledonia". *Palaeogeography, Palaeoclimatology and Palaeoecology* 168, 97-123.

Tiffin M., Mortimore M and Gichuki F. N. 1994 *More people, less erosion: Environmental recovery in Kenya.* London: Wiley.

Trimble S. W. 1976 „Modern stream and valley sedimentation in the Driftless Area, Wisconsin, USA". *23rd International Geographical Congress*, sect 1, 228-31.

Van Vliet-Lamoë B., Helluin M., Bellerin J. and Valadas B. 1992 „Soil erosion in western Europe: From the last Interglacial to the present". *Oxbow Monograph* 22, pp. 101-114

Vita-Finzi C. 1969 *The Mediterranean valleys*. Cambridge: Cambridge University Press.

Waters M.R. and Haynes C.V. 2001 „Late Quaternary arroyo formation and climate change in the American Southwest." *Geology* 29, 399-402.

Wells N. A. and Andriamihaja B. 1993 „The initiation and growth of gullies in Madagascar: are humans to blame?" *Geomorphology* 8, 1-46.

Marina Fischer-Kowalski

Modes of Colonizing Nature

Abstract

Departing from theoretical models of society-nature interactions I will discuss what meanings "exploitation" of nature may have. What then is "overexploitation"? My point is that this question has to be placed within historically different socio-ecological regimes, to be characterized by their metabolism and their colonisation rate.

Paradigms of exploitation and overexploitation

These terms originate from the language of politics, the language of social relations. "Exploitation" usually is referred to as an asymmetrical exchange relation.

What is an asymmetrical exchange relation? To define this, it requires – at least – two distinct entities, that need to reproduce themselves: Let me call them systems. In order to do so, they enter into an exchange relation with one another upon which the reproduction of both systems depends. If we just look at what is being exchanged, we will find different quantities, but also different qualities. They will be hard to compare – so from the exchange itself we will not be able to tell whether it is "equal" or "unequal". But if, as an outside observer, we see one of the systems involved thrive, expand and flourish, while the other system stays small and miserable, we can assume unequal exchange: System A is "exploiting" system B.

How can such a situation of unequal exchange, or exploitation, be maintained over time? At least the following two preconditions have to be met:

1) that both systems maintain the ability to reproduce themselves. If system B is exploited to the extent that it is not able to reproduce itself anymore, it will collapse. This then is the risky case of "overexploitation",

2) that system A is able to control some crucial parameters of system B so as to keep it dependent upon this unequal exchange – otherwise, system B would terminate this unequal exchange situa-

tion, either by making it more equal, or by denying exchange altogether.[1] This control of crucial parameters of one system by another system is what I will explain as "colonizing regime" further down.

Thus, maintaining an exploitative situation is also costly and risky for system A: If it wishes to continue to receive the services from system B, it has to carefully avoid the case of overexploitation. One risk it encounters is the collapse of system B. If this happens, system B will no more provide the services system A used to receive, and system A will therefore be in a position to have to look for a substitute of system B. Risk number two consists in getting involved in a risk spiral of controlling ever more parameters of system B, with all the potentially rising continuous investment that this may require, to the point where system A may be no more able to sustain this effort.

In order to fully understand the risks involved in exploitation, we have not only to look at the victim, but also at the culprit. This helps to go beyond a moral discussion of exploitation and overexploitation as towards discussing them as issues of functional interdependency.

Let me now apply this very general idea to the exchange relation between human social systems and natural systems. What kinds of exchanges take place, and in what sense may they be considered exploitative?

In the past decades of environmental debate, several quite distinct paradigms have emerged concerning the ways in which human societies may harm the environment and in effect may be overexploiting natural systems.

These paradigms, originating from different scientific traditions, refer to different types of exchange: they presuppose different types of sensitivity in natural systems, and they head towards different policy reactions. (see *Fig. 1*)

---

[1] This reasoning is based upon arguments brought forward by Johan Galtung (1969), in analyzing inequity within and between societies, characterizing it as "structural violence" (as distinct from "direct violence").

Figure 1: Paradigms of environmental exploitation

medical scientists, chemists, large part of the public "POISON" pollution with toxic substances **→ human death**	*biologists, climatologists, agriculturalists* "BALANCE" threatening natural systems functioning **→ complete breakdown**
physicists, environmental economists "ENTROPY" wasting natural capital **→ exhaustion of needed resources**	*philosophers, moralists, animal rights activists* "CONVIVALITY" unjustified dominance over other species **→ obvious mass suffering of creatures**

According to each paradigm, "overexploitation" carries a different meaning. The "poison" or "pollution" paradigm, focuses on natural systems such as the atmosphere, the water cycle or soil in their capacity as sinks for wastes and emission from human society. The exchange process involved is a metabolic one, and overexploitation occurs when these natural systems cannot absorb and re-transform these wastes and emissions sufficiently to continue their services for a healthy human livelihood. The policy answer to this risk is emission control.

Paradigm 2, "entropy", again deals with metabolic exchange, but looks only at the input side of human society and its need for natural resources. If resources are used and degraded at a rate exceeding their natural reproduction, they eventually get exhausted. The policy answer to this risk consists in sustainable resource use in terms of quality ("renewable" versus "non-renewable" resources) and quantity, and in taking care to have a substitute at hand before a vital resource is finally exhausted.

Paradigm 3, "balance", refers to the complex requirements of self-reproduction of particular natural systems. This may be the global climate, or certain ecosystems, or species. The services provided by these systems to human society are considered complex and fundamentally unpredictable, and the activities by which these systems can be brought out of balance are not confined to metabolic exchanges, but cover a wide range of possibilities. The overexploitation risk is that these systems either altogether disappear, or substantially change their mode of functioning. The policy reaction against this risk has to consist in various conservation and protection measures.

Paradigm 4, "convivality"[2], covers a meaning of harm and exploitation that reaches beyond the functional arguments admitted as "scientific", and refers to human domination and the infliction of pain and suffering upon other creatures. It is based upon empathy and respect for other forms of life. Overexploitation occurs when there is an unproportional amount of suffering inflicted. The policy response to this is the introduction of something like "animal rights", or change of nutrition towards vegetarianism. What is at stake is something like the moral identity of humans, as fair co-inhabitants of the earth.

The potential harm to the environment, or in the above terms, the exploitative impact of human activities upon natural systems, can be judged more or less independently according to each paradigm – they cannot be reduced upon one another. But taken together, I would claim, they map a pretty complete picture of the qualities involved when talking about the harm done to, and the potential overexploitation of natural environments.

Societal metabolism and colonization of natural systems[3]

Now, I will turn away from qualifying impacts of exploitation, and start talking about exchange processes. I wish to talk about those metabolic processes between social and natural systems that create the risks of overexploitation, on the one hand, and those regulatory processes of colonization that allow to perpetuate exploitative exchange relations over time, and eventually avoid overexploitation.

Let me briefly explain what I mean by these concepts "societal metabolism" and "colonization", and why I consider them as very helpful for understanding historically variable risks of overexploitation, both conceptually and empirically.

The notion of societal metabolism departs from the idea that human societies can be considered dissipative systems that have to maintain a continuous flow of energy and matter from and to their natural environments in order to reproduce themselves. The core of this metabolism is the sum metabolism of society's population, or is the biological metabolism of a certain number of humans. Beyond this biological core, there is a wider range of possible variation: the "characteristic metabolic profile" of a society varies historically, with its mode of subsistence.[4]

---

[2] This expression has been adopted from Ivan Illich (1973) who developed it for characterizing tools and technologies that permit human cooperation and a division of labor under equal, non-hierarchical terms.
[3] For a more elaborate explanation of the concepts introduced here, see Fischer-Kowalski and Weisz (Fischer-Kowalski and Weisz 1999; Weisz et al. 2001).
[4] We use the term „mode of subsistence" as coined by Adam Smith: In contrast to Marx's later term "modes of production" it focuses livelihood and sustenance instead of the ways to provide for this sustenance.

Concerning the exchange relations with natural systems, a „basic metabolism“ can be distinguished from an „extended metabolism”. A society may live from the renewable resources it can draw from the biosphere (or, even more narrowly, from its local or regional biosphere). This *basic metabolism* rests upon the natural reproduction of resources: freshwater, air, and plant or animal biomass. For each of these resources there exists a natural recycling mechanism that transforms the releases from social metabolism into useable inputs again. Most societies in human history had nothing but such a basic metabolism. They could deplete their environment of resources if the rate of consumption exceeded the rate of natural reproduction. Their main over-exploitation problem, therefore, was resource scarcity (or, in the above terms, problems of the “entropy”-type).

An *extended metabolism*, in contrast, largely relies on input from outside the actual biospherical cycles (e.g. fossil fuels, various metals), and thereby may overcome some scarcity problems, but introduces large scale pollution problems.

Figure 2: Material Flows including Population Flows

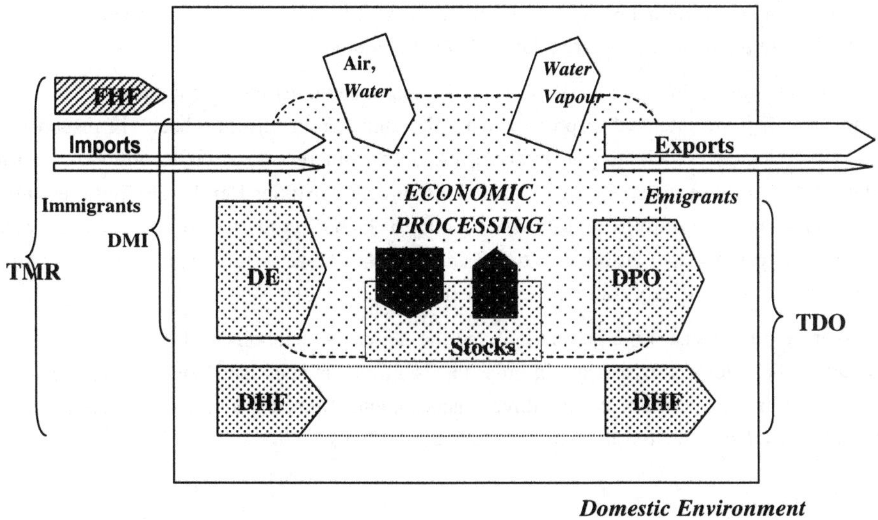

Source: Matthews et al. 2000 (modified)

The input-output model displayed in *Fig 2* is more complex: It was developed as a conceptual tool for material flow analysis of industrial societies and defines certain indicators for (overall) materials input and materials consumption, as I will demonstrate below empirically. It also draws attention to the fact that societies rarely maintain their sustenance upon exchange with their natural environments alone, but typically also in exchange with other societies.

In order to overcome problems of resource scarcity, and moreover, to maintain an extended metabolism, societies have to colonize their natural environments. Colonization refers to society's deliberate and sustained interventions in natural processes / systems aimed at modifying their characteristics so as to better fit society's needs.

Intuitively, one is tempted to conceive of "colonizing natural systems" spatially, as a difference between "cultivated land" and "wilderness". While this concept may indeed be useful for some aspects of land use research, we prefer a sufficiently abstract notion of "colonization". Social activities which colonize natural systems may intervene on different levels. The most obvious interventions take place on the level of ecosystems: agriculture and forestry deliberately transform biotopes in order to make them more productive for types of biomass society needs, and less productive for other biomass. Similarly, technical changes of the water cycle (construction of dams, draining, irrigation, etc.) intervene on this level. But the interference may also take place on levels below, such as the level of organisms or even the level of genomes, which means an intervention into biological evolution (such as traditional breeding or modern biological techniques). While societies invest considerable effort into colonizing interventions, they still control only a few parameters compared to the vast complexity of the natural systems affected – the rest is left to the internal dynamics and regulation of natural systems.

Wherever these colonizing interventions occur, they serve to increase the exploitability of natural systems, and they are intended to prohibit natural systems from "striking back" in response to exploitation. However, societies get involved into an ever-increasing effort to observe, control, regulate and tend those systems (see 'risk spiral' as coined by Müller-Herold and Sieferle 1998). These efforts imply not only a considerable amount of labour on the part of society (e.g. traditional agriculture), but also an organizational adaptation to these tasks. (Most recent challenge: juridical, ethical and property solutions for modern biotechnologies.)

The larger (and the denser) the population, and the larger its metabolism, the more natural systems have to be colonized by society in order to sustain this metabolism. This involves societies in labour and organization beyond the direct management of metabolism, and it generates additional pressures upon the environment, beyond material flows.

On the historical variability of socio-ecological regimes

What I shall now proceed to is an attempt to demonstrate that such a framework can serve well in guiding research bridging historical, anthropological and contemporary „sustainability" approaches across scientific disciplines and across various time periods.

In developing this, I rely upon Sieferle's (1997) analysis of "socio-ecological regimes" that can be equated with modes of subsistence in terms of a particular energy metabolism in combination with a set of colonization strategies.

I will try to illustrate from some of our team's empirical research across time periods, regions and cultures how well the notion of „socio-ecological regimes" may explain major features of society-nature interaction, of socio-cultural organization, of transition processes between modes of subsistence, and finally, of exchange processes between differently organized societies.

The first step is very simple: From various sources of data (historical statistics, cultural anthropological field studies and modern statistical data) one may show that transitions from one mode of subsistence to the next are associated with a substantial (that is four to fivefold) increase in per capita metabolism. This holds true both for energy and for materials. *Fig. 3* and *4* display the energy and materials metabolism for four case studies from different socio-ecological regimes. All four case studies are based upon the same system definitions and analogous operational procedures. While the data for Trinket (see Singh 2001, in this volume) and Sang Saeng (Grünbühel 1998) have been generated by direct observation and measurement in field studies, the case of Austria 1830 has been generated from historical statistics (in combination with some modelling, see Krausmann and Haberl 2001), and the data of Austria 1996 are based upon contemporary (economic and other) statistics and have been part of a large comparative international study (Matthews et al. 2000). The material metabolism is calculated in accordance with the model presented in *Fig. 2 (see p. 25)*, comprising biomass consumed by humans and livestock, fuel wood and other fuels, construction materials for housing, roads and the like[5], and materials incorporated in other artefacts (such as metal tools or textiles, all in metric tonnes). The energy metabolism is calculated analogously[6] (in calorific values) and therefore deviates from the usual energy statistics that only comprise technical energy while ignoring human and animal nutrition. "Direct input" (DEI and DMI, respectively) refers to the sum total of energy and materials that enter the social system annually (be it from domestic extraction or by import from outside), while "domestic consumption" (DEC and DMC, respectively) amounts to direct input minus exports to other social systems. All numbers have been calculated on a system-wide base and then divided by population number.

---

[5] For Austria in 1830, no reliable data on construction materials could be generated. Thus the material metabolism is slightly underestimated.

[6] Beyond energy derived from materials, it also includes electricity generated by hydropower, and imports.

Figure 3: Empirical demonstration of variability of energy metabolism: direct energy input (DEI) + domestic energy consumption (DEC)

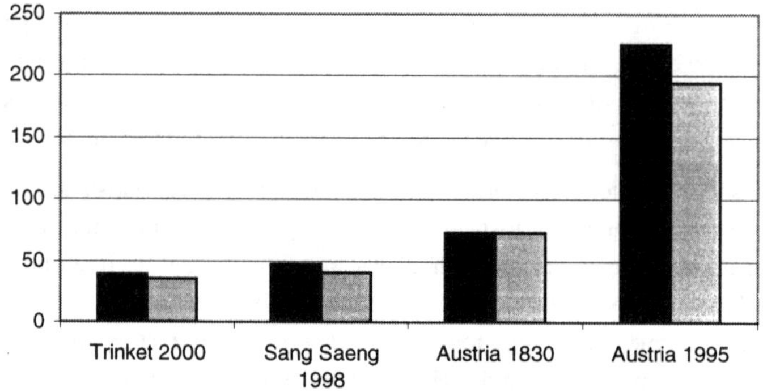

Source: IFF - Social Ecology

Figure 4: Empirical demonstration of variability of material metabolism: direct material input (DMI) + domestic material consumption (DMC)

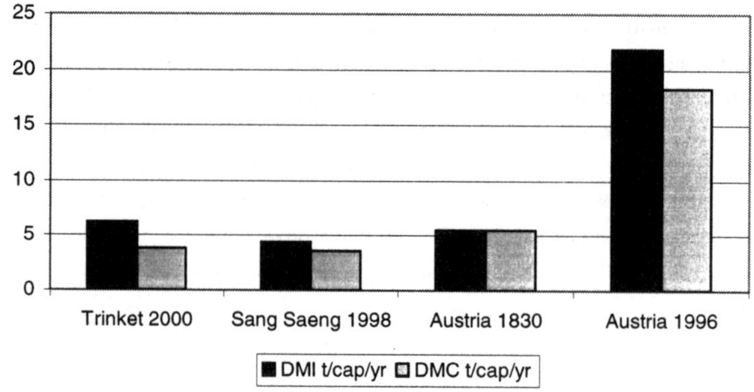

Source: IFF - Social Ecology

Trinket is one of the Nicobar Islands in the Indian Ocean, containing about 400 inhabitants that still partially live a hunting-and-gathering mode of subsistence (mainly fishing), partially harvest coconuts and produce copra (which they exchange for rice). They have very low working hours, are well nourished and healthy and show no signs of deprivation. Sang Saeng is a little village in Northeast Thailand. It is dominated by the agrarian mode of subsistence (rice cultivation), but also bears elements of hunting and gathering (during the dry season), and at the same time is part of a country that undergoes a rapid transition towards an industrial mode of subsistence. Sang Saeng can be said to have about 200 inhabitants at most, while the actual population fluctuates strongly. There is a large number of migrants who, during the dry season, work outside the village and use their salaries to bring industrial artefacts to the village. Sang Saeng represents a local society in transition within the rapidly industrializing country of Thailand. Working hours vary strongly. For the residents that remain in the village they are very low during the dry season, but very high during the wet season when rice is grown. Similarly, the quantity and quality of nutrition varies seasonally. Austria in 1830 (within present-day boundaries) may be considered a highly developed agrarian society before its transition to the industrial mode (Sandgruber 1982; Sandgruber 1978). Working hours, nutritional and health state have not been established, but from general historical records the situation may be considered pretty strained. Austria in 1996 represents a prosperous industrial society.

What we can see from *Fig. 3* and *4* is that the energy metabolism of the two villages that live by the socio-ecological regime of hunting-and-gathering in combination with agrarian features sustain themselves on an annual per capita energy consumption of 40 GJ or less, and on a material consumption of about 4 tonnes. The per capita energy consumption of the Austrian society (which is obviously not a village, but contains cities and a royal court, keeps an army etc.) in 1830 is not much higher, at about 75 GJ. In contrast, contemporary industrial Austria maintains an energy metabolism of 200 GJ per capita and year, and a material consumption of about 20 tonnes. These similarities between different agrarian societies, (and between different industrial societies, as we shall demonstrate below) are all the more striking as we deal with very different natural environments (ranging from tropical rainforest to a semi-arid temperate zone, to an alpine country in the middle of Europe), different time periods and very different cultures. Even if we widen our horizon of comparison to more cases (taking into account a somewhat lesser degree of methodological comparability), we find the pattern confirmed.

Figure 5: Metabolic profiles by mode of subsistence (DMC/capita)

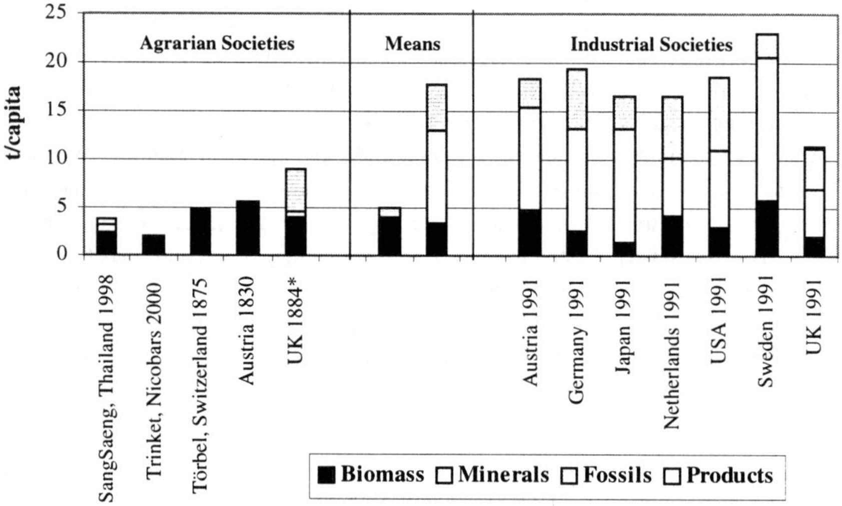

with data from:
Grünbühel (1998), Singh et al. (2001), Netting (1981), Krausmann, Schandl & Schulz (2001), Schandl (2000), Adriaanse et al. (1997), Matthews et. al (2000)

Fig. 5 compares most cases from literature where the annual material consumption has been established so far. As we can see, the average per capita material consumption of industrial societies is about 3,5 times higher than the average material consumption of the agrarian societies. While biomass consumption is about equal (or maybe even a little smaller under industrial conditions), there is a much higher consumption of minerals (mostly for construction), facilitated and driven by the extra amount of energy supplied by fossil fuels. Thus the claim of a characteristic metabolic profile, depending on mode of subsistence, seems well warranted.

Are such different metabolic profiles facilitated by, and linked to, a change in colonization strategies? The answer, most obviously, would have to be yes. Unfortunately, though, colonization strategies have so far received much less conceptual and empirical attention than metabolic processes. Colonizing interventions, according to the abstract notion we employ, take place on all levels of biological organization, from ecosystems (terrestrial, aquatic, marine) to organisms (domestication, breeding, etc.), organs, tissues (e.g., tissue culture) down to the molecular level of the genome (genetic engineering) (Haberl and Zangerl-Weisz 1997). The concept of colonization seeks to provide a theoretical framework for both biophysical and cultural analyses, focusing on the mutual dependencies between the two. For something to be a colonizing intervention, it must be causally effective in changing some biophysical process; it must make a difference in the physical world. Likewise, it must be culturally conceived of, organized and monitored; it must "make sense" in the world of communication. One application of this concept where we have come as far as producing an operational definition is colonizing interventions into the energy household of terrestrial ecosystems. The concept of „human appropriation of net primary production" (Vitousek et al. 1986). HANPP measures the aggregate effect of land use and biomass harvest on processes and structures of ecosystems. It therefore allows us to quantify certain aspects of colonization of terrestrial ecosystems of various social units and to relate them to societal metabolism. Net primary production (NPP) is the biomass production of green plants in a defined region in one year. It can be expressed as material flow (kg biomass production, measured as dry matter per year), substance flow (kilograms of carbon fixation per year) or energy flow (Joules in biomass energy production per year) – these three different ways to measure the process are not identical, but closely related. HANPP can be defined as the difference between the following two quantities (Haberl 1997): The NPP of the vegetation that would prevail in the area under consideration without human intervention (i.e., the 'potential' natural vegetation, see Tüxen 1956), and the amount of NPP actually remaining in the ecosystem after human harvest. This remaining NPP is calculated by assessing the NPP of the actually prevailing vegetation and subtracting harvested biomass. Thus, HANPP is influenced by two processes: 1) Changes in the productivity of ecosystems, caused by human activities; e.g., the conversion of forests to grassland, cropland or built-up area. 2) Harvest from the actual NPP for human purposes. The larger HANPP, the more intensive the colonizing intervention into the energy household of a terrestrial ecosystem is considered to be.

Going by this indicator, we may analyse the intensity of colonization of terrestrial ecosystems across different socio-ecological regimes.

Figure 6: Empirical demonstration of variability in the intensity of colonizing terrestrial ecosystems: Human appropriation of aboveground net primary production

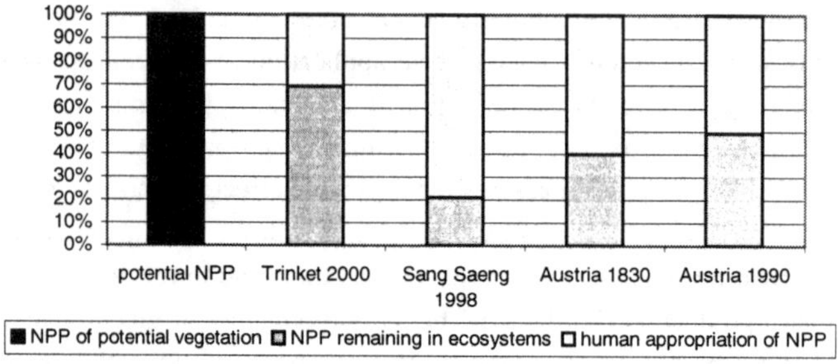

Source: IFF-Social Ecology

Comparing our four case studies above (see *Fig. 6*), we find differences in the intensity of colonization very much in line with what should be expected from Sieferle's analysis of socio-ecological regimes – however unexpected this may be from conventional presumptions. For Trinket, the case still strongly featuring a hunter-and-gatherer pattern, we find only 30% of potential NPP to be appropriated. Even this is more due to deforestation that took place a hundred years ago when European colonizers attempted to establish animal husbandry on this island – nowadays the inhabitants of Trinket do not directly use these deforested areas for livestock, but the forest just has not fully regrown (see Singh 2001 in this volume). The societies that more heavily rely on agriculture, namely Sang Saeng and Austria in 1830, appropriate as much as 80% and 60% respectively of aboveground NPP – which is probably as much as altogether possible.[7] What may come as a surprise is the reduction of NPP appropriation in present day Austria – despite of a much larger population, and a much larger overall biomass-harvest from Austrian territory. This is strongly related to the use of fossil fuels. Fossil fuels substitute wood for combustion purposes, they substitute animal traction, and – in combination with modern techniques of crop breeding - they permit a much higher biomass harvest per area through artificial fertilizers and pesticides, resulting in reforestation of agricultural areas of marginal productivity (Krausmann 2001; Krausmann and Haberl 2001). This very much conforms to Sieferle's analysis of the area-dependency of agrarian societies, and the (relative) area-independence of industrial societies.

[7] That it is less in Austria than in Sang Saeng is probably due to the fact that the territory of Austria encompasses large areas of hardly usable, often not even accessible alpine areas, whereas the territory of Sang Saeng comprises only land usable for colonizing purposes.

Colonizing interventions under industrial conditions focus less on the energy household of terrestrial ecosystems, and more on the biological levels below: the organisms, and increasingly the genes.

Exploitative relations between societies?

So far, we have been discussing modes of subsistence, or socio-ecological regimes, as different patterns of society-nature-interrelation, and as different patterns of (domestic) nature exploitation. For doing so, we have picked our cases across space and time, irrespective of context. Heuristically, this has helped us to establish systematic differences. But if we now wish to put these results in a global perspective and try to understand the dynamics of future development, we have to become aware that the context of the socio-metabolic transitions in the nineteenth century was very different to what it is now. One way to grasp this context is to make one more step and look at the exchange relations *between societies*, between industrial societies and so-called developing societies, societies that still bear some features of agrarian societies. If we look at the past two decades, the core industrial countries have managed to reduce their energy and material intensity. While in absolute terms their energy and material input stagnated or increased at a very low rate, their economies in terms of gross national product continued to rise substantially. Thus, energy and material intensity (defined as Joules or tonnes per unit GDP) were declining. (See *Fig. 7* for some of several similar cases). At the same time, a certain relief of environmental pressure in terms of local or regional pollutants, (Fischer-Kowalski and Amann 2001), and in terms of land-use patterns (as demonstrated above) upon domestic environments can be observed. Are industrial countries, therefore, becoming more environmentally benign, or more sustainable? There is one major indication that this, on a global level, is not the case: their CO_2 emissions, detrimental for the climate system, keep rising. There is another indication, contained in *Fig. 7*, that raises suspicion.

Figure 7: Material Intensity Declining in Industrial, but Rising in Developing Countries

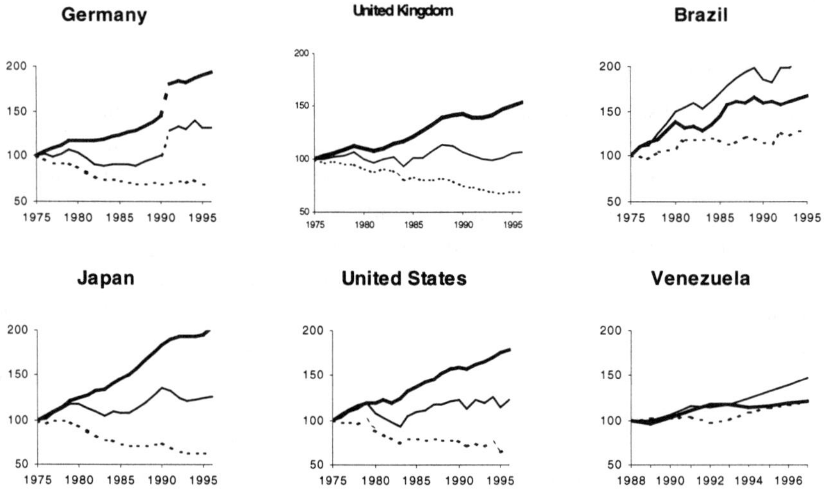

GDP (real, constant)
Material Intensity (GMI/GDP)
Material Input (DMI)

Source: Fischer-Kowalski & Amann (2001)

If we compare the material flow trends for two developing countries, Brazil and Venezuela, with core industrial countries, we can see a different pattern. In both cases the increase in material flows exceeds the growth in GDP – this amounts to quite a substantial rise in material intensity. Moreover, if we compare per capita material flows for those developing countries with some industrial core countries *(Fig. 8)*, we find little difference. This is in sharp contrast to what we should expect from the presumption that these countries are in the middle of a transition from the agrarian to the industrial mode of subsistence. Under such circumstances, according to our analysis above, they should be characterized by a much smaller per capita material consumption. If we now proceed to *Fig. 9* and compare the per capita income of those same countries, we find, as was to be expected, a much lower income on the part of Brazil and Venezuela. In effect, we find a considerably higher material intensity (at least in terms of direct material input per capita) in those developing countries – a material intensity that still keeps rising! *(Fig. 10, see p. 36).*

Figure 8: Materials use per capita 1995

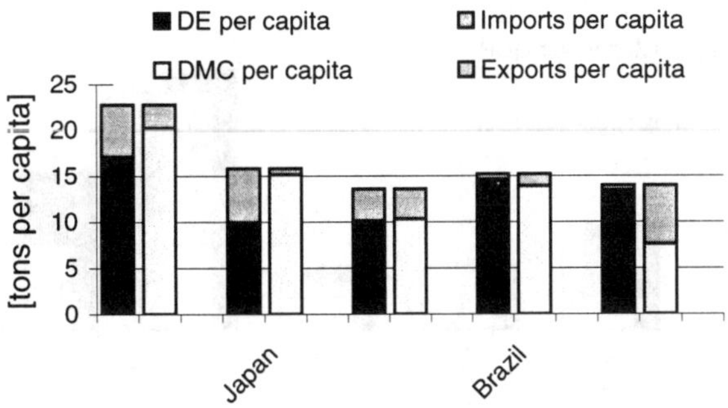

Source: Fischer-Kowalski & Amann (2001)

Figure 9: Income per capita 1995

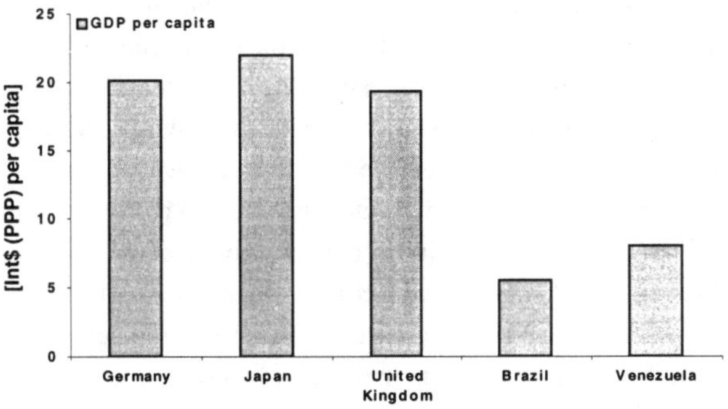

Source: OECD

Figure 10: Material intensity 1995

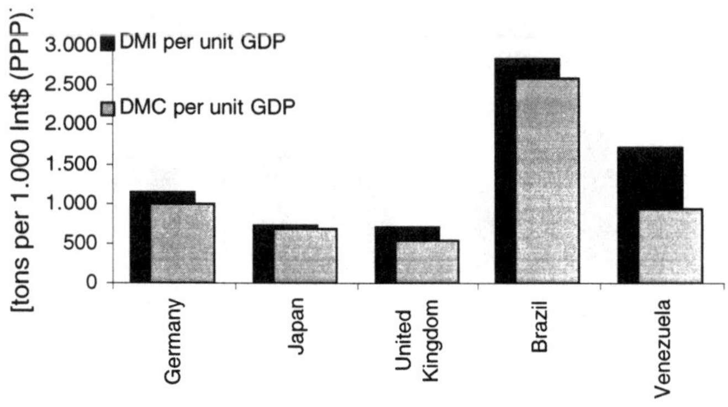

Source: Matthews et al. (2000), Amann et al. (2002)

It may be, of course, that those two developing countries are just special cases. Unfortunately, there exist hardly any reliable material or energy flow analyses for developing countries yet.[8] For the time being, based upon the scarce evidence that exists, we may at least suspect that, beyond the distinction between the agrarian and the industrial socio-metabolic regime, a third regime may prevail: a regime of "extractive economies". These extractive economies would have to be looked upon as a pattern deriving from an international division of labour, in which the industrial core countries externalise their energetically and materially intensive processes to developing countries. Production processes tend to be more materially and energetically intensive, the closer they are to the primary extraction of raw materials, and the closer to basic industrial transformations of these materials. The further down the line of consumption, the less energetically and materially intensive they become (see Fischer-Kowalski and Amann 2001). Thus, industrial countries may progress from pressures upon their domestic natural environments towards pressure upon other countries natural environments. This hypothesis is also supported by an analysis of North-South trade (see Muradian and Martinez-Alier 2001; Fischer-Kowalski and Amann 2001).

[8] In a presentation at the Stockholm ConAccount conference in September 2001, Stefan Bringezu (2001) reported on material flows from Greece and Portugal – as two cases within Europe that may be considered countries in transition. He arrived at a diagnosis similar to the one we found for Brazil and Venezuela – but this still may not be considered strong evidence.

Conclusion

Whatever the conclusions, based upon broader empirical evidence, may be: It is clear that in order to understand global trajectories, one needs not only to investigate historically different socio-ecological regimes in terms of society-nature exploitation, but also in terms of exchange (and exploitation) relations between societies.

So, finally, we may ask what the contribution of the analysis of socio-economic metabolism and colonization regimes may be to guiding a vision, and decision making processes, towards viable futures? What are the options? One conclusion is quite obvious: There is no "way back" into terrestrial biomass based modes of subsistence. A path well paved seems to be the shift of environmental loads from the industrial core to developing countries. What seems to be on the horizon, and meets fierce public opposition, is a path into a massive intensification of colonizing interventions into the biological evolution – as a second transition after the major metabolic transition of the past. Is there a way out, a path towards sustainability on a global scale, managed by reason and democratic participation? Departing from the biophysical constraints we have explored, such a path will not be easy to detect. But for sure it is part of the task of socio-ecological research to contribute in finding out.

References

Adriaanse, A., Bringezu, S., Hammond, A., Moriguchi, Y., Rodenberg, E., Rogich, D., and Schütz, H. (1997): *Resource Flows: The Material Basis of Industrial Economies.* Washington DC: World Resources Institute

Amann, Christof, Bruckner, Willi, Fischer-Kowalski, Marina, Grünbühel, Clemens M., and Schütz, Helmut (2002): Material flow accounting: A tool for monitoring sustainable development in Amazonia. In: *Amazonia 21: Final Report.* forthcoming.

Bringezu, Stefan (2001): *Is the European Economy developing towards a Sustainable Metabolism?*, Paper presented at the ConAccount Workshop "Economic growth, material flows and environmental pressure" in Stockholm, April 2001.

Fischer-Kowalski, Marina and Amann, Christof (2001): Beyond IPAT and Kuznets Curves: Globalization as a Vital Factor in Analysing the Environmental Impact of Socio-Economic Metabolism. In: *Population and Environment* 23(1): 7-47.

Fischer-Kowalski, Marina and Weisz, Helga (1999): Society as hybrid between material and symbolic realms: Towards a theoretical framework of society-nature interaction. In: *Advances in Human Ecology* 8: 215-251.

Galtung, Johan (1969): Violence, peace and peace research. In: *Journal of Peace Research* 6:167-191.

Grünbühel, Clemens M. (1998): Acting as a Cameleon: Material Flows of a Subsistence Economy in Northeast Thailand. In: Kleijn, René et al. (Eds.): *Ecologizing Societal Metabolism: Designing Scenarios for Sustainable Materials Management*. Leiden, CML Report 148: 57-61.

Haberl, Helmut (1997): Human Appropriation of Net Primary Production as An Environmental Indicator: Implications for Sustainable Development. In: *Ambio* 26(3): 143-146.

Haberl, Helmut and Zangerl-Weisz, Helga (1997): Kolonisierende Eingriffe, Systematik und Wirkungsweise. In: Fischer-Kowalski, Marina et al. (Eds.): *Gesellschaftlicher Stoffwechsel und Kolonisierung von Natur. Ein Versuch in Sozialer Ökologie*. Amsterdam : G + B Verlag Fakultas: 129 -148.

Illich, Ivan (1973): *Tools for Conviviality*. New York: Harper & Row

Krausmann, Fridolin (2001): Land Use and Industrial Modernisation: an empirical analysis of human influence on the functioning of ecosystems in Austria 1830 - 1995. In: *Land Use Policy* 18(1): 17-26.

Krausmann, Fridolin and Haberl, Helmut (2001): The Process of Industrialization From an Energetic Metabolism Point of View. Socio-Economic Energy Flows in Austria 1830-1995. In: *Ecological Economics* in print.

Matthews, Emily, Amann, Christof, Fischer-Kowalski, Marina, Bringezu, Stefan, Hüttler, Walter, Kleijn, René, Moriguchi, Yuichi, Ottke, Christian, Rodenburg, Eric, Rogich, Don, Schandl, Heinz, Schütz, Helmut, van der Voet, Ester, and Weisz, Helga (2000): *The Weight of Nations: Material Outflows from Industrial Economies*. Washington: World Resources Institute

Muradian, Roldan and Martinez-Alier, Joan (2001): South-North Materials Flow: History and Environmental Repercussions. In: *Innovation* 14(2): 171-187.

Müller-Herold, Ulrich and Sieferle, Rolf P. (1998): Surplus and Survival: Risk, Ruin and Luxury in the Evolution of Early Forms of Subsistence. In: *Advances in Human Ecology* 6: 201-220.

Netting, Robert M. (1981): *Balancing on an Alp. Ecological change and continuity in a Swiss mountain community*. London, New York, New Rochelle, Melbourne, Sydney: Cambridge University Press

Sandgruber, Roman (1978): Wirtschaftswachstum und Energie in Österreich 1840-1913. In: Kellenbenz, Hermann (Ed.): *Wirtschaftswachstum, Energie und Verkehr vom Mittelalter bis ins 19. Jahrhundert*. Stuttgart, New York: Fischer Verlag, Forschungen zur Sozial- und Wirtschaftsgeschichte 22: 67-95.

Sandgruber, Roman (1982): *Die Anfänge der Konsumgesellschaft. Konsumgüterverbrauch, Lebensstandard und Alltagskultur in Österreich im 18. und 19. Jahrhundert*. Wien: Verlag für Geschichte und Politik

Schandl, Heinz and Schulz, Niels (2001): *Using Material Flow Accounting to operationalize the concept of Societys's Metabolim. A preliminary MFA for the United Kingdom for the Period of 1937-1997*. Colchester: University of Essex, ISER Working Papers 2000-3.

Schandl, Heinz, Weisz, Helga, and Petrovic, Brigitte (2000): Materialflussrechnung für Österreich 1960 bis 1997. In: *Statistische Nachrichten* 55 (NF)(2):128-137.

Sieferle, Rolf P. (1997): Kulturelle Evolution des Gesellschaft-Natur-Verhältnisses. In: Fischer-Kowalski, Marina et al. (Eds.): *Gesellschaftlicher Stoffwechsel und Kolonisierung von Natur. Ein Versuch in Sozialer Ökologie*. Amsterdam: Gordon & Breach Verlag Fakultas: 37-53.

Singh, Simron J., Grünbühel, Clemens M., Schandl, Heinz, and Schulz, Niels (2001): Social Metabolism and Labour in a Local Context: Changing Environmental Relations on Trinket Island. In: *Population and Environment* 23(1): 71-104.

Tüxen, R. (1956): Die heutige potentielle natürliche Vegetation als Gegenstand der Vegetationskartierung. In: *Angewandte Pflanzensoziologie* 13: 5-42.

Vitousek, P. M., Ehrlich, P. R., Ehrlich, A. H., and Matson, P. A. (1986): Human Appropriation of the Products of Photosynthesis. In: *BioScience* 36(6): 363-373.

Weisz, Helga, Fischer-Kowalski, Marina, Grünbühel, Clemens M., Haberl, Helmut, Krausmann, Fridolin, and Winiwarter, Verena (2001): Global Environmental Change and Historical Transitions. In: *Innovation* 14(2): 117-142.

Kai W. Wirtz

Hindcast Effects of Neolithic Land-Use on World-Wide Migration Patterns and Technology Evolution

Abstract

During the Holocene strong gradients in the distribution of technology including food production techniques had emerged on a global scale. These patterns were further amplified in historic times and are now still visible through worldwide differences in national wealth. In order to give possible explanation for the origin of inequalities we here employ quantitative methods. A deterministic but simple model is proposed which is able to simulate the time evolution in different aspects of human culture with special focus on interactions with the environment. This dynamics is formulated in terms of marginal adjustments in interaction strategies leading to higher reproductive success. After compiling existing maps of potential vegetation at 5000 B.P. (Adams and Faure, 1997) the inhabited world is splitted into 230 regions with homogeneous environmental conditions. Suitable variables for the cultural development in the neolithic period are found to be farming to hunter-gathering ratio, number of domesticated species and a technological development index. The model then explicitly describes adaptation, growth and migration of human populations together with the spread of their cultural it characteristics. Implicitly (over)exploitation of natural resources, several mortality factors and the development of societal hierarchies are included. Uncertainties in the few model coefficients are reduced by conducting a very high number of simulation runs with changed parameters. The aim of this study hence goes beyond reproducing region specific trajectories of the cultural characteristics as partially revealed by the archaeological finds. Instead, simulated patterns of regional civilization rise are statistically analysed and the gross effect of biogeographic factors on Holocene human history is assessed. This way we provide measures for a strong but not exclusive dependence of cultural evolution on natural determinants. The overall strength of using mathematical modeling in anthropological sciences is further demonstrated by highlighting some model outcomes which both lit as well as diverge from the state-of-the-art picture.

1. Introduction: A deterministic approach for the neolithic shift

One of the most prominent scientific goals within the last decade has been the assessment of human impacts on global climate (IPCC 2001). Nevertheless it is still an unresolved problem to embed the anthroposphere into the world's physical, chemical and ecological systems (Kane and Yohe 2000, Ramankutty and Foley 1998). In current climate models human impacts thus mostly appear as a predefined scenario, whereas relevant processes like vegetation change due to land-use (Tilman et al. 2001), are not represented in a fully adaptive and dynamic way.

The basic requirement when integrating a feed-back sensitive land-use dynamics into climate model algorithms are simulation tools which can deal with cultural or economic change in relation to endogenous as well as exogenous forces. However, even if one focuses on the early Neolithic period where man-nature relationship can be assumed to be much less complex than in (post)industrial times, no starting basis for a deterministic and quantitative approach is existing. Contrary, many archaeologists and pre-historians raise fundamental doubts against any attempt of reducing historic processes to few generalising explanations (Taylor 2001).

But a second group of scholars persists in searching for primordial causes behind the independent occurrence of agricultural centres in the Old and New World (e.g. Steward 1955, Toynbee1989). Despite the many facets up to date revealed by archaeological evidence, these scientists are fascinated by the idea of finding a generic why for the spatially non-correlated shifts from millions of years of human hunting-gathering to agricultural food production.

Both needs, the one of climate modellers as well as of the latter group of theoretical anthropologists and historians, were recently addressed by Wirtz and Lemmen (2002) who for the first time suggested a deterministic mathematical model able to generate the spatio-temporal pattern of subsistence style alteration in a realistic and robust way. In this paper, the model is shortly described while special emphasis is invested on the formulation used for simulating overexploitation of natural resources. This tool opens the way to systematically analyse the backslash effect of non-sustainable exploitation as one of the outcomes of regional development on the development trajectory itself.

2. The model: Aggregating and integrating process units

A detailed derivation and verification of the mathematical model is given by Wirtz and Lemmen (2002). In brief, the model describes the time evolution of four state variables which quantify relevant characteristics of a regional population with special regard on its food productivity. Beside the classical variable *Population Density* (PD) we have in particular three conceptually new measures:

· *a Technology Index* (TI) which describes the efficiency of resource use comprising the availability of tools, engineering knowledge but also aspects of social organisation like division of labour,

· *the Farming Quota*, i.e. the relative amount of effort put into farming/herding compared to foraging activity,

· and the established Number of Agricultures with which, for example, grain cultivation or grassland pastoralism is intended.

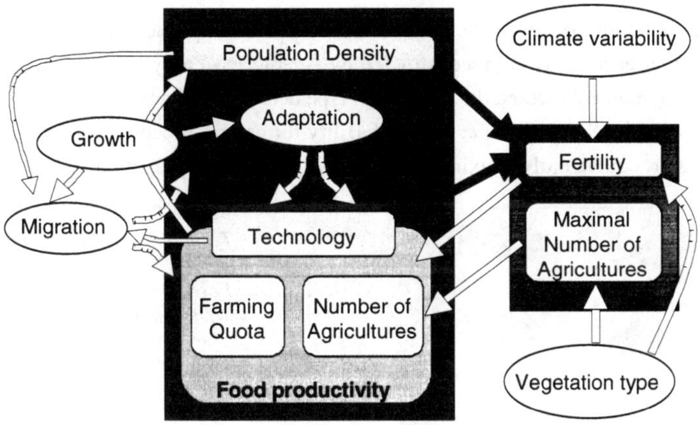

Figure 1: Graphical representation of the model. The central rectangular box ("anthroposphere") contains the four state variables, the right box the two resolved properties of the "biosphere". Arrows indicate dependencies and ellipses the key mechanisms and boundary conditions.

It is a straightforward exercise to relate population growth to food productivity which in turn is affected by the local fertility, as graphically represented in *Fig. 1*. But in order to find appropriate evolution equations for the listed three variables, a major methodological improvement is required. The idea here is to derive their time dependent behaviour on an adaptation assumption: If the actual state is non-optimal with respect to growth, it will change with time towards a better suited value. Direction as well as velocity of this movement can be mathematically derived on the base of marginal changes of growth function under variations of the state variables (Wirtz 2000). With this method a multidimensional regional development including technological innovation and maintenance, domestication and adoption of new ways of life can be numerically integrated.

Though the two variables *Farming Quota* and *Number of Agricultures* build the key units in the model, they are not discussed more profoundly in this work.

Beside adaptation as central element for temporal evolution, all state variables are subjected to changes due to diffusion between neighboured regions. Local exchange is supposed to be unilateral going from the more to the less "influential" zone expressed through spatial differences in the product of PD and TI. Colonisation, warfare and trade are implicitly accounted for by this concept. In addition, spread is enhanced under crisis when the local growth rate becomes negative (see arrows in *Fig. 1, p. 43*).

The spatial distribution of the 196 homogenous regions currently resolved is based on the vegetation type boundaries at 5 kyr BP reconstructed by Adams and Faury (1997). Being a proxy for a series of biogeographical factors, the vegetation type determines the two environmental boundary conditions needed by the model, i.e. habitat fertility for calorie procurement and the diversity in domesticables or, equivalently, maximal number of agricultural production styles.

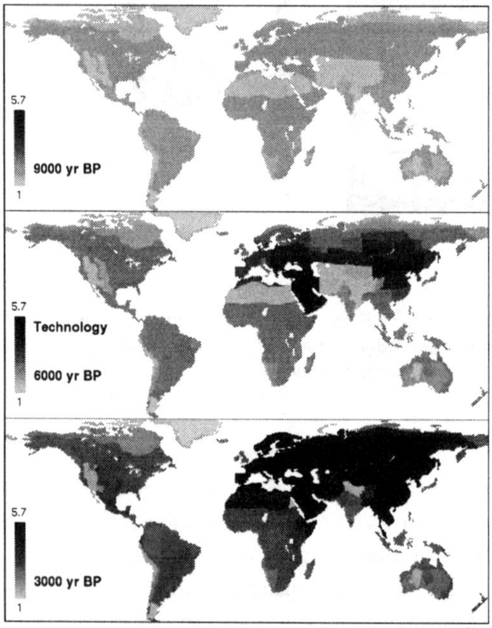

Figure 2: Projected evolution of the Technology Index TI around the globe. Three time slices are shown. For details of the model set-up see Wirtz and Lemmen (2002).

In addition to the stationary distribution of biogeographical properties the model includes a modulation of the fertility which mimics long lasting cooling events repeated at a period of around 1.5 kyr (see also *Fig. 4, p. 47* and de Menocal 2001). Although variations in vegetation type are globally synchronised, the effective fertility change may differ among neighboured areas. That is due to the non-linear relation between the two measures.

The third source of fertility variations originates from human action itself. Food productivity includes the calorie gain achieved by hunting-gathering as well as farming. Both activities may equally lead to a negative feed-back. Macrofauna extinction as well as soil degradation are well-known representatives of long-term fertility loss. Hardin (1993) proposed a quantitative impact proportional to TI and to PD taken to the power of n. In most cases, n should exceed one. But since technology contributes to fertility loss in some but not all of its aspects, the non-linear formula is re-transformed to the product of PD and the square root of the TI, times a specific constant of proportionality, here denoted as *Kover* . According its definition, *Kover* can be regarded as a specific habitat vulnerability.

Even from the brief overview it should be clear that the underlying philosophy is to keep model complexity and parameterisation effort as low as possible. Nonetheless, the model is able to hindcast when and where natural preconditions had led to land-use intensification, and how its negative feed-back on resource availability produces a specific response of the evolving communities.

3. Studies on different overexploitation regimes

3.1 Constructing a reference

A typical simulation result of the global dynamic model is shown in Fig. 2 where the technological development is quantified via the region specific dynamics in TI. In the early Holocene no remarkable gradients can be found: All life supporting habitats are populated with communities sharing essentially the same efficiency of tool manufacture, hunting techniques and social stratification. The situation dramatically changes soon after the mid-Holocene shift, when agricultural societies soon reach a new technological level. The spatial patterns of hot Neolithic spots produced by the model is heavily in line with archaeological evidence. First, one observes in Fig. 2 the two distant Eurasian centres Fertile Crescent and East China from where the new production style together with higher technology is spread to nearby areas. Second, in mid-Holocene times other continents begin to lag behind. Even to the agriculturists of the New World, correctly located at Central Mexico and the Andes, lower TI values are attributed at 3 kyr BP than to the Eurasian societies at 6 kyr BP.

3.2 Sensitivity of technology evolution

For our question, how development is affected by the possible over-use of resources, we assess the sensitivity of the spatio-temporal development pattern to changing overexploitation regimes. These regimes were already quantified by the coefficient *Kover* introduced in the last section. In addition, the continental gradients in technological advancement at 3 kyr BP are well character-

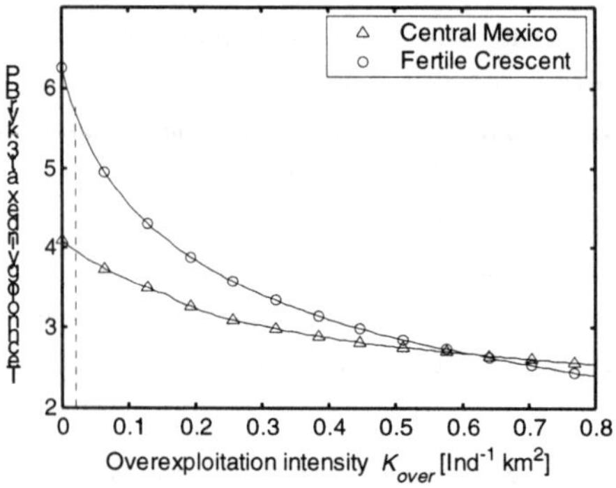

Figure 3: Technology index of the two regions Central Mexico and Fertile Crescent at 3 kyr BP. Simulations were run with different specific overexploitation coefficient K_{over}. *Its value in the standard run (*K_{over} *= 0.02 Ind*$^{-1}$ *km*^{2}*) is represented by the dashed line.*

ised by the TI values of the two kernels Central Mexico and Fertile Crescent. *Fig. 3* shows these values calculated within a series of simulations where only the specific overexploitation intensity *Kover* is varied. Obviously, the variation interval is much too large since reasonable estimates for *Kover* are lower than 0.05 Ind-1 km2 what would set the maximum population density at approximately 5 Ind km-2. Within this realistic *Kover* range the gap between the two worlds remain stable except for some quantitative modifications as final TI decreases with growing vulnerability. That is by part immanent to the adaptive behaviour of the simulated technology dynamics by which production efficiency gains have to compensate losses in habitat fertility.

When leaving the zone of reasonable *Kover* values, the pattern reverts and the less favoured areas may achieve a more elevated stage. This result motivates the following speculation: in a world highly vulnerable to human action those communities with slower developing rates will be better suited in the long run than their rushing counterparts. But vulnerability represents still an abstract concept. Despite the obvious transformations of landscape during and after the mid-Holocene shift (e.g. Louwe Kooijmans, in this volume), it is still unclear to what degree large zones were made less productive on the scale of decades and centuries. In addition, our simple formula neglects variations in vulnerability along distinct landscape types. For example, deforestation acts differently in mountainous Mediterranean regions and plain Alluvial soils.

3.3 Sensitivity of global migration rates

Import of traits via migration works as the second model mechanism leading to structural transformations in prehistoric communities. In *Fig. 4* the global sum of migration rates between each region and its neighbours is plotted over time, once for the standard simulation and for a presumed vanishing human impact on the biosphere (*Kover* = 0). Both runs reveal a highly illustrative example of temporal self-organisation, here visible through the formation of distinct waves. Obviously, these waves are triggered by the imposed climate fluctuation. Their globally averaged effect on local fertility is shown in the lower diagram. The phase locking between fertility and migration rate derives from a combination of many effects. The most relevant one follows from the different impact of variations between adjacent regions (see Section 2). Populations after the Neolithic shift have reached carrying capacity and are therefore always prone to outmigration. Then even a minor spatial decoupling in climatic deterioration can produce a remarkably synchronised response on a global scale.

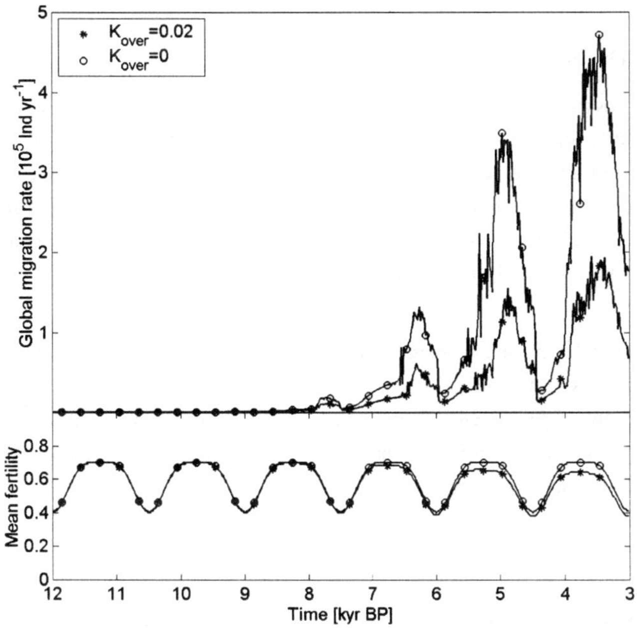

Figure 4 Top: Global sum of net capita exchange between adjacent regions. The two underlying simulation were run with standard and vanishing specific vulnerability K_{over}.Bottom: Globally averaged habitat fertility for the same pair of simulations.

How is such synergy effect amplified by overexploitation? Indeed one may expect that a lower vulnerability, and thus, resource depletion in succession of intruding populations is preventing later out-migration. According the model results, however, the opposite is true: With vanishing

Kover the migration rate even more than duplicates, as obvious from Fig. 4. Among the several mechanism responsible for this trend we have, for example, higher magnitudes of absolute TI *(Fig. 3, seep. 46)* and PD values, in particular in higher developed regions. Since less prolific areas constantly show low densities, gradients become more pronounced which in turn enhances the overall spreading intensity.

When further interpreting the negative correlation between overexploitation and migration intensities one has to be aware of the spatial and temporal scales inherent to the model calculations as well as of the many simplifying assumptions it is built on. The picture may be reverted when going to shorter time periods, sub-regional scales, and in particular to inhomogeneously populated habitats where carrying capacity is not reached.

4. Conclusion: The benefit of system analysis

The two studies shortly presented here provide some evidence for the usefulness of a deterministic model in anthropological sciences. Already due to the spatial coupling of 196 regional trajectories one observes unexpected effects hardly predictable with classical methods. Numerous path-ways of prehistoric communities are strongly aggregated but at the same time not necessarily neglected. The quantitative nature of the approach allows for integrating a spectrum of relevant processes, and, above all, for specifying their relative contribution on the variables of interest.

The sensitivity analysis presented here provides only one of the many possible methodologies. As soon as deterministic models gain acceptance in the "new" field of historic and anthropological sciences, the entire equipment of system analysis developed in the natural sciences can be made profitable. Our understanding of the puzzles left by past (and present) communities will then certainly make a big step forward.

Acknowledgements

Special thanks go to Wolfgang Ebenhöh and Bert de Vries for their encouragement and to Georg Hooss for a critical reading of the manuscript. Carsten Lemmen assisted with the organisation of the model software.

References

Adams J. M. and H. Faure. 1997. Review and Atlas of Palaeovegetation: Preliminary land ecosystem maps of the world since the Last Glacial Maximum. Oak Ridge National Laboratory, TN, USA. http://www.esd.ornl.gov/ern/qen/adams1.html

de Menocal, P.B. 2001. Cultural responses to climate change during the late Holocene, in: Science 292: 667-673.

Hardin, G. 1993. Living Within The Limits. New York: Oxford Univ. Pr.

IPCC. 2001. Climate Change 2001 -- the Scientific Basis. Technical Report, World Meteorological Institution, The Edinburgh Building, Shaftesbury Road, Cambride CB2 2RU, UK.

Kane, S. and G. Yohe. 2000. Societal adaptation to climate variability and change: An introduction. Clim. Change 45: 1-4.

Ramankutty, N. and J. Foley. 1998. Characterizing patterns of global land use: An analysis of global croplands data, in: Glob. Biogeochem. Cycles 12: 667-685.

Steward, J. 1955. Theory of Culture Change: The Methodology of Multilinear Evolution. Urbana: University of Illinois Pr.

Taylor, T. 2001. Explanatory tyranny, in: Nature: 411, 419.

Tilman, D., J. Fargione, B. Wolff, C. D'Antonio, A. Dobson, R. Howarth, D. Schindler, W.H. Schlesinger, D. Simberloff and D. Swackhamer. 2001. Forecasting agriculturally driven global environmental change, in: Science: 292: 281-284.

Toynbee, A. J. 1989. A Study of History: Abridgement of Volumes VII-X. Oxford University Press.

Wirtz, K.W. 2000. Simulating the dynamics of leaf physiology and morphology with an extended optimality approach, in: Ann. Bot. 86: 753-764.

Wirtz, K.W. and C. Lemmen 2002. A global dynamic model for the Neolithic transition, in Clim. Change (in press.).

John R. McNeill

Resource Exploitation and Over-Exploitation: A Look at the 20th Century

Abstract

The 20th century's environmental history was peculiar. Various developments, including a 13-fold expansion of energy use and a 4-fold expansion in human population, created ecological tumult unlike anything in human history. That tumult included accelerated exploitation of natural resources, provoking numerous analyses and forecasts predicting overexploitation and shortages. The most troublesome overexploitation concerned "sinks", that is the buffering capacity of ecosystems, and certain biological resources, e.g. fisheries. Technological change and substitutions mitigated the importance of the exploitation of minerals and fuels.

By the standards of the more distant past, the 20th century was very peculiar. One measure of its peculiarity is its prodigality: its record of resource use. On several occasions, concerned observers lamented the rate of resource use and predicted dire shortages. The shortages predicted rarely occurred, normally because price signals provoked either conservation or more thorough efforts to locate further supplies (or both). Shortages that did occur usually proved less dire than expected, normally because of substitution of one material for another.

This is not to say that the environmental effects of human action in the 20th century were inconsequential: far from it. Rather, it is to say that those effects proved, and are proving, more troublesome in departments other than those usually anticipated. The world in the 20th century did not run short of coal, oil, natural gas, construction timber, nickel, or uranium. It depleted its supply of all these things, but not seriously. It did not even run short of food, despite a four-fold expansion in human numbers from 1.5 billion to 6 billion, although patterns of food distribution meant that famines still took place. The most serious overexploitation was that of sinks for wastes. That is because for many human uses, there are no substitutes for air and water; and because the reigning conceptions in economics and law meant that the price mechanism did not provide useful signals. The second most serious overexploitation was of renewable, biological resources.

1. The magnitudes of 20th century environmental change

First, consider some rough estimates of the size and intensity of environmental changes, world-wide, in the 20th century, and with estimates of the strength of the forces driving these changes.

Raw population growth was, in my opinion, the 2nd most important driving force behind 20th-century environmental change. Whereas throughout most of human history, global population grew very slowly, by much less than one-tenth of 1% per year, by 1900-1950 the rate attained nearly 1%. And by the second half of the 20th century, the rate climbed to 1.7% per year, and indeed at times to over 4% in a few countries. The global population growth rate peaked in the late 1960s, and has since been in decline, although total population continues to grow. Of all the years lived by hominids and *homo sapiens* over the past 4 million years, about 20% were lived in the 20th century.[1]

The world's economy grew even faster than population in the 20th century, which is why we are (on average) richer than our grandparents and great-grandparents. The size of the world's economy has grown by about 130-fold since 1500, and about 15-fold since 1900. Today Japan alone produces as much as the whole world did a century ago. All of us alive today have come to regard such a fantastic expansion of wealth as normal, as it has been throughout our lifetimes with only brief interruptions. But is it anything but normal by the standards of the more distant past. Much of this growth was driven by population; the rest by technological and organizational changes. On a per capita basis, average incomes grew 4-fold in the 20th century. This is an average, which of course disguises gross inequities. The average Mozambican today has an income well under half of the global average of 500 years ago and less than 2% of the average German's or American's. The 20th century saw a tremendous expansion in inequality as well as in the creation of wealth.[2]

A big part of the reason that economic growth outstripped population growth lies in the history of energy use in the 20th century. This I regard as the single most important driving force behind modern environmental change and resource use. The world's total energy use grew by nearly 5-fold in the 19th century and then by another 13- or 14-fold in the 20th century. The chief reason for this was the development of fossil fuels, mainly coal and oil, but since 1950, also natural gas.

---

[1]The data and calculations behind these statements are drawn from Biraben 1979 and Bourgeois-Pichat 1988. See also Haub 1995.

[2]See Maddison 1995.

Nuclear energy and hydropower played much smaller roles. Around 1890 or so fossil fuels came to provide more than half of the world's energy supply, so the 20th century was truly an age of fossil fuels.[3]

In the hundred centuries from the dawn of agriculture to 1900, humanity used only about two-thirds as much energy (most of it from biomass) that we used in the 20th century. Indeed it is likely that humankind used more energy in the 20th century than in all preceding human history put together. From the point of view of energetics, the 20th century was extremely peculiar.

The 20th century was peculiar in many other respects directly relevant to resources and environment. The world's total urban population grew by about 13-fold, and the proportion of people living in cities by nearly 4-fold. Its total industrial output grew by roughly 40-fold, its freshwater use by 9-fold and its irrigated area by 5-fold. All this stood behind the incessant quest for more food, fiber, coal, oil, gas, mineral ores, water, timber, and almost every other resource one can think of. The scope and scale of these changes in a mere three or four human generations should makes it easy to suppose the earth will soon run out of what have become essential resources for humankind.

2. Resource stress and energy shortage in the fossil fuel era

For most of human history, our ancestors made do each year with what energy they could harvest from the annual flows provided by the sun, plus what they could garner by burning wood and charcoal. Plants captured some of the sun's energy delivered to the earth. People ate some of those plants, or ate animals who ate plants. This supplied the muscle power that did almost all the work, supplemented in some societies by draft animals, and, eventually, by wind and water power. All the work done depended on the annual flows of energy from the sun, and no one could store up energy effectively. For heating, but not for work, people also used wood and charcoal, which allowed them to tap solar energy stored over a few centuries (if they cut and burned old trees). But this was the only significant use of energy stocks (as opposed to flows).

That situation changed when the Dutch began to use peat, a source of energy stored over millennia in the bogs and swamps that used to make up most of the Netherlands. From medieval times forward the Dutch enjoyed low energy costs, and built energy-intensive industries such as brewing, glass-making, brick-making, and sugar-refining. They worried that their peat might run out, and not without reason, as their prosperity and power depended on it.

A similar worry on a larger scale occurred in Britain soon after coal became the basis for British prosperity. Coal could do much more than peat once it became practical to use it in iron-making

[3]See Smil 1994 and 1999.

(after 1709) and, with steam engines, in pumping and indeed for countless tasks calling for mechanical energy. Since at least 1789, not long after James Watt's decisive improvement of the steam engine, Britons were calculating how long their island's coal supply might last. The early forecasts averaged around 300-400 years. In 1865 the English logician and economist William Stanley Jevons published a book called *The Coal Question.* He had taken stock of the escalating figures concerning coal consumption in Britain, had consulted the estimates of how much coal remained in the ground, and concluded that a crisis of coal supply lay ahead. While he never said that Britain would run out of coal, he forecast that by 1950 or 1970 the price of recovering further coal would be so high that Britain's prosperity would be a thing of the past. The work won Jevons wide renown and a chair in political economy.

But Jevons was mistaken. There was plenty of coal left underground in Britain. When the price of coal crept upward, as it did from time to time, British miners and geologists found coal in new places and found it worthwhile to dig out more from old places. Eventually the miners and their employers convinced Parliament that coal was so essential that they extracted subsidies from the Government, encouraging the quest for coal that would otherwise have been unrewarding to mine. Even today, billions of tons later, there is still plenty of coal in Britain. Most of it is probably destined never to be mined. And Britain is far more prosperous than in Jevons' day, although it no longer is the richest country in the world. What was true of British coal was true of the world's: the estimated supply of global coal reserves nearly doubled between 1913 and 1990 despite the mining in the meantime of 200 gigatons. It now stands at 250-300 years' worth at current rates of use, although some estimates suggest 600 years..[4]

In the early 1900s, when the United States was pioneering the conversion of both transport and industry to oil, worried observers undertook the same sort of calculation for American oil as Jevons had made for British coal. The first calculations implied only a 10-year supply. In 1930, given the best estimates of existing supply, and the trends in oil use, it seemed the oil might run out by 1940. (If it had, the Second World War would have turned out differently). But these predictions proved as inaccurate as Jevons' and for the same reasons. Oil was found in new places, and price rises and better drilling techniques made it possible to find more in the same old places. Indeed, in the USA more oil was found in the 1930s than in any decade before or since. Prevailing estimates of potentially recoverable oil grew 4-7 fold between 1940 and 1980. In the early 1970s, when political events brought about a tripling of crude oil prices, dire predictions about oil supply followed. The American CIA in 1978 estimated that global production would have to decline by 1988 at the latest because of shortages. But within ten years the proven reserves of oil had jumped to an all-time high: once again higher prices had made it rewarding to drill and pump up more oil. Indeed, since 1920 the ratio of oil reserves to annual production has remained be-

[4]Smil 1999:136-7.

tween 25 and 40, that is a 25-40-year supply (the same is true for natural gas, despite the sharp increase in consumption since 1960).[5]

Throughout the 20th century such predictions for coal, for oil, for copper, for uranium (which in the 1970s was thought to exist in supplies sufficient to last only to 2000 or 2020 and now is expected to last until 2100) and sundry other raw materials have proved wrong. At the moment, the best estimates are that there is about 41 years' worth of oil left at current consumption rates. But those rates will eventually fall, and there will still be oil in the ground in 100 years. It is not, of course, that there is an infinite supply of these things on earth: there is not. But we shall never dig out the last ton of coal or pump up the last barrel of oil, because long before we get to that point it will be economic to substitute other sources of energy. And, for that matter, if we did burn all that coal and oil in only a few centuries, the carbon dioxide levels in the atmosphere would be far higher than at present, and the globe much warmer. This leads to the heart of the matter.

But before we get there, I want to emphasize one thing. While I claim that there was no coal crisis or oil shortage on a global basis, this does not mean that everyone always has enough. Many a family passed a cold winter without coal because they did not have money to buy it, even though there were billions of tons in the earth. Every year many people die of hunger, but the world is not short of food.

3. The overexploitation of sinks

The atmosphere and hydrosphere are used as sinks for all manner of pollutants. So are soils. Air, water, and earth all have the capacity to absorb, break down or recycle certain amounts of certain pollutants. But there are thresholds beyond which pollutants accumulate faster than they can be dissipated. In the 20th century the atmosphere and hydrosphere were obliged to accept overloads. As a consequence they became durably polluted, in places acutely so, with unwelcome consequences for living things in general and human health in particular. These were the most important overexploitations of resources in the 20th century. Happily, they are also among the most easily reversible.

Air pollution, most of which came from the combustion of fossil fuels, increased – very roughly speaking – b y 2 to 10-fold in the 20th century.[6] Ecosystems were affected most by acidic emissions, mainly of sulfur dioxide, but also from nitrogen flux. In the long run, they may be yet more affected by carbon emissions via global warming, but that belongs to the future.

---

[5]In addition to Smil's works cited above, see Deffeyes 2001.

[6]For the basis of this estimate, see McNeill 2000: 63-4.

The most important air pollution problem for human health was the prevalence of particulate matter in urban areas and indoors. Sulfur dioxide and lead emissions also produced health problems. In the 1990s, urban air pollution killed about half a million people annually, a bit less than auto accidents, a quarter of the toll from malaria or tuberculosis. All told, urban air pollution probably killed somewhere around 25-40 million people in the 20th century, numerically about equal to the great influenza pandemic of 1918-19 or the combined casualties of the World Wars. Equal to, but not equivalent to – because the death toll from air pollution came over a century, rather than in a few years, and because the respiratory ailments caused by air pollution tended to kill the very old, the very young, and those already sick, whereas war and influenza killed far more people in the prime of life.[7]

Indoor air pollution, mainly in poor countries where fuelwood and coal are used in domestic heating and cooking stoves, surely killed far more people. I have found no reliable data and will make no estimates. In any case, this is not a matter of overexploitation of resources, unless one considers indoor air as a resource.

The overexploitation of water as a sink for wastes is more important still. For thousands of years people have dumped wastes in the nearest stream or river. Most of these were biological wastes. In the 19th and 20th centuries people started dumping large quantities of chemical wastes as well, occasionally obliterating all life in some bodies of water. From the point of view of human health, however, biological contamination in the form of pathogenic microbes remained by far the most important water problem. Today water pollution kills about 5 million people per year, some 10 times the toll from urban air pollution. Most of these are in poor countries where sanitation infrastructure is weak. A very rough guess of the century's death toll from polluted water is 300-500 million. Most of these were and are small children, but dysenteries, typhoid, and cholera also killed plenty of people in their most productive years. This in itself is a good argument for the proposition that the most serious overexploitation of resources in the 20th century was of freshwater sinks.

4. Pollution control in the 20th century

An encouraging feature of the 20th century was its attention to the problems created by overuse of sinks. For millennia, people had sought to segregate waste water from drinking water, but only rarely with consistent success. Some of the more successful cases are the ancient Indus cities of Harappa and Mohenjodaro, and of course ancient Rome. But their capacity to construct hydraulic engineering works was unusual; most urban societies suffered greatly from bacterial pollution.

[7] McNeill 2000:102-4.

But with the emerging science of bacteriology in the late 19th century, it became possible to take effective action, to convince relevant political bodies of that possibility, and to improve the health of hundreds of millions. The decisive steps – wastewater treatment, large-scale metropolitan waterworks – occurred between 1890 and 1930 in most of the rich countries and in some colonial settings. In poorer countries this "sanitation revolution" took place only after 1950, and is by no means complete today.

Lowering the actual pollution loads of the world's waters was a different matter from safeguarding supplies of drinking water. Efforts in this direction became increasingly common in the 19th century, at least in Britain where rivers were dangerously polluted. But the most effective measures came only after 1970 as part of the worldwide ecology movement. At very modest cost it proved possible to reduce drastically the pollution loads from factories and cities, although not from farms. The modern history of the Rhine river is a prominent example of how quickly waterways – at least rivers – can be cleaned up to the point where fish species long absent will return. The Rhine after 1850 carried heavy loads of industrial pollution, which by the early 20th century had killed off many of its fish species, such as salmon, sturgeon and mayfish. It served, in effect, as the open sewer draining one of the world's great industrial zones. But after 1965 political authorities in Switzerland, France, Germany, and Holland cooperated sufficiently to change the incentives governing pollution of the Rhine, and by 1975 the river was getting cleaner. By 1992 fishermen could catch salmon in the Rhine. [8]

The ambition to control air pollution also long predates the 20th century. Some London regulations go back to the 13th century. But significant reductions in urban air pollution date only from the mid-20th century. St. Louis was a pioneer in this respect, creating an unlikely coalition of politicians, businessmen, crusading journalists and housewives in 1940-41 that together sharply reduced smoke, soot and sulfur emissions from the coal-powered city. Pittsburgh, London, Osaka, and Mexico City – a quartet of poster-children for air pollution – managed sharp reductions in their emissions between 1955 and 1995. They achieved it through fuel substititions, using less coal and more natural gas, through various technical improvements to smokestacks and auto engines, and various regulations, such as limits on driving in Mexico City. The resulting improvements in air quality and human health were correspondingly sharp in the old coal-fired cities of Europe, North America and Japan. They were not in Mexico City, which continued to grow fast, continued to expand its vehicle fleet, and, most importantly, continued to bathe in bright sunshine while resting in a bowl subject to frequent temperature inversions – a perfect recipe for brewing smog.

[8] Cioc 2002 forthcoming; Lelek 1989; Haberer 1991; Reihelt 1986; Malle 1996.

Meanwhile, many large cities at the end of the century suffered from increased, rather than decreased pollution loads. In Delhi, Bangkok, Cairo, and Seoul burgeoning vehicle use and/or reliance on coal combined to make for particularly unhealthy air. In several cities of north China, heavy reliance on a particularly dirty coal created what are probably the most polluted cities on earth today. Urban air quality, which 100 years ago was much worse in the rich countries than in the poor ones, today is among the many reasons life is easier in the rich world.[9]

On a global basis, the whole atmosphere was seriously overexploited as a sink in the 20th century. This was especially true for two classes of pollutants, ozone-rupturing chemicals such as CFCs, and greenhouse gases. These stories are very familiar ones by now, and I shall not rehearse them. I will only say that the consequences of depleting stratospheric ozone and of loading the atmosphere with greenhouse gases are durable across several human generations, widespread around the world, and potentially acute. The full range of consequences is not yet apparent, and not yet possible to predict with precision, but it seems quite plausible that these will one day appear as the principle costs of overexploitation of the atmospheric sink.

5. Renewable resources

It is one of ironies of environmental history – a field rich with ironies – that so-called several renewable resources came under greater stress in the 20th century than the non-renewables such as coal and copper. For example, fisheries and forests: as biological resources these are renewable. But in the 20th century the global marine fish catch climbed from about 2 million metric tons to about 75 million (this does not count inland fish catch or aquaculture). If official figures are at all accurate, the seas surrendered more fish in the 20th century than in all previous centuries combined. As a result of intensifying fishing effort, and lack of effective regulation, one after another marine fishery collapsed in the 20th century. Some recovered, some did not, but the total catch continued to climb as new fisheries were discovered, or perhaps better put, subjected to more efficient methods. The last frontier was the pilchard fishery of the southeast Pacific, opened up in 1971. Since the late 1980s, all marine fisheries have been exploited at or above sustainable levels. To maintain the catch at more or less the same levels, increasingly uneconomic fish are targeted. About a billion people depend on marine fish as their chief source of protein.[10]

The history of the world's forests in the 20th century is another case, somewhat less acute but perhaps more consequential, of overexploitation of a renewable resource. Forest and woodland area shrank by about 20% in the 20th century, accounting for perhaps half of the net deforestation in world history. Of the 20th century's total deforestation, about half occurred in the tropics after

---

[9] McNeill 2000: 64-83.

[10] Jackson 2001; McNeill 2000:243-51.

1960. People clear forests in order to use the timber or to use the land (or, rarely, both). Over the course of the 20th century, about 80% of forest clearance was motivated by the wish to farm the land, about 20% by the quest for timber. [11]

The consequences of this massive forest clearance, one of the hallmarks of the 20th century, are unclear. Surely it reduced biodiversity somewhat, although measurement remains elusive here. Surely it also added plenty of carbon to the atmosphere, perhaps 10-20% as much as did fossil fuel combustion. Surely it changed local climates and exposed millions of hectares of soil to erosion. It will take time and much work to figure out what the full meaning of this history of forest clearance might mean.

6. Conclusion

While I remain persuaded that the most important overexploitation of resources in the 20th century were those of the atmosphere and of fresh waters as sinks for wastes, this must be only a provisional judgment: Because biological resources were also overexploited in the sense that their stocks declined, and in the further sense that their yields declined, sometimes to zero. It is in fact too soon to tell just which overexploitations will ultimately prove the most meaningful. Fish populations sometimes bounce back in a year or two from severe declines. Forests can recover in a century or three. The stratospheric ozone shield will return to its former robust state by 2080 or so, if emissions of ozone-rupturing chemicals are checked, as to a considerable degree they have been. Cheap desalinization of seawater would at a stroke reduce the costs and importance of freshwater pollution. And the future history of global warming will determine how seriously one ought to regard the 20th century's (and the 21st's) loading of the atmosphere with greenhouse gases.

Thucydides wrote contemporary history with such clairvoyance that his judgments on the Peloponnesian War still command respect 24 centuries later. His wisdom overcame the inevitable problems that arise from not knowing how everything will turn out. Despite the best efforts of climate modelers and futurists we do not know how the environmental history of the 20th century will turn out, because although the century is over the processes set in motion (e.g. stratospheric ozone depletion or dramatic greenhouse gas loading of the atmosphere) are still in train. In due course it will be clearer whether my judgments stand the test of time like those of Thucydides – or ultimately fail the test, like those of Jevons.

[11] A recent review of world deforestation history is Chew 2001; McNeill 2000: 229-37.

References

Biraben, J. N. 1979. "Essai sur l'évolution du nombre des hommes", Population 34: 13-24.

Bourgeois-Pichat, J. 1988. "Du XXe au XXIe siècle: Europe et sa population après l'an 2000", Population 43: 9-42.

Chew, Sing S. 2001. World Ecological Degradation: Accumulation, Urbanization, and Deforestation, 3000 B.C.–A.D. 2000 (Lanham: Rowman & Littlefield).

Cioc, Mark 2002. The Rhine: An Eco-Biography (Seattle: University of Washington Press).

Debeir, Jean-Claude et al 1986. Les servitudes de la puissance (Paris: Flammarion).

Deffeyes, Kenneth S. 2001. Hubbert's Peal: The Impending World Oil Shortage (Princeton: Princeton University Press).

Haberer, Klaus 1991. "Die Belastung des Rheins mit Schadstoffen", Geographische Rundschau 43:334-41.

Haub, Carl 1995. "How Many People Ever Have Lived on Earth?" Population Today 23, 2:4-5.

Jackson, Jeremy B. C. et al 2001. "Historical Overfishing and the Recent Collapse of Coastal Ecosystems", Science 293: 629-37.

Jevons, William S. 1965. The coal question; an inquiry concerning the progress of the Nation, and the probable exhaustion of our coal-mines (New York: A.M. Kelley [London, 1865]).

Lelek, Antonin 1989. "The Rhine River and Some of Its Tributaries Under Human Impact in the Last Two Centuries." In: D.P. Dodge, ed., Proceedings of the International Large River Symposium (Ottawa: Department of Fisheries and Oceans, Special Publication of Fisheries and Aquatic Sciences, 106: 469-87.

Maddison, Angus 1995. Monitoring the World Economy, 1820-1992 (Paris: OECD Development Centre).

Malle, Karl-Geert 1996. "Cleaning Up the River Rhine", Scientific American 274, 1:70-75.

McNeill, J.R. 2000. Something New Under the Sun: An Environmental History of the Twentieth-Century World (New York: Norton).

Meybeck, Michel 1979. "Concentrations des eaux fluviales en éléments majeurs et apports en solution aux océans", Revue de géologie dynamique et géographie physique 221: 215-46.

Reihelt, Günther 1986. Lasst den Rhein leben (Düsseldorf: Girardet).

Smil, Vaclav 1994. Energy in World History (Boulder: Westview).

Smil, Vaclav 1999. Energies: An Illustrated Guide to the Biosphere and Civilization (Cambridge: M.I.T. Press).

2. Environmental History

Leendert P. Louwe Kooijmans

Archaeological Approaches to the Long-Term History of the Landscape

Abstract

The paper discusses the two rather controversial approaches to the landscape in prehistoric archaeology. First, the physical landscape is treated as the arena of subsistence activities, second, the 'symbolic landscape' constructed by societies as the context of their social and spiritual lives. It is subsequently discussed how many pitfalls there are not so much in the empirical reconstruction of the physical environment, but especially in the attempts to understand the man-land relationships and their transformations on the very long term: Ethnographic analogy has the danger to degrade prehistory to a clone of subrecent societies and to deprive it of its originality. Ethnocentrism brings modern values in. Ecological determinism reverses the causes and effects.

The second part gives an outline of the man-nature relations in the Lower Rhine basin since the last Ice Age as far as empirical data allow. It is the story of the 'domestication' of the landscape. After the small-scale reclamations of the Neolithic the forests were rigorously opened up in the first millennium cal. BC by the plough farmers of the Bronze Age. The so-called Celtic field system of the subsequent first millennium can be conceived as a measure to restore sustainability on the poor upland coversand landscapes. A restricted number of demographic data together with the long term environmental impact registrations of pollen diagrams allow us to follow the dynamics of environment and society over the last seven or even more millennia.

1. Reflections

Landscape archaeology: The ecological approach

Landscape archaeology deals with the use and transformation of the land surface and its vegetation by man in the past. It tries to trace these transformations through time in their cultural and geographical differentiation and it tries to understand the how and why of the inferred processes. It also tries to grasp the attitude of former people and societies to their natural surroundings and the meanings or symbolic connotations they connected to it.

Nowadays two landscape approaches can be made out as research lines. I will call these short hand the ecological and the symbolical. Let me first deal with the ecological approach. That is the field of study of settlement and subsistence, in relation to the natural environment by field archaeology, in cooperation with palaeobotanists, archaeozoologists and Quaternary geologists: The environment seen exclusively as a source of food and resource of raw materials. It is a very functionalistic and positivist approach of man-nature relations. We should, however, ask ourselves: To what extent we can really *reconstruct* the landscape, and to what extent we can really *reconstruct* subsistence. Are these aspects of the past really knowable or should we better speak of our 'constructions' than of the more pretentious 'reconstructions'?

The landscape

Reconstruction of the physical environment is not very problematical. Landforms in the last few millennia have hardly changed and we can map sediments in the lowland zones, but former soil conditions are often difficult to assess on the basis of the eroded and degraded conditions of today. Dated palaeosols sealed below monuments like barrows or below colluvium or wind blown sand are rare and themselves not untouched as well.

Our view on former vegetation is more problematic. It is mainly 'reconstructed' on the basis of pollen diagrams, together with presumed soil conditions and with modern natural vegetation types as a reference. But pollen bearing deposits are not always available, especially not in the upland zones, and their interpretation is not easy to follow by a layman and not without pitfalls as well. This is demonstrated by a recent discussion in my country with nature conservationists who wanted to use prehistory as a reference for nature management, while we at the same time are using present day nature as our reference! Some environmentalists argued that large grazers, especially bovids, had created a natural park woodland already in Atlantic times, criticizing the traditional view of the closed deciduous climax forests. It appeared to be very difficult to differentiate between both options on the basis of pollen alone.

Subsistence

An even more cautionary tale is subsistence. Agriculture as such is easily established on the basis of animal bones and charred botanical remains, but in all cases the main composition of the menu – the ratio between crop farming and animal husbandry, the role of wild plant food and of fishing – is rather speculative, since the differences in archaeological formation processes, in conservation and recovery processes make the data incomparable. The importance of milk is difficult to assess, even when there are plenty of animal bones. Calculation of population densities should in most cases be distrusted and always have large margins of error that are rarely or never mentioned. This altogether means that we only have a very general view on the range and volume of activities behind documented environmental changes.

Environmental impact

Reasoning from the observations of human environmental impact in the present, it is not difficult to specify the traces of impact we have to look for in the past. These are first of all vegetation changes, made visible in pollen diagrams: by fire, by cutting trees, by grazing and (over)grazing by herds of domestic animals.

Secondly, physical changes can be documented in sediments: soil degradation, slope erosion, colluviation, increased alluviation of valley floors and the formation of inland dunes. The accurate dating is, however, often problematical.

A major issue is to distinguish the anthropogenic effects from those brought about by natural change of climate, sea level and the like. Illustrative is the discussion over decades to explain the so-called elm decline in pollen diagrams around 5300-5000 BP, originally seen as the reflection of large scale pollarding of the lime trees and of extensive leaf foddering of enclosed cattle herds. It is now clear that the scale of the decline is far beyond the capacity of Neolithic farmers, that Neolithic animal husbandry was based on free grazing cattle and at any rate did not include byres, thirdly that the process can be best understood as the result of a natural disease or plague, like the Dutch elm disease.

A main general problem is to generalize from locally observed stratigrafies to more general landscape formation processes on a regional or even continental scale. But this is a general aspect of archaeology, the problem of the representativity of anecdotic observations.

Quarrying and mining

It was not only subsistence that transformed the landscape, but also the exploitation of mineral resources by means of open quarrying and deep mining: flint, igneous rock, copper, tin, iron. The spoil heaps, piled up at the mining sites, demonstrate the non-conservationist and wasting attitude of the miners. The large quantities of firewood needed in roosting the metal ores to obtain the metals must have caused additional deforestation as early as the Bronze Age. To this the enormous consumption of wood for trackways and wooden defensive structures like Biskupin, Poland, and the Celtic oppida of the late Iron Age added to the increased process of the opening of the forests. The concepts of sustainability and conservation seem to be alien to these activities, but at the other hand one might question whether there were any alternatives and whether the offer of nature was so overwhelmingly rich, that the resources seemed inexhaustible, even though certain mining sites seem to have come out of use because of their total depletion.

Landscape archaeology: The symbolic approach

This economic approach has been criticized in the case of hunters for viewing people as 'walking stomachs', by talking about food only, and that even with a 'meat fixation bias' since the botanical component of the menu is hardly visible archaeologically. For farmers we could as a parallel speak of 'settled stomachs'. But people did not live by food alone.

Ethnographic reference

Anthropology tells us that people in subrecent societies tried to understand their being and their environment. They live in a world of miracles that should be understood and in some way be brought under control: life and death, day and night, sun and moon, the seasons, storm and rain, thunder and lightning, fertility of plants, animals and men themselves. In stories and myths people reconcile themselves with the uncertainties of their lives and hand past experience and current knowledge over from generation to generation. They fill the world with powers and spirits of nature and of ancestors, and often link these with locations in the landscape. They seek to get some control over them, or at least communicate with them, by means of song and dance, rituals, offerings and tokens. Most of it is transient and only a part leaves lasting traces, but some acts are very durable.

Monuments in the landscape

We believe to see that these principles worked very similarly in later prehistory: People created in the landscape places of cult, visible to us by rock art and deposition. So we can observe that the landscape was not only exploited economically, but also given meaning: rocks and caves, rivers, lakes and bogs were apparently considered embodied with such powers or at least the media by which communication could taken place. In addition to the impressive body of ecological knowledge an equally impressive body of metaphysical explanations and meanings, much more than physically expressed in the landscape, must have been part of the daily life.

Apart of these means of giving the natural landscape a cultural signature, people transformed and constructed the landscape by reclamation and building of monuments, not only for the dead but for cult as well. The land was 'domesticated', brought under control, structured, brought into culture. We should realize that all of this was a cumulative process, an accumulative investment, inherited from earlier generations and passed on to the next. Once built a stone or earthen structure stood 'for ever', was extended or transformed. So this acculturation of the landscape is a continuous process of structuring and restructuring and extending, of reclamations as well as monuments, depositions and panels of rock art. As observed today many are the outcome of activities over long time spans, covering many generations, palimpsests of symbolic writing in the landscape.

Some biases towards the interpretation of the past

There are some serious restrictions to an unbiased assessment of the relations between man and his environment in the past on the basis of archaeological data:

- the use of ethno-analogies,
- ethnocentric views,
- ecological determinism,
- cultural diversity.

Ethnographic analogy

Yes, archaeologists make lavishly use of ethnography as a reference and even as a simple analogy of the past to better understand and interpret the archaeological remains. This way they try to overcome their often frustrating scantiness and poverty. In a closer look we see the tendency to construct views that surpass the factual information of the artefacts and their patterns by the choice of specific, well-studied ethnicities as a reference, which leaves hardly any space for original aspects of the prehistoric societies involved. So, the specialized Late Palaeolithic hunters become clones of the Nuniamut reindeer hunters, Mesolithic broad spectrum hunter-gatherers are clones of the North American Ojibwa Indians and the early Neolithic farming societies are made a mix of Amazonian Indians, New Guinea Papuas and North American Iroquois. Doing so we deprive the prehistoric past of its cultural uniqueness, of its originality and are in serious danger of circular reasoning: We make constructions of the past based on modern references and subsequently argue that processes and attitudes in the past were strikingly similar to those of today.

Archaeology, after a long period of intense profit from this anthropological inspiration is nowadays more aware of the dangers of this flirtation with the sister discipline. We should be so fair to admit that there is no good counterpart for the European Mesolithic, for the Linearbandkeramik and the complete Bronze Age, just to name a few, and that prehistory was not only different but also more diverse as the present, subrecent ethnographical record. Instead of *assuming* that the anthropological generalizations based on societies in the last one or two centuries are valid for various stages of the past, it is our task to *demonstrate* that this with some degree of probability is the case, or not. So we should clearly *show* that at least some of these anthropological ‘rules’ are the most plausible options to understand the patterns in the archaeological data. This is increasingly necessary when we go deeper into the past and are more remote from the modern men of today, and it is perfectly clear that anthropology does not work anymore when we meet societies that appear to have been fundamentally different: the Neanderthals. Their archaeology is only very partly understood in reference to the present, fundamentally different in many respects and lacking manifestations that we consider common to all humans, like family life, burial of the dead and material symbolism.

Ethnocentrism

Secondly, if we like it or not, we all have some preconceived ideas about the past, especially prehistoric societies, with two extremes: that of ruthless brutes or that of the Rousseau-an 'noble wilds'; ruthless brutes, uncivilized and spoiling savages as part of the wild. Or we idealize prehistoric societies, with their low population densities, living in an unspoiled and 'virgin' environment as 'pure' and in harmony with nature, gratefully cropping from it according to their needs, respectfully exploiting their environs, in a conservationist way that would please Green Peace and the World Wildlife Fund together. Self evidently both attitudes are wrong. Present day ethnography should already be a warning, with the numerous examples of overgrazing and ruthless overexploitation. Neither offers prehistoric archaeology itself arguments for such a conservationist view of the past.

Ecological determinism

A third handicap in studying man-land relations is ecological determinism: The idea that natural conditions would *prescribe* what people do, in such a way that we even can predict human behaviour from ecology. It leaves no room for the deliberate choices that people make, nor for the culture specific structuration processes. Adaptation to environmental conditions, based on intimate native knowledge systems seems such a very general principle, at least for prehistoric societies, that this should not be presented as a remarkable outcome of research, as still often is the case. *Self evidently* people adjusted, within their main technological capabilities, and preferred subsistence strategies to the natural conditions. In different periods people adapted in different ways to the same environment. When we observe that within one culture people lived under divergent ecological conditions it should be no surprise that they did so in a very different way. We should see it as the reflection of a flexible cultural system allowing a wide choice of subsistence and making it possible to optimally profit from specific natural circumstances.

Diversity

The fourth item is cultural and ecological diversity. I listed it because of the tendency perhaps of this congress to develop a world view. I fear that this is as yet far beyond our capabilities. It would mean a synthesis of a representative series of regional landscape histories or biographies, covering at least the last five to six millennia. While such biographies are very specific in climate, landscape, subsistence and cultural traditions, such a synthesis would mean a high level of abstraction. But landscape studies today are still very much bound to specific regions or cases.

2. Observations and interpretations

Hunters and foragers

Early man

Far before people had any impact on their environment they must have given meaning to it and this might very well have been the case far before we, as archaeologists, can conclude it on the basis of material evidence.

The impact of early humans on the landscape will not have been different from that of other scavengers and hunters, making paths and having dens, and far less than all herds of grazing ungulates. Even the important change from scavenging to the hunting of large game will not have made a difference. This must have taken place around 300.000 years ago or even earlier as demonstrated by the spectacular Schöningen javelins. In this way early Neanderthals competed but certainly did not replace the large predators. In subsequent times increased knowledge about animal life and behaviour must have been acquired, leading to the specialised hunting of migrating herds of herbivores in an interception strategy, based on the predictability of seasonal migrations, at least in the Northern hemisphere. The same holds for the properties of raw materials, used for their increasingly complex material equipment. It is the start of the development of an extensive 'native knowledge system'.

Rock art

The first rock art, as preserved in caves and in the open air in *abris sous roche*, from northern Spain to the Ural mountains, is the first positive sign that people had developed a complex system of symbols. These artists were modern humans, from c. 35.000 BP onward, who replaced the earlier Neanderthal man. In this context it is relevant that they expressed themselves not only on their mobile artefacts, but in the landscape as well, as a sign that specific features of it, like caves, played a role in their metaphysical world. We can argue that this is the stage of human evolution in which the scenery around was consciously perceived and so upgraded to 'landscape'. It is not unlikely that many aspects of the surrounding physical world played a part in this symbolism, be it that it is hardly possible to support this opinion with other arguments than the fact that animals are dominant in the pictures.

Fire ecology

We should realize that as a scavenger and later as a hunter and even as a beginning farmer man's impact was negligible as compared to that of the ruminant herbivores. In this respect the discussion is important whether and to what extent use was made of fire in hunting tactics and in manipulating the environment. Structured fireplaces as a sign of fire control go back to Neanderthal times, at least 100.000 years ago, but the first indications interpreted as the deliberate firing of vegetation or 'fire ecology' dates from the Mesolithic. The evidence of charcoal in dated peat horizons is, however, exclusively from Britain, especially Scotland, and completely lacking from the European continent. There are alternative natural explanations, which altogether make us hesitating to accept the argument. Most of it seems a wishful projection of the modern world (Africa. Australia, Indonesia, historical Scandinavia) into prehistory.

Settling down

A main change in the man-land relations took place in the end of the last glacial and the early Holocene when in widely separated regions on earth foragers settled down on fixed locations or in small territoria. This was a new way of life in which the exploitation of the permanent and readily available aquatic resources, inland as well as coastal, played an important role. We find such communities from the early phases of the Jomon cultur in Japan, along the lower courses of the Yang Tse and the Yellow River in China, to the Natufian of the Near East, the so-called aqualithic of Saharian Africa and the Maglemosian of Northern Europe. We can see this development as a specific answer to the new interglacial conditions by the socially and technically much more sophisticated fully modern man, Homo sapiens sapiens, as compared to the Neanderthals and their contemporaries. One innovation stimulated by this new life style independently in various contexts was pottery.

First farmers

In a few of these areas a unique constellation gave independently rise to farming: the settled way of life, based on the presence and exploitation of large-grained grasses. These are wheat and barley in the Near East around 10.000 cal BC, millet and rice in respectively Northern and Southern China around 7000 or even earlier and maize in Middle America around 5000. In the Near East the process seems to have been triggered by the combination of population increase and climatic deterioration, more specifically: the Younger Dryas climatic deterioration.. From then on real environmental impact starts, but small scale and not immediately. Food production means an intensification of land use, a growth of population, more restricted territories, a fixed relation with a small section of the landscape. In a few millennia agriculture had spread over most of the Old World.

Europe

The first *Bandkeramik* farmers of Central Europe opened small enclaves in the 'virgin' forests for their fields with wheat and barley and other Levantine crops. Small parts of the landscape were 'brought into culture' or cultivated. It was the start of the domestication of the wild, according to Hodder. This earliest Neolithic hoe cultivation on soils of permanent fertility, the loess, is barely visible in the environmental record. The confined patches of fields were surrounded by woodland that extinguished most of the pollen signals at the sample points in the brook valleys. People manifested themselves in their domain by means of long houses in fixed settlements, impressive in their times, especially for the people beyond the agricultural world, the hunters of the northern zone.

Native knowledge systems

The aspects of subsistence that archaeologically are documented in the Meso- and Neolithic show an intimate knowledge of what nature has to offer in the case of hunter-gatherer societies. The same holds for the selection of raw materials for the production of tools: the right wood species for the right functions, a careful selection of specific bones for implements. It seems justified to assume that this knowledge was general and also extended over domains badly or not at all documented in the archaeological record and of which the absence can be explained by differential conservation or by a lack of direct evidence. This means that aspects as animal behaviour and soil conditions must have been part of it and will have been used in settlement location strategies. That is exactly what we see. Modern palaeoecological research shows that most site locations are fully rational in the perspective of the agrarian capabilities of the societies involved.

Monumental imprints

New farming communities all over the West and the North of Europe developed a different way of life. Settlements seem to have been small and short-lived. In this pattern of shifting settlements and shifting fields megalithic tombs were erected for the dead. So, fixed points were created in the landscape visually demonstrating the rights on the inherited land and directly connecting the claims on specific territoria to the ancestors. The tombs became locations of offering and cult to the ancestral spirits as well, a function that in regions like Britain later shifted to special communal cult places. Such megalithic tombs were characteristic for most landscapes outside the central European loess zone: from Southern Spain to the Orkney Islands and Southern Scandinavia.

The ritual aspect, as demonstrated by the tombs, generally seems to have been a common factor of daily life, but there are some regions where people in the sequence of many generations concentrated their monuments, as it seems inspired by those visible from earlier times. The older monuments were reinterpreted and quite often even reconstructed to serve the new needs. Famous examples of such 'ritual landscapes' are the regions of Stonehenge and of Avebury in Wessex, the Morbihan with its stone lines or *alignements* in southern Brittany and the bend of the river Boyne in eastern Ireland. Many of these, remained in use well into the Bronze Age. In later prehistory, when the megaliths and the connected burial rituals became out of use, individual barrows took over the function of territorial manifestation, linked with the spirits of the forefathers.

There are still other manifestations of ascribed values to specific features of the land. One is the offering in bogs and in stretches of rivers, in Northern Europe from the earliest Neolithic onward and continued into the Roman Iron Age. Another are the panels of rock carvings from Bronze and Iron Age, well-known from the Alps at Mont Bego and Valcamonica and from many locations in southern Scandinavia. They show us pictures of a differentiated mythological world that are equally difficult to understand as those from the Ice Age, but that by their locations close to the arable show again that the profane and the ritual were two inseparable aspects of one and the same landscape, throughout later prehistory.

The term 'ritual landscape' is, however, more recently toned down since it was realised that even in the most impressive examples domestic sites are found as well. It appears that all landscapes have their ritual and domestic aspects, but that some indeed were more ritual than others or that in some cases their symbolic aspects were more prominently preserved than elsewhere. The domestic is at any rate always underrepresented and often hardly known, while enduring stone monuments strike the eye.

Exotics from the earth

Another sign of the important role the landscape has played in the minds of people, not often mentioned as such, is the apparent value ascribed to objects made of remarkable or 'exotic' materials, derived from specific, often unique and distant locations. These materials strike the eye by their colours or colour patterns, or by their properties and it is generally assumed that these objects were used in wide ranging exchange networks, which clearly demonstrates the ascribed value. Examples amber and jadeite, many types of flint, like the chocolata flint and the banded flint from Krzemionki in Poland and the brown flint from Grand Pressigny. That it is not only the remarkable material itself that made out the value, but the location as well as illustrated by the 'Group VI axes', mined high up at Great Langdale in the Cumbrian mountains, not a type of rock that strikes the eye, but first of all a striking location. In later prehistory copper, tin, bronze and gold, equally mined and linked with specific sources in remote land, replaced the old stone values.

Agricultural change and environmental change

Secondary products

Let us leave now the ritual and symbolic and return to the more profane, from the *imprint* on the landscape by various forms of manifestation to the *impact* by continued exploitation. I have chosen to discuss just an example from my own research experience: Northern Europe in Bronze and Iron Age.

A main economic development in the Later Neolithic is the increased use of so-called secondary products, or products that can be 'cropped' from the animal without killing it: traction power, milk, wool, dung. These secondary products brought about a revolution in farming life. Traction means ploughing and so the possibility of opening up poorer soils that gave lower yields per ha. Traction also means wheeled transport of bulk, increasing the action radius of the settled farmer. This bulk can be harvest, but dung as well, and so the men presumably became more and more involved in crop farming, in the Neolithic considered to have been predominantly the domain of women.

Wool means spinning and weaving, milk implies a dairy house industry, making butter and cheese, both attributed to women. Good proof of these activities is, however, not so easy. Woolen fabrics are rarely preserved, but certainly attested in the beginning of the Middle Bronze Age. Dairy farming can be based on age patterns of the slaughtered cattle and on special pottery types, connected with the making of cheese or butter. All this implies fundamental changes in the activity patterns of men and women, in the roles of both sexes in the farming practice: the men being more important in primary food production, the women being more confined to the house and in charge of activities there.

Expansion and destruction

The integration of animal husbandry and crop cultivation into one unified system of mixed farming is typical for the end of the Neolithic – the Beaker Period – and was fully established in the Early Bronze Age, at least in Northern Europe. It meant a wider environmental impact, as is visible in the pollen diagrams that show an increase of herbs and grasses, reflecting the large-scale opening of the woodland.

Long houses with stable parts, fixed fields surrounded by fences or ditches, arable soils, extensive plough marks all are widely established from the beginning of the Middle Bronze Age, c. 1700 cal BC and certainly have their roots in the centuries before. But in spite of the apparent measures to compensate for soil degradation, we observe that soils were widely exhausted and the rich brown earths transformed into the poor Humic Iron Podzols, the Brown Soils being characteristic for the earlier Beaker barrows, the podzols for the later barrows from the Bronze Age. Overexploitation went so far that the wind got grip on the sand and tracks of wind blown sand deposits became to cover the old arable. The degradation of those poorer soils was compensated for by means of manuring. This can be identified by distinct arable soils, by high phosphate contents of these soils, by thin veils of pottery sherds over extensive areas and by weed associations in the palaeobotanical remains. Manuring can also be deduced from house plans with evidence of cattle boxes. Although these need not necessarily to have been used throughout the full winter, it means at any rate that dung must have been piled up in some periods and removed.

Restoring sustainability

The final answer towards a more sustainable arable farming, at least in Northern Europe, seems to have been the so-called Celtic Field system, developed in the late Bronze Age, between 1000 and 700 cal BC. This is an irregular lay-out of small quadrangular fields, that allowed a good agrarian planning and possibly a protection against wind erosion by hedges and brushwood on the low, separating banks between the fields. A strategic location in a gradient of lower and higher ground water tables diminished the risks of crop failure: the lower parts had a good crop in the dryer years, the higher part in the years with higher precipitation. Systematic manuring and the introduction of new crops, the oil seed *Camelina sativa* and the pulse *Vicia faba*, enabled a shift the from long fallows of the Neolithic to a short fallow cycle and a systematic crop rotation.

For the Netherlands the territories were calculated at c. 100 km^2, with a central 100 ha Celtic Field with three to seven farms, forming an open hamlet, surrounded by outfields and heathland, presumably used for grazing sheep. Tracks of forest that produced wood for house construction, fencing and fire separated the communities. The communities were interconnected by sand roads, along which barrows remembered ancient ancestors and urnfields the more recent forefathers.

In more hilly country slope erosion, colluviation and the filling up of valley floors tell us about exploitation and overexploitation. On slopes lynchets or terracing was constructed to prevent slope erosion. In most valley floors several meters of sediment have piled up since the Mesolithic. Now and then, in deep excavations, Mesolithic remains come to light. Most of these sediments seem to be rather late and to date from Iron Age and historical times. The same is true for sedimentation in the Rhine / Meuse delta, which is most prominent in that period, signifying that in slope wash and all other erosive processes an equilibrium was broken in the end of prehistoric times. We can visualize these trends in a curve for environmental impact, based on a large series of independent pollen diagrams. We can derive from all environmental evidence a scheme for landscape changes, showing the major transformations in the two millennia BC. At last we can compare these schemes with a population curve (on a logarithmic scale) for the same period, to demonstrate how few people with population densities of only 2-5 per km^2 did away with most of the forest *(see pp.78-80)*.

So in large parts of Europe major environmental destruction has taken place in later prehistory, a combination of poor soil conditions and a first 'mechanization' of arable farming in the form of the plough and draught oxen. Soil degradation and slope erosion was compensated for by manuring and a new arable system, or by terracing the fields in a hilly countryside.

From many other countries examples can be given of early overexploitation that is even larger in scale and more impressive. There is the option that – apart from climatic deterioration – large scale cattle herding disturbed the subtle ecological equilibrium in Northern Africa in the 5th millennium BC, and so contributed to or even caused the fast and wide extension of the Sahara desert.

The Mesopotamian irrigation systems of the 2nd and 1st millennium BC were fully dependant of continuous maintenance efforts and suffered from silting up and increased salinity.

The fast extension of the coastal plains in Greece and western Turkey in historical times, but also elsewhere around the Mediterranean, is clearly related to large scale slope erosion in the Hinterland, itself caused by a too intensive use, esp. the herding of sheep and goats. It is interesting to see that in the same landscape spoiled in this way many locations were given high symbolic values as demonstrated by sanctuaries, temples and myths.

Wet rice cultivation on terraced slopes in Southeast Asia, on the other hand, can be seen as an early form of extreme, but sustainable intensification, supporting high population densities, a new equilibrium in an artificial landscape, dependent of the maintenance by its human occupants.

So several statements might be made. Firstly, in the past the relation between man and the land had a very dual nature. On the one hand the landscape was valued, given highly symbolic connotations, filled with spirits and powers as visualized in mounds and temples. On the other hand it was exploited and used, often irrespective and certainly unaware of the long-term effects.

Secondly, it seems that the more destructive stages are not directly linked to agriculture as such: it is very difficult to point to Neolithic examples. This seems to have been a period of relative small-scale impact. The landscape was opened up, but not degraded. The two millennia BC demonstrate, however, a major change, at least in Europe: A combination of population increase and inadequate strategies mark the start of landscape destruction by overgrazing or soil exhaustion. It seems that population density itself should not be seen as a cause, but more the lack of measures to assure sustainability, given a certain population density. We should ask ourselves whether the changes were fast enough that people could be aware of these, or that for them the landscape in essence was static. The changing landscape dynamics - so very visible in our long diachronic perspective – might not have been identified and recognized as such in antiquity.

Biographies of the landscapes

Successive generations and successive culture traditions have made their imprint in the landscape in the course of time, be it in the form of more or less permanent structures, be it in the form of extensions of reclamations and of environmental disturbances. Every generation inherited the landscape and its layout from the generations before, made its interpretations of the old and added new. Manifestations of the past might not have been properly understood, will have been mythologized, denied or adopted and restructured. Old landscapes were replaced by new. So we find ruined megaliths and eroded barrows together with old field parcelling as traces of former active communities in nowadays unused moors. Each landscape is inscribed by successive generations and on the basis of these inscriptions archaeology can write what we call their biographies. These are stories of construction and destruction, at any rate of structuration processes, in increasing intensity. Much information is gone in the course of historical and recent land use, or invisibly hidden in the soil, but in combination of natural and cultural evidence these biographies can be written and teach us about the shift from the wild to the domesticated land, about former attitudes towards the landscape and the struggle for sustainability in the past.

References

Bell, M., and M. J .C. Walker, 1992. *Late Quaternary Environmental Change, Physical and Human Perspectives*, Harlow (Longman).

Bender, B., 2000. Investigating Landscape and Identity in the Neolithic, in: Anna Ritchie (ed.) *Neolithic Orkney in its European Context*, Cambridge (McDonald Institute for Archaeological Research), 23-30.

Bintliff, J., 2000. Landscape Change in Classical Greece: A Review, in: Frank Vermeulen and Morgan de Dapper (eds.). *Geoarchaeology of the Landscapes of Classical Antiquity, Proceedings International Colloquium Ghent, 23-24 October* 1998, Leiden (Stichting BABESCH), 49-70.

Bradley, R. and M. Edmonds, 1993. *Interpreting the Axe Trade. Production and Exchange in Neolithic Britain*, Cambridge (Cambridge University Press).

Butzer, K.W., 1964. *Environment and Archaeology*, London (Methuen).

Butzer, K.W., 1982. *Archaeology as Human Ecology*, Cambridge (Cambridge University Press).

Lemaire, T., 1997. Archaeology between the Invention and the Destruction of the Landscape, *Archaeological Dialogues* 4, 5-21.

Louwe Kooijmans, L. P., 1994. Prehistory or Paradise? Prehistory as a Reference for Modern Nature Development, the Dutch Case, in: G.F.W. Herngreen and L. van der Valk (eds) *Neogene and Quaternary Geology of North-West Europe, Contributions on the occasion of Waldo Zagwijn's retirement* (Mededelingen Rijks Geologische Dienst 52), 415-424.

Louwe Kooijmans, L. P., 1998. Bronzezeitliche Bauern in und um die niederländische Delta-Niederung, in: Bernhard Hänsel (ed.). *Man and Environment in European Bronze Age,* Kiel (Oetker-Voges), 327-339.

Louwe Kooijmans, L.P., 1998. *Between Geleen and Banpo. The Agricultural Transformation of Prehistoric Society,* 9000-4000 BC, Kroon-voordracht no. 20, Amsterdam.

Louwe Kooijmans, L. P., 2000. Living in the Neolithic: Habitation and Landscape, in: Anna Ritchie (ed.) *Neolithic Orkney in its European Context,* Cambridge (McDonald Institute for Archaeological Research), 323-331.

Richards, C., 1993. Monumental Choreography: Architecture and Spatial Representation in Late Neolithic Orkney, in: Christopher Tilley (ed.). *Interpretative Archaeology,* Providence / Oxford (Berg), 143-178.

Roymans, N., 1995. The Cultural Biography of Urnfields and the long-term History of a Mythical Landscape, *Archaeological Dialogues* 2, 2-24.

Simmons, I.G., 1999. History, Ecology, Contingency, Sustainability, in: John Bintliff (ed.). *Structure and Contingency,* London / New York (Leicester University Press), 118-131.

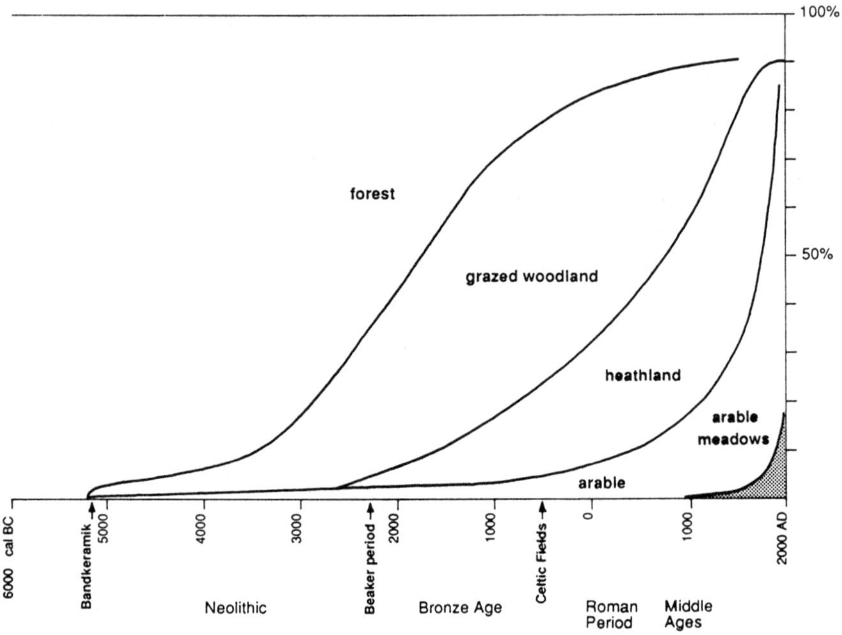

Curve for environmental impact

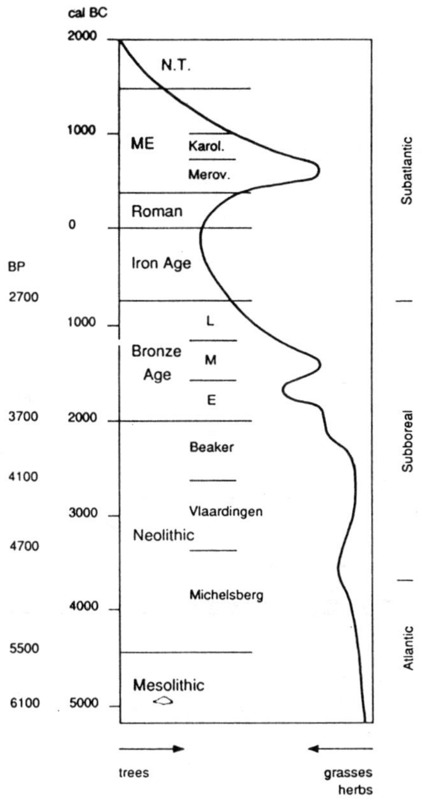

Scheme for Landscape Changes

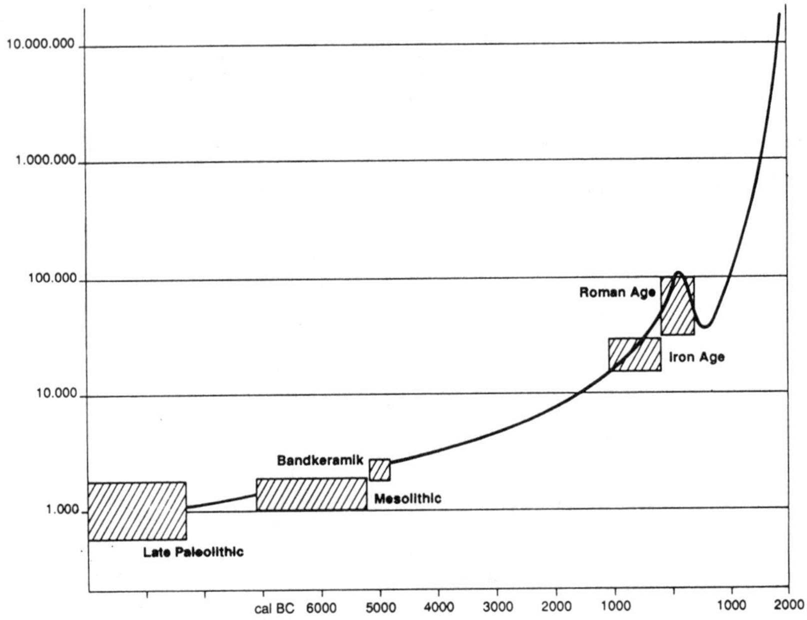

Population Curve

Verena Winiwarter

Agro-Ecological History

Intrinsic Resource Problems of Solar-Based Societies

Human affairs are much complicated
by our capacity to adapt
culturally and individually
to our circumstances.
(John R.. McNeill, 1992:3)

Abstract

Agro-ecological history offers a long-term perspective on the basic questions of sustainable development and on global change. It does so by offering comparative material but also by suggesting different theoretical frameworks for studying such questions.

As quoted above, human affairs are much complicated by our capacity to adapt culturally and individually to our circumstances (McNeill, 1992:3). The most basic complication is the fact that humans have a history. To change nature is a basic prerequisite for having a history. Humans have histories, because they change nature (Godelier, 1990).

The largest part of human history is the history of agricultural societies, of social systems that are based on the harvest of solar energy by means of biomass production. Agriculture, a basic form of changing nature, or, in other words, a basic way of adapting to nature, also is a main cause of complications of all kinds. Changes in human nature are but one of them. I shall focus on these complications and review their explanatory potential.

The OECD recently published a report on "Environmental Indicators for Agriculture". Four groups of indicators are suggested: A first group that investigates agriculture in its broader economic social and environmental context, a second group dedicated to farm management and the environment, a third that deals with the use of farm inputs and natural resources and finally a large group of indicators to determine and describe the environmental impacts of agriculture.

Soil erosion, coping with nutrient losses and the necessities of animal management, to name but three main challenges of agriculture that are taken care of in the indicator system, are also principally applicable to pre-industrial conditions. Starting from the present state of affairs in OECD countries. Other indicators might also be applicable under pre-industrial conditions, highlighting the differences to the present.

Agro-ecological systems are comprised of three realms, which are coupled in many ways:

The realms of human population, production system and agro-ecological system are linked by means of material, energy and information flows. Apart from the flows one has to investigate the depletion or accretion of stocks of nutrients, pollutants and produce, to name but a few.

A set of environmental indicators for pre-industrial agriculture developed from the OECD report, but resting on this tripartite coupled system model is suggested.

Such a set of indicators – which can be useful as sustainability indicators – has to consider agriculture not only as a way of human adaptation to natural conditions, but also as a co-evolutionary process of human societies and nature. Roy Bashkar has argued that living things determine the conditions of applicability of the physical laws to which they are subject, so that their properties cannot be reduced to the latter (Bashkar, 1978: 113). I shall discuss the indicators from such a viewpoint as a means to determine the conditions of co-evolution of humans and nature by means of agricultural practices.

Introduction

The small and by any obvious means insignificant village of Theyern, situated in the Austrian province of Lower Austria, south of the Danube, close to the picturesque town of Krems has recently joined the union of villages well known to a wider, if specialized, audience. Like Törbel (Netting, 1981), Alagna (Viazzo, 1989), Unterfinning (Beck, 1993), Laichingen (Medick, 1996) and Neckarhausen (Sabean, 1991), to name but a few, it was and is the site of an intensive scholarly study. Whether this study can be characterized as micro-history depends on what you want to understand by micro-history, but it is definitely the site of an important development within the historical sciences. Theyern was the first case study for a long-term environmental history in Austria.

A team of researchers from various disciplines started to study Theyern in 1995, and it became the model village for our research into relationships between nature and society in the pre-industrial past (Projektgruppe Umweltgeschichte, 1999a, b). The case of Theyern will be used in an attempt to suggest an analytical framework for environmental histories that can both help us to bridge the gap to other disciplines and provide information relevant for future planning processes targeting the core issue of sustainable regional development.

An agenda for environmental history to link its research with current agricultural policies shall be suggested. Before we will concentrate on Theyern, on the question of indicators for agriculture, on resources and on intrinsic problems of agricultural societies, attention shall be drawn to an exercise in reflecting what we are doing.

Reflections on images

History is a way of reflecting on human nature. It is concerned with societies and their changes over time. But societies do not exist as such but solely in interaction with nature. To change nature is a basic prerequisite for having a history. Humans have histories because they change nature (Godelier, 1990), therefore the study of interactions of humans and nature is the basis of history.

But this kind of history is a difficult thing to come to terms with, as it is – like all other histories – based on human interpretations of the world and cannot easily delve beyond them to gain information on the historical status of natural systems like soil and vegetation.

Historians are working with sources that are the products of human minds. We are thus always reflecting not only our research question but need to reflect the circumstances that led to the production of the sources we are using. One way of reflecting on those circumstances is to look at the images that are used pictorially or invoked in writing. Images are powerful and have a life of their own, they are often indicators of an undercurrent to what is said on the surface of a source. In preparation of this manuscript I encountered images, both pictorial and verbal ones, that have led me to wonder about the hidden agenda of the conference where this paper was presented also about and the plenary lecture I chose to give.

Al Gore, while being Vice-President of the United States, authored the book: "Earth in the Balance". The notions of "Balance", "Equilibrium", "Harmony", are leading rhetorical figures in the environmental discourse. Gore himself wrote one of the articles in the TIME-Magazine Special Issue "Our Precious Planet" in 1997, which had the most powerful image available to concerned citizens on its cover: The "Blue Planet" as seen from space. Vulnerability is conveyed by this image as is beauty, but it is most powerful in changing size relations: The blue gem the astronauts saw from space can be contained in the palms of a caring human. Not so in real life: We are tiny dots on the earth, not visible from space. When one takes into account the 6 billion humans that make up the population, it has to be questioned if the sheer number makes us powerful enough to willingly restore what we have destroyed by our unleashed growth both in numbers and in our material consumption.

Turning back to verbal imagery, the theme of the IUAES congress itself should draw our attention: It is "Exploitation and Overexploitation of Resources". In this notion the image of an equilibrium is hidden, as there is obviously a threshold between the "exploitation" and the overdose of it. Would exploitation then be a harmonious way of interaction? We have arrived at yet another very powerful notion: the notion of the threshold. Thresholds are an image of the quantitative world-view, and not all peoples that have populated and are still populating the earth would subscribe to such a concept. It is still open for debate if such a worldview will be the harbinger of salvation from the global environmental crisis, natural sciences international network of expert advice for politicians notwithstanding.

Sustainable development, a notion that will be dealt with, conveys the verbal image of the quest for a better future, asking the world's current population to leave enough of the earth for our descendants to dwell.

All these images let one wonder what we, as humanity, are actually up to. I would like to suggest that we are – to some extent or in some respect – in search for harmony, for the great harmony that we have come to identify as a basic prerequisite of survival. But one can doubt that the world is a place full of harmony, that an equilibrium can be created willingly by humankind, One can doubt that the world is at our disposal or has ever been. We have always been freckles on the face of the planet, but we have always in some way or other tried to pretend otherwise.

Images are unavoidable, but need to be reflected. Changing course, an image-laden idea of how the ecological history of agricultural societies can help in our quest for survival shall be the focus of the following pages.

Long-term sustainability in agro-ecosystems

Ecological History, Environmental History, Historical Ecology are names given to a way of studying history as a tale of the changing interaction of humans and nature.

Ecology is the study of the relationships among living organisms or between them and the physical environment. In doing Ecological History we study human-induced changes alongside and on equal footing with non-human changes, and our questions are bi-directional: The major question often is to understand the repercussions of social change on the natural environment, but it is equally important to understand the repercussions of natural change on social systems.

To understand changes in the interaction of humans and their environments has recently become a leading paradigm in international environmental research under the headline of "Global Change" research, in particular within the IHDP, the International Human Dimensions of Global Environmental Change Program sponsored by UNESCO.

Global Change Research is based on the central paradigm that humanity is facing global catastrophe unless we are able to change our relationship with nature into a *sustainable* development.

Agro-ecological history offers a long-term perspective for the basic questions of sustainable development and with regard to global change. It does so by offering comparative material but also by suggesting different theoretical frameworks for studying such questions.

The largest part of human history is the history of agricultural societies, i.e. of social systems that are based on the harvest of solar energy by means of biomass production. Agriculture, a form of changing nature, or, in other words, a way of adapting to nature, is also a main cause of complications of all kinds. Changes in human nature are but one of them. But the most visible complication is that of diminishing yields, if natural systems are exhausted by human interventions. In such cases, agro-ecosystems are clearly unsustainable, the ancient civilizations of Mesopotamia are among the best known examples for such a development.

Definitions of sustainability abound. A model based on the question of resources, their use and the capabilities of natural systems to cope with social resource uses and their consequences is suggested as framework hereafter. The model is based on the concept of two interacting systems. Human societies undertake the extraction of resources, produce waste materials and effluvia of all kinds and finally try to change the internal characteristics of natural systems in order to make them more useful for society. Change is possible by means of labor and energy input. Natural systems, on the other hand, are undergoing all kinds of changes, some of them anthropogenic, many of them natural. The coupled system can only be called sustainable if the capacities of natural systems to deal with the effects of social resource management without undergoing degradation are not overtaxed. If the amount of resources extracted by society does not exceed the availability of these resources, if the wastes and emissions are quantitatively and qualitatively not harmful to natural systems which can biodegrade them, and if the structural and ecological demands of natural productivity are not endangered by human interventions into natural systems, a system can be called sustainable. *Fig. 1 (see p. 97)* gives an overview of the model which is derived from the work of Marina Fischer-Kowalski et al. (Fischer-Kowalski, 1997)

This model of sustainability is equally valid for all modes of production and subsistence. Sustainability cannot be assessed through short-term measurements, albeit one can identify unsustainable states of a system by assessing their current parameters.

If one accepts the need for long-term measurements, one has to investigate pre-industrial conditions, hence study agricultural societies. Robert McC. Netting has compiled a list of attributes of sustainable agro-ecosystems (Netting, 1993:136f) consisting of four major points:

1. Relatively stable production per unit of land. No declining yields. System is resilient to short-term or seasonal perturbations.
2. Predictable and relatively stable inputs of energy.
3. Economically favorable rates of return between inputs and outputs, both in energy and in monetary terms. Diversity of crops and agricultural operations limits risk and strengthens stability.
4. Returns to labor and other energy inputs are sufficient to provide an acceptable livelihood to the producers. Sufficient income includes also sufficient savings to meet contingencies and to be able to make the investments necessary for long-term productivity.

Netting argues that in addition to the resource demands, the economic demands of the producers need to be met in order to make a system sustainable. This is a valid observation. It should not lead to the wrong conclusion that economic stability is necessarily coupled with ecological sustainability.

Netting bases his sustainability indicators on "stability" as a central category. While it is true that social systems need to have some degree of stability in order to be feasible, the notion of stability overshadows the importance of dynamics and change in agriculture in order to obtain feasible conditions with stable outcome. Agriculture can be viewed as an ecological process involving co-evolutionary developments of nature and society: Monoculture of crops creates attractive habitats for specialized organisms called "pests" by their human competitors. In addition, new crops bring new pests, for which societies at first have no remedies nor a coping strategy. The Irish potato blight catastrophe is a case in point. While remedies are developed, organisms with short life spans and thus with the ability to mutate quickly become new threats. Micro-organisms drive humans into a rat-race. The most powerful of competitors and parasites might not even be visible to the unaided eye. Co-evolution then becomes a fight in the dark, and human ingenuity is necessary to win it, knowing that all victories are temporary. Coping with erosion, drought, floods and locusts, to name but a few additional challenges demands adaptation and flexibility from peasants societies face as a starting point. Agricultural systems face the basic challenges of declining yields and increasing labor demand, two challenges that can easily combine into a vicious circle. The condition of their soils, both with regard to nutrients and to waterlogging, erosion and salinization is the most important variable. A second type of problem is competition, by pests, weeds and other humans (warfare, population growth). The epidemiological challenge of a close connection of humans and farm animals and their diseases can be problematic, too. Availability and efficiency of labor are probably more important, this means that the health conditions as well as the age and gender distribution of the population are important. Last but not least, availability of capital is also an important feature, as lack of capital means drudgery in times of crop failure and a far longer time of recovery from depression, and capital also determines labor efficiency via the possibility of investing into technology.

These basic challenges are best discussed as questions of input-output relations in a coupled system. Agro-ecological systems can be divided into three parts, which are connected in many ways: The three parts are human population, production system and agro-ecological system. They are inter-linked by means of material, energy and information flows. Apart from the flows one has to investigate the depletion or accretion of stocks of nutrients, pollutants and produce, to name the most important. The "black-box"-Model given in *Fig. 2 (see p. 98)* gives a first impression of the flows that need to be investigated.

Labor is provided within the population system, either by biological reproduction or by migration. The production system comprises both political and technological features. Farm households are the units of coupling population and production, and they are the units that need to be investigated in terms of economic stability. Note that fields belonging to a farm are comprised in their natural aspects in the agro-ecological system but they belong to the household in the social sense. The agro-ecosystem itself comprises fields, meadows, forests, gardens and all kinds of animals in various compositions, these being the anthropogenic parts, whereas soils and water are natural constituents of the system. Climate is a major external factor of the agro-ecosystem, albeit humans can influence microclimatic conditions by means of vegetation cover. Epidemics such as the plague for humans or foot and mouth disease are also important factors that can drastically change the overall yields of the system, they are exogenous impacts, but their impact depends on the internal layout of the system (e.g. population density). Changes in *one* of the parts necessarily vibrate through the entire complex by means of feedback loops, and a new equilibrium can eventually form, but it will affect all parts of the system in one way or other. Resilience of such a system (resilience is a cloudy concept, but the word is used here in a common-sense way) is a question of how it can cope with the changes affecting one of its parts. Resilient systems might be the ones that are sustainable but it would again be dangerous to believe in this coupling without proof. Indicators to measure sustainability and resilience are necessary. Whereas the latter have not yet been developed as such, sustainability indicators are widely known. It might be worthwhile having a look at them.

Indicators for sustainable agriculture

The OECD recently published a report on "Environmental Indicators for Agriculture" (OECD 2000). Four groups of indicators are suggested: A first group investigates agriculture in its broader economic, social and environmental context, a second group is dedicated to farm management and the environment, a third deals with the use of farm inputs and natural resources and finally a large group of indicators is designed to determine and describe the environmental impacts of agriculture.

The OECD- List of Indicators is given in Tables I-III.

Tables I-III: Complete List of OECD Agri-environmental Indicators

I Agriculture in the broader economic, social and environmental context

1. Contextual information and indicators		2. Farm financial resources
• Agricultural GDP	Land use	Farm income
• Agricultural Output	- Stock of agricultural land	• Agri-environmental expenditure
• Farm employment	- Change in agricultural land	- Public and private agri-environmental expenditure
• Farmer age/gender distribution	- Agricultural land use	- Expenditure on agri-environmental research
• Farmer education		
• Number of farms		
• Agricultural support		

II Farm management and the environment

1. Farm management		
• Whole farm management - Environmental whole farm management plans - Organic farming	• Nutrient management - Nutrient management plans - Soil tests • Pest management - Use of non-chemical pest control methods - Use of integrated pest management	• Soil and land management - Soil cover - Land management practices • Irrigation and water management - Irrigation technology

III Use of farm inputs and natural resources

1. Soil quality	3. Land conservation	4. Greenhouse gases
• Risk of soil erosion by water • Risk of soil erosion by wind **2. Water quality** • Water quality risk indicator • Water quality state indicator	• Water retaining capacity • Off-farm sediment flow (soil retaining capacity)	• Gross agricultural greenhouse gas emissions
5. Biodiversity	**6. Wildlife habitat**	**7. Landscape**
• Genetic diversity • Species diversity • Wild species • Non-native species • Eco-system diversity (see Wildlife Habitats)	• Intensively-farmed agricultural habitats • Semi-natural agricultural habitats • Uncultivated natural habitats • Habitat matrix	• Structure of landscapes - Environmental features and land use patterns - Man made objects (cultural features) • Landscape management • Landscape costs and benefits

Whereas one should always keep in mind that indicators are a construction, in fact a kind of second order reality, as I have argued elsewhere, and should not be mistaken for reality (Winiwarter. 2000), they are useful if they enable us to make those features visible and comparable that can help us guide our actions. The OECD scheme could probably be criticized for the approach it takes, but in general it provides a useful picture about the environmental impacts of agriculture. The indicators dealing with the broader economic, social and environmental context of agriculture are specific for industrial societies and can hardly be used in others. The second and third group, however, are partly useful also for agricultural societies at large and thus also for historical examples.

Within the group of farm management indicators, nutrient management, be it the use of animal manure or measures involving an increase in nutrient availablity by addition of lime or marl, can easily be used as an indicator to describe historical systems, even if information will be incomplete. But even for prehistoric times some information is available (Bakels, 1997).

If one takes a holistic view on soil testing, it is also useful in pre-industrial societies. Various effective soil test methods have been known at least since antiquity (Winiwarter, 1999).

To a high degree, pest management was based on magical practices. But as magical practices were often quite time-consuming, they need to be considered, even if they were not effective (Schmid, 1998).

Data on how long soils are covered during one vegetation cycle ("soil cover"), are available as long as one knows the crops. Dates for sowing, plowing and harvest were often contained in calendars, so one can arrive at figures for this indicator, too.

Irrigation technologies are well accessible, both in archaeological remains and in written sources, and a detailed reconstruction is feasible, as e.g. Netting has shown for Törbel (Netting,1981).

Risk assessments for soil erosion in hindsight are feasible if sediments are available downstream of the investigated area. Bork et al. have conducted research at such sites, showing that both extension and reconstruction of a timeline are possible (Bork, 1998). Wind erosion is more difficult to investigate, but in extreme cases data are available. Not only the "Dust Bowl"-events in the United States, but equally disastrous man-made erosion in the Soviet Union in the 1950ies and 1960ies offer quite well documented cases (for the latter, see e.g. Thurner, 1997). Erosion has been the topic of a wide range of historical studies, which document the possibility of historical assessments (e.g. Andel et al. 1990, Bell and Boardman (eds). 1992, Hughes, 1982, Phillips, 1999, Vogt, 1990).

Water quality can only be assessed in such cases where it was bacteriological dangerous enough to cause epidemics, and in most cases such information will not be available.

Land conservation will normally not be directly accessible, but might be, in such cases where archaeologists work together with soil scientists and devise means how to establish data on water retaining capacity and soil retaining capacity of agricultural soils. Such information will necessarily be cumulative, and cannot easily be assigned to single events in the history of the particular place, but cumulative evidence will be especially interesting in the case of abandoned village sites.

Whereas it might be possible to calculate greenhouse gas emissions from historical agricultural sites, this information will be less useful than others, as the general trend is established and detailed data would not change our assessment. Data on genetic diversity will be hard to obtain, as will be reliable estimates of species diversity and other species indicators. A research group at Göttingen University tries to establish methods for investigating historical biodiversity. Habitat matrices can be obtained for the 19th century from the cadastral maps, and land use patterns can in several cases be traced even further back into history.

The overall picture that emerges shows that it is clearly possible to undertake such analysis. For several of the indicators, such as nutrient management, soil cover, irrigation and landscape structure, abundant sources are available, the information for others might be costly to obtain, but investigation would still be possible. Only very few seem to be impossible. Reasons why such investigations are not usually undertaken cannot be discussed here. Theyern is a vivid example of the feasibility of such analyses.

Sustainable Theyern?

Research done in the village of Theyern shows how historical studies can be linked with environmental policy indicators and thus enable a new view on questions of sustainability. The case study cannot be referred here in detail but is available in German in an interactive CD-ROM (Projektgruppe Umweltgeschichte, 1999 a).

One should not forget that the indicators do not allow to see the development of a village over time. Hence, before going into the indicators, a short overview of the situation is given.

Telling the history of Theyern as a stability tale, we can start in the 15th century. From around 1420 to 1550 the first "trial period" brings about quite some fluctuation in holding size and composition. Homesteads are taken apart, others are combined, fields and meadows are assigned to different holdings to build economically feasible units. Later on, the holdings are much more stable. From 1570 to at least 1820 the system is extremely stable if we look at the holding sizes and composition. Each of the villagers' households holds the same parcels of land for almost 300 years. The emerging picture of stability, however is challenged if one looks at ownership. The trial period is reflected in an extremely volatile ownership structure, in some of the years 10 of the holdings change owner, an enormous amount, given that Theyern consists of 17 households altogether. These ownership changes are not changes due to inheritance, but changes involving a new family name of all household members. Political instability is reflected in a second period of volatile ownership, from the 1610s to the l650ies. From then on, peasants seem to stay on their holdings longer and changes become infrequent.

The system has reached a status where most of the holdings are economically feasible units, meeting one of Netting's sustainability criteria. Information on yields per holding is not available, but we can draw one conclusion which seems to be of relevance. It took quite some time to make Theyern feasible. Sustainability might well be a trial and error game, like so many other human endeavors, and modern systems, with their enormous velocity of material and energy flows might simply be to fast to ever be sustainable.

If we look at the village as such, not just at the holdings, we get the overall picture of mixed agriculture with a moderate degree of products for the market, most notably wine. *Fig 3 and 4 (see pp. 99, 100)* show the agro-ecosystem of Theyern in the 1820s. All information comes from the cadastral maps and its estimation registers. It is derived directly from the sources and not based on modern estimates or best guesses.

On a national level, data on the appropriation of biomass in a comparison from 1830 to 1995 are already available for Austria. Fridolin Krausmann has calculated that in 1830 59% of all available biomass in the country was harvested by humans, whereas this figure had dropped to 51% as of 1995 (Krausmann, 2001). Both, the total amount of biomass harvest and the trend, need explanation. The picture is quite typical, in the first place. The agricultural societies of 19th century central Europe were working on the margin of energy availability as e.g. Peter Sieferle has shown in his study on forests and woods (Sieferle, 1981). Neither Netting's criterion of capital accumulation ("savings") nor his criterion of stable yields were met in these days. Lack of energy prevented peasants and their lords to invest into measures that could have increased yields. As yields were low, a large area had to be used, which translates into the almost 60% NPP (net primary production) appropriation figure. Between 1830 and 1995 the amount of harvested biomass nearly doubled in Austria, while in the same period NPP appropriation fell significantly, which can only be explained by the greatly increased efficiency, which again is only explicable if one takes into account the availability of non-biomass energy in large quantities.

Going back to the example of Theyern, solely the indicator of "Landscape Structure" shall be discussed here in some detail. The assessment makes use of information about the production system and about the agro-ecosystem, but does not include information on the population as such *(see Fig. 2, p. 98)*. Using Ecological structure analysis as developed by Forman and Godron (Forman and Godron, 1986), we were able to draw maps of the situation in 1820, the time of the cadastral maps and using information available for 1733. It is important to note that relevant changes in landscape structure do take place prior to the introduction of fossil fuel into agriculture. Anthropogenic disturbance is an important ecological attribute of landscape elements. It is scaled according to the frequency and strength of disturbance events, which in most cases are caused by different intensity of plowing, mowing or grazing respectively. In 1733 one third of the arable land lay fallow according to the medieval three-field system. The fallow land was only extensively used for animal grazing as well as the field balks, small pastures inside the open field and the forest on the limestone ridge. In 1820 the former fallow land was cultivated with fodder plants like clover, fodder beet or cabbage. This enabled the introduction of stable-feeding in summer, which in turn reduces the disturbance caused by animal grazing. In the immediate surroundings of the village some gardens were turned into meadows characterized by a lesser degree of disturbance. Together with spatial information on natural resources such as water availability, information on the introduction of landscape elements (like houses or non-native plant species) and information on those patches which are subject to natural regeneration, the disturbance information can be combined to yield an overall picture. Most clearly visible are changes in forest use and changes in the use of four adjacent agricultural plots within the forest, which had been cultivated in 1733 and were subsequently abandoned due to insufficient yields (for details, see

Project Group Environmental History, 1999). Ecological analysis can go down to the plot level, which makes it possible to link such information with current natural science based policy schemes. If the analysis is taken up to the present, the dramatic loss of landscape diversity becomes clearly visible. Such information can and should be relevant in regional planning and conservation, but is only seldom available.

Sustainability in agro-ecosystems: Can the past inform the future?

A set of indicators to measure sustainability of agricultural societies has to consider agriculture not only as a way of human adaptation to stable natural conditions, but as a co-evolutionary process of human societies and nature. Roy Bhaskar has argued that living things determine the conditions of applicability of the physical laws to which they are subject, so that their properties cannot be reduced to the latter (Bhaskar, 1998:113). In this vein, agriculture has to be viewed as a multi-species cluster in co-evolutionary development, interacting with habitat conditions in complex ways. It cannot easily be predicted if changes in climate, soil fertility and the like have positive or negative effects in a given case, because this depends on the status of the system at the time of the change and what is to be considered as positive or negative or which parts of it are discussed. But the boundary conditions can nevertheless be assessed with some accuracy, and one can investigate the intrinsic resource problems of such systems and determine their weaknesses with regard to sustainability. This kind of information is useful in the development of regional policies, especially when organic farming practices are to be promoted.

Looking at Theyern, it becomes clear that sustainability is achieved in a long-term trial and error process and maintained by constant adjustment. Todays high-speed production cycles of agriculture are dependent on government support and thus quickly adjust to ever-changing support regulations. This happens in close coalition with the company-supported extension service systems prescribing quick remedies. Do such systems have any chance of being sustainable? A set of indicators to connect villages under pressure by the global agri-business with their past can be a useful counter-agent to such developments by showing peasants what their lands were capable of in the past. In showing this, one also makes visible the boundarieswhich cannot be transgressed unless fossil energy is available with all the multi-facetted problems this brings about. Such a long-term view to "limits to growth" will let us re-consider the role of the so called third world. It will also change our assessment of the relative dangers of environmental problems: Soil erosion and degradation might then be considered the most urgent and pressing environmental problem to be tackled.

Final thoughts

Environmental History is neither a-political nor anti-political. It is concerned with one of the major political fields governments have to address in the 21st century, and offers reflexive insights for politicians. Its lessons are usually complex. They might be hard to accept in the age of so-called "neoliberalism", declining concern for the environment and general disregard for agriculture as a form of culture. Without accepting the lessons of the past we are bound to re-enact it, albeit on a much more global, and much more dangerous level.

As scholars we have the responsibility to make our results known and the lessons we have learned available to a wider public. By connecting environmental agricultural policy – as in the OECD-indicators – with historical knowledge once can make such a history lesson available. Doubts as to the feasibility of a harmonious way of interaction between society and nature as such have been raised. But we can surely adapt better to the needs of ecological systems than we currently do. A different way of exploiting nature, under a different general framework, will create societies that differ as much from the one we are currently living in as we are different from our past as in the village of Theyern. Some basic agri-environmental indicators will still be applicable then, nevertheless.

References

Andet, Tjeerd H. van, Zangger, Eberhard, Demitrack, Anne (1990). Landuse and Soil Erosion in Prehistoric and Historical Greece. In: Journal of Field Archaeology 17: 379-396.

Beck Rainer (1993). Unterfinning. Ländliche Welt vor Anbruck der Moderne. München.

Bell, Martin, Boardman, John (eds.) (1992). Past and Present Soil Erosion. Archaeological and Geographical Perspectives. (Oxbow Monograph 22) Oxford.

Bhaskar, Roy (1998).The Possibility of Naturalism. A Philosophical Critique of the Contemporary Human Sciences. 3. ed. London 1998, 1st ed. 1978.

Bork, Hans-Rudolf, Bork, Helga, Daichow, Claus, et al. (1998). Landschaftsentwicklung in Mitteleuropa. Wirkungen des Menschen auf Landschaften Stuttgart.

Fischer-Kowalski, Marina, Haberl, Helmut, Huttler, Walter; Payer, Harald, Schandt, Heinz, Winiwarter; Verena, and Zangerl-Weisz, Helga (1997). Gesellschaftlicher Stoffwechsel und Kolonisierung von Natur. Ein Versuch in Sozialer Ökologie. Amsterdam.

Forman, Richard T.Y, Godron, Michel (1986). Landscape Ecology. New York.

Godelier, Maurice (1990). Natur, Arbeit, Geschichte. Zu einer universalgeschichtlichen Theorie der Wirtschaftsformen. (Sozialgeschichtliche Bibliothek bei Junius 6). Hamburg.

Hughes, J. Donald (1982). Deforestation, Erosion and Forest Management in Ancient Greece and Rome. In: Journal of Forest History 26: 60-75.

Krausmann, Fridolin (2001). Land Use and Industrial Modernization. An empirical analysis of human influence on the functioning of ecosystems in Austria 1830-1995. In: Land Use Policy 18 (1):17-26.

Medick, Hans: (1996). Weben und Überleben in Laichingen, 1650-1900. Lokalgeschichte als Allgemeine Geschichte. (= Veröffentlichungen des Max-Planck-Instituts für Geschichte, Band 126) Zwei Bände. Göttingen.

McNeill, John Robert (1992). The Mountains of the Mediterranean World. An Environmental History. Cambridge.

Netting, Robert McC. (1981). Balancing on an Alp. Ecological Change and Continuity in a Swiss Mountain Community. London, New York, New Rochelle, Melbourne, Sydney.

Netting, Robert McC (1993). Smallholders, Householders. Farm Families and the Ecology of Intensive, Sustainable Agriculture. Stanford.

OECD (2000). Environmental Indicators for Agriculture. Methods and Results. Executive Summary. Paris.

Phillips, Sarah T. (1999). Lessons from the Dust Bowl: Dryland Agriculture and Soil Erosion in the United States and South Africa, 1900-1950. In: Environmental History 4 (2) :245-266.

Project Group Environmental History (1999). Landscape, Labour and Population in Pre-Modem Austria. In: Present and Historical Cultural Interventions in Landscapes. Vienna http:://www.pph.univie.ac.at/kg2/iale98/publ_e.html.

Projektgruppe Umweltgeschichte (1999a). Landschaft hat Geschichte. Historische Entwicklung von Umwelt und Gesellschaft in: Theyern. CD-ROM Veröffentlichung, WUV-Verlag Wien 1999, ISBN 3-850764-62-1. (Projektgruppe Umweltgeschichte).

Project Group Environmental History (Kaus Ecker; Michael Grünweis, Andreas Maimer, Christoph Sonnlechner, Harald Wilfing, Verena Winiwarter, Ilse Wrbka-Fuchsig, Thomas Wrkba) (1999b). Landscape and History: A multidisciplinary Approach. In: Collegium Anthopologicum 23, 2: 379-396. (Projektgruppe Umweltgeschichte).

Sabean, David Warren. (1991) Property, Production, and Family in Neckarhausen, 1700–1870. Cambridge.

Schmid, Martin (1998). Magie in der Kolonie, in: Verena Winiwarter (Hg.), Bodenfruchtbarkeit und Schädlinge im Kontext von Agrargesellschaften. Schriftenreihe Soziale Ökologie 51, Wien: 89-112.

Sieferle, Rolf Peter (1981). Der unterirdische Wald. Energiekrise und industrielle Revolution. ("'Die Sozialverträglichkeit von Energiesystemen). München.

Turner, Michael (1997). Economy, Environment and Environmental History: Case Notes from Agriculture, in: Rural History 8,1: 125-140.

Viazzo Pier Paolo. (1989). Upland Communities. Environment, Population and Social Structure in the Alps since the Sixteenth Century. Cambridge.

Vogt, J. (1990). Aspects of Historical Soil Erosion in Western Europe. In: Brimblecombe, Peter; Pfister, Christian (eds.). The Silent Countdown: Essays in European Environmental History: 83-91. Berlin, Heidelberg, New York.

Winiwarter, Verena (1999). Böden in Agrargesellschaften: Wahrnehmung, Behandlung und Theorie von Cato bis Palladius. In: Rolf Peter Sieferle, Helga Breuninger (Hg.). Natur-Bilder. Wahrnehmungen von Natur und Umwelt in der Geschichte. Frankfurt/M. Campus: 181-221.

Winiwarter, Verena (2000). Soils in Ancient Roman Agriculture: Analytical Approaches to Invisible Properties. In: Novotny, H. & M. Weiss (Hg.), Shifting Boundaries of the Real: Making the Invisible Visible. Zürich: vdf Hochschulverlag: 137-156.

This paper is an extended abstract of the oral presentation at the IUAES-congress 2001, Göttingen, Germany. My thanks go to the Research Group Environmental History at the Institute for Anthropology, Vienna University, especially to Harald Wilfing, the head of the group, for years of successful (and enjoyable) interdisciplinary co-operation. Herwig Weigl has critically commented the paper and my sincere thanks go to him for his enduring interest and critical appraisal. The empirical results were obtained by the Project Group Environmental History under contracts from the Austrian Ministry for Science, Education and Culture in the framework program "Kulturlandschaftsforschung". This presentation was prepared within my current Hertha Firnberg Research Fellowship, T-45 HIS ("Environmental History") of the Austrian Science Fund, FWF, and I greatly acknowledge this support.

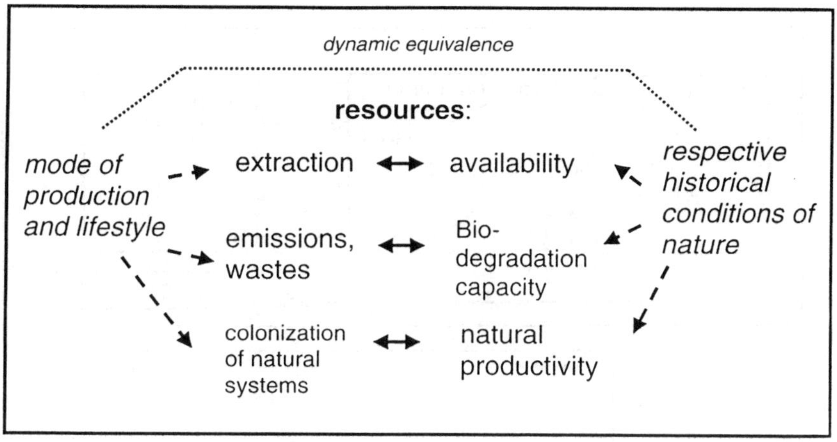

Fig. 1: Sustainability as a dynamic equilibrium of society and nature (translated from Marina Fischer Kowalski et al., 1997)

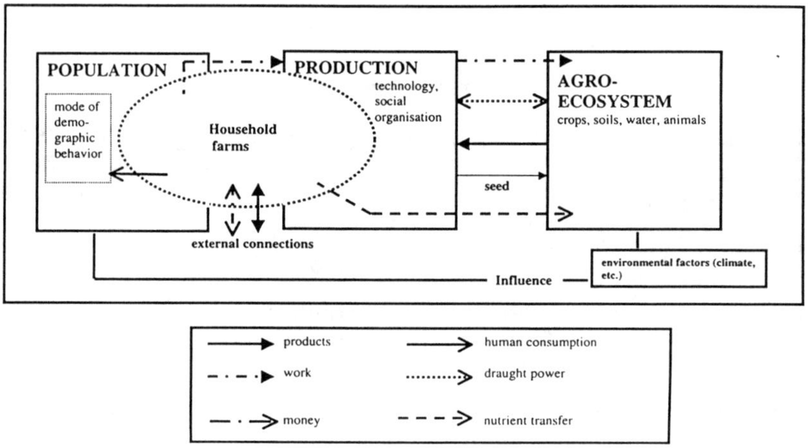

Fig. 2: Tripartite model (overview). Pre-industrial agriculture as coupled system of Population, Production and Agro-Ecosystem

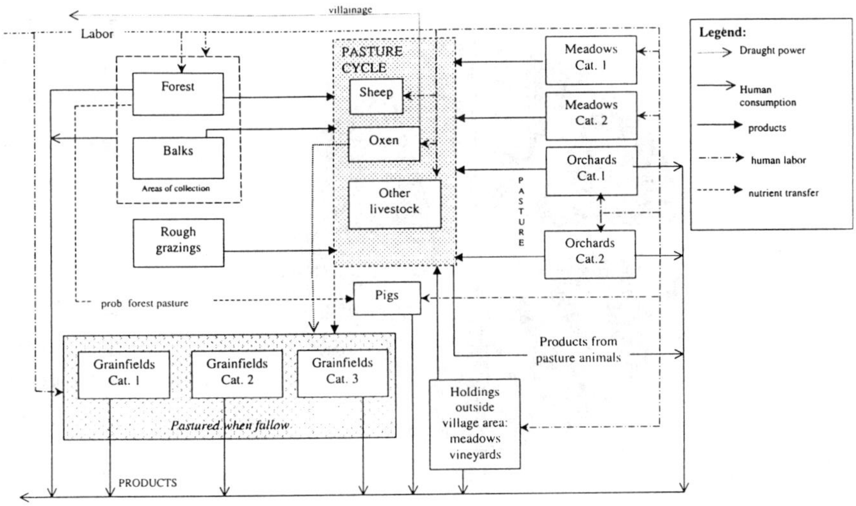

Fig. 3: The Agro-Ecosystem in Theyern 1827, data derived from cadastral maps estimation registers

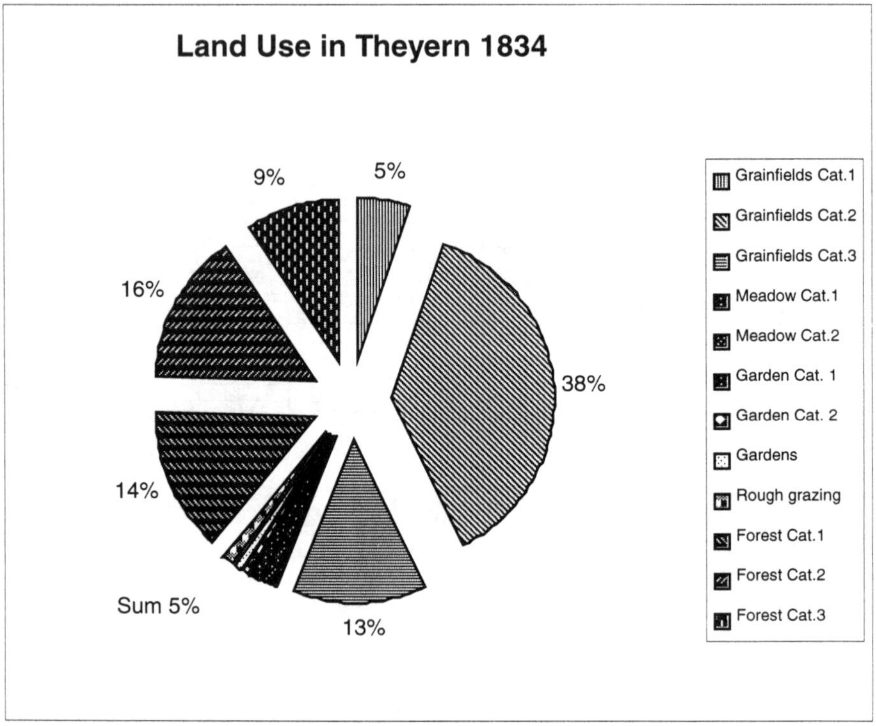

Fig. 4: Land Use in Theyern. Data from cadastral estimation registers

Peter-M. Steinsiek

Bernd Herrmann

Land Transformation and Biodiversity in 18th Century Prussia – A Project Overview

Abstract

The research project aims at evolving a tool to make more reliable judgements on the diversity of ecosystems in the past by considering historical biological information. For that, proxy-data are made available out of the stocks of archives and, standards are set according to which historical species stocks can be compiled from archival sources, be checked and be used as references for changes of biodiversity in former times.

By taking a landscape drained in the 18th century (Oderbruch, Brandenburg) as an example, we are elaborating a method which allows both, a systematic approach to the relevant information stored in the archives, and their efficient analysis. In addition, we are examining the social and political background as well as the strategies of the contemporary actors in order to explain the historical processes leading to changes in biodiversity.

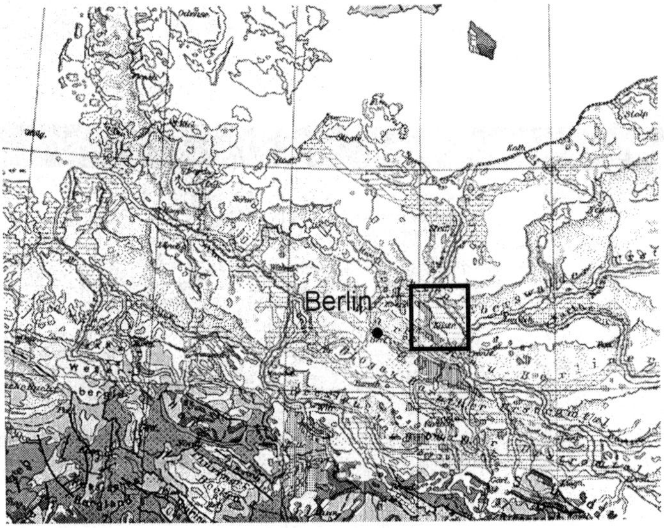

Figure 1: Location of the "Oderbruch" in Brandenburg, Germany

Introduction

So far, archives have not been consulted for measuring historical biodiversity. In comparison with exclusively modern data collections on biodiversity, they represent, however, an irreplaceable source of information for reconstructing the conditions of nature in the past. By presenting historical scales, shifts in biodiversity can be assessed and compared with current findings in order to get a better understanding of ecosystems in terms of their historical dimensions.

Making archives accessible

The first request is to find out whether and to what extent archival records and museum collections are suitable to get sufficient information on the existence of animals and plants in a changing landscape in order to simulate biodiversity. At the very best, there are lists of species and descriptions of ecosystems which enable us to derive the existence of other species not mentioned in the sources and, eventually, to infer which animals and plants lived in symbiosis. By checking for indicator or key species we will apply proxy-data which are widely used in biosciences. Due to their role in the ecosystem, they indicate other species, since they either rely on them (e.g. food web) or those species are tightly linked to them (e.g. pollination or spread of seeds). Thus indicator species can serve as proxy-data also for historical studies. Our ambition is to develop an adequate tool to reconstruct biodiversity at least for certain indicator species, which in turn can be used to determine the consequences of large scale land reclamation for biodiversity.

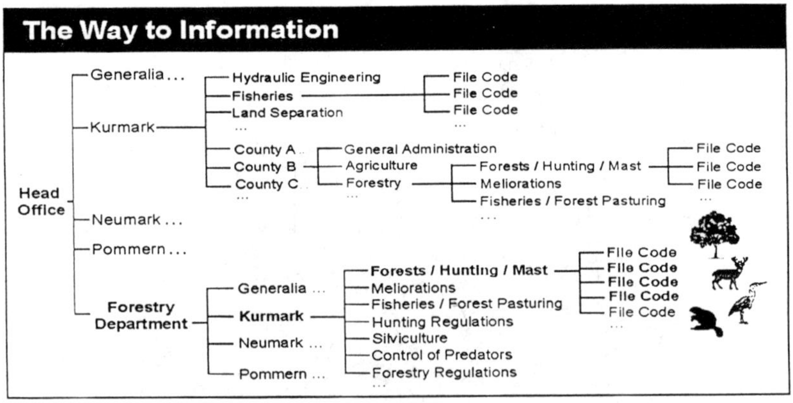

Figure 2

To achieve a quick and successful exploitation of archival sources it is necessary to know the historical structures of the administration. This scheme *(Fig.2)* illustrates the path through the stocks of the State Archive in Berlin-Dahlem leading to the relevant historical information on biodiversity.

In our project, the land reclamation measures in 18th century Prussia and their impacts on plants and animals serve as a general case study. Since the first half of the 18th century, Frederick II, King of Prussia, began to regulate and to dyke the river Oder and to drain the adjacent land, an area of about 800 km². His aim was to reclaim land, to win new workers by offering land to new settlers, to raise bovine meat production, and to increase taxation for the government.

Figure 3: View into the northern part of the "Oderbruch" near Oderberg before its melioration (about 1715 AD).

The scattered groups of shrubs and trees underscore the character of an opened up marshland traversed by many offshoots of the Oder river which are seen in the foreground (Meisner, 1913).

Before melioration, the Oder marshlands were mainly used by fisheries. The process of land transformation resulted in considerable alterations of the respective ecosystems. After more than two hundred years, it is still unknown which faunistic and floristic elements actually disappeared.

First results

The reconstruction of fish stocks of the Oder river in the marshland area at six different times compiled so far from printed sources might be an example of possible results of our research approach. Compared with the oldest historical records we have got, such as Jobst 1571, Bekmann 1700, and von Borgstede 1788, the species we find in our focus area today are reduced in numbers and in composition. Most surprisingly, the differences do not affect small fish which are considered as being without any interest for human use. However, it turned out that even small fish species were used in the 18th century as soil fertilizer and, after being coated with bran, to fatten poultry.

The differences in species concern – except from the barbel – species with low individual numbers, even in historic times, and migratory anadromic fish. We believe that they were affected by consequences from the increasing commerce since the middle of the 18th century on all the banks of the river course, rather than by the drainage measures. Pollution was raised by the end of the 18th and throughout the 19th century. Archival files report on complaints about pollution in the focus area affecting fry as early as in the 1780s. Probably a lingering increase of heavy metal pollution brought in from upstream areas with seasonal flooding had reached a first critical threshold value already in the 1730s. Salmon and sturgeons were most likely overexploited, rather than suffering from consequences from land transformation. As far as the barbel is concerned, which was the dominating fish of the Oder river zone in the 18th century, its decline is surely associated with land reclamation. This is because land transformation changed the character of this riverine eco-zone.

In contrast to the aquatic ecosystem, the terrestrial ecosystem was more and deeply affected. The melioration did not bring about a new type of terrestrial ecosystem, but it extended dry areas and grassland significantly. Any terrestrial animal adapted to swampy environments became seriously endangered, such as the beaver or the swamp turtle, and definitely all amphibious species. The results obtained so far suggest a shift in reproduction of animals (biomass production or abundances), rather than in species numbers. We suspect that many, if not most indigenous species survived, but on a very low or even critical scale.

The reconstruction of the Oder fish stocks in the area under investigation represents a successful example of consulting historical data for the assessment of species diversity *(see Fig.4).*

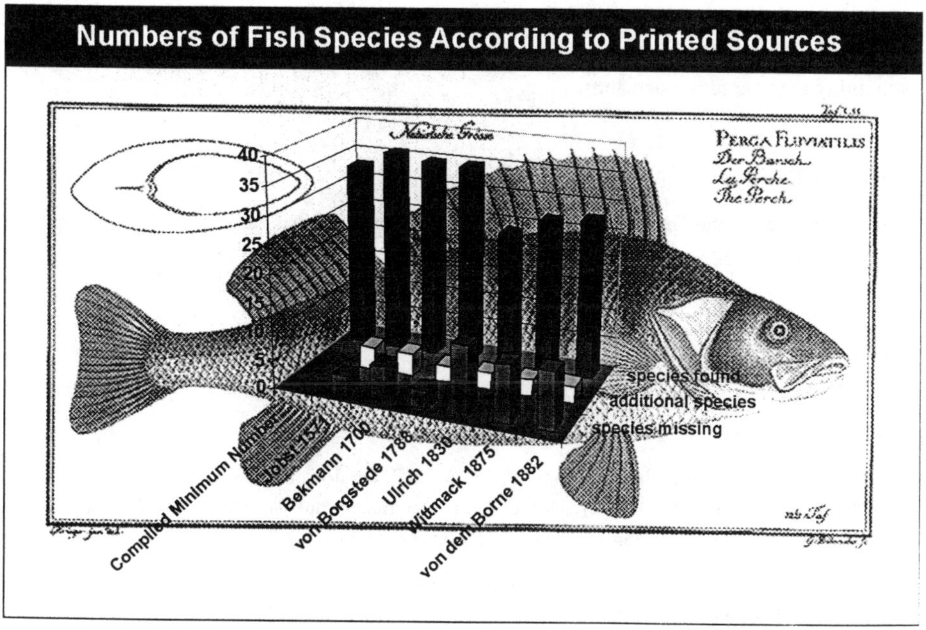

Figure 4

Final remarks

At the time when nations were created and new state territories were to be safeguarded it became necessary to think about the prerequisites of sustainable structures. Once secularisation of life and the rationalization of labour came to the fore, the exploitation and usage of natural resources was increasingly mechanized and hence, planning became important. Large-scale land transformation projects, such as the "Oderbruch" melioration in 18th century Brandenburg, need also to be interpreted against the background of the sovereign's absolute power over his country and people. The extermination and extinction of pests for public welfare on the one hand and the targeted promotion and introduction of beneficial animals and plants on the other are two aspects of sovereign power at that time. Therefore, reconstructing landscape change and its consequences on biodiversity gives insight into the historical socio-economic and biological implications of sustainability, too.

Since the beginning of the early modern times, European patterns of shaping and utilizing the landscape have been transferred by colonists to entire parts of the so called New and Third Worlds. Archives holding historical data of administrative, fiscal and similar concern on overseas ecosystems may be important for nature conservation and reconstruction issues in the former European colonies. The project aims at scrutinizing these sources of human heritage for their suitability to serve future demands.

Acknowledgement

We are grateful to the German Federal Ministry of Education and Research who are sponsoring this research project.

References

Crosby, A.W. 1986. Ecological Imperialism. The Biological Expansion of Europe, 900–1900, Cambridge

Heckscher, E. F. 1932 Der Merkantilismus. 2 Vol. Jena

Herrmann, B. 1997. „Nun blüht es von End' zu End' all überall": Die Eindeichung des Nieder-Oderbruches 1747–1753. Umweltgeschichtliche Materialien zum Wandel eines Naturraums. Unter Mitarbeit von M. KAUP. Münster, New York, München, Berlin

Jackson, J. B. C. et al. 2001. Historical Overfishing and the Recent Collapse of Coastal Ecosystems, in: Science 293 (27 July 2001): 629–638

Meisner, H. (ed.). 1913. Ansichten Märkischer und Pommerscher Städte aus den Jahren 1710–1715 Berlin. p. 53.

Popper, K. R. 1972. Naturgesetze und theoretische Systeme, in: H. Albert (ed.) Theorie und Realität: Ausgewählte Aufsätze zur Wissenschaftslehre der Sozialwissenschaften Tübingen. p. 43–58.

Steinsiek, P.-M. 1999. Nachhaltigkeit auf Zeit: Waldschutz im Westharz vor 1800. Münster, New York, München, Berlin

Lajos Rácz

Environmental Crises in Hungary During the Modern Epoch – Case studies

Abstract

In my study I will try to find an answer to the question: When and why did environmental crises develop in Hungary during the modern epoch?

Before presenting the case studies about environmental crises I have to define two basic elements. The first is the geographical notion of the Carpathian Basin. The Carpathian Basin is a 300,000 square kilometre area in Central Europe that was the geographical site of the Hungarian Kingdom for centuries.

Figure 1: Central Europe in the Middle Ages

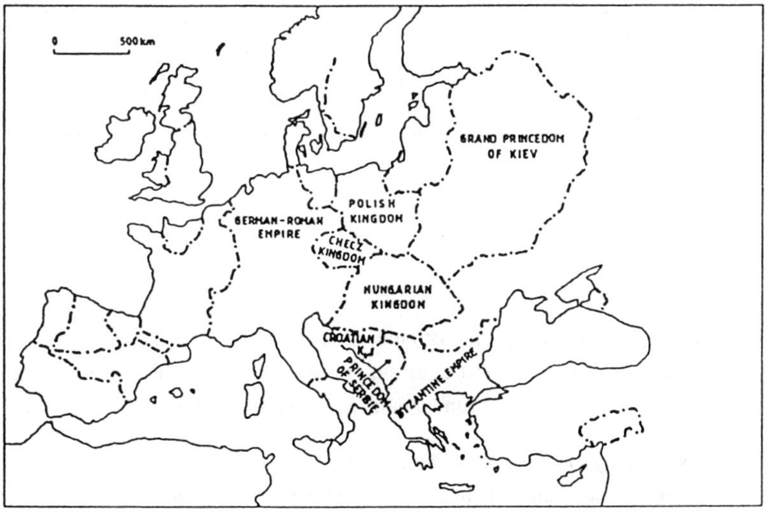

The frame of this basin is the Carpathian Mountains (the highest parts are over 2,000 meters high), inside this basin are four macro-regions: Transdanubia, Highlands (most of which part is now Slovakia) and Transylvania (part of Romania) both of which are broken and hilly areas, and the Hungarian Plain which is the largest with 90,000 square kilometres.

Figure 2: Macro-Regions of the Carpathian Basin: Transdanubia, Highlands, Transylvania and the Hungarian Plain

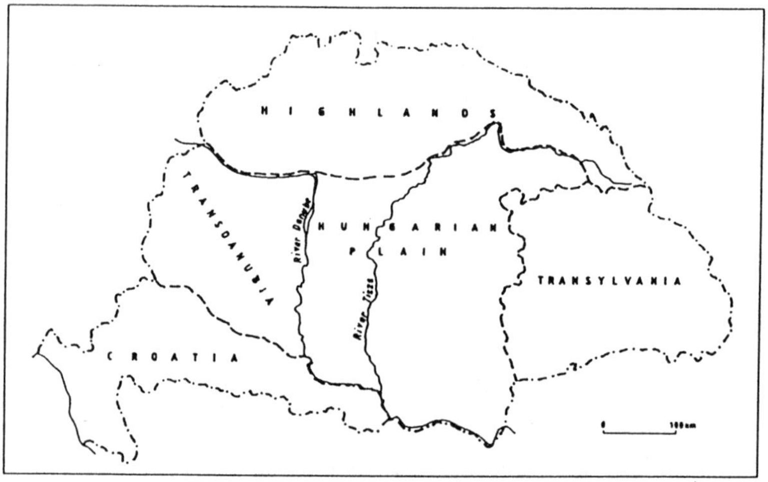

The second basic element is the notion of environmental crisis. There are two faces of environmental crises: Disturbances in natural ecosystems and a crisis in artificial ecosystems or agro-systems. These environmental crises can be induced by natural and/or human causes.

For the analysis of Hungarian environmental history we have to accept two pre-conditions. First, physical environment and society there are in interdependent relation. The physical environment can influence social and economic processes and society can change its physical environment.

Secondly, the carrying capacity of Carpathian Basin was very high but the density of the population during the modern epoch wasn't so high in comparison with the rest of Europe (10-60 inhabitants/km^2). Therefore, environmental crises generally develop in special situations: Socio-political and economic troubles coinciding with physical environmental anomalies.

Historical and environmental outlines of Hungary since the 16th century

Before showing the environmental crisis of Hungary, I will try to give a bold outline of the social-political and environmental processes of the Carpathian Basin since the 16th century.

Historical processes

Since its conception in the 16th century, Hungary changed a lot. At the beginning of the early modern epoch it was one of the strongest kingdoms of Europe, but in the middle of the 16th century the Turkish Empire occupied southern and central Hungary, and the central belt of the Carpathian Basin became a warfare zone for one and a half centuries. The territories occupied by the Turks were finally liberated at the end of the 17th century and the Hungarian Kingdom had lost its independence and retained a special status within the Central European Habsburg Empire. The Austro-Hungarian Monarchy ceased to exist as a state as decided in the peace agreements ending the First World War when a division into the quasi-national states of Austria, Czechoslovakia, Yugoslavia, Romania and Hungary replaced the empire. Finally after the Second World War, Hungary became part of the less desirable area of Europe and stayed there until the 1990s.

Physical environmental processes

There have been two basic environmental processes in the Carpathian Basin during the modern age: Climate changes (Little Ice Age and Recent Global Warming) and humanization of physical environment, mainly by regulation of rivers. During the Little Ice Age the Carpathian Basin was under generally cool and wet climate conditions and Recent Global Warming indicated a drying process.[1] There were basically different structures of natural seasons. In Little Ice Age winter began in January and finished frequently at the end of March, spring began in April and continued until the end of June. Summertime was confined to July and August, autumn was rainy and long, lasting from September to December. The main features of Recent Global Warming are the

---

[1] Rácz Lajos (1999): Climate History of Hungary Since 16th Century: Past, Present and Future. Pécs. 160 pp.

decrease of contrasts between seasons, basically a warming of winter's months and a decrease of whole year's precipitation (1992: 384 mm, 1993: 363 mm).

Figure. 3: Yearly temperature and precipitation 50-year averages over the decades from the 16th century until today. The first diagram (1500-1850) is based on the time series of a history based climate reconstruction, while the second diagram is based on the time series for instrumental observations from the Budapest observatory (1780-1996)

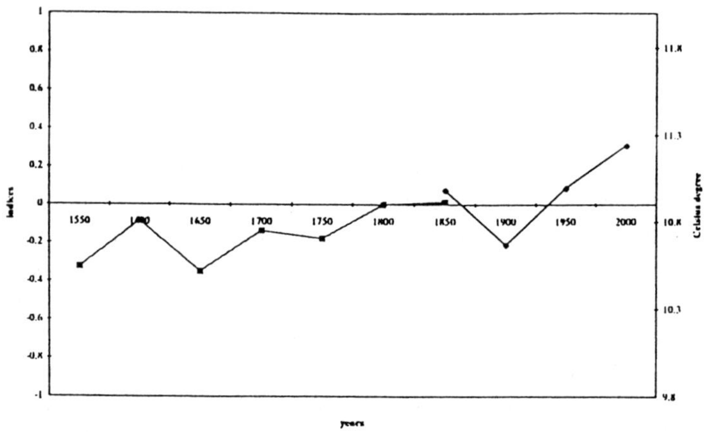

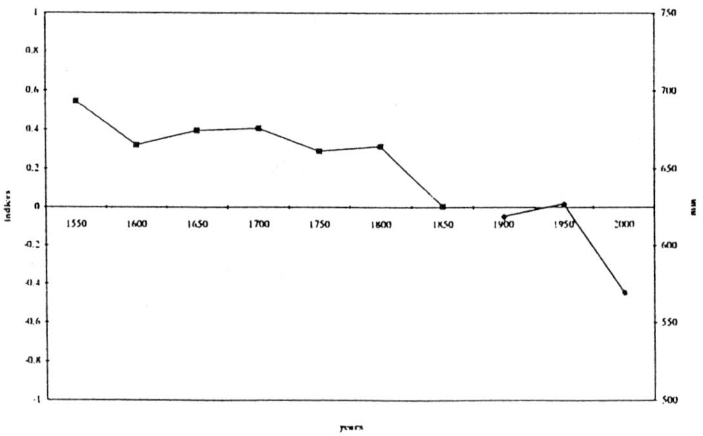

Case-studies about environmental crises in the Carpathian Basin

Environmental disturbances during Turkish wars

In the middle of the 16th century, the Turkish Empire occupied the southern and central parts of the Hungarian Kingdom. In the span of two decades double lines of forts were constructed in the central belt of Hungary; Hungarian forts were built up against Turkish crests. The Hungarian Plain wasn't fortified with rock, therefore military engineers supplied wood for the construction of forts called pile-forts. For construction and reconstruction, the forests of the Hungarian Plain were cut down and this sandy area of the plain lost its vegetation and temporarily became a desert (windy sands).

There was a sad speciality of Turkish wars in the period of continuous warfare: In summertime troops of the sultan used to attack and in wintertime followed the counter-attack of the Habsburg Empire. There were two environmental crises periods during the Turkish wars when physical, environmental anomalies coincided with continuous warfare: 1593-1606 and 1664-1711.

<u>1593-1606:</u> This was the time of the "fifteen years war" in Hungary with continuous warfare that coincided with one of the coldest periods of Little Ice Age. In Switzerland the Low-Grindelwald glacier advanced one kilometre during the last 20 years of the 16th century.[2] In Hungary at the turn of the 16th and 17th centuries the vegetation period became cooler and rainy, grain harvests were continuously very poor in all macro-regions and large areas became a feral landscape. This was a time of collapse of the settlement network of the Hungarian Plain. Documentary sources reported about a famine and about cannibalism in Transylvania.

<u>1664-1711:</u> In this period began the re-conquest of Buda from Turkish troops; wars of repossession of Hungary ended in 1699 but after some years of peace began in 1704 the insurrection of Rákóczi against Habsburg absolutism. The last third of the 17th century was cool and wet in Europe. Long continued warfare and the cold climate regime destroyed the power of resistance of the Hungarian population. The summit of the subsistence crisis was between 1707 and 1711 with a famine and a plague in the central and eastern parts of the country.

Warfare and wet climate increased the size of marshland and the level of lakes in the Carpathian Basin. Lake Balaton at the beginning of the 18th century was 7 meters higher than in 20th century.[3]

---

[2] Pfister, Christian (1999): Wetternachhersage. 500 Jahre Klimavariationen und Naturkatastrophen. Bern. 304 pp.

[3] Bendefy László (1969): A Balaton évszázados partvonalváltozásai (Coastline Change of Lake Balaton Over Centuries). Budapest

Figure 4: Water level changes of Lake Balaton

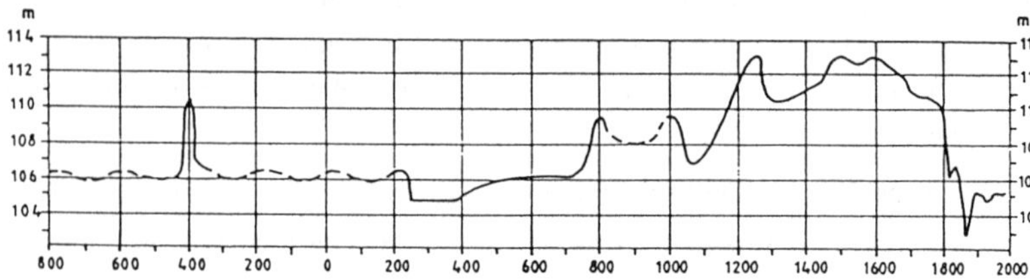

Water problems in the Carpathian Basin

During the Little Ice Age one of the most important environmental problems was a large marshland in the plains of the Carpathian Basin. The regulation of rivers was a crucial element of the Hungarian modernisation program in the 19th century. There were three targets of this program: The improvement of communication, the increase of arable land and controlling the regime of the watercourse. Regulation began in the middle of the 19th century and finished in 1908; it eminently affected the water system of the Hungarian Plain. This was the largest water regulation work in Europe and its balance was very antinomic. Communication improved and became safer, but the quality of new arable land was generally poor. A new water engineering system produced new risk factors: Increased numbers of floods. River Tisza lost 90 % of its fish-stock and a collapse of the ecosystem in the Tisza (vegetation, mew, birds) happened.[4] This was an environmental-ecological catastrophe in the Carpathian Basin.

---

[4] Lászlóffy Woldemár (1982): A Tisza. Budapest

Figure. 5: Temporary and continuously water covered areas in the Carpathian Basin

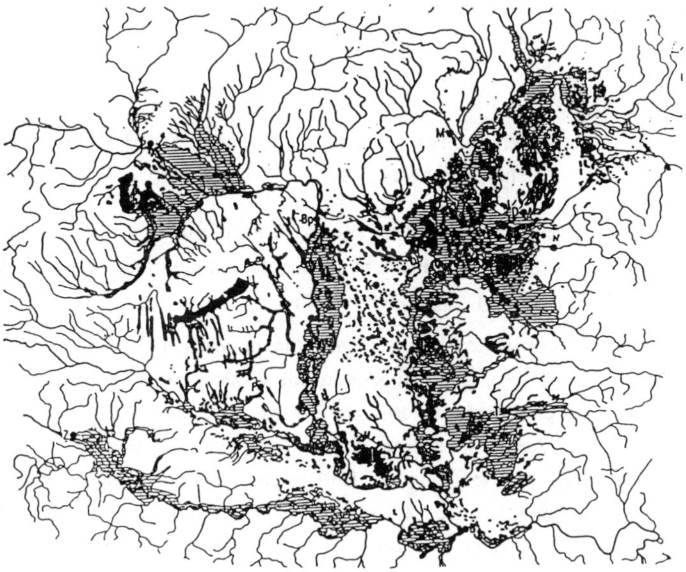

Water problems emerged again in Hungary in the 1980s. The first sign of environmental problems was a sudden ground-water level decrease in the central sandy area of Hungary. In the span of ten years the ground-water level decreased between 4 and 5 meters, the basic reason was an acceleration of a long term drying trend in the 1980s and 1990s. In the opinion of meteorologist János Mika, Hungarian climate changes are developing into a Florence type climate with rainy winter half year and dry summer half year (without the Mediterranean sea). But this climate change is hard hit and challenging for Hungarian agriculture which is the unambiguous loser of political and economical changes of 1990s: Landed properties are subdivided, credit possibilities are restrained and mechanization is very unbalanced. But that wasn't enough, these hits in the last decade became very dangerous for flooding in the Carpathian Basin for the following reasons: New owners of woodlands on the watershed area of rivers cut down large forest areas,

last decade became very dangerous for flooding in the Carpathian Basin for the following reasons: New owners of woodlands on the watershed area of rivers cut down large forest areas, therefore the down flowing of water was accelerated and waves of floods intensify each other. In addition, water control based on the bank system of 19th century became worn out and no longer saved the society against unexpected and very high floods.

Conclusions

I have shown examples of environmental crises in the Carpathian Basin in different Ages but there were some common element of these crises:

In each environmental crisis water overflow, or its absence, played a very important role. I can state that water is the most important element of climate and environmental changes in the Carpathian Basin, much more important than temperature.

Evidently, socio-political crises can induce environmental and agro-system problems. These crises could be Turkish warfare or political-economical system changes of the 1990s. But current warfare can induce great environmental crises in Europe too: I saw (in ex-Yugoslavian republics) a lot of feral landscapes due to the killing of farmers and/or mine danger e.g. around Vukovár (Croatia) and Mostar (Bosnia-Hercegovina). But we can summarize our conclusions by stating that the deepest environmental crises are induced by the coincidence of water problems and socio-political crises in the Carpathian Basin.

Balázc Borsos

From Land-Use to Overuse of Land The Changing of Environment and Land-Use in the Bodrogköz in Northeastern Hungary in the 19th Century Due to the Channelization of Rivers

Abstract

The paper intends to summarize the results of a survey of a period of the environmental history of the Bodrogköz, a flood-plain area in the northeastern corner of the Great Hungarian Plain, which is bordered by three rivers. By analysing historical and cartographic sources as well as carrying out a computer-analysis of the data, the author describes how environmental conditions influenced the pattern of land use during 19th century. Before the regulation of rivers geomorphology and altitude were the decisive factors, while after this soil-conditions became more important, but have played only a restricting role ever since then. Through cartographic comparisons and the computer-analysis he defines regional differences in the Bodrogköz which are due to different natural conditions and different land-use patterns. He also characterizes the two main steps in the changing of those conditions. After the regulation of the rivers in this area (1860-1880) previous meadows and pastures were turned into ploughlands. Following the drainage of marshlands (1895-1910) the rest of the meadows, the woods and pastures, which used to be flood areas, were all followed. The author emphasizes that at the end of this transformation-process the land use in the Bodrogköz was more uniform and simpler than before. Analysing the optimal and real conditions of this certain land-use, he also claims that the region was overused: Areas originally not suitable for intensive use were forced to be ploughed by economical needs.

"Bodrogköz" is a triangle-shaped flood-plain area of 940 km in the northeast part of the Carpathian Basin. It is bordered by three rivers, the Latorca to the north, the Bodrog to the west and the Tisza to the southeast. It is an "island on the mainland": Only a 1,5 km wide neck connects it to the other plain territories. In it we can find nowadays two now nearly completely dried out previous Tisza-branches meandering from east to west: Closer to the Latorca is the Tice and south of it is the Karcsa. As a result of the peace-treaties following World War I. in 1920, it was divided by an international border along the Karcsa, the northern part belonging to the present-day Slovakia, the southern one to Hungary.

The territory of Bodrogköz is a flood-plain lower than 105m altitude with some higher parts. There are two hilly regions above 150 m, the Tarbucka and the Helmeci-hills in the northern part. We can find sandhills, concentrating along the Tice and in the eastern corner between the Tisza and the Karesa. Among the hills and in the lowlands there were a lot of small lakes and runlets. Some of them were active only during the flood-period. The flood usually could not pour back to the rivers, so it formed swamps and marshes fed by precipitation and inland waters, too (Valter 1974:4-6). The main rivers were bordered by oxbow lakes. Some runlets, especially in the southwest areas, had more importance: they separated the territories of the villages.

At the beginning of the 18th century the settlement-structure of today was already developed (Valter 1974:11-33). The villages settled on the natural boundary of the flood- and floodfree-areas in order to utilise the conditions of both (Réfi Oszkó 1987: 37-38). The adaptation to these environmental conditions set up the so-called flood-plain economy that characterised the peasant-economy along the main rivers in Hungary nearly until the 19th century.

The basis of the flood-plain economy in Bodrogköz was agriculture, though its territory was restricted to the - in some villages very small - flood-free areas. To increase these territories, forests were chopped and burned and the peasants - especially those from villages along the Tisza and the Bodrog – leased agricultural land in the neighbouring county of Szabolcs (Valyi 1799/2:288, Pesty 1864). Agriculture in better areas was enough only for self-sustenance. Greater importance had the utilisation of flood- and semi-flood areas, especially in animal husbandry complemented with bee keeping, fishing, hunting and gathering (Dankó 1986:22-23).

The different agricultural zones became settled in accordance with the altitude of the land. Open waters were used for fishing. Lakes, riversides covered by vegetation were subject to gathering. Gallery forests and territories temporarily covered by flood were the scene for orchards and animal husbandry. During the flood the cattle grazed in the upper parts, in dry periods in the lower parts. Hay was collected from the upper parts of marshlands and from meadows below agricultural lands. The flood-free – in some cases very small – areas were the places for human settlements, for the woods being good for masting, and most important of all, here were the arable lands. In the small hills there were usually vineyards and forests and it was also used for grazing.

The extension of the agricultural zones depended on the height of the flood in the given year. This also determined the main factor of supply. However, considering that all kinds of cultivation were practised, they always had a chance of surviving. But in the 19th century, agriculture became the main factor and it also spread to the lowlands.

In the middle of the 19th century, the two most important events in Hungary from the agricultural point of view were the abolition of serfdom and the effects of the corn-boom in world economy. As the old and anachronistic agricultural structure and techniques did not change, the only way to increase agricultural produce and so to utilise the boom was to expand arable land. In the

Bodrogköz the only way to do so was the channelization of the rivers and the drainage of marshlands (Szabad 1979:555-559, Refi Oszkó 1987:88).

Before channelization - taking into account only the natural features - land-use patterns were influenced mainly by geomorphology, altitude and the belonging to subareas. After drainage, soil-conditions became important. These had however only a restricting role:

They did not determine economy as altitude and geomorphology did before. It means that the influence of the natural environment was decreasing, contrary to the economic and the social environment. Briefly, channelization has reached its goal.

As the main aim of channelization and drainage was to change the structure of land-use and to extend the arable lands, the changes were, of course, characterised by this process. After regulation and drainage, the previously typical altitude-zones have lost their importance. The area of arable lands expanded from the hilltops to the hillsides, to the riverbanks and later even to the drier parts of the lowlands. Agriculture has lost its special flood-plain character and became a general type of agriculture. However, the territories of the different villages suffered a different type and measure of change after the regulation and drainage. Due to the measure of the two main processes – the extension of arable and the disappearing of barren lands – we can arrange the settlements of Bodrogköz in groups. The most intensive changes can be seen in the territory of the villages around Hosszúrét (Longmeadow). Settlements in the east and middle part of Bodrogköz have suffered less changes and the territory of villages between the Latorca and the Tice and along the northern part of the Bodrog remained nearly untouched. It means that most thorough changes happened in villages around the lowlands. Settlements along the river Bodrog and those villages that were far from both the Tisza and the Bodrog were less affected. After all, the land-use structure of the settlements in Bodrogköz became more similar to each other. Land-use patterns suffered very little change in the northern and eastern part. The extension of arable land happened in two steps. After the regulation of rivers (1860-1880), previous meadows and pastures were turned into plough-lands. After the drainage (1895-1910), the rest of meadows, woods, and pastures made of marshlands were fallowed. Barren- and marshlands nearly totally disappeared and plough-lands extended to the detriment of a less valued but more flexible branch of cultivation. Nevertheless, the value of plough-lands transformed from previous wet lands was also low. As the best meadows were fallowed, the base of animal husbandry was transferred to pastures that were relatively scarce. So the number of animals decreased and it affected land-use as well. Thus the paralysed structure of land-use and animal husbandry mutually hindered each-other's development.

From the economic point of view, the process was a late and ill-matched adaptation: Because of political and economic difficulties, the extension of plough-lands was completed too late: after the end of the corn-boom. Because of technical problems in drainage and the lack of fertilisation, the value of plough-lands was low. Because of the paralysed economic structure, the new lands were cultivated in the old way and this hindered the development of a more suitable agriculture. In short: The social and economic environment that prompted the natural and agricultural changes at the same time hindered the complete utilisation of the new natural environment.

Besides a historic and geographic description, the natural and economic changes in Bodrogköz due to the regulation of rivers and drainage can also be investigated by a mathematical analysis of the body of data that characterise the natural and economic environment of the settlements. Through a multifactor analysis that aims at exploring the connections between the factors, we can discover inner links that cannot be detected otherwise. This investigation is based upon a cluster analysis that arranges the 53 settlements of Bodrogköz in groups according to natural factors and to land-use factors in the different time-segments of the second part of the 19th century. So, in this territory we can describe subsystems, subareas and subregions. Analysing the correlation of the different clusters the dependency of economy upon the natural environment and the process of change in land-use can be characterised.

These groupings are comparable. Comparison can be done by a visual analysis of the dendrograms and by a correlation analysis of the dendrograms carried out by the computer. Although the numerical values are not high enough to come to firm conclusions, some trends can be detected: The land-use of the villages between 1855 and 1913 is getting more and more similar. Geographical features have more influence on land-use before 1855 than later. It means the generalisation of land-use and the decreasing importance of natural features. The soil type has more influence on land-use patterns after the regulation of rivers than before. The most significant change in land-use happened between 1855 and 1883, namely after the regulation of rivers. Drainage caused a smaller change between 1897 and 1913. The difference between land-use patterns of 1883 and 1897 is the smallest as we can find the highest numerical value of correlation coefficient here.

We can analyse and draw on maps as well, whether natural conditions make some kind of land-use possible or impossible. This method was developed in Hungary by Éva Konkoly-Gyuró (1989) on the example of the Zemplén Mountains. Her method can be adapted to the flood plain of Bodrogköz with some restriction. 1. Her soil valuation system was developed on Hungarian material (e.g.Varallyay 1985), and as Slovak pedologists use another type of valuation, we could adopt this method only to the southern part of Bodrogköz which today belongs to Hungary. 2. In the flood plain we can make differences only among pastures, meadows and arable lands. 3. As soil characteristics can suffer rapid changes under the changes of environmental conditions, recent investigation has only a limited historical validity.

Anyhow we can create an optimal land-use map and it shows that there are very few areas in the south of Bodrogköz suitable for plough-land, most of the territory ought to be pasture or meadow. The projection of this map on the maps showing land-use in 1855 and 1880 leads us to the interesting conclusion that, due to the need of arable land to supply the local population even before the channelization, some areas were overused. After the regulation of rivers in the 1880s, overuse increased and after the drainage in the turn of the 19th to the 20th century the overuse became more intensive. It is the main cause of the recent environmental and agricultural problems of the area (Viga 1989:116).

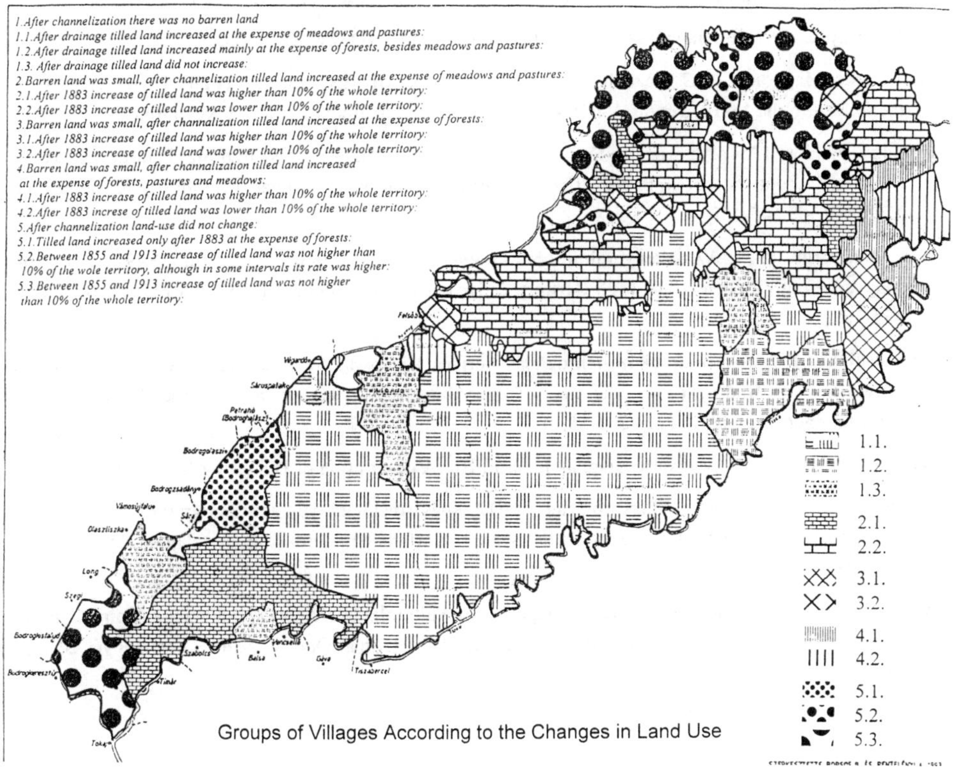

Groups of Villages According to the Changes in Land Use

References

Borsos, Balázs. 1995. Ecosystem - Geographic Area - Economic Region: A Computer Analysis of the Environmental and Economic Changes in the Bodrogköz, NE Hungary in the Second Part of the 19th Century Acta Ethnographica Hungarica 40(1-2): 131 - 184.

Dankó, Imre. 1986. A Bodrogközr régi vizrajza és vizi élete (The previously existing hydrography and life-patterns based on the use of water in Bodrogköz). In: Fejezetek a Bodrogköz néprajzából (Chapters from the ethnography of Bodrogköz) (ed. VIGA Gyula). Néprajzi videkek Borsod-Abaflúj-Zemplén megyében V. Miskolc: 21-28.

Konkolyné Gyuro, Éva. 1989. A területhasznositás optimalizása a Zempléni-hegység térségdben (Optimalising land-use in the area of Zemplén Mountains) Gazdálkodás XXXIII/11: 39-50.

Pesty, Frigyes. 1864. Helynévtéra (~'s Collection of toponyms). (OSZK Kézirattár)

Refi Oszkó, Magdolna. 1987. Gazdálkodás a Rétközben a XVIII-XIX. században (The native economy of the Rétköz in the 18-19th century). (Dissertation. Manuscript) Budapest: MTA Kézirattár.

Somogy, Sándor. 1967. Az árnentesitések és folyószabalyozasok (vázlatos) földrajzi hatásai hazánkban (A sketch about the geographical effects of water-regulation in Hungary). Földrajzi Közlemények XV.(XCI.)/2: 145-158.

Szabad, György. 1979. Az önkényuralom kora (1849-1867) (The age of absolutism [1849-18671]). In: Magyarország története 1848-1890 (History of Hungary 1848-1890 ed. KOVÁCS Endre), Budapest: 435-768.

Valter, Ilona. 1974. A Bodrogköz honfoglalás kori és középkori települléstörténete (The history of settlements in Bodrogköz in the age of the Hungarian conquest and in the Middle Ages). Agrártörténeti Szemle XVI./1 –2: 1-55.

Vályi, András. 1796-99. Magyar országnak leírása I-III. (A description of Hungary I-Ill.) Buda.

Varallyay, Gyorgy. 1985. Magyarország 1:100000-es méretarányú agrotopográfiai térképe (An agrotopographical map of Hungary on the scale of 1:100000). Agrokémia és talajtan XXXIV/1 –2: 243-248.

Viga, Gyula. 1989. Néhany megjcgyzés a néprajz és a kulturalis ökológia kapcsolatához (Some remarks on the connection of ethnography and cultural ecology). Herman Ottó Muzeum Közleményci 26.115-119.

3. Sustainability and Concepts of Sustainability

Rolf Peter Sieferle

Sustainability in a World History Perspective

In the present debate on sustainability descriptive and normative elements are necessarily combined. We do not only ask whether a certain activity is sustainable, but we are mainly interested in recommending how a sustainable practice should look like. This becomes clear regarding the concept of „sustainable development" which combines two different objectives, development and sustainability, implicitly taking it for granted that both aims are compatible.

What is sustainability? An analytical minimum definition proposes „that the material and energetic exchange processes between societies and their physical environment can be maintained over longer periods of time".[1] In a broader meaning aiming at „sustainable development" specifically normative, that is political, social or ethical aspects are added, like justice between regions (industrial countries/Third World), social groups or generations. These criteria of desirability, however, are less matters of analysis than of politics.

In a historical perspective it does not make much sense to include these „soft" criteria into the concept of sustainability. The past cannot be changed at will but in the best case we can try to describe and analyse what happened. Most societies of the past do not follow the ethical standards which prevail today. The agrarian civilisations dominating the history of the last 5000 years had sharp class distinctions, often legally fixed, which set unsurmountable obstacles to individual freedom. If we apply concepts like „equality" or „human rights" to these societies most of them would be qualified as despotic or inhumane. Slavery, caste, torture, feuds, oppression of women, discrimination of religious or ethnic minorities and similar violations of UN conventions were widespread and deemed normal, even in societies like the Attic polis, the historical cradle of democracy.

In political terms, democracy in the modern sense, that is, a form of political rule including the entire population was a very rare exception. Normally, agrarian states were ruled by small privileged minorities who were able to apply the apparatus of political coercion for their own objectives. In most cases they were aggressive and expansive, and it was part of the normal human experience to become subject or object of conquest, plunder and exploitation. In economic terms

[1] Helmut Haberl, et al., Die Kolonisierung der Landschaft. Wien 2001: 7.

the picture is not pleasant, too. Poverty and hunger were widespread, periods of „development" or „growth" in a modern sense remained short and rare exceptions, and the majority of people lived under frugal conditions periodically punctured by subsistence crises, plagues or destruction by war. Most agrarian civilisations experienced some breakdown, not only in political, but also in social and economic respect, often accompanied by a drastic reduction of the populations size.[2]

Were these agrarian civilisations sustainable? If the concept of sustainability has a normative meaning or even if it is used in the sense of „stability" the answer surely must be negative. The convulsions of history as it happened are strictly the opposite of a „sustainable development" as we view it today. In the long term each political, social and economic dimension was exposed to permanent and often violent change. No particular society remained stable or developed continually or in peace. In this sense agrarian societies were not sustainable by definition.

On the other hand we can make the observation that the agrarian mode of production as such prevailed over longer periods of time. Agriculture began about 10'000 years ago, and agrarian civilisations, that is, complex, socially stratified agrarian societies with an urban-industrial sector existed for more than 5'000 years. When we ignore single societies and look at the more general pattern, agrarian societies have been sustainable in the sense that their kind existed in the same regions of the world for several thousand years.

Sustainability in this sense only applies to the physical relations between social and natural systems but not to properties of these systems in isolation. Only the exchange processes between social organisations and their physical environment are meant to be „sustainable", and our historical analysis concentrates on this relationship. In a historical perspective the concept of sustainability should be restrained to this narrow social-ecological relation and only when we restrict it like that research can become fruitful. We can ask questions like these:

- If and how far was a certain mode of production sustainable in the sense that it did not destroy or consume its own physical preconditions?
- If and how far was a single society (or region, or community) sustainable in the sense that it was able to continue certain economic activities without destroying their physical foundations?

Our following reflections deal with the former, more general question, that is with the sustainability of certain modes of production or social-metabolic regimes. This is a rather abstract and highly aggregated matter and we have to subsume a multitude of single societies under common

---

[2] Joseph A. Tainter, The collapse of complex societies. Cambridge 1988; Norman Yoffee / G.L. Cowgill (eds.), The Collapse of Ancient States and Civilizations. Tucson 1988.

concepts. This, of course, doesn't go without serious problems. Agrarian societies in particular depend in a very high degree on specific local or regional ecological conditions. It is much easier to reconstruct ideal features of „industrial societies" than to subsume agrarian societies under a common pattern. After all, automobile factories in Detroit and Shanghai have much more similarities than dry wheat agriculture and wet rice agriculture. We have to move to a more abstract level to speak of common features of agrarian societies. These reflections can provide analytical tools which allow an examination of particular societies – but this, of course, remains a matter of empirical research.

The ecological concept of sustainability used here considers four criteria:

- energy[3]
- material (resources, sinks)
- biodiversity
- population dynamics.

This does not mean that these are the only criteria which could be used. But they are prominent in the present discussion, it is relatively easy to isolate them and they deal with the substantial aspects.

Three different social-metabolic regimes can be distinguished in world history. A social-metabolic regime is defined as a stable form in which the material and energetic exchange processes between human societies and their physical environment are organised.[4] In this definition physical processes (and not social organisations) are stressed. The following regimes are dealt with:

Hunter-gatherer societies, social-metabolically based on an uncontrolled use of solar energy flows. This epoch in world history ended about 10'000 years ago.

Agrarian societies, social-metabolically based on a controlled use of solar energy flows. This epoch began about 10'000 years ago and ended about 200 years ago. The larger agrarian era can be divided into the period of simple peasant societies and the period of complex agrarian civilisations, the latter beginning about 5'000 years ago.

The transformation society which began about 200 years ago is social-metabolically based on the use of fossil energy stocks. This society has not yet developed a stable structure but is involved in a process of accelerating transformation.

---

[3] For energy as a concept of historical analysis see my The Subterranean Forest. Energy Systems and the Industrial Revolution. Cambridge 2001.

[4] Cf. Marina Fischer-Kowalski (ed.), Gesellschaftlicher Stoffwechsel und Kolonisierung von Natur. Amsterdam 1997.

In a first step it is possible to estimate the scope of social metabolism of these three regimes in terms of energy and material. It is relatively easy to identify and quantify the amount of energy flows allowing a comparison between different regimes. With material flows, however, matters are much more complicated. Each social-metabolic activity has a material aspect, but it is not easy to find a common denominator. In a first, rather clumsy approach we can concentrate on the mass of material which flows through a social system. But not everyone will be convinced when 1 kg of gravel, water or wood is dealt equally with 1 kg of gold, dioxin or plutonium. However, this is only a first approach that allows a rough comparison. The benchmark is the basic metabolism of humans, that is the physiological minimum of human metabolism. In energy terms this is about 10 MJ/d, that is 3,5 GJ/y. In terms of materials it is at least 3 kg/d, if water is included, hence more than 1 t/y.

Annual Per Capita Use of Energy and Material in Different Regimes[5]

	Energy	Material
Basic Metabolism	3,5 GJ	1-2 t
Hunter-Gatherers	10-20 GJ (Factor 3-5)	2-3 t
Agrarian Societies	60-80 GJ (Factor 20)	4-5 t
Transformation	250 GJ (Factor 100)	20-22 t

Evidently, the quantitative difference between the three social-metabolic regimes is big enough to make the distinction between these patterns plausible. Our differentiation between these three regimes, however, is not only based on such quantitative effects but on the structure of their activities – which result in such quantitative effects.

[5] Figures according to I.G. Simmons, Changing the Face of the Earth. Culture, Environment, History. Oxford 1989: 379; Marina Fischer-Kowalski / Helmut Haberl, Tons, Joules and Money: Modes of Production and Their Sustainability Problems. In: Society and Natural Resources 10, 1997: 70

1. Hunter-gatherer societies

Paleolithic hunter-gatherer societies tap more or less passively existing solar energy flows without much trying to control these flows actively. They skim off free energy available in their habitat but do not take systematic measures to influence the availability or the amount of these energy flows. Even in energetic terms, however, there is a major difference between prehistoric humans and other primates or mammals: For several 100'000 years hominids actively use fire, and hence (proto-)humans were the one and only pyrophile mammal (or even animal) species.[6] This fire use, especially when savannahs were ignited for hunting purposes could lead to severe and sustained ecological change. Big game hunters thus artificially created the steppe landscapes on which their prey could pasture and insofar a first incidence of a (indirect and unintended) control of the physical environment can be observed.[7]

When we apply our criteria of sustainability to paleolithic hunter-gatherer societies, the following picture emerges:

- **Energy**. They tap given flows without much modifying them, and they could do that infinitely.
- **Material**. They mobilise few material, so that resource- oder pollution-problems may occur on a local level. But they can easily cope with them by migration, mobility being the major method of problem solving in non-sedentarian societies.
- **Biodiversity**. In principle, hunters are able to overhunt and extinguish their beasts of prey. The major waves of human invasion and migration in prehistory coincided with a remarkable increase of the extinction rate of large animals, especially of prey (and their predators). Most spectacular was the megafauna breakdown in America at the end of the last ice-age, that may have been caused by invading hunters from Siberia. For this event, Paul Martin created the term „late pleistocene overkill“.[8] The extinction of megafauna as such is uncontested, the debate only deals with the role humans played in it.[9] As an effect not only hunting resources became scarce in America. There were also severe consequences for the later transition to agriculture because precisely those animals were lacking in America that built the backbone of agricultural production in Eurasia: horses, cattle, donkeys, camels, pigs, sheep, geese.

---

[6] Johan Goudsblom, Fire and Civilisation. London 1992.
[7] Charles E. Kay, Aboriginal Overkill. The Role of Native Americans in Structuring Western Ecosystems. In: Human Nature 5, 1994: 359-398.
[8] Paul S. Martin /Wright, H.E. (eds.), Pleistocene Extinctions. The Search for a Cause. New Haven 1967; Paul S. Martin/Klein, S., eds., Quarternary Extinctions. A Prehistoric Revolution. Tucson 1984.
[9] Peter D.Ward, On Methuselah's Trail. Living Fossils and the Great Extinctions. New York 1992.

- **Population.** It can be assumed that there was no continuous human population growth during the Paleolithic, at least there was no increase of population density. During the last 100'000 years people migrated out of Africa over the whole world. This migration, of course, was combined with an increase in numbers. Local population pressure, however, could normally be solved by migration and did not lead to overpopulation.[10]

Hunter-gatherer societies thus encountered problems of sustainability only in respect to biodiversity. As a matter of fact, these societies could not have any concepts of biodiversity, but in their perspective the extinction of animals meant that resources became scarce which were abundant before. Possibly this scarcity was alleviated by the parallel extinction of predators which disappeared by lack of prey. Reduction of biodiversity may thus have had an ambivalent character for people – when large predators (like sabre tooth tigers) went extinct this was a rather positive event because a competitor if not a dangerous predator of people disappeared. The extinction of megafauna in America, however, was very detrimental for future development, because it led native Americans on a technological and economic path quite different from the one agrarian civilisations in Eurasia took: no draught animals, no carts, no wagons, no wheel, no rotation technology, hence no mills and no machinery; no potting wheel, no high temperature furnaces, no metallurgy. It is possible that it was the late pleistocene megafauna extinction which led to a developmental trajectory in America which resulted in the emergence of „retarded and weak civilisations“[11] which broke down at the first contact with invadors from Eurasia. Even the high native American mortality due to virgin soil epidemics may have been the result of lacking close contact with domesticated animals that were the source of many disease agents in Eurasia. This might be a case of an unintended long term effect of non-sustainable activities.

2. Agrarian societies

The epoch of agrarian societies began about 10'000 years ago, in several regions independently from each other. Now a pattern of human history came to an end which reached back to the dawn of hominids. The history of agrarian societies can be divided into two large segments:[12] During the first three to five thousand years an enormous evolutionary dynamic unfolded, leading

---

[10] Mark Cohen (The Food Crisis in Prehistory. Overpopulation and the Origins of Agriculture. New Haven/London 1977) holds that about 10'000 years ago the carrying capacity of the earth in the context of the hunter-gatherer-regime was overstretched so that the transition to agriculture can be seen as the reaction on an imminent overpopulation crisis.

[11] Fernand Braudel, Capitalism and Material Life. London 1974: 117.

[12] Stephen K. Sanderson, Social Transformations. A General Theory of Historical Development. Oxford 1995.

through different stages of social evolution, until about 5'000 years ago the general pattern of agrarian civilisations emerged showing astonishing common traits all over the world. During the last 5'000 years almost nothing new happened – till the era of agricultural society came to an end 200 years ago. Of course, there were some technological innovations (metallurgy, mechanics), some new cultural and religious patterns (e.g. monotheism), but the social, economic and social-metabolic basic structure remained remarkably stable: There were town and countryside, petty agriculture and petty industry, lords and servants, peasants and warriors, merchants and priests, wars, plagues and famines (all of which did not exist 10'000 years ago and virtually disappeared during the last 200 years in a process not yet completely finished in the present). These features built a stable stage – „history" proper could be acted upon – an endless violent zero sum game about small stocks which could be redistributed but could hardly be increased.

Energy. Like hunter-gatherer societies agrarian societies tap natural solar energy flows, but unlike them their basic strategy aims at controlling these flows. They developed two strategies to achieve this goal:

1. Biotechnology. Energy radiating from the sun is primarily caught and chemically fixed by plant photosynthesis, then it is secondarily converted by animals and finally processed by humans. For this purpose, the agrarian system mainly uses living organisms which serve as food, tools, building material, power source and means of transportation. To achieve this end, humans try to bring the life cycle of their service species under total control. They clear the forests, plow the fields, sow and plant, irrigate and drain, burn down and cultivate, breed and extinguish, propagate and protect useful animals and plants, kill off vermin, weed and predators. Agriculture's strategy aims at destroying primeval „natural" ecosystems, mainly vegetation, to prepare and monopolise the area for its domesticated species.
2. Mechanical devices. Here solar energy flows available in the biosphere (wind or running water) are mechanically converted. The total amount of these energy flows cannot be influenced, but people can increase the efficiency of energy conversion, albeit no great breakthrough can be expected. Technological progress is slowly pushing elastic limits. The most important of these mechanical devices are the sailing boat, which was essential for long range transportation in agrarian civilisations, and the watermill, which was the paradigmatic installation for the machinery of the last 2000 years.

Energy use in agrarian societies has a general structure which can be reconstructed as a technically modified solar energy system. Its main characteristics are dependence on an energy flow, low energy density and the limited possibilities of converting one energy form into another. Thus particular energy forms like heat, movement, light or food appeared as qualities, not as aspects of one energy flow. These features of the agrarian energy system defined a narrow scope of the agrarian landscape that could not be transgressed within the context of the agrarian regime.

There were three distinct forms of energy conversion based on the use of biomass that went together with a tripartite structure of the agrarian landscape (at least in colder regions): Forests provided wood that served as source of thermal energy, for heating and for chemical processes (cooking, industrial purposes). Pasture provided grass or hay as fodder for animals that served as bioconverters for mechanical energy (draught animals), as food or as raw material for industrial purposes (leather, wool, bones, horn). Arable land mainly provided food for the human metabolism. Forest, pasture and arable were the areas from which these different qualities of biomass had to be produced. If people wanted to substitute one energy carrier by another they had to change the form of land use, e.g. if they needed more mechanical energy and less thermal energy, they had to clear a forest and transform it into pasture. A direct conversion of fuel (wood) into mechanical labour was not possible before the steam engine was invented.

The amount of energy an agrarian society could use was very small, due to the low energy density of solar radiation and the low efficiency of technology. To assess this amount we can treat particular elements of the agrarian solar energy system as if they were power plants with a certain installed capacity. For this purpose we distribute the energy product (which becomes available discontinually at the harvest) over the whole year:

Power installed in the agrarian solar energy system

	Power in kW
1 ha forest	1
1 ha arable	0,25-0,5
1 ha pasture	0,7
watermill	3-4

As we can see, the amount of energy that becomes available continually is very small; the agrarian energy flow is a mere trickle. It is virtually impossible to overcome this energy scarcity by transportation because transport costs are exceedingly high and have to be expressed in energy terms, too.[13] The agrarian system can not afford to operate with a negative energy harvest factor,

[13] When transport costs are expressed in terms of grain, 1 t/km costed 4 kg over land, 1 kg over a waterway and 0.4 kg over sea. Paul Bairoch, Economics and World History. Myths and Paradoxes. New York 1993: 60.

that is, it must not use more energy during the production process than is incorporated in the product. This explains why agrarian societies are always decentralised – they have to use areas which are their main factor of production. They live on archipelagos of scarcity, and any tendency towards spatial concentration of production and consumption is counteracted by these physical conditions.

When we take a look at energy stocks available in agrarian societies we can see that „stocks“ are only short-lived intermediate storages, they are not large reserves which could be consumed. The largest energy stock an agrarian society could ever use was a primeval forest with a biomass representing about 300 years of photosynthetic production. But a primeval forest could only be used once, in a pioneer situation, when new land is claimed. When land is continually used people have to economise forest use sustainably, that is they have to treat forests as buffers of chemical energy. In a given period of time they can only consume the biomass yield produced during this period. Forests are no stocks but intermediate storages and this is true for all the others elements of the agrarian solar energy system, too.

Energy Stocks in Agrarian Societies

Stock	representing years
primeval forest	300
middle forest	80
coppice	20
large animals (cows, horses)	10-20
small animals (pigs, sheep)	2-5
poultry	1-2
grain	1-2
fruits, vegetables	1
watermill (dammed water)	1 day
wind (windmill, sail)	0

From these characteristics it becomes evident that energy use could not be but sustainable, for the simple reason that there were no large stocks that could be consumed. Of course, it was always possible to overuse energy resources, e.g. to consume more wood than regrew during the same period of time. But the biomass buffers were generally so small that it was impossible to establish an economic structure based on the consumption of stocks. Agrarian societies were energetically sustainable because there was no physical alternative to sustainability.

Material

Material is mobilised by the use of energy so that in the last instance the social-metabolic material flow is limited by the available amount of energy. The sharp energetic restrictions set by the agrarian regime thus had a limiting effect on material processes. But it does make sense to take a closer look at the material aspect. Two elements deserve a closer examination:

1. Soil is the fundament for the agrarian use of biomass and much of agrarian society's productive potential depends on it. It would be wrong to treat soil merely as a passive durable supply that could be used at will. On the contrary, soil must be understood as an exhaustible resource. It is a complicated aggregate of mineral matter, organic matter and small organisms building a specific ecosystem, with a history and an evolutionary trajectory of its own, independent of human intervention.[14] There is a large variety of different soils with different features, reacting more or less sensibly or resiliently to disturbances. This is the reason why general predictions whether human soil use is sustainable or not are impossible. This remains an empirical question.

The agricultural use of soil is a problematic matter. When forests are cleared or grassland is plowed soil will be exposed to the eroding power of wind and water in a higher degree than if its natural vegetation cover remains undisturbed. Agriculture accelerates erosion and thus may destroy its own physical preconditions. When arid land is irrigated soil may become salinated and finally barren. This happened in early centres of agricultural production in Mesopotamia.[15]

On the other hand, there are examples of long-term sustainable soil use, especially where soil is young and stable, where water is provided by rainfall and where agriculture is extensive, in combination with forestry and pasture. This was the case in central and northwestern Europe where agricultural production was maintained over several thousand years without destroying soil. Other agricultural regions have a less favourable record.[16]

An older tradition of soil science, following the example of Justus Liebig's soil chemistry, focuses on limiting chemical factors in the soil which is regarded as a carrier of chemical solutions, not so much as an ecosystem. Although this view neglects the complexity and inner dynamics of soil, it still provides a useful explanation of some simple processes. One critical chemical is nitrogene, the lack of which diminishes the assimilating capacity of plants. When we look at the nitrogene in- and output in pre-industrial agriculture, the following picture emerges:

---

[14] Antoinette M. Mannion, Global Environmental Change. A Natural and Cultural Environmental History. Harlow 1991.
[15] Daniel Hillel, Out of the Earth. Civilization and the Life of the Soil. Berkeley 1991.
[16] J. Donald Hughes, Pan's Travail. Environmental Problems of the Ancient Greeks and Romans. Baltimore 1996.

Nitrogene Balance of Central European Agriculture[17]

	N Exports (kg/ha)	**N Imports** (kg/ha)
Harvest 1'000 kg grain	20	
Seed (yield factor 5)		4
NO_x produced by lightnings		8-12
N fixed by bacteria		4-10
Erosion, loss by water	2	
Total	22	21

Under these conditions the nitrogene balance was stable even without manuring, that is without exogenous transfer of nutrients on the arable, so that a sustained annual production of 1 t grain per hectar could be maintained. It should be noted that European grain harvest was lower than that during the Middle Ages and in the Early Modern Epoch. This means that even without manuring European agriculture was sustainable, at least in the narrow terms of soil chemistry. On the other hand, this means that any increase of production encountered a physical limit at about 1 t/ ha y. It was possible to approach this limit but it could not be transcended without fundamentally changing the methods of cultivation (manuring by leguminoses, new forms of rotation etc.)

2. Industrial material like metals, salt and other chemicals provided specific resource and pollution problems, above all in settlements. Here we find the classical forerunners of actual „environmental destruction", originating by uncontrolled mining and diffusion of substances into the biosphere, which causes unintended side-effects. Agrarian civilisations always had a non-agrarian industrial sector, and we may ask if and how far it produced specific problems of sustainability.

The first problem was the availability of mineral resources. Mining, smelting and processing of metals were always connected with a rather high energy demand that had to be supplied by the agrarian sector (forestry). The energy scarcity inherent in the solar energy system became sensible here, too. When the easier available resources were exhausted, shafts had to be deepened, ores with a lesser mineral content had to be used, or transport routes had to be extended. What-

[17] R.S. Loomis, Ecological Dimensions of Medieval Agrarian Systems. In: Agricultural History 52, 1978: 478-483.

ever the solution, in the normal course of events metallurgy faced the perspective to be throttled by rising energy costs. People could react by finding new reserves, or by technological progress, but there was inevitably the problem of diminishing marginal returns which was a basic feature of agrarian societies. In contrast to the agrarian sector, the industrial sector's resource basis was non-sustainable in principle, that is its fundament was the consumption of stocks, not the management of flows. Regarding the low dynamics of technological innovation in agrarian societies, severe problems could rise.

The backside of resource development is waste disposal. If mineral resources are scarce and expensive there will not be any major problems with sinks or pollution because the mobilised masses are too small. Global or even regional pollution of the environment was not possible in agrarian societies from reasons of want. Detrimental immission of pollutants only occurred on a local level, in direct vicinity of production plants, e.g. copper or lead mills and their slagheaps. There is no indication that this caused trouble of larger dimensions.

Biodiversity

The physical fundament of agrarian production is the colonisation of natural ecosystems. Agriculture's basic strategy aims at the destruction of natural vegetation and plant societies and their substitution by an artificially controlled biotop moulded for human purposes. To do this requires large labour inputs not just to produce but to maintain these artificial states. But we must not forget that agricultural societies never succeed totally in their venture to control their colonies; there are always undesirable side-effects of colonisation (weed, vermin, zoonoses). Agriculture has very complex effects on the issue of biodiversity, and it is not possible to name an unequivocal tendency.

On the one hand, biodiversity decreases because peasants compete with other organisms for the use of land and biomass and try to eradicate these competitors as pests. When a certain plant society is removed by clearing and plowing, the niches for heterotrophic organisms feeding on these plants disappear, too. This is not necessarily intended, but it happens. More spectacular is the direct elimination of large predators who compete with humans for prey (bears, tigers, wolves, eagles etc.). Agriculture tries to monopolise the biomass production on its colonised land and this requires that other organisms will have to pay the prize of destruction or marginalisation.

On the other hand we should not forget that agriculture produces new organisms and ecological niches precisely as a side-effect of its basic strategy of colonisation. This is the case with artificial selection and breeding of plants and animals which produces new life complexes which are coevolutionarily and symbiotically connected with humans, thus augmenting (phenotypic) biodiversity. Active and intended selection, however, is accompanied by passive and unintended selection, as an effect of coevolution. New kinds of organisms originate, which may be a nuisance, above all parasites that switch vectors and acquire the status of agents of endemic disease.

Finally, transportation and migration of organisms are to be mentioned. Most important agricultural plants and animals spread over the whole continent of Eurasia during the last thousands of years, so that it is almost impossible to identify the region of their first cultivation. Many domestic organisms have left their origin many centuries ago and were cultivated in other regions, sofar ecological conditions allowed this. Wheat was first cultivated in Mesopotamia, but soon spread to Europe and China. Apples and lemons come from East Asia, rice and sugar cane from South East Asia, but they can be found in the Mediterranean since more than 2000 years.

Migrating domestic plants and animals brought their parasites with them. The most widespread rat species, *Rattus rattus* and *Rattus norvegicus*, had their origin in South East Asia from where they conquered the whole world as people's companions. [18] Similar is the case of parasitic microorganisms like the agents of smallpox, plague or malaria who spread in all agrarian civilisations supported by animal or human vectors.[19]

Most spectacular and part of human memory is the bioinvasion connected with the discovery of America. Domestic plants like (sweet) potatoes, maize, peanuts, tomatos and peppers are to be found all over Eurasia since mid 16th century. On the other hand, many organisms were carried from Eurasia to America, among them many agents of disease.[20] Horses for example, who originally had invaded Eurasia from America, had died out in the continent of their phylogenetic origin 12'000 years ago, were reimported from Europe after 1492, and spread rapidly over the whole continent again.

Bioinvasion does not produce new species but it increases regional biodiversity. The loss of species caused by agriculture is thus compensated, if not over-compensated by breeding and spread of new varieties. Per saldo regional (not global) biodiversity may have increased during the agricultural epoch.

Population

The population regime of agrarian societies differs from that of hunter-gatherer societies. Most important is the drastic increase of population throughput, that is of the combined rates of fertil-

[18] Cf. F. di Castri et al. (eds.), Biological Invasions in Europe and the Mediterranean Basin. Dordrecht 1990.

[19] Emanuel Le Roy Ladurie, Un concept: L'unification microbienne du monde (XIV-XVIIIe siècles), in: Schweizerische Zeitschrift für Geschichte 23, 1973: 627-96; William McNeill, Plagues and Peoples. Garden City 1976; Mark Nathan Cohen, Health and the Rise of Civilization, New Haven, London 1989.

[20] Alfred W. Crosby, Ecological Imperialism. The Biological Expansion of Europe, 900-1900. Cambridge 1986.

ity and mortality. This is the effect of basic characteristics of the agrarian mode of production.

Agrarian production allows a higher population density because peasants can reserve a larger part of biomass available in a certain area for their particular purposes. This higher population potential materialises by means of several ecological and cultural processes. Birth rates are higher in agrarian societies than in hunter-gatherer societies. There are some reasons for that. Sendentary life allows women to reduce the birth intervals because they no longer have to carry small children with them when the group is migrating. Shorter births intervals increase fertility because it becomes possible for a woman to give more births during her lifetime. Another reason is that agrarian societies have baby food like milk or gruel available so that children can be weaned earlier. This leads to female hormonal change with the effect that another pregnancy becomes possible at an earlier time. In addition to these biological reasons children become useful in peasant households. At an early age they can do some simple work so that they provide for their own costs of rearing. This has the effect that birth control sets in at a higher level than with hunter-gatherer societies.[21]

Mortality, too, is higher in agrarian societies, that is individual life expectancy decreases. The most important reason for that is higher population density, producing the critical mass for the spread of parasitic microorganisms. Only in agrarian societies infectious diseases are endemic. Another reason is the close contact with animals provoking a change of hosts. Most agents of infectuous diseases have their origin in (domesticated) animals.

The nutritional basis of agrarian societies is much smaller than that of hunter-gatherers, that is they use less organisms as permanent food sources. This strategy makes them dependend on the life- und growth conditions of these few favoured organisms. Bad weather, pest invasion or other uncontrollable disasters may destroy the harvest with the consequences of severe famines and increased mortality.

In agrarian societies warfare is widespread. It is true that hunter-gatherer societies, too, have a record of violent conflicts with a (statistically) high mortality rate[22] (if one member of a local group of 50 is killed, the mortality rate is 2%), but in agrarian societies war has more fundamental effects. They result in crop failure, famine and epidemics with a drastic increase of mortality which is only indirectly the effect of homicide.

The combined effect of higher fertility and mortality in agrarian societies is a higher fluctuation of population numbers, as compared with hunter-gatherers or with the transformation era. Life expectancy is relatively low, population throughput is high, and there is a low level of security.

---

[21] Marvin Harris / Eric B. Ross, Death, Sex, and Fertility. Population Regulation in Preindustrial and Developing Societies. New York 1987.
[22] Lawrence H. Keeley, War Before Civilization. New York 1996.

One particular problems are larger settlements: towns of agrarian civilisations were places of higher mortality. They may be regarded as population sinks and were demographically dependent on a permanent level of immigration from the countryside. On the other hand, this allowed agricultural regions to produce a population surplus which could be absorbed by towns. The combination of these two activities favoured the high fluctuation of population levels.

Demographic Regimes in World History[23]

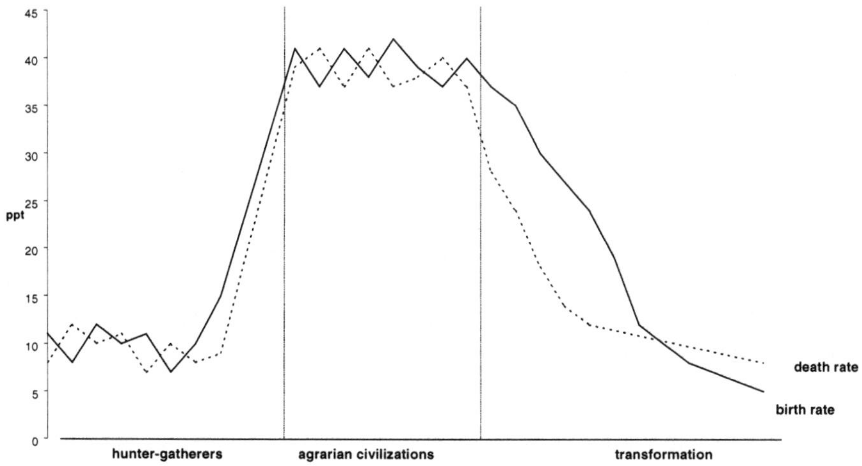

Was there a general tendency towards population growth during the epoch of agrarian societies? There is no doubt that human population has grown since the transition to agriculture. 10'000 years ago world population was about 5 million and during the following several thousands of years it increased by a factor 25. About 2'500 years ago world population may have been about 100 Million, and at the beginning of the industrial transformation about 500 million people lived on earth.[24] However, if we contemplate particular agrarian civilisations, we get the impression that there was a high volatility but no clear trend. Global population growth during the epoch of agrarian civilisations may rather have been the effect of the fact that the number of agrarian civi-

[23] Cf. Josef Schmid, Das verlorene Gleichgewicht. Eine Kulturökologie der Gegenwart. Stuttgart 1992, 107.
[24] Joel Cohen, How many people can the earth support? New York 1995, 400f.

lisations increased and that they dominated larger territories, but not so much of population growth in older agricultural regions.

It is now possible to summarise the basic features of agrarian societies:

- small stocks
- organisation of flows
- dependence on area of photosynthesis
- scarcity of material, hence poverty
- paradigm of zero sum game
- main strategy: management by optimising given flows
- tendency towards a stationary state
- hence: sustainability.

3. The Transformation Society

The transformation era began about 250 years ago and it seized all elements of the agrarian societies. Here I will not go into details of the social-metabolic transformation about which much has been said.[25] I will just concentrate on the energy and material aspects in the early phases and will neglect the development of the nearer past.

Energy. The energetic foundation of the transformation is the switch to the use of fossil energy carriers: coal, mineral oil and mineral gas. This has two major implications: Very large stocks became available within short periods of time, and the mobilisation of material was fed by comparatively cheap and abundant energy supplies. A new social-metabolic regime was formed which soon transgressed the physical boundaries of the agrarian solar energy system.

What this meant can be illustrated by the development of the British coal production which can be expressed in terms of the basic unit of the solar energy system, that is land. 1 t coal has the thermal equivalent of 5 cubic meters wood, that is the annual yield of 1 ha forest. Given these data we can express the evolution of coal production in terms of area equivalents:[26]

[25] John R. McNeill, Something New Under the Sun. An Environmental History of the Twentieth Century. London 2000.

[26] Coal output figures according to N.K. Buxton, The Economic Development of the British Coal Industry. London 1978, 86; Sidney Pollard, A New Estimate of British Coal Production, 1750-1850, in: Eco-

Area equivalents of British coal production

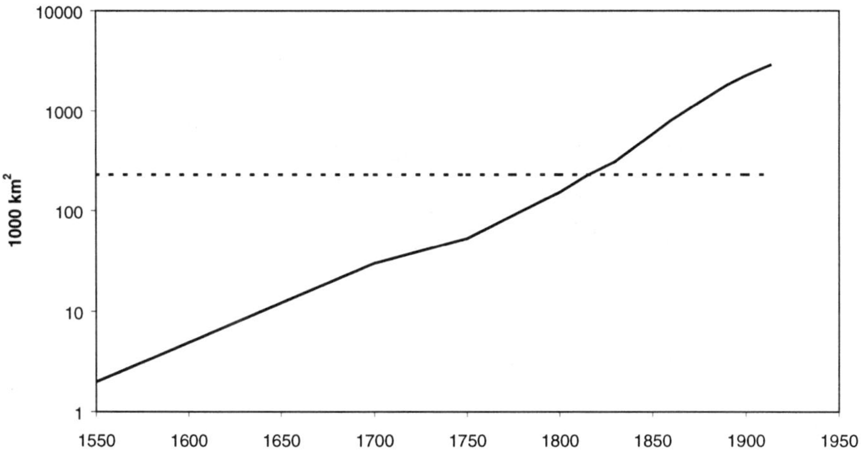

The dotted line represents the surface of England and Wales (150.000 km²). That means that already in the first decade of the 19th century the virtual area won by coal use was as large as the whole surface of the country. It becomes clear that the fossil energy system broke the bounds of the agrarian solar energy systems, and „something new under the sun" came into existence. The new energy regime moved far from the sustainable scope of the older regime and reached dimensions which were uncomprehensible in the context of an agrarian society. It is self-evident that this is the physical basis of an unsustainable economic and ecological regime.

Material. The availability of large energy stocks allowed to mobilise material in similar dimensions. This can be demonstrated with the development of global metal production during the last 150-200 years (as far back as data seem reliable).[27]

---

nomic History Review 33, 1980: 229; Michael W. Flinn, The History of the British Coal Industry, vol. 2. Oxford 1984: 26.

[27] Database cf. R.P. Sieferle, Rückblick auf die Natur. München 1997: 155-158.

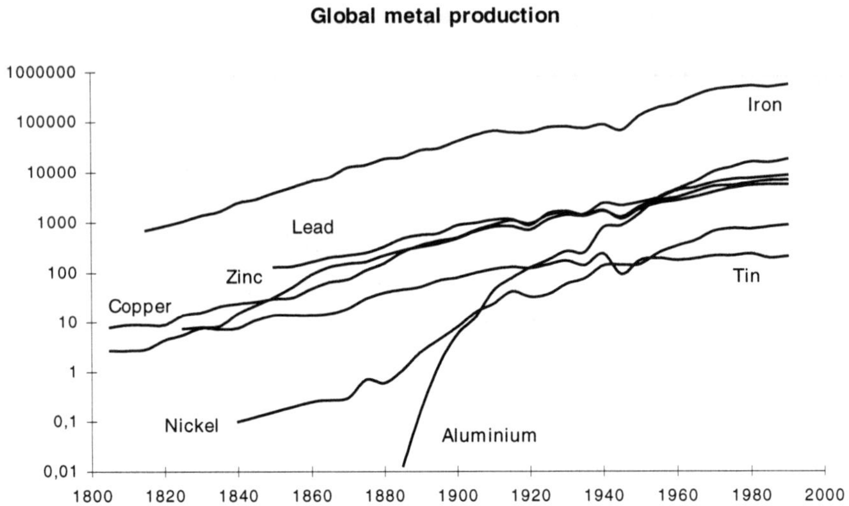

We have an exponential growth of metal production over 200 years, fed by fossil energy. Pollution problems are just the backside of this process: They provide the sink aspect of material mobilisation.

Biodiversity. It is not self-evident that biodiversity decreased during the transformation era, because human impact on land could have been substituted by technological processes. But as a matter of fact biodiversity suffered, as more parts of the earth became actively colonised for human purposes. At the turn of the 20th century about 40% of global net biomass production was somehow affected by human activities, if not appropriated by agro-business or forestry. This, of course, left fewer niches for other species. The transformation regime did not forgo intensive land use, but on the contrary, biomass appropriation increased.[28] But there are some exceptions: Only transformation societies can afford to protect natural reservations. Conservation, species protection and the establishment of parks and reserves are exclusive features of these societies which are (in contrast to agrarian societies) rich enough to dedicate land for species which do not serve them directly.

---

[28] Fridolin Krausmann, Rekonstruktion der Entwicklung von Materialflüssen im Zuge der Industrialisierung: Veränderungen im sozioökonomischen Biomassenmetabolismus in Österreich von 1830 bis 1998. Stuttgart 2001.

Population. As everybody knows, human population increased by a factor 10 since the beginning of the transformation. In the following diagram humans are represented in terms of their yearly energy intake (basic metabolism: 3.5 GJ/y) so human population growth can be compared with the availability of fossil fuel. This suggests that modern population growth has something to do with the transition to a new energy regime.

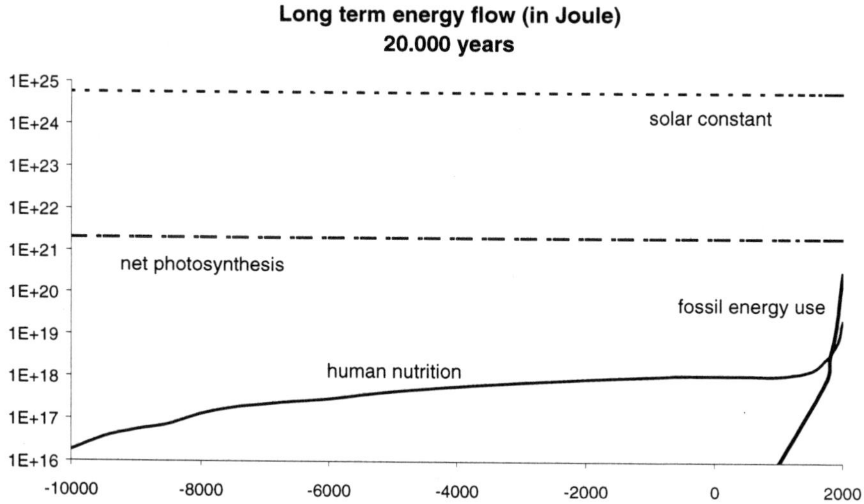

Conclusion

To come to a conclusion, lack of sustainability is not something totally new. Sustainability problems occurred in different settings in the past, but they were connected to the general features of the respective societies. The transformation society, however, is not sustainable because its physical foundation is the consumption of stocks, not the management of flows. As there are no infinite stocks, it is impossible to sustain their consumption infinitely. This means that sooner or later the transformation regime will have to acquire a different material fundament that may be sustainable in metabolic terms. To answer the question if and how this can be achieved, however, lies outside the scope of this historical paper.

William I. Woods

Soils and Sustainability in the Prehistoric New World

Introduction

Herein, three case studies will be briefly outlined, whose implications suggest that it is best to consider closely what we think we know before making any attempts at generalization. As anthropologists and geographers we are all well aware of the concept of evolution, that is: change in form through time. We apply this concept and its corollaries routinely; however, when it comes to soil landscapes our retrospective view is often a static one. This is, of course, deadly for projecting the past in regard to questions of productivity and sustainability.

During the last century, a number of researchers looked seriously at development scenarios for various parts of the ancient world and attributed great importance to natural soils and their cultural management or mismanagement. One sees in the literature much discussion of salinization in the Tigris-Euphrates Valley, soil erosion throughout the Mediterranean, and nutrient depletion in lowland Central America as leading to the fall of empires. In the case of Amazonia, the extremely poor soils present were cited as the fundamental cause for lack of cultural attainment; while in the Mississippi Valley the rise of temple mound centers during the late prehistoric followed the eternal Egyptian model of fertile, annually renewed soils. So soils were used deterministically as an explanatory mechanism when they presumably suited a preconceived notion of development or decline, but little in-depth study was undertaken of what soils were actually present on the microscale and how these had been affected by different management strategies through time. In the following discussion the problems that can occur with such an intellectual stance will be illustrated. Moving from the mid-latitudes to the equator three distinct trajectories taken in quite diverse environments in North, Central, and South America, respectively, will be examined *Fig. 1 (see p. 144)*.

Soils, along with energy from the sun, water, and the cultivated plants themselves, constitute the major environmental resources for agricultural societies and are, therefore, critical to discussions of sustainability. For the inhabitants of the late prehistoric centers at Cahokia, Xunantunich, and Santarém and their hinterlands, maize was a principal crop; although for all of these agriculturalists, other produced and gathered foods provided significant adjuncts to the diet. Each of these

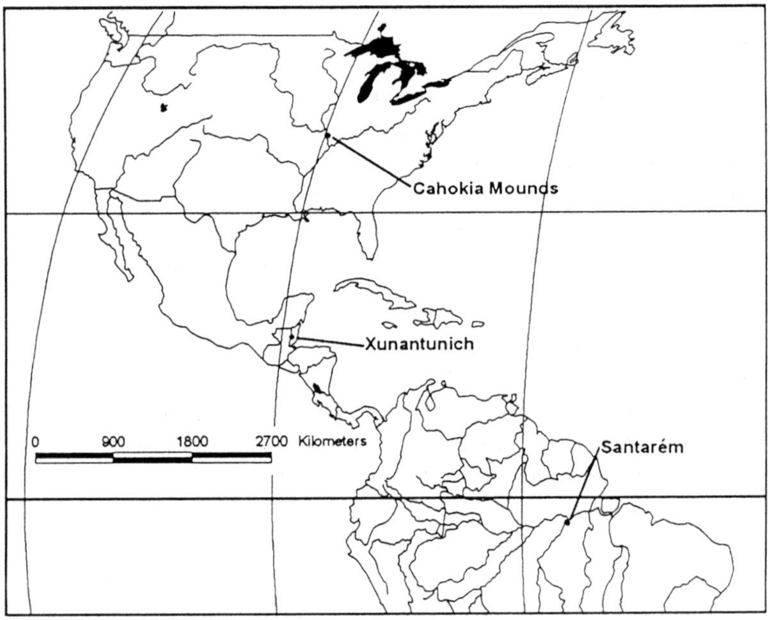
Cahokia Mounds
Xunantunich
Santarém
0 900 1800 2700 Kilometers

Fig. 1

three sites presents a different regional soil context. Illinois is termed "the Prairie State" and at the macro-scale one finds organic- and nutrient-rich soils developed under grassland vegetation; similar to those of the Pampas and the Ukraine. Certainly, one would expect no problem for sustainability here; these soils now feed the world. However, the late prehistoric inhabitants of the region did not till the prairies, but rather placed their fields in zones of annually renewed, alluvial soils in the Mississippi and tributary valleys. The thin soils in the Maya Lowlands of Belize and adjacent Guatemala developed under dense forest foliage on limestone terrain. These soils have some nutrient problems and a tendency for high concentrations of aluminum which may be toxic to some plants. One would expect problems with agricultural sustainability here, particularly with nucleation of population. Finally, in the lower Amazon region, often depicted as a "Counterfeit Paradise" or "Green Hell," the highly weathered, very acidic soils are thought of as extremely forbidding. With few available nutrients and having aluminum in concentrations high enough to mine, one couldn't imagine a worse regime for agriculture. Indeed, even in the flood plain with somewhat better soils, crop production is a risky endeavor because of the unpredictability of the flood regime.

So, one would from the macro-view have to state that problems for the prehistoric New World agriculturalists would increase exponentially from the mid-latitudes to the equator. However, it's a matter of scale when dealing with humans and the environment; and, for soils this is particularly true. Continental or regional depictions simply are not appropriate. Rather, one needs to look at the microscale and here one finds enormous pre-Columbian modifications of the soil landscape and unexpected answers to questions of sustainability.

The Cahokia situation

One thousand years ago an immense prehistoric community, now termed Cahokia, developed on the Mississippi River flood plain directly to the east of the present St. Louis and existed for over three centuries. Its rise is coincident with the regional development of temple mound centers, hierarchical political and religious organization, and a largely maize-based agricultural economy (Dalan et al. 2002). Cahokia's position was quite favorable being situated on high ground proximal to extensive water resources and quality soils coupled with ready access to the largest interior watershed in the local region, *Fig. 2 (see p. 146)*.

Estimates for the peak population at the Cahokia center have ranged from less than 5,000 to over 40,000 individuals (Fowler 1997). However, it is agreed that the order of magnitude was in the thousands, making it the largest prehistoric settlement to the north of central Mexico. Cahokia happened as a result of rapid intensification of food production with a maize based economy. It can best be viewed as an enormous rural community wherein the vast majority of its inhabitants were primary producers engaged in the food quest, most importantly that associated with agricultural production.

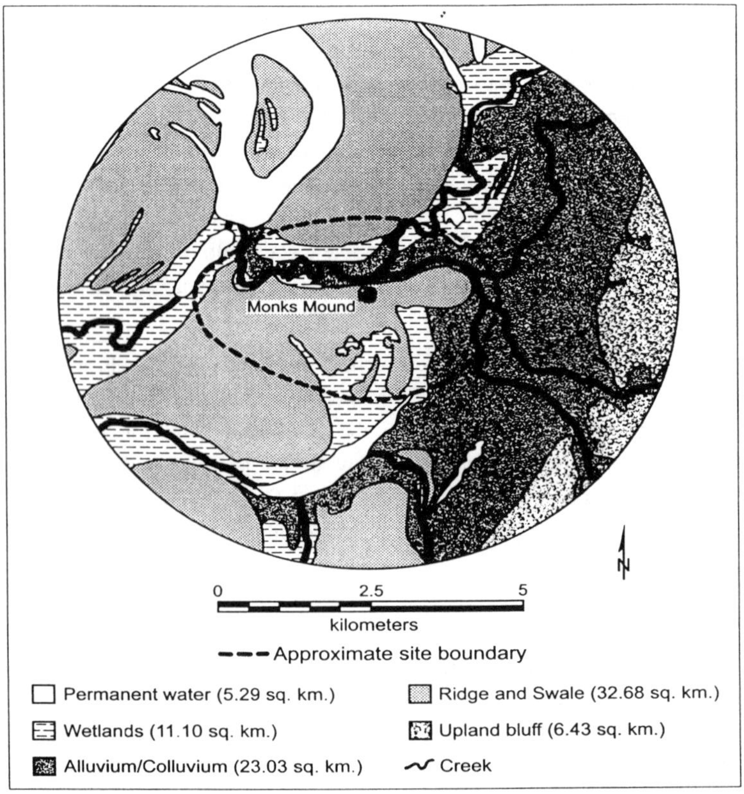

Fig. 2

At Cahokia, agricultural production took place in three settings (Woods 1987, 1993). One, the multi-crop gardens within the habitation zone on soils which had often been enriched by prior occupations. Two, the large, commonly worked, mono-cropped outfields found on natural levees, overbank deposits, and alluvial fans to the east of the site with the soils characterized as optimal for hoe cultivation without fertilization ("Alluvium/Colluvium" in *Fig. 2*). And, three, in more distant ancestral lands northward along the base of the bluffs and into the upland stream valleys to the east and north. The nature of this production did not include swidden or field rotation as an option for the Cahokians. Due to the restricted areas of suitable lands, annual re-cultivation and planting was necessary with slash and burn only utilized for initial field clearance.

Over the years many causes have been advanced for the decline and abandonment of Cahokia. Disease, climatic change, warfare, failure of leadership, internal rebellion, and usurpation of external relationships by more dynamic groups have been posited and, to an extent, may all have been contributory factors (Woods and Holley 1991). However, within the local setting, it is clear that the seeds for the destruction were inherent and included the nucleation of a large population coupled with a subsistence base centered on maize and that anthropogenically produced environmental degradation occurred widely and exerted a great impact on the food production capabilities of the Cahokia society.

Demands on forests for fuel and construction were great and, in addition, timber clearance was extensive for fields (Lopinot and Woods 1993). Major changes in the local hydrologic situation would have been brought about by overexploitation of upstream wood resources in bottomland, slope, and bluff-top settings. More rapid runoff coupled with decreased channel capacity from sedimentation would have produced major flooding after each heavy rain. The results of such flooding during summer would have been catastrophic for bottomland communal maize fields and Cahokia with its heavy reliance on such settings for crop production would have been particularly vulnerable. Significantly, these projected events co-occur with a dramatic increase in fortifications and burned structures (Pauketat and Woods 1986; Holley et al. 1990; Woods and Holley 1991), a documented movement of habitation structures to higher elevations within the flood plain (Milner 1986), and a general trend of migration back into interior upland settings (Woods and Holley 1991). By A.D. 1350 the complex nucleated community present during the previous centuries at Cahokia had been largely abandoned (Woods 2000) and all indications are for a regional settlement pattern of sporadic, relatively short-term, low-density habitations (Dalan et al. 2002).

In order to describe the Cahokia phenomenon one needs to define the conditions of base line existence for the vernacular Cahokians and their everyday engagement with the environment. Significant anthropogenic alterations to the environment did occur as a result of population nucleation. As a result, the agricultural basis for life at Cahokia was literally being smothered. On the sloping fields and disturbed woodlands at the margins of the valley each rain would have progressively eroded surfaces. In fields at lower elevations, the increased rates of sedimentation would have been accompanied by flooding, standing water, and saturated soil conditions and during the growing season crops would have suffocated through drowning. The economic and social consequences of declining production and localized crop failure were disastrous; particularly at Cahokia with its downstream location and large resident population so reliant on the production of the maize outfields proximal to the site. Unfortunately, the relatively slow rates at which the anthropogenic alterations changed the regional hydrology insured that adequate countermeasures were not implemented.

A Mayan example

Soils have long been connected with views of the ancient Maya (Cowgill 1961; Olson and Puleston 1972). Initially, focus was placed on the concept of infertile tropical soils sustaining only low-density populations practicing swidden cultivation of maize. As an increasing population overused the productive capacity of these soils the fall of Classic Maya society naturally occurred as a result. It has become clear though that this simple scenario is not valid (Woods et al. 1996). More intensive and diverse systems of forest and crop management, often employing drained fields or terracing, had been operant on a large scale. Although prehistoric soil erosion and nutrient depletion have been identified, collapse theories no longer rely on soil degradation as the primary causative factor (Culbert 1973; Santley et al. 1986; Turner 1993).

Our research is associated with a study area in western Belize near the Xunantunich site along the Rio Mopan (Holley et al. 2000). Archaeological deposits buried by anthropogenically-induced processes within the Maya area have largely gone unreported and methods to identify buried sites have not been widely applied. Though the magnitude of broad-scale surface modification for the creation of centers and villages and agricultural pursuits is apparent (Binford et al. 1987; Jacob 1992; Wingard 1992; Dunning and Beach 1994), the effects of environmental degradation have largely lacked integration with survey and excavation strategies. Our work concentrated on the implications of the emplacement of slope terrace features and the dynamic prehistoric riverine geomorphology evident on the surface and in a series of test units.

Within our field area, the present river has cut a steep bank. Moving east and up onto the terrace is a raised cobble bar about six meters above the current river level. Abundant habitation mounds are strewn on this terrace. Further to the east, a river paleomeander, located at the toe slope of a hill marks the edge of the uplands. The excavation revealed near – surface cultural fill and debris relating to Late Classic occupations on the terrace. Stratigraphically below the Late Classic horizons were coarse deposits comprised sands, gravel, and cobbles. Contained within these deposits were water – worn sherds whose ceramic diagnostics included Preclassic rims. Below the coarse materials we uncovered evidence for a Preclassic occupation that included Middle and Late Preclassic sherds, a Late Preclassic structure delineated by postmolds, and a possible earthen mound. The Preclassic occupation surface was located on clayey overbank deposits and contained evidence of well developed soils, indicating a long period of depositional stability.

A reconnaissance of the hillslopes abutting the paleochannel revealed extensive cultural terrace systems along the valley walls. These features had been ignored by prior investigators because they do not contain stonewalls and are only distinguished by microrelief. Habitation mounds are also associated with these terraces.

Our investigations permit us to offer a synthetic interpretation of the dynamic characteristics of the landscape within the central portion of the Rio Mopan. Initially, a Preclassic settlement was established, probably during the Middle Preclassic period along the riverbanks, *Fig. 3 (see p. 150)*. The catastrophic flooding, which buried this Preclassic village, took the form of a significant and rapid discharge of poorly-sorted cobbles, gravels and sands that were deposited to attain the present elevations of the terrace. Intermixed within these coarse textured deposits were weathered Preclassic sherds, likely deriving from upstream settlements positioned near the Rio Mopan. The size of the gravel and the absence of stable horizons within the strata indicate that the river migration was rapid. The gravels were deposited during the migration of the channel eastward towards the hill that was curtailed by the footslopes of the valley margins, where an elevated new channel was formed.

We argue that these flooding events were initiated by broad-scale anthropogenic modifications upstream from our study area that derived from the construction of major Maya centers and clearance of land for cultivation before and during the Early Classic Period (Ball and Taschek 1991; Ford and Fedick 1992; Fedick 1994). We see this valley-wide initiation of construction and population aggregation as the causative factor in the catastrophic flooding evident along portions of the Rio Mopan.

The raised channel formed by the river migration was cut off from the main stem and the river likely returned to its present course to the west due to upstream hillslope modification including agricultural terracing. The erection of house mounds on the river terrace occurred during the Late Classic and the presence of residence mounds within the filled channel attests to the cessation of slope erosion and stabilization of the present channel by the erection of agricultural terraces both locally and upriver. This coincides with the rise of Xunantunich, located a few kilometers upstream, as the regional center; a role which continued into the Terminal Classic, when it declined precipitously and was by the 11th century abandoned (Leventhal et al. 1993). Significantly, this pattern of environmental degradation followed by stabilization has been reported in a number of other settings in the Maya Lowlands (Dunning and Beach 2000).

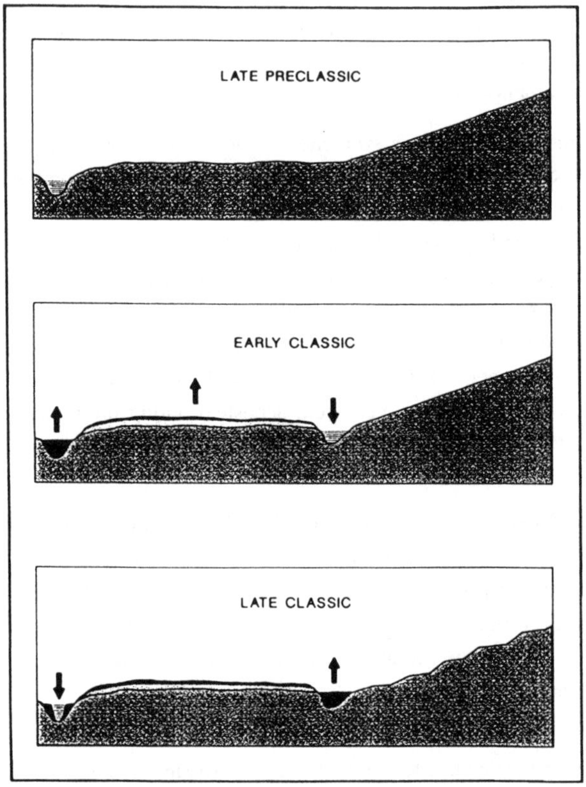

Fig. 3

Amazonian Dark Earths

Despite its great resource concentration and diversity, the Amazon Basin has been seen as a region capable of sustaining only a low population density based upon non-intensive subsistence activities (Evans 1969; Meggers 1971). However, questions have been raised about this traditional viewpoint and it has been proposed that complex societies with large, sedentary populations were present for at least a millennium before European contact (Roosevelt 1987; Heckenberger 1996; Petersen et al. 2001). Early explorers described dense villages extending for kilometers along river bluff edge settings with roadways linking these to settlements in the interior (Carvajal 1934). Associated with the presumed village locations are soils termed "Indian black earth," or *terra preta do Índio*. The heightened fertility status of these soils has long been recognized by the indigenous and *caboclo* inhabitants of the region, as well as by current colonists (Smith 1879; Smith 1980; Woods and McCann 1999). Throughout Amazonia *terra preta* occurs in a variety of landscape contexts, in circumscribed patches ranging in size from less than a hectare to many square kilometers (Smith 1980; Woods and McCann 1999). Currently, most researchers believe that the dark earths are cultural deposits created through the accretion of waste around habitation areas (Sombroek 1966; Smith 1980; Rodrigues 1993; Woods 1995; Kern 1996; Costa and Kern 1999).

My colleagues and I investigated dark earth sites in the Lower Rio Tapajós region of Brazil, the center of the prominent pre-European Santarém culture (Woods and McCann 1999; Woods et al. 2000; McCann and Woods 2001; McCann et al. 2001). Although often not previously identified in the scientific literature, these sites are known to local *caboclo* residents, who value their high fertility, planting on them the most nutrient-demanding crops, including maize, beans, squash, sweet potatoes, melons, and tobacco. They also recognize a distinctive vegetation structure and species composition, and exploit a unique and abundant assemblage of useful wild and semi-domesticated plant species occurring on them.

Soil scientists from the University of Bayreuth have shown unambiguously that organic residues of incomplete combustion of woody materials are the key factor for the high organic matter levels and the enhanced fertility of the *terra preta* soils (Zech et al. 1990; Glaser 1999; Glaser et al. 2001). However, we were surprised to find that only small portions of most dark earth expanses showed clear evidence of long-term human *habitation*; calcium and phosphorus levels were not elevated, cultural artifacts were rare, and the soil was typically not black but rather dark brown. To distinguish it from *terra preta*, we call this dark brown soil *terra mulata*. *Terra mulata* does not appear to form under conditions of natural burning frequencies, or under the long fallow shifting cultivation and forest fallow agroforestry currently practiced in Amazonia.

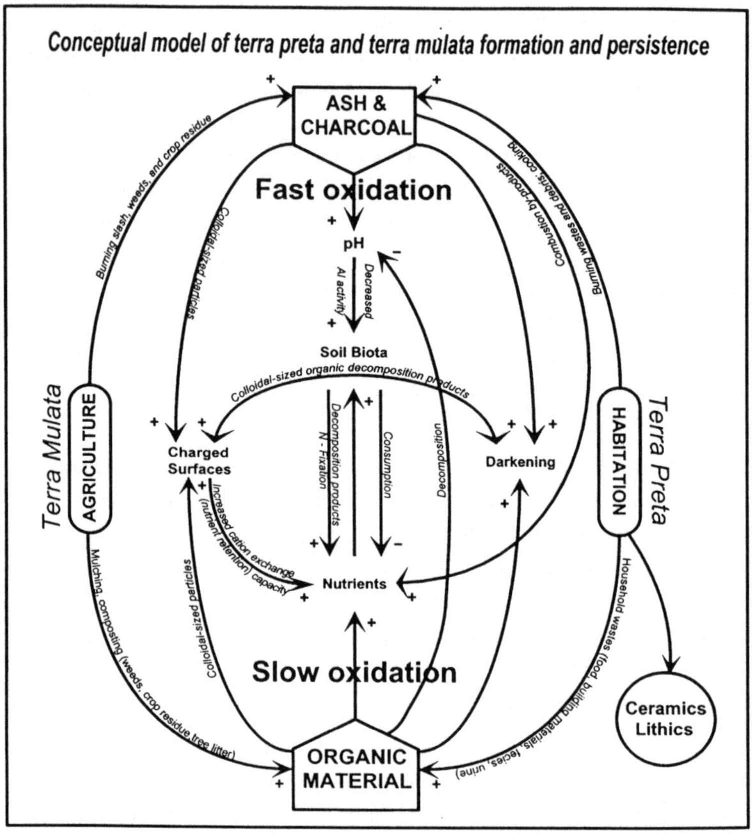
Conceptual model of terra preta and terra mulata formation and persistence
ASH & CHARCOAL
Fast oxidation
pH
Decreased Al activity
Soil Biota
Colloidal-sized organic decomposition products
Charged Surfaces
Darkening
Decomposition products N - Fixation
Consumption
Decomposition
Increased cation exchange (nutrient retention) capacity
Nutrients
Slow oxidation
ORGANIC MATERIAL
Colloidal-sized particles
Burning slash, weeds, and crop residue
Combustion by-products
Burning wastes and debris; cooking
Terra Mulata
AGRICULTURE
Terra Preta
HABITATION
Mulching, composting (weeds, crop residue, tree litter)
Household wastes (food, building materials, feces, urine)
Ceramics Lithics

Fig. 4

We suggest that some combination of long-term mulching and frequent burning under intensive prehistoric agriculture produced the heightened organic content and dark color of the *terra mulata* expanses. Fire contributes charcoal and ash, which increase soil pH and thereby suppress aluminum activity toxic to plant roots and soil microbiota, *Fig. 4 (see p. 152)*. The consequent increase in microbiological activity adds colloidal-sized organic decomposition products to the soil matrix. These, along with the byproducts of incomplete combustion, provide charged surfaces largely absent in the local soils and increase nutrient retention capacity. The spatial associations of dark earths, with *terra preta* patches typically occur nearby or embedded within larger *terra mulata* expanses, support this hypothesis and bring into focus a pre-European landscape of long-term settlements and associated fields.

Intensive permanent cultivation is consistent with the stone axe technology in use before Europeans introduced iron and steel cutting implements. Stone tools are inefficient in felling large trees and opening clearings, and provide a strong disincentive for the frequent and repeated clearing of secondary growth forest that shifting cultivation and settlement mobility require (Denevan 1992). However, once fields are established; the effort required to maintain them through weeding, mulching, burning of crop residues, and other soil enhancement activities would compare favorably to the more arduous task of making new openings. In contrast to the methods of most of today's Amazonian farmers, soil enhancement practices by ancient Amerindians allowed them to intensively cultivate the land, without needing to continually clear new fields from forest.

Conclusions

Three instances of complex, agricultural societies with nucleated settlements relying to a great extent on local soil fertility for subsistence and sustainability have now been reviewed. In each case these complex societies ceased to exist and their major centers were abandoned. The question is: to what extent did soils play a part in their downfall? We have seen at Cahokia the perils of combining population nucleation, flood plain agriculture, and deforestation. Regardless of the natural fertility of the soils, the society did not respond adequately to the danger and ultimately failed. A similar scenario existed in the Rio Mopan valley of Belize and Guatemala with catastrophic results initially, but here the slope management and stabilization brought about through the emplacement of terracing resolved the erosional situation and provided planting beds whose soil properties could be manipulated toward greater productivity. Societal collapse occurred hundreds of years later at the end of the Terminal Classic Period and was most likely due to regional and extra-regional political change, rather than problems with the subsistence base. In lower Amazonia, the agriculture was faced with a dismal situation of highly weathered, infertile upland soils and lowland soils whose potentially greater productivity was threatened by unpredictable flooding. In response, the aboriginal cultivators developed field management mechanisms which mimicked the process long operant within habitation areas where basic soil properties were radically changed through the addition of ash and other organic materials. As a result, long after the decimation of these peoples during the early Historic Period, their enriched soils still provide a major resource for agriculture in Amazonia.

Earlier, the problems with base line soil data, including questions of scale, were referred to. As has been seen, culturally influenced soils and sediments do not conform to the norms anticipated from standard soil perspectives and should not be expected to. Anthrosols and cultural sediments are characterized by great heterogeneity at all scales of investigation. This should not be surprising since we are dealing with dynamic cultural landscapes in which the effects of many millennia of occupation are present. In addition to consideration of areal diversity on the microscale, one must address the specific system of past agronomic micro-management operant when interpreting the soil results for any projections of fertility to productivity and, ultimately, sustainability.

Acknowledgements

It should be noted that these three case studies have been presented in greater detail in a number of indicated publications. Co-authors for these include: Rinita Dalan, George Holley, Joe McCann, Don Meyer, Mick Watters, and Christy Wells. The figures were prepared by Andy Martignoni and Mick Watters. Finally, Bernd Herrmann and Brigitta Benzing are gratefully thanked for organizing the excellent congress that led to this volume.

References

Ball, J. W., and J. T. Taschek. 1991. Late Classic Lowland Maya Political Organization and Central-Place Analysis: New Insights from the Upper Belize Valley. *Ancient Mesoamerica* 2:149-165.

Binford. M. W., M. Brenner, T. J. Whitmore. A., Higuerra-Gundy, and E. S. Deevy. 1987. Ecosystems, Paleoecology, and Human Disturbance in Subtropical and Tropical America. *Quaternary Science Review* 6:115-128.

Carvajal, G. de. 1934. *The Discovery of the Amazon*, H. C. Heaton (ed.). New York: American Geographical Society.

Costa, M. L., and D. C. Kern. 1999. Geochemical Signatures of Tropical Soils with Archaeological Black Earth in the Amazon, Brazil. *Journal of Geochemical Exploration* 66:369-385.

Cowgill, U.M. 1961. Soil Fertility and the Ancient Maya. *Transactions of the Connecticut Academy of Arts and Sciences* 42:1-56.

Culbert, T.P. 1988. The Collapse of Classic Maya Civilization. In *The Collapse of Ancient States and Civilizations*, edited by N. Yoffee and G.L Cowgill, pp. 69-101. Tucson: University of Arizona Press.

Dalan, R. A., G. R. Holley, W. I. Woods, H. W. Watters, Jr., and J. A. Koepke. 2002. *Cahokia: A Landscape Perspective*. DeKalb: Northern Illinois University Press. (In press).

Denevan, W. M. 1992. Stone vs Metal Axes: The Ambiguity of Shifting Cultivation in Prehistoric Amazonia. *Journal of the Steward Anthropological Society* 20:153-165.

Dunning, N. P. and T. Beach. 1994. Soil Erosion, Slope Management, and Ancient Terracing in the Maya Lowlands. *Latin American Antiquity* 5:51-69.

Dunning, N. P., and T. Beach. 2000. Stability and Instability in Prehispanic Maya Landscapes. In *Imperfect Balance: Landscape Transformations in the Precolumbian Americas*, edited by David L. Lentz, pp. 179-202. New York: Columbia University Press.

Evans, C. 1964. Lowland South America. In *Prehistoric Man in the New World*, edited by J. Jennings and E. Norbeck, pp. 419-450. Chicago: University of Chicago Press.

Fedick, S.L. 1994. Ancient Maya Agricultural Terracing in the Upper Belize River Area Computer-Aided Modeling and the Results of the Initial Field Investigations. *Ancient Mesoamerica* 5:107-127.

Ford, A., and S. Fedick. 1992. Prehistoric Maya Settlement Patterns in the Upper Belize River Area: Initial Results of the Belize River Archaeological Settlement Survey. *Journal of Field Archaeology* 19:35-49.

Fowler, M. L. 1997. *The Cahokia Atlas: A Historical Atlas of Cahokia Archaeology*. Urbana: Illinois Transportation Archaeological Research Program, University of Illinois.

Glaser, B. 1999. Eigenschaften und Stabilität des Humuskörpers der „Indianerschwarzerden" Amazoniens. *Bayreuther Bodenkundliche Berichte* 68. Bayreuth.

Glaser, B., G. Guggenberger, L. Haumaier, and W. Zech. 2001. Persistence of Soil Organic Matter in Archaeological Soils (Terra Preta) of the Brazilian Amazon Region. *Sustainable Management of Soil Organic Matter,* edited by R. M. Rees, B. Ball, C. Watson, and C. Campbell, pp. 190-194. Wallingford: CAB, International.

Heckenberger, M. J. 1996. War and Peace in the Shadow of Empire: Sociopolitical Change in the Upper Xingu of Southeastern Amazonia, A. D. 1400-2000. Unpublished PhD dissertation, University of Pittsburgh.

Holley, G. R., R. A. Dalan, W. I. Woods, and H. W. Watters, Jr. 2000. Implications of a Buried Preclassic Site in Western Belize. In *Mounds, Modoc, and Mesoamerica: Papers in Honor of Melvin L. Fowler* edited by Steven R. Ahler, pp. 111-124. Illinois State Museum Scientific Papers Vol. 28. Springfield.

Holley, G. R., N. H. Lopinot, R. A. Dalan, and W. I. Woods. 1990. *South Palisade Investigations*. Illinois Cultural Resources Study No. 14. Springfield: Illinois Historic Preservation Agency.

Jacob, J. S. 1992. The Agroecological Evolution of Cobweb Swamp, Belize. Unpublished Ph.D. dissertation, Texas A&M University.

Kern, D. C. 1996. Geoquímica e Pedogeoquímica em Sítios Arqueológicos com Terra Preta na Floresta

Nacional de Caxiuanã (Portel - PA). Unpublished PhD dissertation, Universidade Federal do Pará.

Leventhal, R. M., T. Jamison, L. LeCount, J. McGovern, and J. B. Braswell. 1993. Xunantunich: A Late/Terminal Classic Center in the Belize River Valley. Paper presented at Aniversario Katun Mesa Redonda de Palenque, Palenque.

Lopinot, N. H., and W. I. Woods. 1993. Wood Overexploitation and the Collapse of Cahokia. In *Foraging and Farming in the Eastern Woodlands*, edited by C. M. Scarry, pp. 206-231. Gainesville: University Press of Florida.

McCann, J. M., and W. I. Woods. 2001. Suelos oscuros antropogénicos en la Amazonia: Implicaciones para la sostenibilidad. In *Desarrollo Sostenible en la Amazonia: Mito o Realidad?*, edited by M. Hiraoka and S. Mora. Quito: Editorial Abya-yala. (In press).

McCann, J. M., W. I. Woods, and D. W. Meyer. 2001. Organic Matter and Anthrosols in Amazonia: Interpreting the Amerindian Legacy. *Sustainable Management of Soil Organic Matter,* edited by R. M. Rees, B. Ball, C. Watson, and C. Campbell, pp. 180-189. Wallingford: CAB, International.

Meggers, B. J. 1971. *Amazonia: Man and Culture in a Counterfeit Paradise*. Chicago: Aldine-Atherton.

Milner, G. R. 1986. Mississippian Period Population Density in a Segment of the Central Mississippi River Valley. *American Antiquity* 51:227-238.

Olson, G.W. and D.E. Puleston. 1972. Soils and the Maya. *Americas* 24:33-39.

Pauketat, T. R., and W. I. Woods. 1986. Middle Mississippian Structure Analysis: The Lawrence Primas Site (11-Ms-895) in the American Bottom. *The Wisconsin Archeologist* 67:104-127..

Petersen, J. B., E. Neves, and M. J. Heckenberger. 2001. *Terra Preta* and Prehistoric Amerindian Occupation in Amazonia. In *Unknown Amazon: Culture in Nature in Ancient Brazil*, edited by C. McEwan, C. Barreto, and E. Neves, pp. 86-105.

Rodrigues, A. J. 1993. *Ecology of the Kayabi Indians of Xingu, Brazil: Soil and Agroforestry Management.* Unpublished PhD Dissertation, University of Cambridge.

Roosevelt, A. C. 1987. Chiefdoms in the Amazon and Orinoco. In *Chiefdoms in the Americas*, edited by R. D. Drennan and C. A. Uribe, pp. 153-184. Lanham, MD: University Press of America, Inc.

Santley, R.S., T.W. Killion, and M.T. Lycett. 1986. On the Maya Collapse. *Journal of Anthropological Research* 42:123-159.

Smith, H. H. 1879. *Brazil: The Amazons and the Coast.* New York: Charles Scribner's Sons.

Smith, N. J. H. 1980. Anthrosols and Human Carrying Capacity in Amazonia. *Annals of the Association of American Geographers* 70:553-566.

Sombroek, W. G. 1966. *Amazon Soils. A Reconnaissance of the Soils of the Brazilian Amazon Region.* Wageningen: Centre for Agricultural Publication and Documentation.

Turner, B.L, II. 1993. Rethinking the "New Orthodoxy": Interpreting Ancient Maya Agriculture and Environment. In *Culture, Form. and Place: Essays in Cultural and Historical Geography,* edited by K.

Mathewson, pp. 57-88. Baton Rouge: Department of Geography and Anthropology, Louisiana State University.

Wingard, J. D. 1992. The Role of Soils in the Development and Collapse of Classic Maya Civilization at Copan, Honduras. Unpublished Ph.D. dissertation, The Pennsylvania State University.

Woods, W. I. 1987. Maize and the Late Prehistoric: A Characterization of Settlement Location Strategies. In *Emergent Horticultural Economies of the Eastern Woodlands*, edited by W. F. Keegan, pp. 273-292. Occasional Paper No. 7. Center for Archaeological Investigations, Southern Illinois University at Carbondale.

Woods, W. I. 1993. A Study of Prehistoric Settlement-Subsistence Relationships in Southwestern Illinois. In *Proceedings of the First International Conference on Pedo-Archaeology*, edited by J. E. Foss, M. E. Timpson, and M. W. Morris, pp. 175-184. Special Publication 93-03. Knoxville: The University of Tennessee Agricultural Experiment Station.

Woods, W. I. 1995. Comments on the Black Earths of Amazonia. In *Papers and Proceedings of the Applied Geography Conferences,* Vol. 18, edited by F. A. Schoolmaster, pp. 159-165. Denton: Applied Geography Conferences, Inc.

Woods, W. I. 2000. Monks Mound Revisited. In *Preprints. Terra 2000. 8th International Conference on the Study and Conservation of Earthen Architecture*, edited by N. Sterry, pp. 98-104. London: James & James Ltd.

Woods, W. I., and G. R. Holley. 1991. Upland Mississippian Settlement in the American Bottom Region. In *Cahokia and the Hinterlands: Middle Mississippian Cultures of the Midwest*, edited by T. E. Emerson and R. B. Lewis, pp. 46-60. Urbana: University of Illinois Press.

Woods, W. I., and J. M. McCann. 1999. The Anthropogenic Origin and Persistence of Amazonian Dark Earths. In *Yearbook 1999 - Conference of Latin Americanist Geographers*, Vol. 25, edited by C. Caviedes, pp. 7-14. Austin: University of Texas Press.

Woods, W. I., J. M. McCann, and D. W. Meyer. 2000. Amazonian Dark Earth Analysis: State of Knowledge and Directions for Future Research. In *Papers and Proceedings of the Applied Geography Conferences*, edited by F. A. Schoolmaster, Vol. 23, pp. 114-121. Denton: Applied Geography Conferences, Inc.

Woods, W. I., C. L. Wells, H. W. Watters, Jr., and D. W. Meyer. 1996. Cautions on the Use of Soil Data for Prehistoric Reconstructions: A Belizean Example. In *Papers and Proceedings of the Applied Geography Conferences,* Vol. 19, edited by F. A. Schoolmaster and J. A. Harrington, pp. 209-217. Denton: Applied Geography Conferences, Inc.

Zech, W., L. Haumaier, and R. Hempfling. 1990. Ecological Aspects of Soil Organic Matter in Tropical Land Use. In *Humic Substances in Soil and Crop Sciences: Selected Readings*, edited by P. MacCarthy, C. E. Clapp, R. L. Malcolm, and P. R. Bloom, pp. 187-202. Madison: American Society of Agronomy and Soil Science Society of America.

Anke Höltermann

Sustainability and Rationality in Forestry

Abstract

Different rationality criteria are discussed with regard to their suitability to elaborate a satisfactory model of sustainability in forestry. It is shown that under today's conditions the most promising concept is the concept of strategic rationality that consists of maintaining the system's potential on the one hand and of facilitating further evolutionary processes by giving more importance to diversity and flexibility on the other hand.

Sustainability and rationality in forestry

The elaboration of a satisfactory model of sustainability in forestry requires the adoption of a suitable rationality criterion which is necessary for choosing the best procedures to ensure sustainability. It is shown that the rapid change of the basic conditions of forestry in the past decades has lead to the conclusion that the concept of substantive rationality nowadays has to be refused. The concept of procedural rationality often cited as 'alternative' also has to be refuted as it does not go along with a 'conservationist' strategy like sustainability. As a third option we will discuss the concept of strategic rationality that consists of maintaining the system's potential which has proven to be reliable in evolution and of facilitating further evolutionary processes by giving more importance to diversity and flexibility.

1. Intention of the article

Starting from the actual debate about the validity of different concepts of sustainability the aim of this article is to analyse the notion of rationality underlying these concepts. The analysis allows us to show that the way in which sustainability is defined largely depends on our concept of rationality and the way how we interpret the future: whether we see the future as a mere extrapolation of the present, whether we think it is predictable, or whether we conceive of it as something entirely new. We will plead for a broadening of the traditional rationality criteria which is substantive rationality, to a more realistic concept of rationality that takes into account uncertainty and historicity of changing systems. This 'change of mind' is seen as the prerequisite for a new conceptualisation of sustainability.

The article is structured in the following way:

After a short overview over the history of the notion of sustainability in forestry, chapter 3 outlines the difficulties of giving an operational definition of the term sustainability and introduces the two most important concepts of sustainability in forestry currently discussed. In chapter 4 the assumptions underlying these concepts when they are used as practical management instructions are outlined from a decision theory perspective. It is shown that the assumption of substantive rationality implicitly underlying these concepts is no longer adequate. Procedural rationality and strategic rationality are discussed as alternative rationality criteria that help to elaborate a more satisfactory model of sustainability in forestry.

2. The history of sustainability in forestry

The idea of 'sustainability' in German forestry goes back to the 18th century and has its origins in the tradition of late-medieval forestry.

The principle of sustainability was born of necessity: Earlier than in other parts of the world, excessive clear-cutting for the production of fire wood, wood processing and particularly for the supply of saltworks, mines and iron-works resulted in acute scarcity of wood in the late middle ages. People realized that the continuation of the exploitation practises employed in those days would lead to a shortage of wood and rise in price – doing harm to the whole national economy.

The transition to sustainable forestry therefore is characterized by a shift away from an overexploitation of forests to a forest management more in harmony with the natural productivity of forests. It was in the mercantilist period that the idea of sustainability emerged for the first time. Forests now were defined as a 'bonum commune' and took a new place in public opinion. In order to ensure a regular maximum harvest the absolutist state put short term capitalistic interest of the individual behind the principle of a sustained use of forests.

The turn of the 17th to the 18th century was also marked by the end of absolutism and the beginning of the Enlightenment. Newton's mechanical theory of the world infiltrated nearly every aspect of life. It not only influenced the organisation of public administration, an increasing division of labour, and the military training, but also had consequences for forestry. Foresters now were striving to develop methods of silviculture and forest planning in order to establish spatial and temporal order in the forest and guarantee a sustained supply of the raw material. In 1713, the term 'sustainable' was mentioned for the first time by Hanns Carl von Carlowitz, a mining officer from Freiberg (Saxony).

Only a few decades later the term 'sustainability' was used by nearly all foresters in central Europe. Forest sciences were flourishing in the late 18th and 19th century and the notion of sustainability, understood as sustained timber yields, gained acceptance as a guiding principle of forest management in Germany. Sustainability has thus been a central principle of forestry during the last 250 years.

3. Concepts of sustainability

3.1 Sustainability: an equal distribution of welfare

The importance of sustainability in today's forestry is underlined by its enactment in German forest legislation. The German Federal Forest Law, for example, prescribes in § 11 that forests have to be managed 'properly' and 'sustainably' regardless of their ownership. Similar formulations can also be found in other Central European countries.

However, legislature usually does not define in detail what is to be understood as 'proper' and 'sustainable' management. Concrete directives from this vague legal term cannot be deduced. In view of the rapid social changes that many countries have experienced recently, it is not surprising that the idea and realisation of sustainability generate so much controversy even in the present.

From a normative point of view there seems to be general agreement that sustainability is based on a demand for intergenerational justice among humans. But we have to state that, while on the one hand only the explicit integration of distributive aspects justifies the use of the term sustainability, it is notoriously difficult on the other hand to sketch an operational procedure for 'intergenerational justice' (e.g. Kant, Rawls, Habermas). A pragmatic approach therefore suggests an equal distribution across human generations.

The question then arises, *WHAT* has to be distributed justly or equally. At a quick glance this question seems to be easier to answer:

In forestry a constant level of 'welfare' is typically proposed as the underlying measure of sustainability. The German forest law defines in § 45 "that the state forest has to contribute particularly to the welfare of society. The goal of forest management consists in a sustained and greatest possible supply of valuable timber while also ensuring protectional and recreational functions."

It becomes apparent that providing a definition of welfare is nearly as difficult as defining 'intergenerational justice'. It is therefore not surprising that the different concepts of sustainability in forestry differ in their interpretation of what is welfare and how to realize it: Some concepts rather emphasize economical aspects while others give more importance to the ecological functions of forests.

3.2 Multifunctional forest management

The most generally accepted concepts in the current discussion on 'the correct' sustainable forest management are 'multifunctional forest management' and 'ecologically oriented management'.

The concept of multifunctional forest management is based on the assumption that forests are an essential basis of life. Its proponents maintain that this basis can only be guaranteed by keeping forest enterprises economically profitable. The obligation to guarantee public welfare however requires the consideration of all functions of the forests when establishing the strategic goals of forest management. Since the ecological and social benefits of forestry cannot be commercialized this justifies the financial support of forestry through taxes. The position of multifunctional forest management is best reflected by Speidel's widely recognized definition of sustainability:

"Sustainability is the capacity of a forest enterprise to produce permanently and optimally wood, services and other goods to the benefit of current and future generations. Those actions and services are 'sustainable' that provide or ensure these capacities to the forest enterprise." [1]

3.3 Ecologically oriented management

The ecological position can be characterized by demands to restrict private property rights on forests because of environmental arguments. The follow-up meetings of Rio (Helsinki 1993 and Geneva 1994) have defined principles of ecological forest-management. For instance, within the Helsinki Resolution H1, sustainable forest management is defined as "the stewardship and use of forests and forest lands in a way, and at a rate, that maintains their biodiversity, productivity, regeneration capacity, vitality and their potential to fulfil, now and in the future, relevant ecological, economic and social functions, at local, national and global levels, and that does not

[1] Speidel 1984: 43

cause damage to other ecosystems".

4. Concepts of rationality

Based on these two definitions several efforts are made nowadays to give specific content to the vague term 'sustainability' in order to submit it to forest inspection and to sanction non-conform behaviour.

Yet two assumptions have to be made if these vague concepts are not only supposed to serve as guidelines but as a basis for precise instructions for forest management:

- the benefit of forests for current and future generations has to be known, so that the management objective of an equal distribution of welfare can be defined operationally;
- empirical or theoretical knowledge on how ecosystems can be managed according to this objective has to be available.

In the next chapter we will focus on these prerequisites from a decision theory perspective and particularly highlight the possibilities of consciously steering ecosystems.

4.1 Substantive rationality

The rationality criterion that is usually assumed to underlie decision-making is substantive rationality. Substantive rationality is deduced from the degree of agreement between the actual results of a strategy on the one hand and the intended results on the other hand. It assumes that any decision made by a person will be the best possible and that in conditions of certainty the results of a strategy examined ex post will not differ from this person's expectations. Thus substantive rationality assumes the absence of systematic mistakes ex post. Differences found in comparing the results of an actual decision with the best possible decision that could have been made are entirely depending on stochastic factors. "A substantively rational agent is bound to make mistakes in conditions of uncertainty just because the information is incomplete. However he utilises the available information avoiding any sort of mistake which could be detected ex ante on the basis of the same information set. (...) This permits the reduction of a sequence of choices to be taken in successive time periods to the single choice of a strategy (...) to be taken in the initial time period."[2]

---

[2] Vercelli 1998: 261

In a model of sustainability substantive rationality assumes the possibility of predicting the future development of a managed forest (including all its welfare functions and services) in a deterministic or probabilistic way. Hence the predictability of the ecosystem's development becomes a prerequisite for such a model of sustainability, thereby creating - as we will see – too high expectations in models of forest ecosystems and ecosystem management.

Let us therefore have a closer look at the situation in forestry practice, particularly as it evolved in the last decades. Since that time, decisions in forestry seem to include a higher level of uncertainty which is reflected in an increasing loss of practical expertise. In previous decades empirically based knowledge of managed forest ecosystems could be obtained over long periods under roughly the same ecological conditions without, at the same time, reaching a thorough understanding of the underlying ecological principles. At present, though, the dynamics and increasing complexity of societal expectations of goods and services from ecosystems[3] along with unforeseen changes in the natural framework (take e.g. the forest decline) have led to a loss of planning reliability. Currently the environmental, societal and economic conditions of forestry are changing at such a pace that existing (empirical) predictive tools become unreliable and outdated (e.g. production tables). And science has not yet replaced the loss of empirical knowledge with a proper understanding of these changing systems. To the contrary, the theory of self-organised complex dynamic systems argues that the complexity of forest ecosystems forbids - even in principle - any long-term prediction.[4]

What does this mean for substantive rationality? It means that if the interaction between society and the natural system is so complex, and available knowledge about these complex systems so limited, the decision maker's beliefs cannot be represented in a deterministic or probabilistic way which is reliable enough to guide his decisions. Hence substantive rationality is not consistent with irreversibility and historicity that typically characterize the evolution of forest ecosystems and thus is not an appropriate rationality criterion for sustainability in forestry.

What alternative criteria of rationality are there, that could be taken as a basis for a performing model of sustainability?

4.2 Procedural rationality

The observation that decisions in practical life are taken - even if the results of an action are

---

[3] see for example Weber & Mann 1997
[4] see for example Bröring & Wiegleb 1998: 52, Breckling 1993: 26, Hauhs & Lange 1996: 101

strongly unknown - triggered the development of a concept known as 'procedural rationality'.[5] Procedural rationality rather emphasizes the procedure of choice than its results. It is based on the observation that a person - instead of choosing the optimal solution - uses as a decision criterion the correspondence of his actions with a socially shared set of convictions of what the 'right' action in a certain situation should be.

So procedural rationality discards the idea that a rational agent will never regret his choice ex post and therefore is consistent with uncertainty, irreversibility and learning.

Nevertheless an adaptive conception of rationality that is characterized through trial and error methods and heuristic procedures is not adequate in the case of sustainability in forestry. As Vercelli remarks, we have to keep in mind that "the consequences of uncertainty in forest management could have catastrophic and irreversible effects such that no therapeutic instrument could give a sufficient relief ex post. It is therefore necessary to take immediate actions to eliminate, or at least to reduce, this sort of hard risk; otherwise the set of available options could shrink in an irreversible way ..." [6]

4.3 Strategic rationality

So, if we conclude that hard uncertainty in forestry cannot be reduced by scientific means and that we can neither afford a strategy of 'trial and error' or even one of " 'wait and learn', because while waiting the acceptable options could disappear"[7], there is only one more way to overcome the limits of the two discussed concepts of rationality: strategic rationality.

Strategic rationality here is understood as the striving of today's generation to preserve a set of options that is at least as large as the one at the disposal of the current generation in order to ensure the intertemporal flexibility of the decision strategy. Intergenerational equity in this case is defined in terms of an effective freedom of choice inherited by future generations. According to Dryzek strategic rationality therefore requires "that all decisions in the present be subordinated to the goal of ensuring the strategic problem-solving position of the next time period (...)."[8]

There seem to be two ways to maintain the freedom of choice, either by conserving the proven potential of a system or by trying to extend its options.

---

[5] Hargreaves Heap et.al. 1992: 17 ff.
[6] Vercelli 1998: 270
[7] Vercelli 1998: 270
[8] Dryzek 1983: 36

The first perspective is best represented by Hauhs[9]: In his opinion sustainable management of complex ecosystems is impossible without reducing the historical influence on the managed system. In the past this has been done by an effective biological reset of the managed system, e.g. by planting operations, successive thinning etc. By freezing the history of the system, the opportunities existing in the past (the proven potential of the system) were maintained for the future.

Nowadays, as we saw above, the environment of ecosystems is changing so rapidly, that the essential knowledge about sustainable management is lost and the question arises, how to preserve the potential of forests under today's conditions?

Hauhs is taking an interesting approach here: He proposes to use the empirical management competence of foresters as the point of reference. By doing so he assumes a privileged internal view of human beings with regard to managed ecosystems. In his opinion this privileged view is justified by the long evolutionary time spans in which men accumulated practical expertise in sustainable management techniques. Because the accumulated forestry expertise seems to be non-verbal to a large extent he suggests that future research should focus on developing a model supporting the communicability of experience-based-knowledge, thus making it accessible for the development of sustainable management strategies under changing conditions ('flight simulator' for foresters).

Trying to extend the capabilities of forest ecosystems means to give more importance to the values 'diversity' and 'flexibility'. Diversity can be increased for example by allowing non-conform management objectives next to the established ones or by testing unusual silvicultural strategies - only to mention the most obvious examples. History provides us with eloquent examples to underline the unpredictability of future demands that only could be satisfied by pure chance. See for example the importance of oak trees that are nowadays precious suppliers of veneer but were planted to feed pigs in ancient times.

By increasing the diversity we can add new capabilities to the existing ones, thus providing chances to realize demands of future generations entirely unknown today.

Nevertheless by encouraging diversity we have to keep in mind that we cannot assume that future generations will appreciate every offered option in the same way. Quite to the contrary: a maximal satisfaction of the prevailing social demands seems to be very unlikely. Thus a flexibilisation of the actual capital stock can be linked perfectly with a loss of social welfare. So we definitely

---

[9] see for example Hauhs & Lange 1996, Hauhs et al. 1998

have to accept inefficiencies.

Unfortunately current developments in public forest administration rather take another direction. Several German state forest administrations e.g. intend to prescribe binding silvicultural directives to all public forest enterprises. Conformity and uniformity once more seem to dominate over creativity.

To summarize we can conclude that even in forestry which is the cradle of the notion of 'sustainability', the discussion of how to implement it is only at its beginnings. It will remain one of the most challenging questions for the future how to ensure the freedom of choice for coming generations under conditions of uncertainty and unpredictability. In our opinion, the principal aim of further investigation in the field of strategic rationality will be to find the right balance between the conservative way of maintaining the system's potential that has proven to be reliable in evolution, and a future-oriented way facilitating further evolutionary processes by giving more importance to diversity and flexibility.

References

Breckling, B. (1993): Naturkonzepte und Paradigmen in der Ökologie: Einige Entwicklungen. Wissenschaftszentrum Berlin für Sozialforschung, Forschungsschwerpunkt Technik, Arbeit, Umwelt, FS II 93-304. Berlin: WZB.

Bröring, U.; Wiegleb, G. (1998): Ecological Orientors: Pattern and process of succession in relation to Ecological Orientors. In: Müller, F.; Leupelt, M. (Hrsg.) (1998) Eco targets, goal functions, and orientors. Berlin, Heidelberg: Springer, 34-62.

Dryzek, J. (1983): Don't toss coins in garbage cans: A prologue to policy design. In: Journal of public policy, (1983) 3: 345-367.

Hauhs, M.; Lange, H. (1996): Perspektiven für eine (Meta-) Theorie terrestrischer Ökosysteme. In: Mathes, K.; Breckling, B.; Ekschmitt, K. (Hrsg.) (1996) Systemtheorie in der Ökologie: Beiträge zu einer Tagung des Arbeitskreises "Theorie" in der Gesellschaft für Ökologie: Zur Entwicklung und aktuellen Bedeutung der Systemtheorie in der Ökologie. Schloß Rauischholzhausen im März 1996. Landsberg: ecomed, 95-105.

Hargreaves Heap, S.; Hollis, M.; Lyons, B.; Sudgen, R.; Weale, A. (Hrsg.) (1992): The theory of choice: A critical guide. Oxford, U.K., Cambridge, USA: Blackwell.

Hauhs, M.; Lange, H.; Lischeid, G.; Kastner-Maresch, A. (1998): Möglichkeiten und Grenzen in der Modellierung naturnaher Ökosysteme. Proceedings 51. Deutscher Geographentag 1997: Global Change - Konsequenzen für die Umwelt, 3. Band, 188-206.

Speidel, G. (1972): Planung im Forstbetrieb: Grundlagen und Methoden der Forsteinrichtung. Hamburg, Berlin: Parey.

Vercelli, A. (1998): Sustainable development, rationality and time. In: Faucheux, S.; O'Connor, M.; van der Straaten, J. (Hrsg.) (1998) Sustainable development: Concepts, rationalities and strategies. Dordrecht: Kluwer Academic Publishers, 259-276.

Weber, N.; Mann, S. (1997): Der postmaterialistische Wertewandel und seine Bedeutung für die Forstwirtschaft, Forstarchiv, 68, 19-24.

Simron Jit Singh

Heinz Schandl

Socio-Economic Metabolism in the Nicobar Islands[1]

Empirical Research in Society-Nature Interactions

Abstract

Based on empirical research, the paper presents patterns of society-nature-interactions among a semi-subsistence non-industrialised society in transition. Fieldwork was undertaken on Trinket Island in the Nicobar archipelago located in the Bay of Bengal, off the east coast of India. Despite its remoteness, but owing to its geographical location, these islands have been ceaselessly contacted over time by traders, mariners, colonisers and missionaries. The role of the world market today and the western paradigm of development has had an added influence on the Nicobarese society and its relation towards the natural environment. By being exposed to these historical and recent social and technological influences, the Nicobar islands are currently in a state of accelerated social and ecological transition.

The presentation focuses on the preliminary results of an on-going research project that attempts to outline current society-nature-interactions in the Nicobars following these historical processes. Though the overall purpose of this project is to conceptualise the coevolution of society-nature relatedness both on a material and on a symbolic level, however for the purpose of this presentation, the paper offers an analysis based on results pertaining to current material and energetic exchanges taking place between the society under investigation and its environment.

Socio-economic metabolism is seen as a key concept for describing material exchanges with nature. Local Material and Energy Flow Analysis constitutes the methodology for defining socio-economic metabolism in the study area. Additionally, indicators for the colonisation of nature will be presented by data on land use, Human Appropriation of Net Primary Productivity (HANPP), time budgets and energetic efficiency of labour for altering and maintaining the local ecosystem.

---

[1] Paper presented at the IUAES Inter-congress "*Exploitation and Overexploitation in Societies Past and Present*", Göttingen, Germany. July 18-21, 2001. All data presented in this paper have been published as part of a more detailed paper in Singh et al., 2001. The authors are grateful to Clemens Grünbühel and Niels Schulz for their contribution in the earlier paper.

1. Introduction

It has often been argued that societies environmental relations and related processes of environmental degradation changed dramatically, when societies moved from a predominantly agrarian mode of production to an industrial mode of production (see Sieferle, 1990; Fischer-Kowalski & Haberl, 1993). This "great transformation" in the sphere of production as well as in social relations happened first in North and Central Europe as an endogenously driven process. The transformation has caused changes in the environmental relations and changes in natural resources utilisation, and use of ecosystems services to a degree unknown before (see Fischer-Kowalski & Haberl, 1993 & 1998; Haberl & Krausmann, 2001).

Obviously, this process of industrialisation has not come to a standstill yet. Still, a huge number of the world's population is living under agrarian conditions. These societies gradually or even rapidly move towards the "new" industrial mode of production. Whatever similarities we might find, the current processes of extension of the industrial system and the inclusion of the agrarian regions is externally driven. Hence, the pathways the process of change will take might differ considerably from the first transition in Europe. Nevertheless, potentials of environmental exploitation might be rather similar.

In this paper we describe the changing environmental relations of a local population living on the remote island of Trinket belonging to the Nicobar archipelago between India and Indonesia. Using the concept of social metabolism we present several indicators to show an economic portfolio of a community that combines horticulture, hunting and gathering activities with elements of industrialisation and market economy.

We begin with a brief explanation of the theoretical assumptions that provides us with the necessary framework for establishing such a physical accounting of a society. This will be followed by a brief description of the geographical and ethnological background of the study area. The remaining sections will be devoted to the results and the ensuing discussion concerning present and potentials of future environmental burdens.

2. A physical portray of a society's natural relations: conceptual clarifications

The theoretical background and also the operationalization of a society's physical interaction with its natural environment - termed as "social metabolism" - has been described in great detail elsewhere (Fischer-Kowalski, 1997; Ayres & Ayres, 1998; Fischer-Kowalski & Weisz 1999; Foster, 2000). The concept of "social metabolism" stems from the theoretical framework of viewing societies as not merely systems of communication and symbols, but as an organised set comprising a cultural system and those material elements (such as livestock and a whole range of artefacts) accorded preferential treatment within the cultural system (Weisz et al. 2001). For societies to create, reproduce and maintain their material or biophysical components (including human population) they organise - similar to organisms – material and energy flows with their natural environment; they extract primary resources and use them for food, machines, buildings, infrastructure, heating and many other products and finally return them, with more or less delay, in the form of wastes and emissions to their environments. This is achieved within the labour process where a society intentionally intervenes into natural systems to gain access to the resources it needs or to make use of certain services of ecosystems or to enter into trade relations with other societies.

The material and energetic demand for a society varies quantitatively and qualitatively depending on the mode of production, distribution and consumption of that society that can be empirically accounted for with the application of a Material Flow Accounting (MFA) and an Energy Flow Accounting (EFA) (Ayres & Simonis, 1994; Adriaanse et al., 1997; Fischer-Kowalski, 1997; Schandl & Schulz, 2000; Haberl, 2001a & 2001b). The amount of material and energetic throughput a society requires for its mode of production and related way of living is termed as *characteristic metabolic profile* of that society (Fischer-Kowalski, 1997).

Both MFA and EFA have been widely applied for national economies such as USA, Germany, Austria, UK, the Netherlands and Japan (Adriaanse, 1997; Mathews et al., 2000) and have gained strong political grounds (EUROSTAT, 2001). They have, however, been under-represented for local-level case studies. It must be noted that MFA and EFA were designed primarily as indicator tools for framing national environmental policies and hence have a somewhat different purpose than to be used at the local level. Macro-level studies are more engaged in issues such as possible delinking of material input with economic growth (De Bruyn & Opschoor, 1997), or North-South material flows (Muradian & Martinez-Alier, 2001).

In contrast, our local-level study, while borrowing the same systems approach and generally accepted methods as for national-level studies, primarily attempts to achieve an in-depth understanding, in physical terms, of the dynamics of environmental relations between a local society and its natural environment. In the context of Political ecology and transition studies we are able to explore the interactions between systems and sub-systems – local-global, local-regional and local-national – over a period of time. In other words, we are able to view a particular society and its inter-relations in its bio-political complexity (see also Bates & Leess, 1996; Kottak, 1999; Giampietro and Mayumi, 2000).

Furthermore, a local material and energy flow analysis provides a micro-perspective or a zoomed in image for identifying factors (such as external dependency) that lead to social change and transformation at a local level, both qualitatively and quantitatively. Quantitative data thus generated from local-level studies only complements national material flow data especially in the case of those nations where most of the population living on subsistence; so that these flows do not enter the market economy and are not reflected in national statistics. The national flow accounting would be highly under-represented if estimates of subsistent-level flows were not taken into account.

However, some of the basic indicators for both macro-level and micro-level studies remain more or less the same. They have been used in this study as well, namely in calculating the *Direct Material Input* (DMI) and *Direct Energy Input* (DEI) - both of which are the sums of material/energy imported and domestically extracted. Consumption indicators[2] are *Domestic Material Consumption* (DMC) and *Domestic Energy Consumption* (DEC) – both of which are the actual amounts of material/energy consumed by the society after subtracting exports from DMI and DEI. If a society is based on an extractive, export-oriented economy, then DMI and DMC might differ considerably. The units used are metric tons (in case of materials) and joules (in case of energy) per capita/year.

3. The geographical and cultural context of the study area

Field work was taken on a remote island of Trinket in the (prohibited) Nicobar archipelago in the Indian Ocean some 1,200 km off the east coast of India. The island is narrow, long and rather flat with a total area of 3,626 hectares. Spread over three villages, the total population comprises of 400 people who derive their sustenance from raising coconut plantations, fishing, hunting-and-gathering, pig rearing and (more recently) trading copra - dehydrated coconut - in exchange for rice, cloth, sugar, and other consumer goods (Singh et al., 2001).

Owing to its location on a historically important sea route to Southeast Asia, these scattered islands between mainland India and Indonesia offered an attractive resting harbour for traders and mariners for a very long time. Trade was used as a pretext to the natives for the use of their safe harbours. Later, from the 15th century, the islands drew the attention of several European powers (mainly the Dutch, the Portuguese, the Danes, the Austrians and the British) who saw them as a strategic military location for maintaining supremacy over trade and territory in Southeast Asia (Chakravarti, 1994; Gupta, 1994).

The Nicobar Islands have remained a sensitive military area and entry into them highly regulated ever since 1869, the year when the islands were officially handed over by the Danes to the British. Even under independent India since 1947, the Indian government has followed the same restrictive policy under the *Protection of Aboriginal Tribes Regulation* of 1956. At the same time,

[2] The term "consumption" in our case includes resources that are not only finally consumed but also those resources required in production processes.

the local population has been subject to several tribal welfare programs such as medical service, primary education, electrification of villages etc.

4. Material flows on Trinket Island

Departing from the old ecology of Vayda and Rappaport of the 1960s and 70s, we conceive Trinket society, despite its apparent isolation, as an open system which has in more than one way been influenced by outside interventions both historically and in present times. Bates and Lees (1996) have aptly stated that "[in] contemporary human ecology there is never an assumption of timelessness or total isolation. While historical change and external influence might once have been regarded as annoying distractions or distortions of indigenous systems, they are now the focus of attention".

Figure 1: Systems Boundaries and Material Flows on Trinket Island

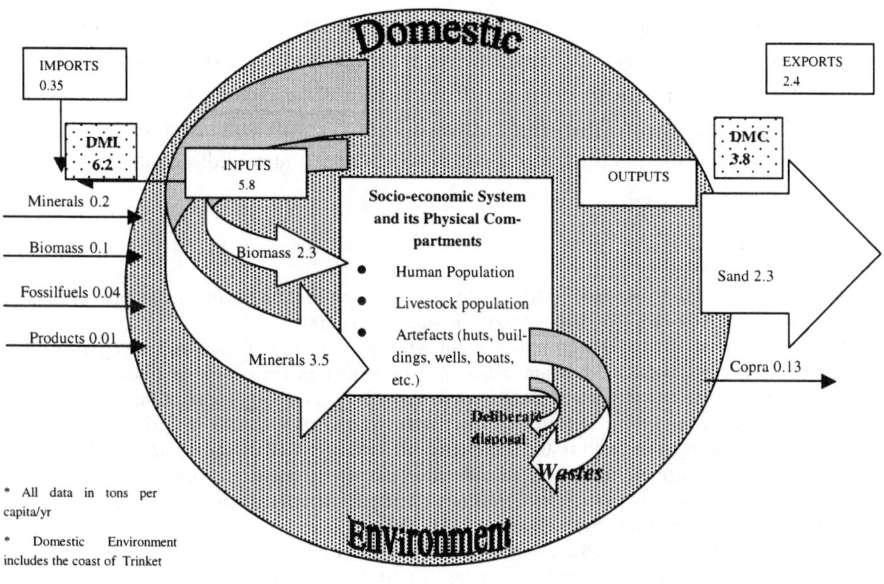

The actuality of this statement is reflected in an overview of the quantitative and qualitative material flows for contemporary Trinket (*Fig. 1, p. 173*)[3]. In this figure we notice two system boundaries that differentiates between the levels of dependency on domestic resources and between that of dependence on other systems. Hence, the first boundary distinguishes the socio-economic system (comprising of the physical compartments of the society i.e. human and livestock population and all human conceived artefacts[4]) and its domestic environment. The second separates the entire social system (including its domestic environment) from other social systems. In the same vein, the figure makes a distinction between "inputs" (when they are extracted from within their domestic environment) or "imports" (when they arrive as traded commodities from other societies). Similarly on the output side, the flows are termed as "outputs" and "exports" respectively.

Quantitative data indicates a Direct Material Input (DMI) - which is the sum of all imports and domestic extraction - of 6.2 tons/cap/year.[5] However, it is evident that imports (0.35 tons/cap) are far below the domestic extraction (5.8 tons). Major imports consists of minerals in the form of construction material (0.2 tons), biomass – mainly rice and sugar - (0.1 tons) and fossil fuels (0.04 tons). A substantial amount of cement and steel is brought to the island each year for construction of buildings such as school, health centre, wells, etc. under tribal welfare schemes. Rice, now a staple diet, gradually replaced *pandanus* that once was the main source of carbohydrate as a result of the occassional barter trade between the islanders and passing ships enroute South-east Asia for over 1,500 years. Fossil fuels are a recent introduction and have now become a necessity for the local people to run motor driven boats for transporting materials to and from the island. Most imports are primarily regulated by the local administration as part of a tribal/rural welfare scheme and is made available to the islanders at subsidised rates.

---

[3] Due to limitation of space, we have intentionally excluded the section on the generation of data and accounting methods. For a detailed methodology see Singh et al., 2001.

[4] Theoretical considerations have been raised about whether to include plants as a component of the socio-economic system insofar as they are maintained by labour in agriculture and forestry. Here we suggest for pragmatic reasons that plants should not be considered as a component of the socio-economic system (Fischer-Kowalski, 1997). Therefore, in the same way as they appear in agricultural statistics, plant harvest can be seen as an input to the socio-eonomic system whereas manure and fertilisers are an output to nature. If agricultural plants were considered as part of the socio-economic system, the boundary between this system and its natural environment will be pushed outward, to the mineral level, except for fishing, hunting and gathering (Schandl and Schulz, 2000).

[5] Compare with - Sang Saeng (1998), an agrarian, ethnic Lao village in northeast Thailand [4.4 tons]; Austria (1830) [5.5 tons]; and Industrial economies (1996), based on the unweighted averages of UK, Austria, Germany, Japan and the Netherlands [20.6 tons]. Sources for *Sang Saeng*: Weisz et al. (2001) and Grünbühel et al. (submitted); for *Austria 1830*: Krausmann (2001); for *Industrial*: own calculation based on Matthews et al. (2000) and Schandl and Schulz (2000).

Most of the biomass requirements (2.3 tons) for the Trinket socio-economic system is met domestically from the harvest of fuelwood, coconuts, tubers, fish, and other minor forest produce. However, Figure 1 indicates that minerals (sand and gravel) account for the majority of materials (3.5 tons) extracted from within the society's domestic environment. These minerals are partly consumed on the island as building materials while most of the sand being exported to the neighbouring island of Kamorta for construction of government headquarters.

Here we see that, to sustain imports, it becomes imperative for Trinket island to organise exports. In other words, the economic viability for Trinket largely depends on these exports. Major exports identified were sand and copra. Although, by weight sand far exceeds that of copra, economically it is copra that sustains most of the imports. It can be said that the islanders are highly dependent on copra trade which makes them vulnerable to the global copra demand and its price fluctuations. Severe fluctuations in both demand and prices were noticed in the two years of field work with grave consequences upon the local population.

The Domestic Material Consumption (DMC) - or the actual consumption after subtracting exports from DMI - for Trinket was calculated to be 3.8 tons/cap/year.[6] Table 1 shows details of DMI – DMC difference of biomass, minerals, fossil fuels and products. The DMI – DMC difference suggests how much a society must produce or harvest in addition to its own domestic consumption in order to enter into a trade relation with other societies for its own sustenance and reproduction. Our data suggests Trinket to be an extractive economy evident in the huge DMI – DMC difference in case of minerals alone *(see Table 1)* being directly exported without further processing (see also Bunker, 1988).

[6] Compare with - Sang Saeng (1998) [3.2 tons]; Austria (1830) [5.5 tons]; and Industrial economies (1996), based on the unweighted averages of UK, Austria, Germany, Japan and the Netherlands [16.1 tons]. Sources: see footnote 5.

Table 1: ***DMI – DMC on Trinket (2000)***

	Direct Material Input (DMI)	**Exports**	**Domestic Material Consumption (DMC)**
	[tons/capita]	**[tons/capita]**	**[tons/capita]**
Biomass	2.4	0.1	2.3
Minerals	3.7	2.3	1.4
Fossil fuels	0.04		0.04
Products	0.01		0.01
Total	**6.2**		**3.8**

In view of the universally agreed accounting methods, water and air, although theoretically part of societal flows, are excluded from the material flow balance sheets (EUROSTAT, 2001).[7] However, we calculated water consumption on Trinket (for humans alone) to be 47,450 litres per capita. While only 3,285 litres is consumed within the household for cooking, washing dishes, cleaning and drinking, the remaining 44,165 litres is consumed at source for bathing and washing clothes. In the absence of artificial agriculture, there is no need for water for irrigation and for kitchen gardens and coconut plantations, natural rain which is abundant is sufficient.

5. Energy flows on Trinket Island

See Fig. 2: Energy Flows on Trinket Island, p. 177

[7] Water, owing to its immense weight as compared to other resources that are consumed by a socio-economic system, is not included in the DMI-DMC indicator as it only downplays the quantity of other materials in relation to it. Water, however, is a crucial resource, especially for countries in the south and therefore it is important to atleast report water consumption as an independent indicator if not as part of DMI-DMC.

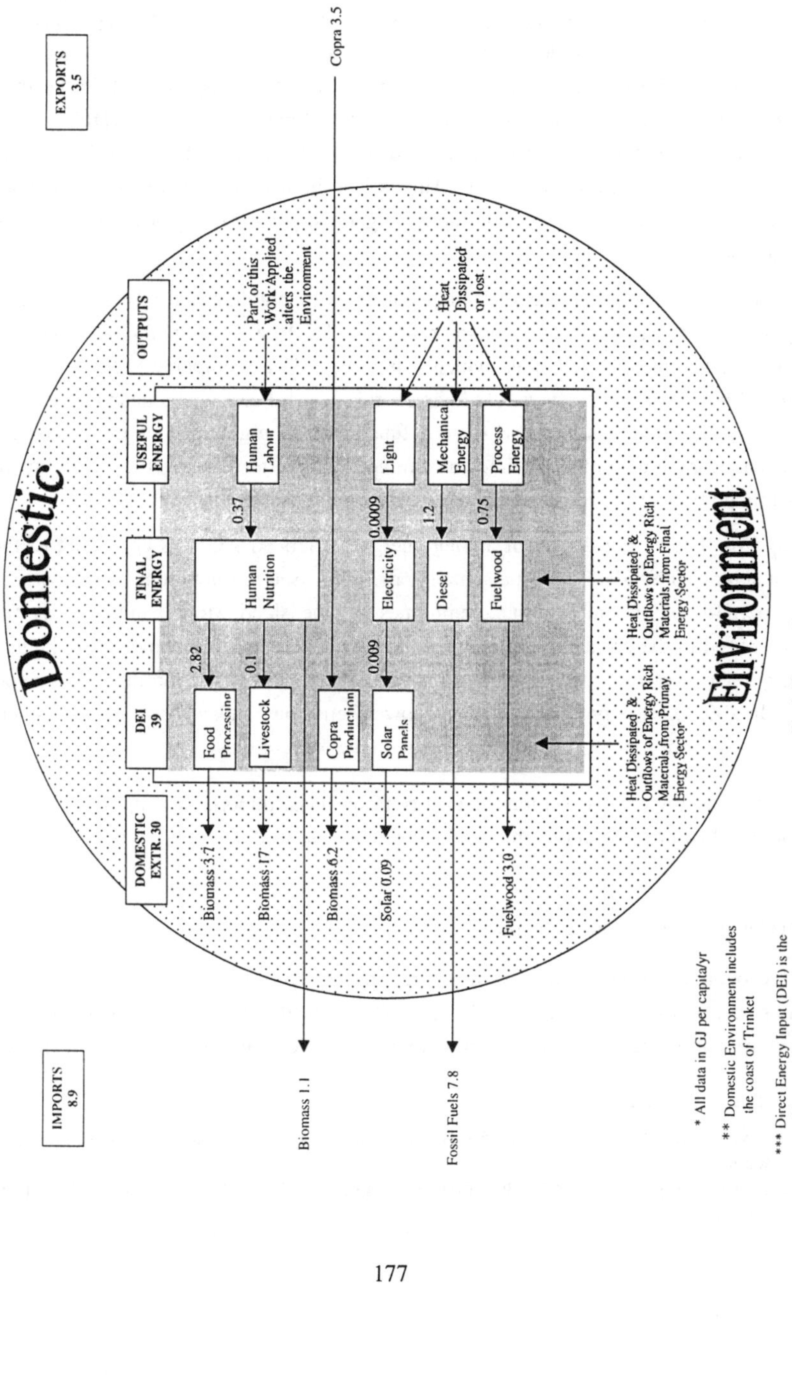

Fig 2: Energy Flows on Trinket Island

Using similar systems boundary as in case of material flows, the study accounted for energy inputs and consumption on Trinket. Figure 2 shows the flow of energy through several energy processing sectors on Trinket. We distinguish primary energy sector, final energy sector and useful energy sector. We notice that 23% of the energy inputs is imported while the remaining, mainly biomass, comes from domestic extraction. The Direct Energy Input (DEI) - sum of imports and domestic extraction - was calculated to be 39 GJ/cap/year.[8] From this 31 GJ is biomass energy and only 7.8 GJ from fossil fuels. This is just the reverse in industrial economies. Subtracting exported energy in the form of copra we got a slightly less Domestic Energy Consumption (DEC) of 35 GJ.[9]

For the purpose of this paper, we shall limit ourselves by highlighting only four things that are striking in the energy flows and conversion processes. The first is the highly inefficient system of animal husbandry (pigs and chicken) which is not even 1% as compared to the 10% average in rural animal husbandry. Idealists would interpret this as a cultural phenomenon which is evident in the place a pig holds in a Nicobari society; functionalists might attribute more ecological reasons such as storage of protein in times of dire need, convertors of vegetable carbohydrate into high quality protein and as being part of a food chain (Rappaport, 1971).

Secondly, fossil fuels are dominant among energy carriers (6.4 GJ) as compared to fuelwood (3 GJ) or solar (0.009 GJ). Fossil fuels, mainly diesel, is used to run motored out-boats for transporting copra for export, and in turn, commodities into the island. More than half of the fuelwood (1.6 GJ) is used in the production of copra while 1.4 GJ is used up in domestic cooking. The solar energy plant was introduced on the island by the local administration in 1990 for household lighting. In 2002/03 it is proposed to start a power house on Trinket for an initial 7 hours a day that will add an additional 3 GJ/cap/yr of energy in the form of diesel.

Thirdly, we find the export of biomass energy far exceeds imports causing a one way nutrient flow and fourthly, on Trinket only human labour is used as useful energy for delivering work.

6. Material stocks on Trinket Island

A socio-economic system, as discussed before, comprises all bio-physical components such as human and livestock population and all man made artefacts like buildings, roads, infrastructure etc. In other words, materials that remain within a socio-economic system for longer than a year

---

[8] Compare with - Sang Saeng (1998) [47.6 GJ]; Austria (1830) [73.3 GJ]; and Austria (1990) [223.2 GJ]. Sources: see footnote 5.

[9] Compare with - Sang Saeng (1998) [40.5 GJ]; Austria (1830) [73.3 GJ]; and Austria (1990) [198.3 GJ]. Sources: see footnote 5.

are considered to be that society's material stocks.[10] The weight of all material stocks are aggregated as tons/captia. For reasons of data comparisons with other studies we have excluded the weight of human and livestock populations, although, according to the logic of material flows these must also be accounted for.

The stocks for Trinket were accounted for two subsequent years (2000 and 2001) to observe on-going changes. Obviously, the two years provide only a hint of the transition on Trinket and they might not be representative of what would happen over a longer period. However, we calculated that the total material stocks on the island increased from 8.3 tons per capita in 2000 to 9 tons per capita in the following year. Table 2 provides a detailed picture of the quantitative increase of the different materials in the two years. This increase occurred primarily due to an increase in the number of wells (from 21 to 23), construction of a teacher's residential block, and a 650 mt. long concrete footpath under government induced welfare schemes. Excluding such buildings promoted by the local administration the per capita stocks would (not surprisingly) dwindle to a modest 635 kgs.

*Table 2: **Material Stocks per Capita for 2000 and 2001 on Trinket Island***

Type of Material	Year 2000	Year 2001	% increase	per capita ratio
	[kgs/cap]	[kgs/cap]	[%]	[%]
Cement	862	952	9	10
Steel	55	59	9	0.6
Wood	376	378	10	4
Sand	2614	2880	9	32
Gravel	4349	4838	9	53
Grass	40	39		0.4
Total	**8296**	**9145**	**9**	**100**

---

[10] Other definitions of stocks can also be used such as: all artefacts and components where constant labour and/or money is invested for maintainance; those that are owned.

Two things stand out in our stock accounts. First is the presence of a high ratio (in terms of weight) of non-traditional material (cement, steel, sand and gravel) as against traditional ones (grass and wood). Secondly, the decrease in the use of a traditional building material, i.e. grass (for roofing), in favour of corrugated roofs made of tin. What follows is not only an increase in material stocks but an indelible change – from the raised beehive-shaped huts – in traditional architectural and housing patterns; rather ill-suited to the local climate and environmental conditions.

7. Conclusions

Trinket appears to follow a more or less similar pattern of an externally driven transition and transformation largely representative of the global south. These third-world patterns are explicit on Trinket in its extractive economy, growing dependency on trade and a permanent doom of following the ideal of materialism while being exposed to the inherent inequality of the global division of labour (Goldfrank et al., 1999).

The MFA and EFA data unequivocally indicate towards a society that is at the same time dependent on domestic resources as well as trade relations. Not that this is a recent phenomenon for Trinket as, owing to its geographical location on an important sea route, the islands have had a long tradition of barter trade with passing ships ever since olden times. The important change that is evident here is that the former barter trade is not permanently replaced by an alternate system dependent on an "all-purpose" currency as the central exchange value and is destined to the dictates of the so called "totalising systems", i.e. capitalism and the world market. It provides a revealing example of "encompassment" of a sub-system by an overarching world system (Hornborg, 1996).

Development programs are directed at changing the characteristics of the local economy, lifestyle and consumption patterns. The traditional economy is very much embedded into other aspects of social life, and resource exploitation is tuned to seasonal cycles and availability of resources. Due to these limitations of resources and economic power traditional economies live more or less sustainable lifestyles. Government interventions attempt to reduce these limitations but, at the same time, institutionalize the economic process as a separate entity in the society (Polanyi, 1957). This, inevitably, has effects on the social structure and its corresponding environmental relations. New quantities and qualities of (industrially processed) materials are introduced onto the islands, markets are created, needs and wants are made to surface, as well as new values adopted by the society. The three dimensions of environmental relations – material, socio-structural, and cognitive – are transformed, and together they make up a new set of interactions with nature.

References

Adriaanse, A., Bringezu, A., Hammond, A., Moriguchi, Y., Rodenburg, E., Rogich, D., and Schütz, H. (1997). *Resource Flows. The Material Basis of Industrial Economies.* Washington DC: World Resources Institute.

Ayres, R.U., & Simonis, U.E. (1994). *Industrial Metabolism. Reconstructing for Sustainable Development.* Tokyo, New York, Paris: United nations University Press.

Ayres, R.U., & Ayres, L. (1998). *Accounting for Resources 1. Economy-wide Applications of Mass-Balance Principles to Materials and Waste.* Cheltenham: Edward Edgar.

Bates, D. G., & Lees, S. (1996). Introduction. In Bates, D.G. and Lees, S. (eds), *Case Studies in Human Ecology.* New York and London: Plenum Press. pp 1-12.

Bunker, S.G. (1988). *Underdeveloping the Amazon: Extraction, Unequal Exchange and the failure of the Modern State.* Chicago: Chicago University press.

Chakravarti, A. (1994). Andaman and Nicobar Islands: Early History. In Suryanarayan, V. & Sudarsen, V. (eds) *Andaman and Nicobar Islands: Challenges of Development.* Delhi: Konark Publishers Pvt. Ltd.

De Bruyn, S.M. & Opshoor, J.B. (1997). Developments in the Throughput-income Relationship: Theoretical and Empirical Observations. *Ecological Economics,* No. 20. pp: 255-268.

EUROSTAT, (2001). *Economy-wide Material Flow Accounts and Derived Indicators: A Methodological Guide.* Theme 2: Economy and Finance. Office for the Official Publications of the European Communities, Luxembourg.

Fischer-Kowalski, M., Haberl, H. (1993). Metabolism and Colonisation: modes of production and and the physical exchange between societies and nature. *Innovation in Social Sciences Research,* Vol. 6, No. 4, (pp. 415-42).

Fischer-Kowalski, M. (1997). Society's Metabolism. On the Childhood and Adolescence of a Rising Conceptual Star. In M. Redclift and G. Woodgate. S., *The International Handbook of Environmental Sociology* (pp. 119-137). Cheltenham: Edward Elgar.

Fischer-Kowalski, M., Haberl, H. (1998). Sustainable Development: Socio-economic Metabolism and Colonisation of Nature. *International Social Sciences Journal.* Vol. 158. pp. 573-587.

Fischer-Kowalski, M., Weisz, H. (1999). Society as Hybrid Between Material and Symbolic Realms: Towards a Theoretical Framework of Society – Nature Interactions. *Advances in Human Ecology* 8, JAI Press Inc. pp. 215-251.

Foster, J.B. (2000). *Marx's Ecology. Materialism and Nature.* New York: Monthly Review Press.

Giampietro, M. & Mayumi, K. (2000). Multiple-Scale Integrated Assessments of Societal Metabolism: Integrating Biophysical and Economic Representations Across Scales. *Population and Environment* Vol. 22(2). pp: 155-210. Kluwer Academic Press, NY.

Goldfrank, W.L., Goodman, D., & Szasz, A. (eds.) (1999). *Ecology and the World System,* Westport: Greenwood Press, Contributions in Economics and Economic History.

Gupta, Arun Das, (1994). The Andaman-Nicobar Islands in the Trade and Navigation of the Bay of Bengal 1500-1850. In Suryanarayan, V. & Sudarsen, V. (eds) *Andaman and Nicobar Islands: Challenges of Development.* Delhi: Konark Publishers Pvt. Ltd.

Grünbühel, C.M., Haberl, H., Schandl, H., and Winiwarter, V. (submitted). Socio-economic Metabolism and Colonisation of Natural Systems in a Northeast Thai Village: Material and Energy Flows, Land Use, and Cultural Change in Sang Saeng. Submitted to *Human Ecology.*

Haberl, H. (2001a). The Energetic Metabolism of Societies, Part I: Accounting Concepts. *Journal of Industrial Ecology* Vol 5(1). pp: 11-33.

Haberl, H. (2001b). The Energetic Metabolism of Societies, Part II: Empirical Examples. *Journal of Industrial Ecology* Vol 5(2). In Print.

Haberl, H. & Krausmann F. (2001). Changes in Population, Affluence & Environmental Pressures During Industrialisation. The Case of Austria. *Population and Environment* Vol. 23(1). pp: 49-70. Kluwer Academic Press, NY.

Hornborg, A. (1996). Ecology as Semiotics. In Descola, P. & Pàlsson, G. (eds), *Nature and Society: Anthropological Perspectives.* London and New York: Routledge.

Kottak, C.P. (1999). The New Ecological Anthropology. *American Anthropologist* 101 (1). pp: 23-35. American Anthropologist Association.

Krausmann, F. (2001). Land Use and Industrial Modernisation. An Empirical Analysis of Human Influence on the Functioning of Ecosystems in Austria 1830-1995. *Land Use Policy*, Vol. 18, No. 1, pp. 17-26.

Mathews, E., Amann, C., Fischer-Kowalski, M., Bringezu, S., Hüttler, W., Kleijn, R., Moriguchi, Y., Ottke, C., Rodenburg, E., Rogich, D., Schandl, H., Schütz, H., van der Voet, E., & Weisz, H. (2000). *The Weight of Nations: Material Outflows from Industrial Economies.* Washington: World Resources Institute.

Muradian, R. & Martinez-Alier, J. (2001). South-North Material Flows. History and Environmental Repercussions. *Innovation: The European Journal of Social Sciences* Vol. 14(2). Interdisciplinary Centre for Comparative Research in the Social Sciences, Vienna.

Polanyi, K. (1957). *The Great Transformation. The Political and Economic Origins of our Time* Boston: Beacon Press.

Rappaport, Roy. A. (1971). The Flow of Energy in Agricultural Society. *Scientific American* 224(3):116-32.

Schandl, H, & Schulz, N. (2000). *Using Material Flow Accounting to Operationalise the Concept of Society's Metabolism. A Preliminary MFA for the United Kingdom for the period 1937 – 1997.*

ISER Working Papers, Number 2000-3. Institute for Social and Economic Research, University of Essex, UK.

Sieferle, R.P. (1990). The Energy System. A Basic Concept of Environmental History. In Brimblecombe, P., and Pfister, C., *The Silent Countdown*. New York: Springer. pp. 9-20.

Singh, S.J., Grünbühel, C.M., Schandl, H., & Schulz, N. (2001). Social Metabolism and Labour in a Local Context: Changing Environmental Relations on Trinket Island. *Population and Environment* Vol 23(1). pp: 71-104. Kluwer Academic Press, New York.

Weisz, H., Fischer-Kowalski, M., Grünbühel, C.M., Haberl, H., Winiwarter, V. (2001). Global Environmental Change and Historical Transitions. *Innovation: The European Journal of Social Sciences*. Vol 14 (2). pp: 117-142. Interdisciplinary Centre for Comparative Research in the Social Sciences, Vienna.

Huang Fengxiang

Relationship Between Human Activities and Changes of Natural Environment – On Changes of Ecological Environment in China's Northwestern Region

Abstract

At present, China is putting into effect the "Go West Movement"-strategy. High attention there should be paid to the protection of natural environments. The article will raise some suggestions regarding how to protect natural environments in western China on the basis of an overview of the evolution of these natural environments. It consists of three parts:

1. *Natural geographic environments in western China in past and ancient cultures*
2. *Analysis of the main causes and results of ecological destruction in western China*
3. *Suggestion to the human being resulting from the historical evolution.*

In history, China's northwestern region was once a rich area with abundant vegetation. It has now turned into an area with serious soil erosion and ecological environmental problems. The ecological environment deteriorated with increasing population burden and damages done to it by human activities.

In order to narrow down the gap between China's eastern and western regions in economic and social development and promote an overall development of the state, the Chinese government implemented the grand strategy of "develop-the-west". How to integrally combine this development with the preservation and reconstruction of the ecological environment in the west has become an important topic for researchers and government institutions from all areas.

Through discussion on historical changes of the ecological environment in China's northwestern region, the thesis tries to provide some beneficial inspiration on the current dealing and preservation of the ecological environment in the northwestern and even the whole western regions.

1. Historical natural scenery in China's northwestern region

According to some historical data, as long as 3000 to 8000 years ago, there were forests and grasslands on the loess plateau in China's northwest. The climate at that time was humid and temperatures were 2°C -3°C higher than at present. This has provided sound natural conditions for people's living and working in ancient times. In ancient human civilization history, there appeared a splendid painted-pottery culture in China's northwest region. During this period, the loess plateau had a thick layer of black soil (with a thickness of 0.5m-1m), distinct for forest and grassland environment. Since then, although the climate on the loess plateau had the trend of becoming colder and dryer, its natural scenery remained the same. Most regions still are covered with forest and grassland environment. Historical records showed that, during the West Zhou period (1066 B.C.~771 A.D.), the forest coverage the of loess plateau had reached over 50%, while other areas were wide grassland. During the Qin and Han dynasties (221 B.C.- 220 A.D.), people in the northwestern region mostly lived in "wooden houses", which proves that forests at that time were quite luxuriant. Until the Ming dynasty (1368 A.D.-1644 A.D.), historical records showed that there were still wide areas of forest and shrubs near Xining city in the Qinghai province.

Thanks to the beneficial natural environment and convenient transportation in some plain areas of China's northwest, it has been China's political center with a most advanced economy and culture for quite a long time in history. It has been the center of 13 dynasties such as Zhou, Qin, Han and Tang.

2. Main factors for the damage of the ecological environment of China's northwest region

In Chinese history, the ecological environment changed to some extent influenced by the natural movement of the Earth and climate changes. Yet, the main reason of the deterioration of the ecological environment and extinction of the forest on the loess plateau for the past 2000 – 3000 years are human damages that include wars, palace construction, overfelling, indiscriminate cultivation, exploration, overgrazing, etc.

A. Effect of wars and large scale construction on the environment

China's ancient civilization was splendid. Yet, with the development of social production forces and cultural prosperity, damages to the environment caused by human beings have been on an increase. The most serious harmful act was overfelling. During ancient times, pottery and bronze industries were quite advanced, but costed a lot of wood. There have, for example, been discovered thick wooden ashes in Yin ruins. Moulding each big pot would fell a large area of trees as fuel.

The Qin and Han dynasties opened China's large-scale construction of palaces and royal houses and this has soon gone to extreme dimensions. The amount of timber used for the construction of the Epang and Lishan tomb under the Qin dynasty has surpassed the timber in Sichuan.

The construction of the Great Wall under the Qin dynasty has mobilized almost one third of the national labor, and the forests along the Great Wall have been ruined. Countless timber disappeared for the laborers' cooking, living and heating.

Under Southern and Northern dynasties, constant wars led to extensive damages of numerous forest vegetation.

During the late Sui and early Tang dynasties, with the improvement of people's livelihood, the population grew rapidly. The population in Changan, capital of the Tang dynasty, was over one million, but burning logs had caused great threat to the forests in the area.

During the Qing dynasty with Qianlong as the emperor, barren hills appeared widely.

During the 1920s and 1930s, the only forests left in Huanghe valley were once again felled by local rival forces and foreign merchants.

Besides, conflagration has also caused serious damages to the forest vegetation. For example, the forest in Inner Mongolia's Wula Mountain has experienced two conflagrations in the past hundred years. One was in 1893. The fire spread tens of miles away. The other was in 1931. The fire lasted for months.

B. Effect of extensive farming on the environment of the northwestern region

In early periods of civilized society, humankind utilized land by way of exploitative development such as burning the mountain vegetation, deforesting to reclaim wasteland and hoeing up weeds for farmland. Such activities have seriously damaged the ecological environment. According to textual researches, during Spring and Autumn and in Warring States periods, China's farming area on loess plateau was mainly in plain areas, while mountainous and most other areas in loess plateau were still covered with forests and grass. Under the Qin and Han dynasties, with promulgation of the policy of "stationing troops to open up wasteland" and "emigrating to support border areas", large scale deforestation and reclamation of wasteland was conducted. As a result, great damages were done to forests in mountainous areas and areas north of the loess plateau. Gradually, sand land appeared.

After the mid Tang dynasty, land annexation and tyranny were heavier than ever. Farmers had no means but to open up wasteland to make a living. The ruling dynasties did not terminate such acts, but ever more intensified them. As a result, plains, valleys and wastelands in middle and lower reaches of the Huanghu River were basically left with no more land to be cultivated.

Textual researches showed that, ever since the Ming dynasty (1368 A.D. - 1644 A.D.), as rulers called on stationing troops to open up wasteland, a greater wave of deforestation and wasteland reclamation was implemented that led to a further deterioration of the ecology on loss plateau.

Under the Qing dynasty, the deforestation and wasteland reclamation were on an increase. The area of reclamation moved from north of Shangxi and Shangxi itself to southern Inner Mongolia. Millions mu of grassland on loess plateau and Ordos plateau were transformed into farmlands. Such reclamation was at first only on plain areas. It then developed into high mountainous areas with no areas left out.

The agriculture on the loess plateau has long been applying a system of land rotation. Fertilizer was not applied in farming and after several years, the lands' fertility would disappear. Then another area of grassland would be chosen to be reclaimed. As a result of such turns, land that had formerly been covered with forests and grass became all barren. We can say that this is the source of a thorough destruction of the ecological environment on loess plateau.

3. Aftermath brought by the damage of the ecological environment of China's northwestern region

As the most powerful natural adjusting force providing sound ecological environment for humankind, forests have such functions as adjusting the climate, preserving the soil, checking the wind and fixing the shifting sand, preventing air pollution and providing forest products. After the damage of vast forests in China's northwestern region, it lost its ecological protective screen and damaged the ecological balance. A series of devastating aftermath appeared then.

A. Deteriorating rivers and creeks' hydrologic situation

Damaging forests means damaging conditions for preserving water resources and it definitely leads to a deterioration of rivers and creeks' hydrologic situation. It is recorded in historical books that the Huanghe River in ancient times was called "big river" with large and crystal-clear water volume. It was under the Tang dynasty that its name was changed to "Huanghe River".

B. Serious soil erosion

On nowadays loess plateau, 3700 tons of soil are lost annually per square kilometer. The amount of nutrient lost annually in this area equals nearly ten times the total volume of fertilizers applied all over the nation. Moreover, the most serious soil erosion areas on loess plateau are hills and gullies, with an average number of topsoil erosion above 10 thousand tons per square kilometer. The highest quantity can reach over 30 thousand tons.

C. Ever intensifying droughts and excessive rains

The severe damage of forest vegetation on loess plateau has reduced the air humidity and lowered conditions for forming rain. The ever deteriorating ecological environment has led to constant natural disasters as drought, flood, mud-rock flow.

D. Increasing sandy wind disasters

Before the Han dynasty, China's northwest was originally a flourishing plain with cities and towns founded one after another. The sea of sand has ruined them all. There were many ancient countries called " 36 countries in the west region" along the Silk Road which was once an important business route. What has been left now are only some ruins and names of places. Their rise and fall has a close relation with desertification. Some scholars estimate that, in the past 2000 years, the Takmakan Desert has expanded northward more than 100 kilometers.

E. Agricultural production has fallen into the abyss of a vicious circle

A large area of deconstruction of forests on loess plateau has made agricultural production losing its ecological protective screen, with fertility of farmland reduced by the years and large areas of farmland wasted. Then grassland was reclaimed to make up for the lost farmland. As a result, the agricultural production has fallen into a vicious circle of "more cultivation leads to poorer life and poverty leads to greater cultivation". The former is reflected in the reduction of rice production and the latter in lower bearing abilities of population on the original land.

F. Destruction of natural environment has led to a southward movement of China's civilization center

Over 3000 years from the Xia, Shang, Zhou to Tang dynasties, the Huanghe valley has always been an economic, political and cultural center and the region with most condensed population for most dynasties. Through five dynasties and until the Song dynasty, China's economic center has gradually moved toward the south, especially to the lower reach of the Yangtze River. At the time when the Huanghe Valley was no longer able to provide ecological guarantees for agricultural development, the social, political and cultural center has moved to the south of Yangtze River. No later dynasty after has ever established capitals or a national civilization center in Huarighe Valley.

4. Inspiration from the historical changes of ecological environment in China's northwest

After several orogenic movements in the Yan Mountain and the Himalayas, China's topology has generally formed three big steps from west to east. The highest step is the Tibetan plateau. Next step is Yunnan and Guizhou plateau, loess plateau and Inner Mongolia plateau. Apart from such ancient lands as Tarim and Chaidamu and mountainous basin and Hetao Area in the west of Sichaung, most of China's west are high elevation areas, sources and upper reaches of big rivers. They are also upper reaches for thc climate. The ecological environment in these regions has not only determined subsistence and sustainable development of local areas, but also contributed to development and security of some developed regions at the lower reaches of big rivers.

Population, resources and environment are three major topics for the development of all nations around the globe. Seen from the history of human development, these three have internal connections of population growth – demand increase – resources development, environmental impact. During such a process, the leading role is the human act. Acts that are in conformity with the natural law are those able to promote the sound circle of ecological environment while satisfying human's own demand. Otherwise, it would cause damages to the ecological environment. In China's implementation of the grand strategy of "develop-the-west", in dealing with the relationship between the economic construction of China's western region and population, resources and environment, importance should be attached to the fact that the ecological environment in China's western region has been deteriorating for the past 1000 years. We should at the same time avoid following the old way of "pollution first, transformation second" adopted by some developed countries. Instead, a significant strategic choice of combining resource development with preservation, economic development with ecological environment preservation so as to realize a sustainable development should be adopted.

A. An understanding of the natural resources must be improved

The subsistence and development of the human society could hardly go without resources. People's consumption of resources in production, living, entertainment and other activities is not only huge, but also with a wide range and since a long period. A lot of resources are limited and not renewable. In order to enjoy subsistence and further development, humankind must strengthen its consciousness of saving resources and deal well with the relations between man and nature by changing the way of developing and utilizing natural resources from an exploitative type to an intensive type. An integral combination of economic development with resources' saving and ecological environment preservation must be adopted to reduce resource consumption and upgrade the resource utilization rate.

B. An integral combination of transformation and development

The basic situation of China's western region is its large mountainous areas and small plain areas. Land is scarce. There is a saying that "80 % is mountain, 10% is water and 10% is farmland". Therefore, a rational utilization plan on state resources should be drawn out in accordance with the current land situation so as to integrally combine transformation of ecological environment with economic construction in an effort to gain mutual progress.

C. Resources' saving type of economic system should be established

In order to realize the objective of establishing a resources' saving type of economic development in China's west, one must rely on technological advance. Without technological progress and scientific management, sufficient rice and other agricultural products would hardly be produced on the limited farmland.

D. Managing resources in accordance with laws

The Chinese government has promulgated a series of laws, regulations and decrees to protect resources and prevent environment destruction. For example, we have a Water Law, Forest Law, Grassland Law, Land Management Law, Mineral Resources Law, Wildlife Protection Law and State Planning on Ecological Environment Construction. The promulgation and implementation of these laws, regulations and measures have had great effect on preserving and improving the ecological environment and rationally utilizing natural resources. Yet, actual situations are complex and laws and regulations are yet to be improved. There still exist many problems which need to be settled in view of preserving the ecological environment and promoting the reasonable development of resources. Therefore, constant efforts should be made in improvement of laws and regulation systems on the basis of strengthening law enforcement so as to achieve the purpose of saving natural resources, protecting and improving the ecological environment.

E. Integrating the objective of rebuilding a western region with "beautiful landscape" into the western development plan

China's implementation of the grand strategy of "develop-the-west" would not only be developing and utilizing resources, but also transforming the environment. During the "develop-the-west" drive, clear rules and regulations for implementation must be set up, and preserving and improving the ecological environment must be integrated into the objective of development. For measures that would cause ecological environmental destruction, no matter how much economic returns they would bring about, their implementation should be strictly prohibited.

Keiichi Omoto

Human Self-Domestication as Metaphor Revisited

Abstract

The concept of self-domestication put forward by German anthropologists during the 1930s does not seem to be a valid evolutionary hypothesis. Yet, it is an interesting metaphor when we try to understand the nature of humanity under modern civilisation. "The Eight Deadly Sins" of Konrad Lorenz is also well-understood under the metaphor of self-domestication. Some key concepts developed from this metaphor will be proposed to cope with the future relationship of humanity, culture and nature.

Recently, I have organized an inter-disciplinary research project entitled "Human Self-Domestication and the Modern Civilization" at the International Institute for Advanced Studies (IIAS) in Kyoto. The aim of the project was to examine whether the metaphor of self-domestication is useful to understand the problems we face in the modern urbanized societies. The members of the project represented widely diverse disciplines such as physical and cultural anthropology, human genetics, parasitology, dentistry, veterinary science, psychiatry, sociology and law. I shall introduce some of the case studies presented and try to show the significance of the given metaphor.

1. The concept of self-domestication

This concept was originally proposed by German physical anthropologists such as Egon F. von Eickstedt in the 1930s. The basic idea came from the morphological observation that some human characters are similar to those of domestic animals. For example, human jaw and teeth are markedly reduced in size compared with those of apes, paralleling pigs compared with wild boar. It was explained that during human evolution the decrease of mechanical stress on biting organs has led to the reduction in size.

It was considered that the similarities of humans to domestic animals are due to the specific nature of human evolution, i.e., the culture-dependent evolution. Humans are unique to develop "culture" as tools for adaptation in the varying environmental conditions. Humans are unable to survive without culture, and as the result of cultural adaptation they became more and more protected from natural selection. Thus, humans without intention made themselves a kind of domestic animal, hence "self-domestication".

While there is no room for self-domestication in modern theory of human evolution since it is hardly testable, I think the basic idea of culture-dependent evolution of humans is important. It seems that self-domestication is a useful metaphor rather than an evolutionary hypothesis to understand human nature in the modern urbanized societies.

2. Konrad Lorenz's "Eight Deadly Sins" of civilized humans

Konrad Lorenz (1903-1989) wrote a popular book in 1973 entitled "Civilized Man's Eight Deadly Sins" (Translation by Marjorie Latzke in 1974). He considers humans to be deviating from all the other animal species by virtue of "positive feedback" of cultural adaptation.

Populations of wild animal species in general are genetically controlled by a negative feedback of natural selection. For example, population size may fluctuate, and sometimes drastically increase, but in the long run it is kept nearly constant. On the other hand, humans have been put into the automatic cycle of positive feedback resulting in a number of behavioral features found in modern urbanized societies, which appears to be contradicting the "natural law" of living systems.

Lorenz's eight processes that may endanger modern human survival are as follows:

(1) Overpopulation. According to Coale (1974), the world population at 10,000 years BP just before the Neolithic Revolution, was a mere eight million. Probably, this is the maximum population size of the human species at a simple subsistence level. After the appearance of major urban civilizations the population at 0 AD was approximately 300 million. Thereafter, the figure rose exponentially, and particularly after the Industrial Revolution in the late 18th Century in Europe, it literally exploded, now approaching 6 billion.

Overpopulation is serious not only because it brings about shortage of food and energy resources, but also struggle for territories. In addition, Lorenz emphasizes the hazard of crowdedness known in animal groups to result in maladaptive behaviors, such as cannibalism and abnormal sex.

(2) Devastation of the environment. Lorenz emphasizes the danger of uncontrolled technological developments, short-sighted land-use and unlimited exploitation of resources such as woods. The problem is not only the exhaustion of resources and loss of biological diversity, but also loss of the sense of awe for the nature that our ancestors used to have. So, humans become more and more arrogant, and go on in the destruction of the environment.

(3) Man's race against himself. Competition is harsh not only among human individuals, but also among "nations", which, like different animal species, destroy each other. Lorenz calls the nations "pseudo-species".

(4) Entropy of feeling. This means the deterioration of sensitivity and passion. By developments of science and engineering, medicine and pharmaceutics, people in the so-called developed countries are physically and mentally so weakened that they are unable to resist a small discomfort.

(5) Genetic decay. Thanks to the development in medical technology, natural selection in modern human populations works only limitedly, at least in the "developed" countries. However, given the extremely high cost spent in medical challenges to natural selection, it is hard to apply all the techniques to all members of humankind. The ethical issue may be raised as to whether modern medicine serves only for a small but rich proportion of humankind.

(6) The break with tradition. Lorenz argues that there is a rapid change in the value judgement features of modern civilization. Thus, there is lack of communication between generations, parents and children, teachers and students, etc. It is doubtful that, in such a situation, the human society will give benefit to our species.

(7) Indoctrinability. The fact that humans are culture-dependent animals leads to another problem in modern societies: education. There is ample evidence in history that humans are easily mind-controlled. Even in the democratic societies, mass-communication, uniformity of school curricula, "a laissez-faire principle" of parents, etc., are all hindering the development of the individual personality and creativity of the children.

(8) Nuclear weapons. For Lorenz, their production and use is a mere addition to the previous seven important processes.

While Lorenz did not use the word self-domestication, I find that all these processes, except the threat of nuclear weapons, perfectly fit in the metaphorical idea of self-domestication.

3. Case studies in Japan

We Japanese face typical examples of the processes pointed out by Lorenz mentioned above. Since the Meiji Restoration in 1868, Japan has been an honorary student of modern technological civilization of European origin. Most Japanese are endowed with a personality of "Wakon Yosi", meaning "European knowledge and Japanese spirit", which may have led Japan to the economic success of the 20th Century. However, there are so many problems arising in the present Japanese society that I feel the Lorenzian expression of "deadly sins" quite true. Here, I will introduce some topics discussed during our project at ILAS mentioned above.

1) Change of food and dental abnormality. Dr. Kazuro Hanihara, Professor emeritus of the University of Tokyo and physical anthropologist, and Dr. Mieko Kuwabara, a dentist, studied teeth of Japanese children and found that, a variety of severe abnormalities is now

common. They concluded that change in food habits in the last 30 years is responsible, including very soft weaning food and juice drinking during infancy.

2) Parasite control and hypersensitivity to Sugi pollen. According to Dr. Koichiro Fujita, Professor of parasitology at the Tokyo Medical and Dental University, the dermal parasite Ascaris was once very common in Japan, the incidence being about 60 percent until the 1950's. This parasite causes no severe pathological symptoms to humans, but the governmental authority considered the high incidence to be shameful for a "civilized" country. After nation-wide campaigns to eradicate it, the incidence dropped to nearly zero percent during the 1960s.

3) Following that, however, the incidence of hypersensitivity to the pollen of a Japanese cedar, Sugi, increased dramatically in Japan. Dr. Fujita investigated the relationship between the two events and concluded that the eradication of Ascaris led to the turbulence in the IgE producing mechanism, causing hypersensitivity to an allergen like Sugi pollen.

4) He also warns against the popularity of "germ-free" goods. Supported by commercialism and mass-communication, such goods like "germ -free" pencils and erasers, as well as skin-cleaners are very popular in Japan. Since they may also kill the beneficial microorganisms on human skin, there is a potential danger to loose the natural ability of immunity response.

5) Frequent outbreaks of E. coli 0-157 mass-infection in schools are a big problem in Japan, but it may also be the result of self-domestication. In Japanese elementary schools, uniform lunch is cooked and provided to all pupils. The reason for this habit had been a financial one during early postwar times. However, it is still kept because many parents don't want to send their children to school with a home-made lunch-box. The problem is that, if infection occurs, all the pupils will be affected at once.

6) Problem of the pets. Dr. Masumi Yoshida, Professor of Law at the Doshisha University in Kyoto, studies the problems now arising in Japan caused by pets such as dogs and cats. These pets are human partners, and in the Japanese society where children are few, people love them and sometimes feel as if they were their real babies, resulting in the "pet-loss syndrome" if their pet dies.

4. From self-domestication to self-controlling evolution

Julian Huxley, a renowned British biologist, wrote in the early 1960's that there are three different levels of the evolutionary change in the earth's history: (1) the evolution of physical matters giving rise to the universe, (2) the evolution of life based on DNA sequence changes, and (3) the evolution of human beings featuring culture-dependent change.

The human evolution is characterized by its extreme rapidness. Our species, Homo sapiens, appeared in a certain time of the earth's history. Humans have developed a cultural system called the urban civilization only in the last several thousand years, and entered into an ecological niche entirely new to the earth. During this short period of time, it is unlikely that human DNA changed considerably. Thus, the phenotypes rather than the genotypes characterize recent human evolution giving rise to modern urban societies. We must be endowed with the same brain and hence the same genetic basis for behavior as those of our preagricultural ancestors, who survive sporadically even today as small groups of indigenous hunter-gatherers around the world.

Julian Huxley also pointed out that theoretically there is a fourth level of evolution, i.e., the self-controlling evolution of humans. Humans are unique in the ability of conceptualization and value judgement on themselves. Thus, humans are the only animal species that can control its own evolution.

Now, we should seriously consider how to realize a self-controlling system as a strategy for human survival. We need to modify fundamentally the economical system of our present industrialized societies, so that "self-control" becomes the key concept. I think that our future depends on this possibility. Several key issues may be as follows: (1) Consider "earth" and "humans" above all! (2) Turn to a "circulating" technological system, rather than a " consuming" one! (3) Start by the "developed" countries! (4) Open scientific and technological knowledge to the general public! To study the realization of these issues is, I think, is an ultimate goal of anthropology in the 21st Century.

References

Coale, A. J. 1974. The history of the human population. Scientific American 231(3): 40-51

Eickstedt, E. F. von. 1934. Rassenkunde und Rassengeschichte der Menschheit. Stuttgart: F. Enke.

Huxley, J. 1963. "The Human Crisis". Seattle: Univ. of Washington Pr.

Lorenz, K. 1974. "Civilized Man's Eight Deadly Sins" (Translated from German by Marjorie Latzke). London: Methuen.

4. Indigenous Knowledge and Sustainable Development

Viatcheslav Roudnev

Indigenous „Know-How“ and the Modern Epoch

Abstract

Increasing the meaning of empirical data about nature qualities for modern science was unexpected for theorist scholars (working in natural sciences) at the end of the 20th century. Investigation of Folk experience in diagnostics of illness, earthquake prediction and weather forecast gave to scholars new concepts about the interdependence of nature and the spiritual culture of indigenous peoples. Indigenous „know-how" has assisted to choose the optimum way in organizing the use of land in zones of risk. This paper examines the role of indigenous „know-how" in modern practice, in the context of the strategy of sustainability.

Traditionally, cultural polymorphism (apparent in the diversity of humankind's achievements in life-support activity) is in focus of human attention. World-wide interest in the variety of national cuisine can illustrate this thesis, but the main subject of interest is the variety in solving analogical problems in life-support activity. History witnesses that first contacts between peoples (belonging to different cultures) favour both: Discovery of the new and recomprehension of the own culture.

First contacts between navigators from the Old World and South America gave new technical data about ships with balance and ocean rafts (constructed from balsa wood) to European navigators. Communication with Chinese navigators helped develop the construction of European ships with separate compartments.

Researchers of the 20th century, epoch of grand prosperity of high technology, paid a lot of attention to investigate indigenous knowledge in life-support activity. Discovering the positive value of indigenous knowledge/experience in diagnostics and medical treatment (for instance, a special study of traditions in diagnostics of man's diseases by changes in the iris of the eye, initiated a new direction in medicine - iridodiagnostics), in forecast of earthquakes and weather, in agrotechnics, had been unexpected in the natural sciences. Problems of ecology, which became apparent in the last decade of the 20th century, were the precondition for calling natural scientists and ethnologists to investigate indigenous culture, especially indigenous knowledge, indigenous „know-how“.

Ecological crisis is the distinctive peculiarity at the beginning of the third millennium. This crisis has a global character and is of great danger for humankind as a whole. This ecological crisis is specifically caused by the development of the industrial societies in the last decades of the 20th century.

At present, more than 80% of the territories of the planet are under anthropogenical influence. As a result, landscapes have changed, conditions of soil, water, air, flora and fauna have changed too. In the process of human transformation activities, materials were created which have no analogues in nature. Consequences of this interference into the living nature have results in changes on a cellular level. Modernization of the natural environment of the planet which begun at one time from quite primitive interferences of man into the life of nature, through adaptation to the nature's features and copying some of nature's „decisions", leads today to a global change in the shape of the planet and humankind itself. New technologies have allowed the people of the twentieth century to be compared in the effect of power influence with the natural (for instance, geological) forces, but have not proved capable to create a mechanism for adequately compensating negative collateral consequences of human, similar to natural, activity.

The attributes of excessive human pressure on nature can be observed already for a long time on a local level, but only in the last years did this process acquire dangerous global features, indicative of the irreversibility in nature degradation. Constant fall down on manufacturing grain and fishing (per head of the world's population), decrease of soil fertility, reduction of the forest resources, reduction of water quantity (by hydrological cycle), reduction of the variety in flora and fauna, marked climate changes everywhere, are, in sum, exceeding the limit of „economic capacity" of the biosphere by humankind and, most dangerously, infringe the natural processes of self-regulation in the biosphere. The infringement of a natural mechanism in biosphere self-regulation is, according to ecologists' opinion, the precursor of a global ecological crisis.

Few researchers showed in their works (V. I. Danilov-Danilyan and others) that the biosphere has already emerged from the stationary condition, characterized by the observance of the Le Chatelier principle, and rapidly degrades. The borderline until which the biosphere was conserving the ability for self-sustaining its biogeochemical cycles was crossed at the beginning of the 20th century. Researchers have different opinions about rates, character and consequences of this crisis, but they agree in understanding the threat to mankind, as well as the limitations of our opportunities to prevent such a development.

Global threat determines the specific character of measures which should be undertaken for its prevention. Alongside with researching on the level of technologies, these measures also include references to human ethics and, in particular, optimization of the human consumer sphere.

Actually, to survive, mankind should change: Re-orientate interests from anthropocentrism to nature preservation (pass from an economic primacy to a primary role of nature). Aurelio Piccei

(President of the club of Rome) has noted: „If we want to change the world, we should first change man".

This task is difficult in itself, and is aggravated by the specific character of mutual relations in mankind - nature in industrial societies.

The technological civilization has generated among its „citizens" a definite vision of the world as a system in which the priority of values relating to „artificial" surroundings is practically indisputable. Under such conditions, realization of the urgent problem of mankind's transition from the attitudes in the „human-nature" - system, oriented anthropocentristically, to a nature-preserving model, constructed on ideas of „ecological ethics", „ecological mentality", looks especially complex, directly connected with the problem of formation of a new culture. At the same time, in conditions of global ecological crisis, ecological problems take priority very quickly, and the transition to a new model of thinking promises to be accelerated.

The decision to improve the attitudes in a „human-nature" - system guarantees restoration. First of all, in order to change the gear to biosphere self-regulation, many ecologists look at wild nature (to the model of original processes). If the probability to convince modern city-dwellers to adopt the mode of life in preindustrial society is small, the deep study of the wild nature and, first of all, of the system of interdependence in it with the aim of „ecologization" our technocratic civilization, is promising.

The new understanding of the nature's role, in particular, the understanding of the absolute value of system organization in wild nature, comes together with the crisis of the transformation concepts of nature in the industrial society, and makes quite urgent this problem of cognition of wild nature. If primordially, in the model of mutual relations „man - wild nature", the aspiration to transform wild nature (to domesticated it) prevailed, later, wild nature was perceived as the reserve for perfectioning the qualities of domestic flora and fauna (improvement of the genofond); today the necessity is recognized to conform the own activity with nature. In this connection, cognition of nature through revealing the specific character of interdependence in wild nature is urgently needed for the solution of modern problems. Norbert Wiener, the founder of cybernetics, wrote: „We have changed our environment so radically that now we must change ourselves in order to exist in these surroundings".

Among a few main models suggesting ways out of the crisis (main plans are: improvement of the technocratic civilization, adaptation of our civilization to nature, and a strategy of co-evolution) each one needs detailed knowledge of nature and changing ourselves.

It would mean a transition from anthropocentrical brain orientation to an ecocentrical orientation connected with the revision of stereotypes of world outlook.

Numerous cases of successful application of folk methods to diagnose and treat various diseases, of agrarian skills and of other economic techniques in contemporary practice show the significance of empirical observations of nature for filling gaps in the modern model of world outlook.

It is well known that indigenous peoples have deep knowledge about wild nature. These peoples have unique data, received in processes of multi-generation life activity in concrete ethnoecological systems not known to natural scientists.

Ethnological research has testified that in the traditional culture of each nation, there is a file of knowledge reflecting experiences in wild nature observation in a particular local natural niche in the pre-industrial period.

Characterizing these data, one should note, first of all, the "density" of such folk supervision over the environment in borders of a certain niche (practically each plant as well as each local natural phenomenon has a certain name), as well as the original and practical value of such folk supervision (medical doctors, biologists, agronomists, physicists and other experts actively incorporate this empirical material in the analyses).

The systematic character of the environment assimilation in folk society is one of the features which can be observed on the basis of the analysis of Russian folk culture.

Russian peasants have created a specific form of nature use, in which opportunities and interests of man and the specific character of regional natural conditions of East European plains were balanced. Being commited farmers, Russian peasants have blended organically their economic activity with local nature. They have actively involved wild flora and fauna as a component of nutrition, in medical purposes - for treatment and as indicators of the environmental condition. Knowledge about wild nature was useful for peasants in solving daily problems and it objectively promoted harmony in the "man-nature"-system, at the level of economic pressure of the human on nature. Folk experience of Russian peasants in agriculture and weather forecast can illustrate this statement.

Russian folk phenological signs, for example, as well as signs setting connections between weather conditions of certain "integrated" dates or periods, have a positive value until today, though modern meteorologists have not found explanations for it yet. So, rain on Samson Day (July 10th) predicts „seven rainy weeks", temper of weather in Pokrov (October 14th) predicts the character of „future winter". The practical value of folk phenological observations has been revealed. For instance, „if bird cherry trees (Padus) begin to blossom, there will be no "light frost", if bees close up the notches with wax making only a small hole, winter will be cold with severe frost.

Such examples demonstrate the specific character of folk experience in nature use, particularly wild nature use, and reveal the process of cross-cultural research, high potential level of this original empirical folk data for modern natural science. Comparison of different points of view about the world always offers interesting data for analysis.

In 1960 at the International Conference "Alive prototypes of the artificial systems – key to the new technics" (Deiton City, Ohio, USA), attention was paid to the prospects of investigation into nature for perfectioning technologies and creating a new engineering. There, a new direction of science, „Bionica" was born. Bionica has radically influenced the notion in 20th century about nature and the world. After 40 years, we can evidently see results of this new thinking in the technologies. Indigenous experience in the use of nature for modern interdisciplinary research is another way for the harmonization in the system "man-nature". This cannot be reduced to copying the technology of life-supporting activities in pre-industrial society. To do so would be an impossible and unrealistic endeavour. The problem is rather seen in the necessity to add some folk experience in wild nature use to modern high-technology.

A data bank of „indigenous knowledge" which will accumulate folk experience in different branches and areas is extremely useful for the realization of a project "sustainable development for mankind in the 21st century".

Y. M. Lotman noted that signs or tokens are remnants of a different truth going back to another type of culture. Today this "other culture" is being discovered anew by physicians, biologists and agronomists. In analyzing the traditionally developed forms of economic activities in the areas with unfavourable natural-climatic conditions (tropical, highland, circumpolar areas) modern science tries to determine their optimum character from the point of view of modern technologies. Thus, for instance, in preparing a project of economic development of the Amazon area, specialists of the USA have recognized the local technologies of growing crops traditionally used by the population of Amazonia as the most effective and optimum.

Having created an artificial world, after his abilities and notions concerning the relations in nature and the system of interdependences in the world, man of the industrial society has destroyed, sacrificed and rejected many of the possibilities offered to him by nature, mostly without even making an effort to understand their significance and meaning. Thus, for example, in using chemical preparations to fight vermin, man has been unsuccessful but has destroyed the natural enemies of the pests he hated. Such examples are very numerous and embrace nearly every sphere of human activities.

As of today when faced with the urgent necessity to find ways out of the ecological crisis, man of the post-industrial society has come to understand the need to live in peace and harmony with nature, and the knowledge about nature and its laws becomes particularly valuable in this respect. Under these circumstances, studies in the empirical knowledge of man in traditional society, who is close to nature and knows its laws well, is important, as it can objectively assist in developing concrete steps to harmonize relations in the „man-nature-society" system. Appropriate attention to the traditional folk experience in sustaining vital activity and use of ecologically clean technologies can be a fruitful step in developing programmes to find ways out of the ecological crisis and to create a new model of ecological development of human society in the 21st century.

Making use of folk experience in nature observation for harmonious interrelations in the „nature-society"- system and for the elaboration of a new model of world outlook is quite an important aspect in the process of implementation of „Sustainable Development", as fixed in the form of the „Agenda 21" at the United Nations Conference on Environment and Development (Rio de Janeiro, Brazil, 1992).

Salomón Nahmad

Anthropology in Social Analysis and its Role in the Efforts to Eliminate Exploitation and Poverty in Traditional Ethnic, Minority, and Peasant Groups in the Context of Global Society

Abstract

Applied Anthropology must generate proposals, with new concepts and definitions of development and sustainability, that incorporate anthropological knowledge and tools, so that the advances from all branches of the Anthropological Sciences can reach, and contribute to, the development projects of these vulnerable populations intended by themselves, as well as those planed by governments, the associations of civil society, and international organizations.

Introduction

The accelerated national development in the 21st century demands a reflection upon and a proposal for sustainable social development in the context of cultural diversity. Applied Anthropology has an essential role to play in efforts to guarantee that the millions of poor peasants and indigenous population of the world, as members of societies, can maintain their own cultures and social organization and their own political and cultural institutions. They are actively excluded and don't benefit from these national development processes in ways that foster their own distinctive paths of economic, political, cultural, and social development. In order to fulfill this role, Applied Anthropology must generate proposals, with new concepts and definitions of development and sustainability that incorporate anthropological knowledge and tools. The advances from all branches of the Anthropological Sciences can reach vulnerable populations as well as governments, the associations of civil society, and international organizations.

History at large

The installation of the colonial system 500 years ago meant not just a military invasion and an economic restructuring of the indigenous economies, but above all an overturning of the juridical, administrative and political order which had been developed on a continental scale, and which had incorporated national, cultural an linguistic diversity to a marked degree, organized in states, chiefdoms, tribal groups and sometimes in complex geopolitical units. The rules concerning the appointment of their own governments, judicial officials, priests and military officials was smashed by the new western model which, in Latin America, was the Spanish or Portuguese version.

After the initial contact with Spaniards a new form of life project was generated which tried to exclude or destroy the earlier experience of the original villages of Mexico. From this moment on the indigenous world was progressively impoverished, and compelled to exchange its own projects of evolutionary development for projects of resistance to an alien project.

Neither the contributions nor the heritage of these civilizations have disappeared; quite the contrary, they are very much alive as a hidden, subterranean social and cultural world where practices that are apparently western have, in fact, deep roots in this ancient heritage.

Any policy which tries to favor the interests of the indigenous peoples has to be based in the real situation, and not in the kinds of utopian plans which the Mexican government has been promoting for the past two decades. Every project should be closely inspected to make sure that it has beneficiaries other than local leaders or a regional elite. One has to recognize the kinds of pressures that indigenous communities have to deal with, and not derogate their long-suffering efforts to overcome their problems. The ethnic groups of Mexico and Latin America already have trained and qualified personnel, and projects should include them and their wisdom. Planners should take into account other examples of community-driven development projects, which will be different in the various groups and countries. These policies should be scrutinized to see how they fit with a national plan for development, and plans should include specific goals both short and long term.

Actually indigenous peoples have lost control over and access to their own natural resources, and even over their own labor power. This has led directly to the transfer of a large part of their production and labor power to others, which is precisely why there exists the global phenomenon of widespread, extreme poverty. The loss of their best lands, the erosion of their soil, the loss of irrigation resources, the overexploitation of the forest reserves, and the use of their best lands for the production of products aimed at the national and international markets has led to the undernourishment of the indigenous populations, as well as to the loss of the self-sustaining productive system which had endured for hundreds of years.

The situation in Mexico

The indigenous regions of Mexico, in great part, have been undergoing a slow process of impoverishment to become the poorest of Mexico's poor. Even although the statistical information and poverty indices are highly aggregated and do not distinguish between indigenous people and others, it is easy to infer the conditions under which they live by looking at the poverty indicators in such areas as: Oaxaca, Chiapas Guerrero, Hidalgo, Yucatan etc. where the World Bank and the Inter-American Bank have initiated special projects to attend the terrible deterioration of subsistence agriculture in thousands of indigenous households. In these states the greatest poverty is to be found in the rural zones, and in these zones the indigenous communities are the ones that display the highest indexes of poverty, consistent whit the very low amount of public and private investment. People leave the rural areas and move to the city in the hope of being incorporated into the productive system of the country. This worsens the human problems of the city, not only in Mexico but also in many of the cities of the United States.

The conditions of poverty arise because people do not have access to land, or they own lands of the most inferior sort, working conditions on the commercial farms and plantations are backward and unjust. The processes of agrarian reform are only partly finished, and now with the constitutional reform the country is entering upon a retrograde period during which secure tenancy of the land is going to be jeopardized by having to pass through the bureaucratic agrarian management and the agrarian courts. Violence in the indigenous regions was a constant in the past decade, and this new reform is going to increase it and complicate land tenancy so as to divide up the ejidos into private lost and to create commercial associations with outside investors. The crisis conditions of the past decade have smoothed the transfer of thousands of hectares of the best community lands to agribusiness. For the indigenous communities and for the peasants the present period is even worse than the period of the crisis of the 1980s.

Now the poverty of these regions is being accompanied by the destruction of the environment which is being affected by industrial development projects, or modernization projects, which have changed the natural habitat as well as the mode of production and quality of life.

In general, the indigenous communities have very little access to education, health services, and sanitation, housing and public health. They are under the control of professionals, technicians or bureaucrats belonging to the dominant society.

The forms of government of the communities which are currently designated as "Indian" (as in colonial terminology) sought to redefine their juridical order in the colonial context by naming their own authorities and governments in order to maintain the same kind of community control and governance as they had before. After 500 years of colonial domination, and all over the continent, the constructed political categories that appeared to be those of the colonial regime preserved shreds of their original autonomy. At the time of Independence, a new version of domination was created by the native born Mexicans, who had every intention of continuing the colonial project of their fathers for the indigenous peoples, keeping them in forms of economic servitude, under racial discrimination while negating their culture and their languages.

Democratization

Democracy and the philosophy of western governance hold that only the individual is a proper social subject, and pays little attention to collective identities which predominate in the ethnic communities, and are embedded in their forms of governance and administration. It is limited because it only permits the expression of civil rights by the vote, and then denies the vote to those who do not belong to the political class. A member of the political class had to speak the language of the conquistadors, and later, read and write it.

The many native languages on this continent are denied their place, just as the cultures, politics and democratic practices of the original inhabitants are swept aside and denied recognition. Western democratic ideas have bypassed the indigenous community in the sense that the right of collective voting as a community has been denied to the indigenous people, except if it can be manipulated by the official parties. The Communities have been forbidden to designate their own candidates to the legislatures and the judiciary, and most of all to the executive positions on all levels. They have been denied the right to form their own political parties with platforms that are appropriate to their political and social demands and to present election candidates that will represent them. In no country have they been permitted to mobilize themselves and direct their own electoral campaigns, while their needs have been systematically overlooked in the campaigns of the national parties. In academic or intellectual circles when the talk turns to democracy, the topic of the role of ethnic groups and their rights hardly ever arises.

The indigenous groups were beaten down in the colonization process, but they have not given up their historical claim to their human and community rights. In the last twenty years their voices have been heard through the rebellion of zapatistas in Chiapas or in academic and political forums which have slowly opened up tiny spaces for listening to them in a truly democratic fashion. The new international realities which have abounded in recent years, the voices of the original ethnic groups of this planet have been quoted in the headlines of the daily papers of the world, just as they have in Mexico. Democracy as it is presented is rigid, closed and conservative, and refuses to begin a theoretical discussion on a truly democratic society which includes all the indigenous groups. The discourse avoids any confrontation with the indigenous peoples, and fears the breakup of the imaginary national project, which Mexico has constructed over the past 200 year and which has so little to do with "the real Mexico".

The prediction of the anthropologists and sociologists about ethnic and minorities' wars have turned out to be true, although they take the form of violence against the indigenous communities. There is neither political force nor sufficient will to terminate these reactions of inequality and injustice which the dominant groups exercise over millions of inhabitants, the inheritors of the ancient cultures of the continent. It is not just that there is no protection for the human rights of these groups, there in no intention of redistributing resources in their favor either. There is no real democracy nor even a democratic project if the indigenous groups are not included, and the whole national project is not reordered.

Incorporation to the global market

The new system of production has changed the patterns of dietary consumption in rural Mexico. The penetration of industrial foods, usually in the form of junk foods, has taken place to the furthest corners of the Republic. As a result a worrying deterioration of the diet has occurred.

It is worth noting that hundreds of thousands of indigenous families working the common lands of their communities managed for years to be self-sufficient in food production within their villages. But in the last decade, in general, communities have lost self-sufficiency, and have turned to the market place for food purchases. There are now indigenous regions where, because of the absence of any incentives, nutritional levels have fallen because families have not been able to produce subsistence foods, in spite of the availability of land.

If Mexico were to regain self-sufficiency in food by incorporating the peasants and indigenous peoples into the milpa (traditional) system once again, billions of pesos would be saved in food imports. At the same time the peasants would be converted into consumers better enable to participate in the national economy and in defending that part of the environment which has historically provided the society with a great variety of products to complement the basic diet.

The fact is that the three countries, the United States, Canada and Mexico, are all engaged in a policy of NAFTA treaty. What people of good will ought to do is set aside the censuses and other statistical data that show the integration of the Indian peoples, and recognize their inclusion and existence as a distinct entity. The white populations in Mexico have always wanted to show that there were few Indians here, despite the abundant evidence of Indian faces, and Indian images. For example, recently, the official parties of Mexico's elites, the Creole inheritors of our colonial tradition, declared that for the neoliberal "modernizers" the indigenous communities are hindrances from the past that ought to disappear. But at the same time the official line is a multicultural society, born originally in its many villages and ethnic communities protected by the law, with a government that supposedly promotes the development of their languages, cultures, customs, resources and unique forms of organization, that they can decide for themselves about their life-styles, and that the communities have the resources to attain this goal.

National and international emigration

The emigration to Mexico City or to the United States which has been observed in the indigenous communities increases each year, as does the rate at which the young men of the communities give up agriculture, leaving it to the responsibility of the women, old folks and the children.

One can see in the principal cities where the banks and telegraph offices are located, the lining up of women and old people trying to cash money orders which the members of their families have sent them from outside. And when the emigrants return to their villages, they bring clothing, electric gadgets, toys etc. which are of importance to the peasants who stayed at home. U.S. airlines are filled with villagers going to and coming from their jobs abroad.

We estimate that the number of indigenous women in the economically active age amounts to 3 million. The majority of them are engaged in agriculture, and they receive no credit for the domestic work they put in. As producer and as reproducer the work of women is invisible and devalued in Mexico, and doubly so if the woman is indigenous. In Mexico the majority of the domestic servants in the cities are indigenous people who work under difficult working conditions. They are supporting their own communities and, at the same time, reducing the number of people at home who have to be supported during periods of crisis.

Regional development schemes usually do not include women's contributions or their prospective development neither in the way they are thought out nor in practice.

The system of subsistence production has enlarged its productive networks through emigration, and through market production for the urban areas. This permitted significant changes in cultural patterns, but it also has continued to support population growth, which in turn produces a greater demand for goods bought in the market, and promotes the articulation of the village with the industrial outside.

Ethno-development and applied anthropology

Ethno-development has been defined by an expert group invited by UNESCO in San José, Costa Rica: "The expansion and consolidation of local culture through the strengthening of the autonomous capacity for decision making of a culturally differentiated group in order to guide their own development in the exercise of self-determination, in what every way this be defined, so long as it implies social equity and self-empowerment". This particularly means the development of decision making power in the area of self-initiating development.

The idea of modifying the integrationist project and of generating a model of self-development was not supported by governmental regimes which have continued in the shop worn model of increasing injustice and control of the indigenous communities by the political elites. The im-

increasing injustice and control of the indigenous communities by the political elites. The implementation of the reform of the economic neoliberal model is going to lead to the transfer of better quality land to the agribusiness and to commercial contract farmers and leave only the worst lands in the hands of the poor peasants. This reform is supposedly generated to transfer urban capital to the rural areas, as well as to promote international investments in the countryside, but I frankly think that it is yet another way of more aggressively exploiting the peasant, and at the same times it decapitalizes the rural zones.

The different regions of Mexico demonstrate how the dominating system of centralized planning does not promote the autonomous participation of the beneficiaries. Their active participation must be at the fundamental base of rural and indigenous development projects,wheras such non-participative focuses have filled the rural zones with modern debris (that today constitute an archaeology) supposedly destined to change and elevate the quality of life of peasants and indigenous peoples. It is imperative that the government agencies and technocracies that design these policies progress from a paternal type of politics to one in which the beneficiaries of the programs actively participate.

The participation in one's own autonomous project must remain realistic, avoiding the interference of foreign interests to the project and, furthermore, avoiding the dependence and redirecting of the bureaucracies in charge of the development. The evaluation and monitoring must take a collective form and avoid the favoring of privileged social classes. Those social actors that are to benefit from the project must be the actual recipients of the programmers aimed to help them in order to achieve efficiency, equality and justice.

In Mexico, the work of Applied Anthropology, and even more its results, have not been able to channel the potential of the communities to eliminate all forms of discrimination, exclusion and poverty of close to 60 million Mexicans that live outside the boundaries of economic, cultural and social transformations. The new generations of anthropologists will have to continue building specialized theoretical bases to modify the anthropological praxis within an updated context that points to the politics of development, which includes the participation and the appropriation of the beneficiaries of projects. The enormous quantities of badly-spent money and the developmental work of thousands of active men of which no advantage has been taken, has generated great discouragement and a loss of faith towards the government institutions and, occasionally, towards anthropologists.

References

Arizpe, Lourdes. 1996. The cultural dimensions of Global Change: An anthropological approach. Culture and development series; UNESCO Ed. United Nations Educational, Scientific and Cultural Organization 7, Place de Fontenoy, Paris

Bonfíl, Guillermo, Verissimo Domingos, Ibarra Mario et al. 1982. *América Latina: etnodesarrollo y etnocidio.* Ed. Flacso. Colección 25 aniversario, San José. Costa Rica

Collier, George.1994. Basta! Land and the zapatista rebellion in Chiapas. The Institute for Food and Development Policy, Oakland, California, U.S.A.

Comas, Juan. 1964. La Antropología Social Aplicada en México: Trayectoria y Antología. INI Serie Antropológica Social 1, México.

Escobar, Arturo. 1998. *Antropología y desarrollo.* Revista de la UNESCO, U.S.A.

Hamelink Cees; Smeets; Shiva; Lim; Kagarlitsky; Boyd-Barrett; Norberg-hodge; Gendzier; Bales; Lintner; Karliner y Falk. 1999. Global Dialogue: The Globalisation Phenomenon J.G. Cassulides & Son Ltd Nicosia

Hoebel E. Adamson y Weaver Thomas. 1985. Aplicaciones de la Antropología. En Antropología y experiencia humana, Ed. Omega 5ª. Edición, Barcelona, España.

Hubinger, Václav. 1998. Antropología y modernidad. Revista de la UNESCO, U.S. A.

Nahmad, Salomón. 1980. Perspectivas y proyección de la Antropología Aplicada en México. América Indígena.- Vol. XL, no. 2 abril-junio.

– 1991. Los derechos humanos de los pueblos indígenas de México a su propio desarrollo político, económico y cultural. Del libro: "Nuevos Enfoques para el estudio de las etnias indígenas en México". CIIL Ed. Porrúa. México.

– 1995. Una experiencia indigenista: 20 años de lucha desde investigador hasta la cárcel en defensa de los indios de México. Suplemento antropológico Vol. XXX, ns. 1-2, Universidad Católica, Revista del Centro de Estudios Antropológicos, Asunción, Paraguay.

– 1997. Mexican applied anthropology: from founder Manuel Gamio to contemporary movements. In The global Practice of Anthropology, Studies in third world societies, Publication no. 58, Williamsburg, Virginia, U.S.A.

Nahmad, Salomón; González, Álvaro; Rees, Martha. 1988. Tecnologías indígenas y medio ambiente: Análisis Crítico en Cinco Regiones Étnicas Centro de Ecodesarrollo México D. F.

Nayara, Deepa. 1996. Toward Participatory Research. World Bank Technical Paper No. 307, Washington, D. C., U.S.A.

Partridge, William L., Uquillas, Jorge E. y K. Johons. 1998. Inclusión de los excluidos: El etnodesarrollo en América Latina. Bogotá, Colombia 30 de junio-2 de julio. Segunda conferencia anual del Banco Mundial para el desarrollo en América Latina y el Caribe. Colombia

Partridge, Williams. 1998. Social Assessment in the Latin America and Caribean Region. B de Walt. U.S.A.

Psacharopoulos, George y Patrinos, Harry Anthony. 1994 Indegenous people and poverty in Latin America: an empirical analysis. Ed- The World Bank. Washington, D. C.

Scott, David. 1998. El Colonialismo. Revista de la UNESCO, U.S.A. Secretaría de medio ambiente, Recursos Naturales y Pesca Delegación Oaxaca

– 2000 Conservación y manejo comunitario de los recursos forestales en Oaxaca (1ª edición) Oaxaca Oax.

Stevenhagen, Rodolfo. 1991. Nuevo enfoque del sistema internacional. Del libro. "Nuevos Enfoques para el estudio de las etnias indígenas en México". CIIH. Ed. Porrúa. México.

Toledo, Victor. 1992. Etnoecológica Volumen I (número 1)

Centro de Ecología de la Universidad Nacional Autónoma

Wolf, Eric. 1987. Europa y la gente sin historia. Sección de Obras de Historia. Fondo de Cultura Económica, México.

Shen Lin

From Classical Evolutionism to Cultural Ecology – On Ethnological Topics in the Development of West-China

Abstract

In China, there is a gap of economic and educational level between the West and the East. To reduce this gap, the government launched the "Go West Movement" and put it in practise. Most of the minorities in China live in the west and there are a lot of natural as well as traditional cultural resources. This gives great chance to the development of anthropology in China. This paper discusses how anthropological research can influence public policy in China.

The 9.60 million km^2 territory of China is close to the size of Europe and there are 56 ethnic groups living in the unified multiethnic country. The development-area of West-China is 6.87 million km^2. That constitutes 71.50% of the total territory. In this vast region, 355 million, or 28.4% of the total Chinese population, have their home. Among them, the ethnic groups amount to 80% of the total (106 million). All this indicates the importance and prominent role of ethnology/anthropology (hereafter ethnology) in the overall development strategy of China's western region.

My understanding of an ethnic group is a community of people who, in social interaction, identify themselves or are being identified as having a common origin, history, culture, and thus having common interests and rights in a social system. Culture is a mode of thinking, acting, feeling and its products are shared by the ethnic group. Ethnology is a discipline that tries to understand various ethnic characteristics through comparative study of cultures in order to promote ethnic equality and sustainable development. These concepts and data, plus the fact that I am an administrator of ethnic affairs, instead of being an ethnological professional, makes my topic a rather difficult one. For this reason, I have to apologize before going into my topic.

1. Please accept me as an outsider of the discipline who is willing to share his personal opinions with you and is willing to bring your knowledge into this work for expanding the benefit of academic communication.

2. Please excuse me for not observing some academic norms, including not listing references. But please, do believe that what I present is my personal experience gained from my daily work in a governmental department.

With these preconditions, I will divide my topic into 3 aspects: First, my understanding of China's development effort in its west region. Secondly, ethnological issues in this campaign. Finally, how to put our research into application.

My understanding of developing West-China

Developing West-China is a part of global modernization. The process of global modernization initiated from Western Europe. It affected East Asia in the mid-19th century, when European and American Powers had partitioned the world. The only exceptions in East Asia were Japan and China. In the following decades, Japan, thanks to its social structural similarity with Western countries, rapidly modernized itself and claimed hegemony in Asia for some time. Nowadays, it is still an economic superpower in the world. China, on the other hand, hesitated a long time in whether or not copying the Western model to participate in the global process. In fact, from 1860-1970, China has tried, time and again, some new ways to avoid the Western Model and take its own way. This effort brought about remarkable results in national integration and social reforms. However, it missed many opportunities for taking part in the world's economic mainstreams.

Since the 1980s the Communist Party of China finally was determined to lead China into the process of global modernization. Though the road is not smooth, the direction is correct. Chinese people of all ethnic groups benefit much from it, and the world also does. However, the process of opening to the outside world and modernization brings new challenges for China. One is the unequal development between the economic and social development in different parts of China. The other is the accelerating deterioration of ecological environment. Moreover, since West China has a higher portion of ethnic groups, the different regional developments also have ethnic connotations. It is this situation that drove the Central Government of China to initiate the campaign of developing West-China, which in turn ushers us in our current topic of ethnological subjects in the campaign.

Ethnological topics in developing West-China

I select the ethnological point of view not because I am a member of an ethnic minority, nor because I am doing administrative work on ethnic affairs. I select it because, in my opinion, it can best reflect the fundamental issues, including ecological ones and those about ethnic minority rights and interests. Moreover, it can offer the most promising answers.

I need not address the importance of ecological environment. The Green Party in Europe demonstrates it to us all the time. What I want to point out is the fact that West-China is one of the most vulnerable areas in the world. It is a vast region with very thin outer soil. Moreover, because of massive mountains with little soil in the south and vast lands with scarce water in the north, there is extensive no man's land due to a lack of vegetation.

Unfortunately, nearly all the surfaces with vegetation have been overpopulated in West-China for a long time. The limited primordial vegetation has been overexploited. Mountains deprived of vegetation would flood the lower land. Plains and plateaus deprived of vegetation are not only subjugated to desertification, but also produce dust storms in the windy East Asia. Currently, the Central Government of China is trying to take strict measures, including the withdrawal of farming for reforestation. The renewal of the ecosystem has also been established as an important goal in the campaign of developing West-China.

The ecosystem in West-China is not only related to local ethnic people's survival and development, but also to the ethnic relations and social stability in China in general. Moreover, it is closely correlated with mainstream culture's attitude toward the ethnic minority cultures. Ethnic minority peoples have been living in West-China for thousands of years, and thus they have sustainable mechanisms for exploitation of local resources. But too often in the context of modernization and market economy, these traditional cultures were regarded as obstacles to development and as target for social reform. As a result, both ethnic cultures and ecosystems in ethnic area are under the pressure of modernization and development. The past 50 years' experience in China is an example.

In the late 1950s, as China barely accomplished its ethnic identification, the mainstream scholars classified the social forms and stages of social development according to the classical evolutionism (rather than cultural ecology) originated in the West. Consequently, most ethnic groups in China were classified as being in the stages of primitive communism, the slavery system or serf system respectively, while the mainstream Han society was labeled as feudal landlord system. All these cultures belonged to the pre-modern, pre-industrial stages. Therefore, all were targets of socialist reform. As soon as the socialist reform in China proper was completed in 1956, the democratic reform in ethnic areas, especially in those in southwest China, was staged. Besides social institutions, cultural practice as marriage customs, language and writings, traditional beliefs were all on the list for reform. It is true that this reform under the orientation of classical evolutionism did achieve some positive results. China became more integrated and the class and personal oppression systems were abolished. Individuals gained more space for personal development. However, these achievements cannot countervail the negative connotations and consequences of the classical evolutionist approach.

First, it negated the value and rationality of local traditional cultures. It turned the synchronic spatial differences between cultures into diachronic differences in social development stages. This discourse (including that of living fossils and primordial poverty etc.) put ethnic minorities and their cultures into a disadvantaged position and thus reduced their capacity to defend their own cultural rights and economic interests. Secondly, it provided an easy pretext for local officials' misplay in decision-making and defects in work, to the effects of covering up the actual cause for the slower economic and social development in ethnic areas. Thirdly, it fostered the self-conceit of the mainstream culture while weakening the right to equal participation by ethnic minorities to tap local resources and to protect local environments. In fact, this is the very reason why the ecological environment deteriorated so badly. It is difficult to expect an effective check of this vicious cycle until this issue gets considered and resolved.

Closely related to this is the classical theory of ethnos (nation). It is rooted in Stalin's version of nation-theory. The kernel of it was that ethnic or cultural differences are bound to social-economic levels and that the gap should be eliminated sooner or later by the socialist state power with planned economy. This theory is ivory-towered and misleading in many aspects. First, we have seen that ethnic identity retains its vitality in changing social circumstances and shows no sign of fading with the increase of material assimilation or economic development. Secondly, the means of the state-planned economy could not become fully effective in the system of market economy. Therefore, the economic affirmative actions granted by the state to ethnic minorities couldn't be fully materialized. Thirdly, the theory of ethnic/national amalgamation, just as the erroneous assumption of living fossils, gave no orientation in practice but aroused strong antipathy of ethnic minority people.

For these reasons, we can no longer use this outdated theory in the development of West-China. Instead, we can adopt the theory of cultural ecology. The cultural differences between ethnic groups should be understood and explained in relation to their ecological circumstances. In this way, all ethnic groups would find an equal intersubjective footing in China as "an entity of diversity in unity". In other words, ethnology in today's China, as in the case of the Red Army in the 1930s, should take a long march to implement the transfer from classical evolutionism to cultural ecology. Under this premise, I see the following issues having the most direct connections with ethnology:

1. **The single notion of development and various developing subjects (hosts)**. It requires ethnology to develop a system of classification for reflecting the diversified natural and cultural ecosystems in West-China. On this basis, different patterns of development should be proposed for different regions or ethnic groups to reflect their features.

2. **The mechanism of sharing risks and benefits for exploiting resources and protecting environments.** Ethnology should investigate a legal framework for compensating ethnic minorities in West-China that bear the risk of resource exploitation and the costs of environment protection. People in East-China as beneficiaries should share the risk and cost for social justice as well as for narrowing the gap between West and East China.

3. Ethnic minority's livelihood, migration and employment. Market economy lacks ethic dimensions. Therefore, it should be under the surveillance of law, especially in the campaign of developing West-China as a multiethnic region. Ethnology should help the state to formulate an operational anti-discrimination law to guarantee the basic rights of ethnic minority people in livelihood, migration and equal competition. They should have nationwide equal rights for employment and should have priority for employment in their home area.

4. The coordination of traditional lifestyle with market economy efficiency. Lifestyle includes traditional beliefs, taboos and customs. With more and more foreign investment and construction projects located in ethnic minority areas, the contradiction between efficiency and traditional lifestyle will be frequent. For the sake of retaining ethnic identities in smooth development, ethnology should take preventive actions to make different cultural lists in different places and among different ethnic groups. In this way, the new-comers would know what can be reformed and what has to be respected or accommodated.

5. Integration of state-law, ethnic-regional autonomous law and native customary law. Ethnic minorities in West-China as "Gemeinschaft" societies have a rich deposit of customary laws for managing and regulating their internal social conflicts. Since these "laws" have a more humanistic connotation, they are widely accepted by local people. However, the West-China development will bring a steady flow of immigrants who are more inclined towards the modern state law. Ethnologists should pay attention to the interaction of these two systems and try to identify the possibility of reconciling their discrepancies with the ethnic-regional autonomous law. Closely related to this issue is the legal position of ethnic traditional religious beliefs. Ethnologists should have some say in the recognition and regulation of this social reality.

6. Ethnic educational system and job market of graduates. In the past decades, ethnic education in China has evolved into a unique system. In near future, the competence of this system will be subjected to the trial of West-China' development. We should create conditions for its survival and development by our own research and suggestions for improvement. Special attention should be paid to guarantee the equal entrance to the job market for graduates from this system.

7. China's cultural diversity and Chinese identity. West-China's development is a long process. This process will be paralleled by the integration of China's Mainland and Taiwan and thus has a profound influence on Chinese identity. In light of this, ethnologists should bear in mind the ethnic minorities in West-China, the development of Taiwan, Hong Kong and Macao, and the situation of overseas Chinese as well for proposing a solid and cohesive discourse on Chinese identity. This discourse should be able to offer an acceptable explanation on Chinese diversity in unity.

The above-mentioned points certainly cannot give a full picture of ethnological topics in developing West-China. However, we do see that each topic involves the deepening of reforms and consummation of the legal system in China. This is a clear indicator that under the vision of cultural ecology, West-China is by no means a synonym of poverty, backwardness or target for development. On the contrary, it is the motor for further economic and social reforms in China. While East-China has offered a pattern for developing a market economy in the framework of a planned economy, West-China has the potential to offer a socio-political model for accommodating plural cultures in the mechanisms of a market economy.

How to put our research into application

As Geertz said, man is an animal dangling on the self-woven web of meaning. So are ethnologists. The raw material of this ethnological web of meaning is composed of our disciplinary tradition and current practice. It has the function of cognition as well as orientating practice. As a governmental worker, I emphasize its function of orientating practice. We all hope that our research will benefit the ethnic minority peoples in China and the mankind as a whole. We should carry out positive research for an objective assessment of ethnic issues and ethnic relations in China. The assessment should constitute a foundation for constructing a new framework of theories, policies and legal systems in regard to ethnic minorities. The resources for this construction lie both in historical tradition and in current practice. Historically, China has a rich deposit in treating ethnic minority issues. Some of them are still relevant today. The founding leaders of the People's Republic of China have effectively tapped such resources in formulating the framework of ethnic-regional autonomy. We also have to rely heavily on local facts and local knowledge.

Mou Benli

Develop-the-West Movement and the Preservation and Development of Ethnic Cultures in China

Abstract:

The "Develop-the-West"-Movement in China does not only mean economic development, but development in a broader sense that includes the development of ethnic cultures in the Western region. China's West is the region with the most abundant ethnic traditional cultural resources. In the new situation, where economic knowledge is on the rise and economy and culture are conceived as mutually complementary, an effective development of the rich ethnic cultural resources is of great significance for the smooth implementation of the strategy of developing the west and the realization of a sustainable development in the western region.

"China's West" consists of 12 provinces and autonomous regions, with a total area of 6.86 million square kilometers and a total population of 350 million, which account 71.4% and 27.8% of the total respectively. Due to reasons as historical background, natural geography, population resource and economic and social development, its economic and social development is quite backward. After more than 20 years of reforms and opening up, China's overall state power has been strengthened constantly and implemented the second strategic objective ahead of time. By 2000, China's GDP has reached six times that of 1980. Eastern coastal regions have enjoyed a sound environment for development and realized „self investment, self accumulation and self development". Throughout 20 years of drastic development, the western region has acquired some fundamental conditions and advantages for further development. Therefore, the central government seizes the opportune moment to set forth the grand strategy of "Develop-the-West". Develop-the-West is directly linked with expanding domestic demand, promoting economic growth, ethnic unity, social stability, frontier strengthening, a co-ordinate development between eastern and western regions, and a final realization of common prosperity of all ethnic groups. As the western region is a major concentrated living area of China's ethnic minorities, the implementation of Develop-the-West, to some extent, puts emphasis on development in ethnic minority areas as such. This would not only have profound impact on the economic and social development of the western region, it would also promote the economic and social development of China's ethnic minorities and ethnic regions. Seen from the development strategy and its implementation, common views are held by the government and social circles focusing on ethnic regions and taking advantage of ethnic traditional cultures.

1. Munificent ethnic cultures are important resources for the development of China's western ethnic region

The western region has more than 40 ethnic minorities that have lived there for generations. It roughly accounts for two third of the ethnic minorities all over the nation. The nation's 154 ethnic localities are mainly spread in that region. There are 5 autonomous regions, 27 autonomous prefectures and 83 autonomous counties (banners), accounting for 96.72% of the total area of national ethnic autonomous localities and 86.47% of the total area of the western region. Yet, its per capita GDP only equals 60% of the national average level. Most populations that haven't settled their food and clothing problems are living there. In terms of the overall development of the nation, if the economic development in the western region fails to catch up, there would exist an even greater gap between eastern and western regions. A lot of social issues would come up that would not only lead to a long-term poverty in the western region, but would also curb a sustained and fast development trend in the eastern region. That is to say, the development of the eastern region would hardly sustain unless the western ethnic region develops itself. Neither would the national modernization course be realized. In order to change such a situation, the Chinese government has set up many preferential policies and adopted many kinds of effective measures to promote a faster development of the western ethnic region. Significant achievements have been reached through such efforts. Yet, due to such factors as low social maturity level, weak basis and harsh natural environment, the development in the western ethnic region is not that satisfactory, with quite a big gap with Chinese government's consistent demand that all ethnic groups in the nation should realize common development and prosperity. Therefore, the Chinese government has proposed the grand strategy of Develop-the-West by the end of the 2Oth Century. Its aim is to fundamentally change the "backwardness" of the western region through a long term comprehensive and sustainable development with the help of people all over the nation.

Develop-the-West, although its contents and form are more or less reflected in economic acts, this is not the whole meaning of development. Instead, it should be understood in an over-all way. Its ethnic cultures are undoubtedly advantageous resources for development, together with natural resources. As a cultural ancient nation with a development history of 5000 years, culture has almost entered every aspect of social life. The role of cultural factors in social development has always been of great importance to China as a whole and all ethnic groups. The denotation and connotation of ethnic traditional cultures are therefore expanding, their density and multiplicity becoming more obvious. Therefore, starting from foreign experience and the accumulation of domestic cultures and its effects, the development of ethnic traditional cultures

tion of domestic cultures and its effects, the development of ethnic traditional cultures should occupy an important place in the Develop-the-West course and become an important entering point for the grand development.

2. Great significance for the development of ethnic cultural resources in the western region

To attach great importance to ethnic cultural development has direct or indirect effects on the development of the economy of the western region. The two are complementary. For example, focussed on establishing a big cultural province, China's Yunnan province has not only held the International Horticulture Exhibition to promote its tourism, construction, service and transportation industries, but also done a lot in comprehensively developing traditional cultures of ethnic minorities. In regions like Dali, Lijiang, Xishuangbanna, Chuxiong and Diqing, ethnic cultures have been regarded as important resources to be developed. Although these regions are remote, they have become destinations that are longed for by tourists both at home and abroad. In this way, Yunnan becomes famous, and remarkable economic returns are gained at the same time. It is a successful example for a good combination of cultural development and economic development.

Meanwhile, we have to realize that strengthening ethnic cultural developments in the western region would also promote understanding and unity among all ethnic groups, so as to promote a prosperous development of ethnic affairs. One of China's fundamental national reality is its multi-ethnicity, and multi-culturalism. During a long time of contact, the ethnic groups have formed the same cultural core, which is the ethnic spirit of the Chinese people. Such a spirit has become a basis for the link and unity of all ethnic groups in China. Yet, the reflection of such a spirit is not always the same. Different ethnic groups would show such a core within their particular cultures. Ethnic cultures with different characteristics have enriched the cultural garden of the Chinese nation. Of course, if the contact channels were not smooth, there would arise obstacles for ethnic communication. Therefore, in order to break away such obstacles, it will be important to promote actively a wide range of cultural communication among ethnic groups. All ethnic groups would be mutually recognized and identified through culture, and the coherence of the Chinese nation would be strengthened. The strategy of Develop-the-West has provided an extremely favourable opportunity for a further realization of such an objective. A thorough communication of cultures in the western region and preservation, development and utilization of ethnic cultures in such a multi-ethnic region would undoubtedly promote great unity of the Chinese nation as well as prosper cultures of all ethnic groups. As a result, besides economic purposes of protecting and inheriting outstanding ethnic cultural heritage, a deeper connotation of developing and prospering ethnic cultures in the western region has arisen.

Of course, the development of ethnic cultures in the western region has some further meaning. We would, for example, show the world the extensiveness and profoundness of the cultures of the Chinese nation, leading to an understanding of China, and this would strengthen our cultural communication and links with other countries in the world.

3. Major characteristics of ethnic cultures in the western region

During the long historical development process, ethnic regions in the West have not only created rich material cultures, but also extensive and profound historical and spiritual cultures, including folklore. Distinctive characteristics have been formed.

A. Long history

Historically, the ancestors of many ethnic minorities lived in this western region. They have accumulated many songs, dances, oral literature and historical books. Some of these ethnic minorities have established local administrations one after another since centuries or generations.

Palace relics, famous ancient temples, gardens and cultural relics are numerous. In the case of Lhasa (Tibet) and Dali of the Bai ethnic group, both have city histories of thousands of years.

B. Multiplicity

In China, the multiplicity and richness of ethnic regional cultures in the western region are hard to describe. Originally, they carry traits of both external cultures as Buddhism from South Asia and Islam from East Asia and of native cultures of the Han and ethnic minorities. Geographically, they have mountainous culture in Yunnan and Guizhou provinces, frigid culture in Tibet, prairie culture and desert culture in China's northwest. Industrially, they have nomadic culture, farm culture as well as commercial culture in towns. They also vary in their belief-systems: Buddhism, Islam, Christianity, and aboriginal religion and Taoism.

C. Ethnicity

Many ethnic minorities in the western region have their comparatively independent compact living areas in terms of regional distribution. Different compact areas are always an independent ethnic cultural unit. It is worth pointing out that different regional distribution of one ethnic minority would cause obvious differences in customs and language. For example, the Dong and Yao ethnic minorities living in the North and South cannot understand each other.

D. Simplicity
Due to geographical encirclement, the impact from external cultures is quite weak, which brings about that the cultures in the western region are quite simple and original in content and form. This is obvious in many ethnic minorities' singing, dancing and customs.

4. Help ethnic cultures to walk on a sound development track through developing Chinas' West!

Economy and culture are two wings for a nation, for regional development and progress. The two are promoting each other. There cannot exist an economically developed but culturally backward area. Even so, such would hardly exist long. At the primary stage of implementing the grand strategy of Develop-the-West, the Chinese government and all social circles have emphasized the development of ethnic cultures. By closely combining economic and cultural development, we should ensure ethnic cultures to walk on a sound development track.

Generally speaking, the main ideas of the Chinese government in its implementation of developing ethnic regional cultures in the west are:

Consistently carry out the policy of preserving and developing ethnic traditional cultures by taking construction and preservation as prerequisites, utilization as means and development as purpose.

Construction

Facing the reality that the construction of ethnic regional cultures in the western region is quite backward, the State Council stipulated Notice on Certain Policies and Measures in Implementation of Develop China's West, which has clearly proposed an input on cultural construction to be increased step by step. The Ministry of Culture has put forward a series of specific measures on basic and group constructions of ethnic cultures in the western region. They are being implemented at present.

Preservation

Cultural resources are not renewable. So preservation must be conducted. Currently, the preservation of China's traditional cultural resources still has some weak links like smuggling of cultural relics and requires further strengthening. Natural erosion also is still quite serious. With the economic development, in particular, some ethnic cultures and regional cultures are facing the danger of extinction. In this respect, the Chinese government has mainly focused on two fields: One is to rebuild and preserve the natural outlook of historical relics and natural villages. For example, the ancient cities of Loulan and Gaochang in Xinjiang are undergoing urgent preservation. Effective management is conducted on the ancient city of Lijiang in Yunnan province. On the other hand, effective measures are taken to urgently save and preserve them for the future with plans and visual technologies, document and record in pictures and words, preserve them in local libraries, museums and ethnic folk museums, by training and educating cultural specialists.

Utilization

We have gained a lot of experience in this respect. A successful example is the preservation and utilization of Mogaoku. Its preservation and utilization have undergone decades. Another example is the state allocating special fund and establishing special institutions to collect, investigate and publish some important historical books and documents of ethnic minorities. We have some successful examples recently as well. For example, the development and utilization of the ancient city of Lijiang and Naxi Gule in Yunnan province are quite successful. Such development and utilization would not damage the living environment for traditional cultures, but would inherit and develop their essence. During the development of China's West, the Chinese government has emphasized that the development of ethnic traditional cultural resources should be: Preservation first, utilization second! The reasons for this approach are very simple. To develop cultures without proper sealing of preservation matters, would damage traditional cultural resources. Meanwhile, the government has demanded that promoting the economy by way of cultural development should be banned, having realized that it can hardly achieve cultural prosperity fundamentally. Instead, a "win-win" method should be adopted to gain mutual improvement.

Development

Insisting on the principle of "making the past serve the present", the Chinese government has stressed the development of cultural resources in the western region by adopting a development concept. We should not only focus on traditional cultural resources, but also explore some modern contents with ethnic characteristics so as to develop the essence of traditional culture in the grand development. The Chinese government attaches great importance to explore ethnic cultural heritages by modern technologies. For example, investigating historical books in Dongba characters with computers, or developing traditional medicines of ethnic minorities through modern medical technologies. Strengthening communications is one important link in cultural spread and development. In order to ensure the heritage and development of ethnic cultures, the central and local governments have organized all kinds of activities such as joint performances of national ethnic minorities, like traditional sports meetings. They have tried their best to provide opportunities for the intercultural contact and exchanges of ethnic cultures.

Éva Sebestyén

Medical Plants and Indigenous Approaches to Healing in Sobral. Afro-Brazilian Cults and a Health Program in Ceará State (Brazil)

Abstract

In Northeast Brazil the low income population usually prefers the cure administered by indigenous healers, but at the same time respects the treatment given in the Health Centers. This preference is based on the social context of the cure: The indigenous healer and the patient belong to the same social strata, therefore their communication has no embarrassment and the cure is a socio-cultural event with participation and support of the neighborhood. The indigenous treatment belongs, as a very active part, to the local indigenous belief system. The healer cures by the transfer of energy received from the spirits of the Afro-Brazilian cult "umbanda", which is a long process. On the other hand, the western medicine represented by the Health Centers introduced the notion of quick cure by effective pills.

This papers deals with a recent process in the State Health Program intending to establish a continuous intercommunication among the healers of western and folk-medicine. This kind of integrative medicine plans to create "the living pharmacies" in the Health Centers which are in fact a representative medicine plant collection of the local indigenous knowledge. It is the first step into a dialog between these two medicines. The western medicine usually presents the following claims against the indigenous medicine: Indigenous knowledge of herbs has an insufficient categorization, ignores how to organize, how to use them, and is unable to formalize their effects. The idea of the holistic medicine influenced the western doctors to recognize the important role of the "hidden" healing system of the indigenous physicians based on a familiar doctor - patient relation characterized by touching, feeling, embedded in the same socio-cultural background. Hopefully, the next step will be for the Health Centers to organize courses about the local indigenous healing and the use of medicine plants for their workers and another course about the proper use and posology of the clinically tested medical plants for the indigenous healers.

The Northeast Brazilian Health Program in Ceará State focuses on improving medical services by distributing medically controlled therapeutic plants among local Health Centers. According to the present state of scientific knowledge there are approx. 700 medical plants in Northeast Brazil in use. Only about 50 have been formally tested in laboratories for their therapeutic effects. The sources of information for this program are, mainly, published materials written by natural scientists. They do not conduct their own research on the use of medical plants. This paper suggests that anthropological research conducted in some local Afro-Brazilian cults in one of the impor-

important towns of Ceará State, in Sobral, may uncover a hitherto neglected set of sources concerning local knowledge about medical plants and their use. These cults, called *umbanda*, have about 200 officially registered ceremonial houses which function as living museums of local Indian and Afro-Brazilian medicine.

Searching the hidden healing system

I have conducted a preliminary pilot research on indigenous health practices which could, I believe, contribute to such a future project.

This pilot research tried to gain knowledge about a "hidden healing system", which official medicine ignores. It is located in the field of indigenous medicine. I shall refer to three subdivisions of indigenous medicine:

a) Afro-Brazilian cults such as *umbanda* represented by the *mae de santo* – female chief of the cult – as healer,

b) Brazilian Popular Catholicism represented by the *rezadeira* (preacher),

c) a combination of the two represented by the *curandeiro* (medicine man).

My history with the pilot research

As a visiting professor of Anthropology and teaching Medical Anthropology and Introduction to African Studies at the State University of Vale de Acaraú in Sobral (Ceará State, Brazil) between October 2000 and December 2001, I conducted a preliminary fieldwork with my students about the African heritage in Sobral. After some months of this pilot research at Afro-Brazilian cult houses, I started to pay special attention to the healing activity of the spiritual leader of the cult. The concepts of illness, health, cure, treatment, seemed to have different meanings in this setting than in those well-known textbooks of Medical Anthropology which form the basis of the discipline. At the same time, there was a new Health Program to be launched in Ceará State called "living pharmacies". The idea was that every Health Center must have its own garden where it can grow about 20 basic medical plants, controlled by laboratories, so that they can be distributed among the low income population. These two facts gave me the idea to start a research about medical plants in order to detect the kinds of healers who cure with plants, their practice, and their knowledge about them. The study of the use of plants obliged me to study first the process of healing, the relationship between healer and patient, the pluralistic use and prescription of products of official and folk pharmacology.

My initial entry to this enquiry was to visit experts in medical plants, also at times, when my students or I had some concrete health problem. In one year I have visited about 40 cult houses and healers of different specialities in town and in the hinterland. I conducted a weekly research in one cult house and occasionally in two others for purposes of comparison.

After finishing my research, I came across a very sensible book about another fieldwork done among Amazonian Wayapi Indians which made me raise many questions about the effect on my

personality and my relationship with my interlocutors. In the final part of the book I found a marvellous sentence for this complex interaction:
"Instead of discarding one diagnosis of 'what they are' in favour of another, passing it on to them like a label, all of us who get involved should take the responsibility for the accounts we give of them and accept that what we say to the outside world is a result of the intermingling of our experiences with theirs."

The cure and its processes

The participants of a cult form a community called "*aldeia*" (village in Portuguese). This conception of village is ritually used by the healer. During the session different spirits are called for cure and are incorporated in the body of the healer. These spirits are deceased Africans and Indians. Firstly, the patients' case is presented to the healer in the presence of all the participants of the session, sometimes loudly, sometimes in low voice. The treatment is processed publicly. Depending on the illness, it may be classified as spiritual one. The presentation will be followed by advice and declaration of support from the part of the spirit in the patient's recovery. If it is a physical illness, you will see ritual acts of expelling its cause.

The concept of illness in Afro-Brazilian cults in Sobral

There is a holistic view about the diseases in these cults. Illness is understood as a disorder in the everyday life which can be any kind of misfortune in private life (bad luck in work, love, etc.), spiritual disturbance and physical diseases. To restitute the order you should consult a local healer. There is a very common trajectory of cure. The town of Sobral is historically a very traditional Catholic town. Therefore, firstly, the patients visit a healer of popular Catholic healing line, the so called *rezadeira* (the preacher). In the case of failure or wishing a more effective cure, the patient looks for the next type of healer, the medicine man, *curandeiro,* who uses some Afro-Brazilian elements in his cure, mixed with the technique of Popular Catholic healing. If this treatment is not successful, the patient has an open mind for cure, beyond socially well accepted healing, and will visit an Afro-Brazilian cult house. It is an interesting fact that, albeit the healers of the Afro-Brazilian cults consider themselves Catholics as the majority of the population in Sobral, they receive a lot of criticism for being practitioners of black magic.
Interestingly, the new sects of Protestantism, and not the Catholics, are forbidden to have any contact with them. In fact, the Afro-Brazilian cult healers are traditionally religious people, going to mass and participating in pilgrimages. The initial and final part of the cult session consists an invocation of God, or a prayer to the Virgin Mary and they frequently request the help of the Virgin Mary and of saints.
The healers have two different activities. One is in the public section of the cult, where participants are people seeking cures. During the healing part of the ritual the healer will make his diagnosis and suggests the treatment. In the case of further consultation, the healer will invite the

patient to visit him in his private consolatory in order to administer an extra cure. All healers confirm that there are two different types of illness: the paid and the free ones. All physical diseases belong to the unpaid category, which the healer has to cure by charity. The cure can be compensated according to the conscience of each patient in either products or money. The ethic of the indigenous healers makes it immoral to ask any kind of reimbursement for the cure of physical illnesses. In misfortune in private life, a payment is obligatory because if you do not pay, the cure would not exercise its effect. This category, which includes troubles in love affairs, punishment, etc., demands works which oblige the healer to make a lot of costly rituals.
Therefore the indigenous illness and its treatment develops in the local social context. Even some physicians of Health Centers, in the case of unsuccessful treatment, suggest that the patient may look for the strongest indigenous "Health Centers", i.e. the houses of Afro-Brazilian cults.

Struggles with research methodology

The famous methodological label in anthropology called "participant observation" causes a permanent dilemma for researchers. The question is whether we stress in our research the role of our participation or our observation, or both of them and how intensively. In other words: Should we be in or be out and distant in relationship with our interlocutors during fieldwork activity? I have always thought it must be a conscious choice. My personal idea was to be objective and distant without any personal involvement. My intention was to be respectfully friendly and distant with the interlocutors in my research. At the same time I considered important to have the clear notion that they and I belong to different cultures, and I always would be an outsider in the Afro-Brazilian cults. This preconcept changed completely during my recent fieldwork. I became their friend, emotionally got involved with their problems, and when I could solve some small problems, I did it. I became deeply touched by their beautiful and free way of treating all kind of diseases and the patients. Illness got a new meaning for me. I came to see the healing of illness as social interaction which involves the whole community. I saw the ritual with the healer as a treatment of the ill person through all elements of the traditional culture (audio-visual: songs, dance, words, body-language, transfer of force, massage, syncretic beliefs in Catholic saints as well as in African spirits).

Limitations of the indigenous cure

Indigenous healers make a clear distinction between diseases which they can cure, and others which belong to the official medicine. They do not deal with cases like pneumonia or AIDS, which they consider to be cases for the hospital. There is no concrete list of this selection.

The other limitation is the social behaviour. If the patient appears as drunkard, or on drugs, or disturbing other persons' life, he/she will be expelled from the cult house. The improper behaviour is possibly an African tradition which punishes the repetitive criminal with obligatory exile.

Comparison of the notion of illness by official medicine and by indigenous healing systems

The indigenous concept of illness is embedded in a holistic medicine, with a strong stress on the social context. In the majority of cases the actors of a cure (doctor and patient) are from the class of lowest income, share the same cultural background, a similar standard of life, the same language and life experiences. The dialog, therefore, is familiar without any fear, discomfort which they usually feel towards the white physician who represents a class of rich people, often their bosses at work is absent. The real communication between a patient of low income class and the expert of official medicine happens more easily with persons in intermediary position, such as nurses of the health service, employees in the pharmacies. Experts of the official medicine concentrate on the physical aspects and the pathology of the illness making diagnoses without considering the whole social background and personal features of the patient. I met only one physician, Doctor Cesar of Sumaré District in Sobral, who was very careful to introduce a holistic view into the official medicine. He opened a new way in the treatment, having a deep interest in the local knowledge, maintaining very friendly relation with all the population, during and beyond the consult. The indigenous healers usually have great respect for official medicine and special recognition for the pioneer physician who started with a holistic approach similar to that of indigenous medicine.

The knowledge and use of plants

The position of official medicine is still very divided about the use of medical plants. Even those who agree with the necessity to create a living pharmacy of plants, prefer, in practice, to prescribe pharmaceutical products. One reason is their lack of knowledge about the therapeutic effect of the plants and their responsibility in the effectiveness of the recipe. They even use the argument that the people nowadays do not value plants anymore, and feel more secure curing themselves with a pill than with a plant.

Alternative medicine uses plants which belong to a general knowledge of oriental medicine, or well known plants from all over Brazil. In the case of folk-healers, there is a big difference between "*rezadeira*", "*curandeiro*" and "*mae de santo*".

The *Rezadeira* (preacher) is usually a woman of old age, who prays silently, and cures not more than 10 illnesses, using sometimes plants in her hand in order to help her pray. She does not suggest the use of any medical plant, and her own knowledge about such plants is very limited. It is said that she heals by the transfer of the force of her prayer. The *Curandeiro* (medicine man) uses and prepares some products, teas, juices of medical plants, and he cultivates them around his house. He uses plants in his cure, and suggests pharmacy products at the same time.

The *Mãe de santo* (healer of the Afro-Brazilian cult): These persons have great knowledge of local medical plants, ten times more than any other healer. Usually they have their own "living pharmacy" e.g. a section of medical plants in their garden, and collect others from the riverside, from the meadow, or in trade with neighbours. These Afro-Brazilian cult leaders have an actual-ised knowledge about the present local plants and their traditional use, which is based on Indian habits and African traditions.

The role of healers in their community

The best approach to healers in general was made by Alan Tomaid Campbell, defining the notion of the Amazonian Indian healer called *paye* (Portuguese pajé) saying that "It wasn't just a role or an office. *Paye* was a whole way of being in the world, an outlook on the world and a relationship with the world, that everyone was involved in." (1995: 185) He made a very important statement on the fact that all members of the community belong to the very same world and even share a common knowledge about the symptoms of illness and its cure. So if they share the very same ideas about the treatment, why are healers wanted? Because they are the illuminated figures of the cure. They have the special strength which can be their own one (*rezadeira, curandeiro*) or received from spirits, and the cure is based on the transfer of energy plus some concrete medical plants and methods of cure indicated by the healers.

Campbell further looks for a more precise understanding of "*paye*" that the other reality yonder, revealed by shamanistic knowledge, has been thoroughly humanised. It is full of creatures all of whom appear as people we talk to and learn from. The world of these creatures and the world of humans become shared. That is to say, the heart of that shamanic reality reveals a human relation between ourselves and the natural world." (1995: 200)

The spirits whom the healer incorporates during an *umbanda* ritual represents the different forces of nature (earth, water, forest, etc.) who speak to the participants, criticise them, cure them, even have a dialogue with them. The healers control, help to solve problems regarding everyday life. Any kind of problem or disorder is considered illness, may they concern the fields of health, misfortune, love affairs, work. Therefore to study only the therapeutic effect of the medical plants without considering the role of the medicine man as a link between our world and nature in a given community would miss the core of the indigenous medicine. The plants have a more effective action if the medicine man prescribes them and also indicates the treatment.

The patient-healer relationship

In the whole complex of folk-medicine there is one common feature. The patient and healer belong to the same cultural background, use the same colloquial language, and usually belong to the same low income strata of the population. That is why the communication is friendly, without any stress, both of them using a lot of signs and silent communication with touch, face expressions, etc. There is a clear hierarchy which is based on the recognised knowledge of the healer as a wise grandmother by the patient. The western physician-patient relationship is a very distant one, the silent communication is very rare, the language, the hierarchical status is very different, even the access to a good cure is very complicated.

The role of the public in the cure

There is an interesting feature in the folk-medicine cure. The patient is not alone, is accompanied by other patients waiting for their turn. When the diagnosis is made by the healer, the participants express their opinion, their experience with the suggested cure. This process of the cure makes the patient more convinced and, in the case of some doubt, there is always a chance to ask others for more explanations in the cult.

Impact of the cure on the patients

There is one very important characteristic of Northeast Brazil folk-medicine which one would not find in the official medicine. It is the transfer of the healer's strength to the patient. The common feature in all the different types of cure is that the patient has to have faith in his healer and the treatment. But only in the folk-medicine will the patient receive vital energy from his healer. The sources of this energy are different. In the case of Afro-Brazilian cults it comes from the spirits of the cult who represent the water, the earth, the forest, thus the forces of nature. In the case of *curandeiro* and *rezadeira*, they share their own forces with the patient. After a well done cure, the patient feels himself recharged like a battery, and become dependent on this transfer of energy during the whole process of his cure.

The folk-medicine offers a complex system of treatment, where the effect of the cure must be studied in a concrete situation, ideally in the concrete language, and comparing the different local healing systems and their cure from the point of view of the patient. In the case of a long-term-cure, the same patient usually visits healers of different specialities for one and the same illness. The social strata and the link to the Catholic Church still exercise their effect in the selection of the healer. The lowest strata still prefers the Afro-Brazilian cults, the middle and high class requests more the service of the other two popular healers, but this class division does not exist any more in the big cities in the Southern part of Brazil.

The study of medical plants, their repertory and their use in the given social context would be very desirable. This fieldwork has proved that the knowledge of their physical utilisation alone cannot be satisfactory, because the concept of the cure deals with the union of the patient's body and spirit which needs, through silent and verbal communication, the transfer of energy of his healer as well.

Indigenous healing as a social performance

In the rationally cold daily life of "western" reality which exists even in Brazil, the Afro-Brazilian cult houses are small oases where any person with problems is treated as friend, as family member. Besides the healer, the visitors and active members of the cult house will express their opinion about the problem and its cure, so the whole healing process is a shared experience without any hierarchy among the participants. The healer is a respected person, the symbolic mother or father of all the members of the cult community. That is why the ritual reference to him or her is father or mother, depending on the sex identification of the spirit he or she incorporates.

The symbolic father-son relation is an energy transfer realised in touches, embraces, drink offers. The strong feeling produced in the follower can cause some kind of dependence without disturbing his everyday life. The member of the cult looks for protection against any negative forces which can disturb his life, and this appeal will be reinforced during the cleaning ritual of the cult. This touching feeling is reinforced by his active participation in dance, song. My view is, that to be regularly, once or twice a week, in a cult house ceremony based on general charity causes a psychological comfort for the participants and makes them forget their hard life. The other important aspect is social recognition, in the house he is a member with full rights equal to all other participants; beyond the house he is a poor person of the lowest social class. Therefore to be in a ritual as a member of a cult house means a good touching feeling for people who usually miss this in their everyday life.

Emerging problems in the indigenous healing system

1. Lack of systematisation of herbs and their effect

The so called indigenous system of knowledge has no western order of ideas, which causes a lot of problems for the researchers. There is no way to make an interview based on categories, or lists of herbs for a concrete illness. The healer's argument is that this knowledge about medical herbs and their cure belongs to the spirits and can only be transmitted when the healers are in trance, and spirits inhabit them. They add that the cure will happen not only with the administration of the herbs but with the help of these spirits. The patient who believes in these spirits will receive their strength and their support to attain his recovery.

This "insufficient" categorisation challenges the researcher to make a western systematisation of the fieldwork data without losing the spiritual component.

2. Lack of a schedule and quantitative use of the herbs

The healer indicates the herbs, the way of using them without giving any idea about the measure, the daily schedule and their possible side effects. The same happens sometimes when he indicates some well known pharmacy products.

Some proposals for use of sustainable indigenous knowledge

The Health Secretary of the Municipality of Sobral recently organised a meeting for all the active traditional healers of the town in order to share their experiences with the experts of the official medicine. It was a big success, the healers became very satisfied with this sensibility and interest of the local government towards their knowledge. On the base of my pilot research experience it would give good future results if the very same Secretary or the local Health Centers would follow two parallel approaches at the same time in one joint action. Therefore I would like to present two ideas concerning the introduction of the indigenous knowledge into the practice of official medicine, and to supply the indigenous healers with basic scientific information about their medical plant administration. The fruit of this co-operation could be a publication about the mainly used medical plants and their characteristics and utilisation according to both medicines. The aim would be to share the local indigenous knowledge with the local population and eliminate incorrect or even dangerous applications, and side effects of improper use.

1. The Health Center would organise a course where traditional healers will speak about their healing experience and present the most utilised herbs in their treatment. Representatives of official medicine (physicians, nurses, pharmacologists) would explain the therapeutic effect and the administration of the medical herbs already checked by science. At the same time they will give information about the effects and the problem of side effects of the most used pills among the population which are indicated by the traditional healers as well. These two groups together will set up a living pharmacy based of the most common and medically controlled herbs in the garden of the Health Center with the necessary jointly prepared information about the healing characteristics and administration of the plants.

2. Undergraduate and graduate students who would be future health workers would prepare their dissertations about one type of indigenous medicine.

Epilogue

Indigenous knowledge is still a mystery for the experts of official medicine and for the population of middle or high class origin. Instead of giving any kind of label from afar, it is time to go closer in order to be acquainted and to save for the future the historical result of another empirical medicine. As it is well known, both of the medicines (indigenous and "official") are based on empirical observations and investigations, and were used in the past to complement each other. The rift between them is recent, basically resulting from the concentration, systematisation and technical experiments of official medicine in the 20th century. It is a basic change which deals more and more scientifically with our body and forgets our spirit, our mind, our social embeddedness. On the other hand, indigenous societies suffer a lot of western influence: Many of Indian and Afro-Brazilian communities disappear for ever, the shamans will be substituted by city Health Centers. Therefore one of the few reserves of local indigenous knowledge can be found among their healers, and in more concentrated form among the Afro-Brazilian cults. Therefore pioneer research should not only concentrate on some badly studied Indian communities somewhere in Amazonia, but should be directed towards the houses of Afro-Brazilian cults over the country. We, the outsiders, have still the chance to get to know a more natural way of life, a dialog between man and nature.

It is time to have a touching feeling of how good it is to share our problems, to recover with the help of our social surroundings. Our biological heritage, our basic needs for survival will have a noble complement in sharing our joint experiences with people of different social and spiritual background.

References

Alan Tomaid Campbell, 1995. *Getting to Know Waiwai. An Amazonian ethnography*, Routledge, London.

Liz Hosken,1999. 'Biodiversity: Green Gold or Sacred Teacher?' *Compas Newsletter*, October 1991, pp. 18-19.

5. Exploitation of Space and Urban Environment

Heidi Dumreicher

Bettina Kolb

Seven Theses on Town and City Quality

Abstract

The way in which public and private space is used, organised, shaped and furnished expresses both the degree of societal coherence as well as the meaning this space has for the individuals. We understand that the shaping of public space is the counter-form of the image that individuals and societal groups have of public space. The physical organisation of public space, on the other hand, shapes the life that is led in that space. Both factors reciprocally influence one another in an iterative process and in a mutual relationship.

The seven theses on town and city quality are part of a sustainable city-scenario: The first practical application field of a sociological theory for urban sustainability. The seven theses have emerged through the methodology of objective hermeneutics. Texts of a photo-questionnaire formed the data -set that we used (Photobefragung, Wuggenig 1990), combined with interviews in the technique of circular questioning (Selvini-Palozzoli). Our team, a researcher of sustainability and a sociologist, followed the steps of interpretation described by objective hermeneutics theory after Ulrich Oevermann (Oevermann 1993). We used, for the first time, a combination of photo-questioning and hermeneutical sequencial analysis. The vivid, active and associative quality of the interviews de–monstrates that we have found a way to reveal the tacit knowledge of the interview partners and therefore managed to go a long way in developing participative social-scientific methods through the art of interpretation.

The seven theses on urban quality are a result of the research grant "Ein urbanes Nachhaltigkeitsprojekt" and they are in line with a research paradigm of sustainable interdisciplinary research work. Project leader: Oikodrom – Institute for urban sustainability; Auftraggeber: bm:wv, BMLF, country Lower Austria, EFRE, City Vienna (MA18 and MDEU).

Overview

1. The Urban Diversity

The city in its complexity generates dichotomies with manifold equivocal images: human scale versus anonymity, freedom versus loss of control, the small scale of a village versus contradictory urbanity.

2. Urban Life needs a town which provides services

A town's acknowledged attraction derives in part from the provision of basic urban services, from proximity supply to public utilities and infrastructure. Conceptualizing the Sustainable City means reconceptualizing the way in which the city administration and ordinary citizens share roles and responsibilities, and do so comfortably without resorting to excessive moralizing.

3. The emotional co-ownership of the city

Usage creates signification. Only if the dwellers use the potential of the city and what it has to offer (including the amenities of public space) will they be able to fully identify with the place, releasing space from abstraction.

4. The city as a stage

The town is a place for self-representation. Today, this quality has been marginalized by the tyranny of intimacy and by over-commercialisation.

5. The near, the foreign, the far away in town

The quality of urban life is a function of the quality of the dwelling and workplace environment, in combination with the opportunities offered by the city-centre together with its integrated suburbs and its immediate surroundings.

6. The city map in the mind

Points for orientation in the city are on the one hand the sightseeing sites and major foreground buildings, and on the other hand the places which attract and support urban life through their functional quality and through built-in history.

7. Space is formless, but it is shaped by objects with form

Space itself is limitless, but its quality is determined by the ways in which it is shaped and limited - from the scale of buildings and groups of buildings to the scale of urban furnishings within the space.

Thesis one

The urban diversity

The city in its complexity generates dichotomies with manifold equivocal images: human scale versus anonymity, freedom versus loss of control, the small scale of a village versus contradictory urbanity.

The classy hotel and the refugee asylum, the city park and the tiny open space next door, the multi-story office building and the coachman-hut: the very nature of the city is diversity - the dense neighbourhoods of diverse structures and the multiplication of possibilities. The city with all its opaque complexities creates dichotomies, which paint a picture of mutual contradictions.

The social know how, which townspeople have acquired over time, to cope with the numerous rules of the urban realm, is today reaching its limits.

Until the recent past, towns were like islands within a larger society, organising the society but also exploiting it, and shifting the output into its own direction. " In the present tense the towns are faster and clearer tending to become a structure of this society by themselves. Therefore city-planning transforms into immediate society planning and last but not least into the planning of the towns' exterior relations." (Reiterer 1998b: 240)

The yearning for clarity and orientation stands in contrast to the desire for anonymity in the large city. But this anonymity is also to be understood as a dichotomy. If the "number of possible social relations is growing according the formula nx(n-1)/2 " (Reiterer 1998b: 245), the organisation of the relations on a personal basis is not possible any more and the capacity of the whole society to steer and control its own relations is overextended. Even with the assumed number of 5000 people who would be living in a district like the Vienna Westbahnhof City-as-a-hill (LEVINE 1999) the limits for the organisation of personal relations is exceeded. According to the mathematical formula above there would be a number of nearly 13 million possibilities of social contacts between all dwellers in a district of 5000 dwellers. So it is evident that such a system is remote from the possibility of control as well as of planning.

The fear to loose control may very likely be a part of the discomfort with towns. On the other hand the absence of oppressing social control can be felt as a big relief. In the confusing street patterns of the old European towns or in the winding passages of the oriental bazaar the stranger, the refugee, the pariah can hide and escape the pursuer – be it the law as well as the gang of criminals. In its opaque and diffuse diversity, town is a place of social security in a double sense: The town enables security and safety by the possibility of encounter – or security and safety by the possibility by of escape. "Stadtluft macht frei" - "Town air makes you free" is a common saying from the European middle ages where farmers could get free from their fief by getting inside the town walls. Within the social closeness of neighbourhoods anonymity gets cancelled, anonymity cancels the social control.

The city as social eco-system requires a mental integration of the single household, neighbourhood, district and town, and lives from diversity at small scale, for instance a good mix of branches. Likewise towns need diverse social patterns ranging from neighbourhood integration to global networking. The offer of diverse livingstyles is a good argument for a life in town especially for young people.

The town is a place where new societal developments with their new requirements are conceptualised and negotiated. In contrast to the small town the metropolis needs controversial architecture. The architectonic language should not be a homogenous soup. In the diversified town there is a wide realm of human standards ranging from the spaces of inhospitability to the needs of human scale, lest of philistinism. There is an aesthetic language for the cosiness and well-being and one for the sinister and bulky. The shape of town (Gestalt) will not be decided in ballot processes but the biographical connections rouse the needs concerning the spatial structure.

"Out of accommodation and diversity the urban situation rises." (Feldtkeller 1984: 38)

Thesis two

Urban life needs a town which provides services

A town's acknowledged attraction derives in part from the provision of basic urban services, from proximity supply to public utilities. Conceptualising the Sustainable City means reconceptualising the way in which the city administration and ordinary citizens share roles and responsibilities, and doing so comfortably without resorting to excessive moralizing.

Besides a social diversity of living patterns, economic diversity supports the service aspect of a town. In the beginning of the 21st century this service aspect of town has developed a new character. In some countries there are concrete moves to reorientate public offices and administrative institutions towards a more user-friendly customer relationship. (In Italy: City bureaus "Tempi della città"; in Hamburg: Service point "Zeiten und Qualität der Stadt", opened in 1997)

“Shop opening hours, traffic hours, school-, caring-, Kindergarten- and opening hours of diverse institutions are not per se urban topics, but they are only interesting for people when linked with the organisation of their own everyday-life which is basically interest bound respectively bound to the own life under changing societal conditions." (Krämer- Badoni, in Mückenberger 1998: 94)

As working hours are constantly getting more flexible and more variable, the client develops a need for modifying the opening hours of services to accommodate these new conditions. In the course of our research the interview partners described the aspects of urban services and the town itself as a place where convenience in everyday life is particularly valued. It is characteristic that the dwellers assume the qualities of urban services as a given, an a priori. They judge the service aspect as an unalterable functional basis and premise of the town. This refers to shopping opportunities and to administration services, but also to an ever increasing mobility. Convenient public transport clearly raises the life quality of a residential area.

The availability and convenience of public transport as well as many other, often invisible, self regulating systems are a major part of the urban services supporting everyday life. The basic supply aspects of the town consist of an available administration, assured infrastructure, fluid mobility, an extensive health care system and sufficient leisure time possibilities. The remark of Karl Kraus: "I expect from a town in which I want to live: asphalt, cleaning of the streets, house-door key, air-heating, warm-water-pipeline. Homey I can be by myself." supports the contention that the services aspect is part of the traditional equipment of a town. Places with service profile give various opportunities for social and cultural exchange and at the same time they are places with many opportunities for an economic life, added value and employment. Being asked the explicit question of the advantages of living in a town all interview partners confirmed exactly these values. But these issues are also mentioned quasi incidentally when superficially other topics are discussed in the main cause. In these cases, they are often formulated as normative expectations, which not only concern the individual alone but also his or her environment. Not only the next grocery shop is at stake, the opening hours of the district's post office or the intervals of the tramway, it is the short-distance supply (Nahversorgung) for the collective neighbourhood and the whole town.

The interview partners are far from neglecting these semi-public interests: There is an awareness that specific groups of the population need specific services. In this way the connection of economic and social considerations show their links already at the level of the service aspect. One of our interview partners speaks about the service in his neighbourhood and it is evident to him that the dwellers of an almshouse nearby benefit from living next to a drugstore and on the other hand the almshouse guarantees the drugstore a permanent stock of customers. In this sense the link between social and economic life is also described as an important characteristic of the town. Even if the discussion about the almshouse does not concern our partner, he is still aware of this service and considers it a value beyond his individual interest.

Environmentalists often assume that in a sustainable town all dwellers would have to check and verify every single action in terms of environmental consequences in a series of minimal daily decisions ranging from cleaning the milk bottle to using the bicycle. Yet the majority of people would be hopelessly overtaxed in doing so, especially if on top of that they would also have to keep a composting toilet working by themselves. Fundamentalist ecologists tend to assume the highly unlikely prospect that people living in the sustainable town would be willing and able to follow such a highly complex and difficult lifestyle. It would be difficult to raise their interest in such issues, yet even more out of the question that they would engage on collegially sensitive action. The key to dealing with this difficulty is to take it from the deliberate activities of each individual or each household and shift it to the level of services provided by the town's public administration.

A successful strategy for urban sustainability would be to establish an environmentally based range of basic services from short-distance supply to separated drinking and grey water pipelines. This relieves people from infrastructure concerns and enables them to shift their attention to more relevant questions of living quality. They may trust that environmentally based services are accomplished as a matter of course within sustainable city scenario of the city-as-a-hill (Dumreicher 1999). In history, the dwellers of a town have experienced that the instance at which the service questions are dealt with is the administration (and not the household), they consider it a distinct historically proved right to rely on the town administration in these topics. In this respect the theory of the sustainable town relieves the town-dweller of the excessive ethical burden of continual involvement with rules imposed in accommodating the many basic services. With such an approach, the dwellers of a sustainable district will be able to assume that the town management is using the systems and technologies that will have no negative effect on the environment or on the city system and that the administration is constantly self evaluating the status quo.

In urban architecture in the broad sense, the shape of space is the basis for social and cultural life and is designed to support that social and cultural life. Accordingly, the physical town provides the infrastructure as well as the spatial conditions within which the social town may flourish. Not only do groups who are willing to act in public space have to learn their lessons to become professionals in bureaucracy, but similarly the town administration has to develop an understanding of its role as the professional purveyor to the citizens of the necessary know how such as: easy-to-handle-submission processes for district events and demonstrations, cleaning services after those events, even the provision of outlets with the required voltage – these are the new realms of activity for the future citizen service of public space. The aim is not that the administration must incorporate the ideas of the civil society and execute them by itself. First of all it is necessary to acknowledge the emerging civil society as such, and then to support it as equal partner and vivacious actor in the public culture of the town. In this way a new balance seeking a tying process between civil society and the society of power will be established.

Thesis three

The emotional co-ownership of the city

Usage creates signification. Only if the dwellers use the potential of the city and what it has to offer (including the amenities of public space) will they be able to fully identify with the place, releasing space from abstraction.

The quality we can see in the town is a structure which is the product of an evolutionary process taking hundreds of years. In this respect the town can be understood as collective piece of art, which accommodates to each societal situation in a permanent process of provision, usage and testing, changing and adapting. Today, we find strong tendencies to misunderstand the city as a kind of self-service shop and to dilute the qualities of a person living in a town to a person using the town. ("From the urban dweller to the urban user.")

Our research shows that only the usage of urban service creates identification with the place. Only the personal use of public space, like parks and streets and semi-public spaces, like shops in the neighbourhood and cinemas enables people to realise its value and to create a personal nearness to the place. It's the specific social actions like shopping, playing, etc. that produce this kind of personal vicinity, which creates a relation with a town district. People who don't show interest their living environment and know neither neighbours nor town spaces are also uninterested in it's design as well. They tend to give very negative comments and feedback.

This potential of significance can substantiate either in the rejection of the city qualities or in their acknowledgement and thus be taken as a resource. Georg Simmel (1903) showed in his sociology of space the inseparable link of social action and fixed place in the example of a religiously defined space of action: a church. If people are to feel well in a town, it needs clearly defined spaces, to which the collective memory can attach. Even for people who have never in their lives been in the Vienna opera house the symbolic value of the opera is so essential, that large expenditures for conserving it are justified in their eyes. So even the non-individual use as place creates a meaning for the individual at the symbolic level.

Urban space which is not used loses its symbolic value and its function: If for instance cultural contradictions in a district lead to conflicts in a public park and when this escalates to violence, the park cannot be used anymore and as a consequence the park loses its function as a communication and recreation area. On the other hand, local initiatives can take over the responsibility of negotiating new rules for communication among the users, they can establish new way of using the place and thereby rediscover the positive attributes of the green space making it again usable by the diverse communities.

The thesis that only usage creates meaning may sound trivial, but it stands at the very beginning of social conflicts, which appear in the adoption of places. As a general reduction of meaning of public spaces is evident, amongst others because the new media have taken over some of their functions, the question arises, whether it is sufficient if the town supplies its dwellers with public space. It rather seems necessary to care for new stagings, new productions, new acitvities. Such productions can be directed by social initiatives, which act at the interface between spatial and social frameworks with their district festivals, flea markets on shopping streets, attendance in parks and other kinds of haunting social work. In this way, public space can be experimental space, where actors apply their social know-how and develop it further.

Due to the current tendency to clear out the public space, the usability and furthermore the possibility to build up personal relationships among the town dwellers gets lost. If on the other hand a town is furnished in a way that enables multifunctional usage, it is - as a supplementation to an exactly defined space - a crucial element for the quality of town. As diverse usage is possible in a principal way, but nevertheless uncommon, traditional planning causes one-sided usage: Bicycle trails have to be there just for cyclists, children playgrounds have to be separated by age, railway stations are only places for arrival and departure, but none for experience. Benches have their assorted users – but in case of usage by other, uncommon groups or even for other purposes than just sitting, protest arises.

Various examples how park users deal with benches differently show that an object of utility can be a starting point for creative usage. A wooden bench can be a bicycle stand, a soccer-goal, a chat-corner and a sunbath deck chair. You can even hang it between two children swings and have great fun swinging on it. Especially the youths who are evidently under-equipped in the Viennese parks are using these opportunities. This multifunctional usage of town furniture may cause protests from the other park visitors, but it shows at the same time that a very simple infrastructure – in this case the park benches - may be a prerequisite for the quality of the town. The personal use, maybe not the one foreseen by the planners, creates a new space of opportunity (Möglichkeitsraum) and vitalizes the public space. "I have some drugstores nearby", one interview partner relates. He could have used the more neutral wording: "There are some drugstores in the district" (Interview 1) When he chooses the verb "have", relating it to himself – "I have"– he indicates that he feels to be an "emotional co-owner" of the town. This very personal saying arising from personal need and benefit points toward a participational ownership even at the level of infrastructural facilities. It is first of all this stakeholdeship of the dwellers that creates a vital town.

The concept of sustainability takes into account that human beings are aware of their environment, that it is important for them and above all that they are interested in investing in its modification and shaping (Gestaltung). If the public space is given back to the people as their property and if they are encouraged them to use it, one basic condition for a sustainability process has been accomplished. In the compass of sustainability (Dumreicher 1999) developed by Oikodrom, the term "Verortung" was introduced for this phenomenon. The acquisition of space by the individual finds its reflection in public: If I (co-)own the street, in the emotional rather than in a classical economic sense, then I (co)-determine by my use what is going to happen there. Therefore I define a limited power over the used space for myself. Space indeed does not only represent the power of the various controlling devices and authorities, ranging from the town administration to multi-national companies, but also the individual claim of each single person, by using it as anonymous car driver, who demands street space for parking and driving, or as anonymous dog-owner, who wants a territory for his/her pet, or as a demonstrator, who protests against globalisation, or finally as a children's group, that plans to have a lantern feast. The emotional accesses are highly divergent: "This is my bench, I'm sitting here." (vagabond) "This is my bank (bench) and it reaches the sky." (official from the World Bank.

Thesis four

The city as a stage

The town is a place for self-representation. Today, this quality has been marginalized by the tyranny of intimacy or by over-commercialisation.

The texture of the town in its very different spatial forms is a stage for different performances at a time. The flaneur is his own director. The director of a demonstration eventually is the global policy, the director of a network-breakfast in the district is a handful of engaged citizens. The actors define and shape the place: "democrats sit in the parliament and slobs or anarchists march on the streets" that's the perspective of an interview partner to the commentator on the radio. (Mittagsjournal Ö1, 5.12.2000) Beside the existing and predefined locations, there arises a culture of time-limited stages: let us call them "ad-hoc places". Building gaps are ephemeral playgrounds, useless pedestrian underpasses mutate to become a fashionable dancing field for excluded groups, who present themselves as important part of the population via their spatial presence and in so doing cannot be overlooked any longer.

The town as space is experienced in different functional connections and shaped, used and demanded from different actors: In the texture of the town, streets are places of meaning for the dwellers, they are places of activities and identification with the urban district. Frequently emerging out of historic village centers, the streets remain carriers of special meanings, where the visible and invisible energies of the town melt into one another. In these places one can find business-world and administration, service facilities and cultural societies, restaurants and private, most beloved places.

The city as a "stage where concrete living styles can be developed" was demanded in an interview and understood as basis of urban life. For city planning that would mean to understand the planned place actually as stage and to understand city planning itself as designer of the stage, which then is made available for the dwellers. The citizens are the ones who shape the show and they get the inspiration for their drama through the circumstance that the urban stage of the city is still part of the collective memory.

"In the city there is a constraint to representation. In the age of growing anonymisation the dwellers cannot rely anymore on the fact that their counterparts are able to understand and interpret them according their history, origin and living connections. Selfpositioning becomes essential unless one wouldn't be noticed and understood at all." (Novy 1993: 55; according to Bahrt 1961: 38)

Though the street is no longer a place for kissing and children's games at the beginning of the 21st century, the remembrance of such a state is still present in our conversations.

In Europe, the dwellers are obliged to give a precise announcement about the location of their main living place (obligation to register / Meldepflicht), in this respect, too, the place becomes a coordination system of urban respectively governmental control. This communication pattern about urban space is the basis for usage by the public administration: only he who has an officially registered address is able to use the service aspects of the town. In addition, the assignment of the place through a personnel address marks the interface between public and private space. The importance of the address when people want to build up a relation to their living place can be filtered out of a report over the Rennbahnweg city expansion area in Vienna. The reporter describes the atmosphere in this living complex for 10.000 people and resumes that the wish for diversification of the people was not respected at all in the planning process: "12.000 people live at one single house number." (Die Presse, 20.2.1999: 12)

The topic "address" is present even in the virtual space, the Cyberspace: Yet there, the internet address provides information about the professional and social embedding of the website provider. The American media artist Paul Garin has picked up this topic: Instead of the currently usual - in his perspective – military - like codes of the internet addresses (diacritic signs and interpunctuations), he proposes new aesthetics of the internet address, which should fulfil an artistic as well as an everyday life claim. His project additionally touches a socio-political realm when he puts forward that internet addresses are dealt in a manner similar to the way in which highly valuable addresses in physical space are assigned. "And so speculation began... They have sold the names for ten-, hundred-, thousand-times of the value – if they managed to do so. For example "business.com" was sold for 150.000 dollars." (Nova Ö1 feature, 2./3. 2. 1999)

When even in cyberspace the spaces dissolve and the address nevertheless remains important, this is even more the case for the built city, its streets and house numbers, which have materialised in a long lasting process. The address here has a similar meaning as the threshold (Schwelle), which symbolises the interface between inside and outside and marks the entry into the private sphere.

The interface guarantees reachability and availability for all the other dwellers and for the public administration, but it is also "door-guard". Here it will be determined who is allowed to step over the interface of the door-threshold and who isn't. By tradition and default this threshold was controlled and secured by a porter or a caretaker (the famous Viennese Hausbesorgerin), meanwhile they are step by step replaced by technical equipment: a talk-back circuit enables control from the person living within that territory. An intermediate system is the one used in Paris, where you open the door of the house by entering a code. This system provides the opportunity of access to an enlarged, yet limited group of affiliated persons: Those who own the key by owning the code. In public buildings the control happens through the use of video cameras, a development which will be extended to private houses in the future: in the first phase highly protected, remote one-family houses, later on even densely settled city areas will install them. Especially in Japan a "smart-house", which should automatically control and scan visitors with a camera is in the planning stage.

The governmental control respects the described interface "addresses" by law and assumes that all things happening behind the threshold doors are running well and are within the law. In a democratic system the state abstains from control of the private sphere, which is over the threshold and concedes that the private space of acting and moving is off limits.

The citizen who leaves the private and secured space and walks on the street enters a place where he/she has to be in line with the public order and rules. If his/her behaviour steps beyond the common codes, the citizen needs the benevolence of the administration or even the permission from a public bureaucracy (for instance permission to hold a demonstration). This may be an inconvenience in the single case, but generally speaking this codex of rules for the public space is necessary in order to make the community work. How far a kind of "rulification" (Verregelung) of the public space results from specific regulations from the public authorities, is in discretion of the political representation and is determined culturally. Therefore it can be seen as a field of conflicts for the society as a whole. The small festival event of a civil initiative or a non-profit organisation has to overcome the same sort of regulations and hurdles at the hands of the public authorities as would a big political rally or a commercial event.

Recent events prove that today public space is still a place for carrying out diverse conflicts. At a demonstration of Kurds on 20.2.1999 in the Viennese Mariahilferstraße, there arose not only a political conflict, but also one about the usage of space between the demonstrators and the shop owners. The use of the streets for non-profit purposes was seen as interfering with business. "There's no business then. Just the regular customers are coming" the initiator of a petition against demonstrations on shopping Saturdays claimed. (Die Presse, 27.2.1999: 12) In 1998, the strongly frequented Mariahilferstraße was a site for demonstrations seventeen times. Proposals to establish a detour for the demonstration through the neighbouring Burggasse or a shift to the Heldenplatz miss the point: actually the fact that people use a public place intensively, attracts more people to that place and triggers a process of vitality to that place.

Along the usage of the public space a commercialisation process of the public space is coming up: Space as economic resource gains significance and relevance and designs the economic and cultural framing conditions. Staging and commercialisation processes are also pushed forward and supported by politics and administration. The Viennese Rathaussquare is meanwhile managed the whole year, from Christkindlmarket, to circus, ice-skating and opening of the Wiener Festwochen till the summer music-film festival: different interest groups may find corresponding offers. But commercialisation alone doesn't provide a permanent ticket ("Persilschein") for the usage of public space in a non-established way. In case such initiatives in the public space are carried out by non-governmental organisations (instead of the city administration itself like on the Rathausplatz), these events are taken as starting points for cultural politic discussions: This was the case, e.g. in Vienna, with like the highly frequented "movies under the stars" (Kino unter Sternen) or the open-air movie-series in the Krieau which have appropirated green fields. They are standing under permanent justification pressure and furthermore, despite their commercial success, they are even forced by administrative side paths to give up. For smaller projects for/in the public space the overcoming of bureaucratic and political hurdles very often is so demanding, that initiatives are extinguished at the very beginning. The question is, if and how the obeying of the regulations for the public space has to be controlled, who has to execute this control and which methods are eligible.

By their control of the public space the authorities administrate the freedom of movement of the citizens, the interests of the abutting owners at such an event, the public security as well as the existing abstract mental pattern of well behaviour and order. The state of interests of the involved persons is various and quite often contradictory. In this respect the interests for a undisturbed private sphere and protection from noise is according the vigilantes prior to the interests of a community based city for which vivid street-scenaries are essential. In the measurement program of the still valid Viennese traffic concept it regrets that the street space above all is considered an "ordered regulated nationally prescribed space" (Traffic concept Vienna 1994), (Verkehrskonzept Wien 1994), which the concept is interpreting as loss of urban living quality. Thus the traffic concept designs measures, which open new alternatives to old functions of the public space.

Something new on the streets is quite often sensed as very threatening even though its just the small street event of a civil initiative. To be peaceful and quiet is not only said to be the first civil duty but for many people it simply seems to be the epitome of an ideal situation. But empty and swept out streets containing nothing frightening or strange are only seemingly safe: What at first glance seems to be safe and pleasant can become very quickly a threatening and nightmarish place, which to enter no one dares.

When the streets are left of people they don't invite to be used anymore and there arises a self reinforcing process which furthermore depopulates the public space.

Instead of getting security via social presence the spiral is spinning towards insecurity via social absence. As counter-strategy you could choose the unimaginable because resource-consuming omnipresence of public vigilantes. A measure easier to be financed yet much more effective and human would be: Securing the diversity in the public roles and the presence in the public space.

This can be done by daily users of the streets as well as by individuals and groups who understand the city as stage and additionally stage it in their sense. On this stage you find actors as well as observers, both – just because of their presence in the public space – reclusively demand the security and the rules for a community stimulating behaviour on the stage.

For debates about sustainability, the public space as a stage for participation is a crucial point. Civil movements (Bürgerbewegungen), local initiatives, protest movements have rediscovered the street as a medium for their interests and raised a claim for their emotional ownership. Meanwhile the civil initiatives tend to move away from their self-understanding as protest movements. A development from being *against* something to being *for* something has taken place. One example for this trend is the project "Permanent Breakfast" in Vienna and Graz, in which small groups occupy public space for performing peaceful rituals, for instance a breakfast. They produce a nicely covered table and take a lot of time for a breakfast in the middle of a place crowded with automobile traffic and invite other passers-by to enjoy together with them this unconventional moment of public presence.

Thesis five

The near, the foreign, the far away in town

> The quality of urban life is a function of the quality of the dwelling and workplace environment, in combination with the opportunities offered by the city-centre together with its integrated suburbs and its immediate surroundings.

On the one hand, the large city is metropolis and distance, it contains the far away and the strange, on the other hand it's a place where the need of closeness is satisfied. Village-like structures which are still expressed in the current district-names (Fünfhaus, Sechshaus, Floridsdorf) bestow the dwellers some reference points for a spatial and social way of being at home. In that way the anonymity of the large city can be cancelled to some extend. A diversity of contacts, of pathways and acquaintances in the own close living environment was eminently important to the female interview partners. They describe the close and concise communication, they sense and reflect themselves as part of this communication, they watch it, as they take part in it and are its stakeholders. Here again the importance of the "emotional co-ownership" (thesis three) as crucial factor for urban living quality is implicitly referred to by the concerned persons.

It seems to be evident that especially in the age of globalisation and the world-wide reachability of places and availability of the communication media the closeness again achieves bigger relevance. The supplement of high tech with high touch is described by the future-researcher John

Naisbitt by means of his personal dwelling biography. He chose to live in a village of 1400 people in the Rocky Mountains, in 3000 metres altitude. (Nova; Ö1 feature, 18.5.1999)

Talking to one another doesn't include any coincidental person in the public space, but it is codetermined by your own patterns of solidarity.

The small-scale communication is even present - at least as idealised imagination - among persons who are telling about themselves that they don't even know the people in their own living house. But the small-term village-like communication can also be unwanted and reach a character of control: It's not just you to observe, you are being observed as well. The ambivalence towards close neighbours appears in the dialogues: One interview partner complains about the "neighbour boys who are coming to make us angry. Normally I don't like this kind of village-thing, but in the city it's okay."

In the city you find both, the near and the far away, at the same time. Emmanuel Levinas talks about the "neighbourhood of the unknown", and our interview partners speak about the village-like closeness and the city-like distance nearly during one take of breath. While in terms of closeness it's important to get along well and to look through the local and social structures, in terms of distance to the unknown, the unexpected, the surprising and scary may be and shall be a distinct part of the metropolis-puzzle. While speaking about the village-like closeness, the service aspect of the city comes into expression. An interview partner points out how many institutions he can reach on foot: " everything I have is nearby" and he tells at the same time that he regards the sometimes near and sometimes far city centre, which he uses now and then, as supplement to the cosy living environment in his village: "If I want to, I'm outside town very quickly and if I want to go for a walk, I am downtown in no time". This shows clearly that he sees the urban diversity as a self-evident and somehow natural urban quality. Even a ride to other districts in the same town (in our case the Viennese districts between Ring and Gürtel) is a kind of Sunday trip to our interview partner. In this context, the service character of the city means that the citizen is offered a metro or a tramway nearby which allows him or her to comfortably use the multiplicity of the urban districts.

Another attraction of the large city is the fact that the dweller may develop native feelings of homeliness for different places without the need to decide for one of them exclusively. A dweller from the Viennese Alsergrund will find his or her social and economic networks in the nearby neighbourhood and enjoy a very different, yet familiar urban atmosphere in the quarter around his or her working location. If the own district (Grätzel) is getting too boring, the dweller can choose to go to the Graben in the city center looking for a very different urban quality. You have a different relationship to the strange and "other" in the city differs as opposed to the feelings in your village-like urban environment. Even in the metropolis, the village-like closeness needs to include urban diversity: "I have grocers, some four or five large markets, butchers, a tobacconist,

I get everything nearby, shoemaker, hairdresser." Even in the contemporaneous city, the medieval structure has survived in which similar sellers offer their services in the same street, one just beside each other. Streetnames in the Vienna Inner City like Fleischmarkt, Kohlmarkt, Heumarkt – (meat market, cabbage market, hay market)... remind us of those practies which still seem to function even in the age of competition.

The success of such apparent mono-structures could result out of the fact that they are capable of fulfilling very individual wishes within the range of one branch. Markets grant a big diversity in an economic as well as in a social respect and link the service character of the city with the closeness of a village square. If similar products are for sale at a market or in a shopping street, this animates the dweller to a specific behaviour: He distributes his shopping and visiting activities to different booths, and this leads to an equitable distribution of the money flow. The intuitive rule for the market is: At one stand you choose your apples, at the next the pears and you pay your visit to the whole market.

Markets have the prime function of economic supply, but they are also important centres of communication. In the large city, markets of every special kind emerge: Flee markets develop an independent dynamics far away from the common urban order and straightness. There are less social and economic regulations and the accepted behaviour can be negotiated form case to case: The city as a stage has a different character on different occasions. The Viktor-Adler-market, the Brunnen-market, the Meisel-market or the Nasch-market have their own corporate identity, their own strategies for marketing and customers. The markets function within different spatial and temporal structures: The Brunnen-market has a different shopping public than the Nasch-market, and the differentiation process also happens along temporal lines. The flaneur combines a visit to the Saturday flee market with the usual weekend shopping tour, with a ramble at the junk dealers and the antiquity stores or with a visit to an Italian coffee bar.

During the daily flow, very diverse patterns can be detected in the visitors patterns. Structures similar to the old marketplace are increasing again – a proof for the fact that the atmosphere of the market is still attractive.

While the traditional markets mute into centres which attract visitors beyond the shopping interest, at the western railway station an inverse process is taking place: what has begun as a mere crossing point of different traffic streams now expands into a place of economic and social communication. At the big scale, similar phenomenona emerge at other traffic crossing points. Every airport has its duty-free zone, every bus station has its café. City planning would be on the right trail to bear in mind these tendencies: Stop zones of the public transport system can be upgraded to centres for service, information and social exchange, even for economic short-distance supply, instead of leaving it to the gasoline station to become the market leaders for small scale shopping.

In the sustainability discussion, the question of closeness and distance is permanently present and described with the slogan "think globally, act locally".

This kind of thinking is a survival question for the large city. The town requires the relation of its dwellers with the local interests, the identification with the happenings at local level and the engagement for the closeness. Yet in parallel, the large city is an arena for regional, national and global developments. The city is the area in which relevant societal developments are bursting out. Just as the big revolutions in history which arose in the city, the new issue of sustainability is also part of urban thinking tradition. In the research landscape, sustainability still needs to make an effort to include the city as a topic. "The city is our thoroughly dug and well-trained disputation field for social responsibility and innovation. We would fail in making happen sustainability as a socio-political century task, if we give up this disputation field and take refuge to an appearing harmony of sub-urbanity. Politics has necessarily to do with polis." (von Winning, 3.3.1999, Internet)

Thesis six

The city-map in the mind

Points for orientation in the city are on the one hand the sightseeing sites and major foreground buildings, and on the other hand the places which attract and support urban life through their functional quality and through built-in history.

In order to find his ways through life, the city dweller permanently carries around a citymap in the mind, as a means for orientation and for differentiation. It's interesting to see which points or buildings appear as a coordination system in this map-in-the-mind: the interview partners do not primarily hold on commercial institutes like a supermarket, but rather cite proeminent architectonic points, the railway stations or the Danube channel bridges. Both places are defined by their static, stony qualities as monuments as well as by the people who grant these places their dynamics. Following the thesis "usage creates significance" it also turns out in this connection that places with an intense socio-cultural significance are much more constitutive for the map in the mind than just simply built structures. The big number of people and the corresponding social presence is responsible for structuring the city. The architectonically significant buildings may serve on the other hand more as a basis of communication with those people who are not familiar with the district. The village-like closeness is described via the own movement through the urban space.

While in a classic perspective the big architectonic deals, the cathedral of St. Stefan, the Tower of London, the Arc de Triomphe, are represented as essential building events, on a pragmatic and symbolic level the points of orientation are much more differentiated. Really important are places of dynamics, places where something is in move, is happening, places of societal movement: A bridge, a station, a market. Something "show-able" can also be a point of orientation, an attraction, a sight-seeing object, which - if possible - attracts people, raises the value of the neighbourhood and provides it with higher significance.

The life feeling in the flat is an outcome of the surrounding buildings, and of the dynamic life they can create through and beyond their physical quality. Its not irrelevant what you see when you are looking out of your window. In the ideal case your window, this interface between interior and exterior, between private and public, provides you with a diverse urban outlook.

The wideness of the large city can even be a reason to move. In choosing the points of reference for your orientation, you show objective urban qualities like the places of movement or the built artefacts. But they get their supplement in your subjective impressions. Especially remarkable to us was that our interview partner mentioned the almshouse. The reason may be that this building has some personal relevance to him, as he is in advanced age and may want to know what architectural setting will be the precondition for his own future; on the other hand, the almshouse stays for the yet unknown, for a place you are not supposed to enter – the almshouse as the built counterform of a big taboo of our time.

When discussing urban sustainability, this means that it is desirable to create places characterized by diversity. The need for closeness mustn't lead to a uniform planning style of a whole city district. The need for dynamics and mobility, in supplement to quiet neighbourhoods, can be linked with a resource saving paradigm of planning. If, instead of the single buildings, the city of short distances ("Stadt der kurzen Wege") with its many details, with connected pathways through the city and their junction points are top priority aspects for the planner, then an urban Gestalt may arise in which people can combine urban living quality with the needs of the future generations.

Thesis seven

Space is formless, but it is shaped by objects with form

Space itself is limitless, but its quality is determined by the ways in which it is shaped and limited – from the scale of buildings and groups of buildings to the scale of urban furnishings within the space.

The theses described so far are the result of an analysis of space from the perspective of social usage. The seventh thesis turns the instrumentarium around and interprets the social living from the perspective of space. Topics which have been determined socially are now appearing in their spatial dimension. The aim to connect social aspects with spatial Gestalt is claimed in some innovative city planning projects, yet this approach hasn't been imposed as a standard so far. Aesthetics, beauty, shape and similar questions are marginalized in the sustainability discussion, but they could establish the basis for a higher acceptance of its values. With our theses, we follow the track of a dynamic balance between social life and its special counter form.

Public space in the city appears often in the form of a green spot-in-between, of interim green („Abstandsgrün"), as a traffic area without room for urbanistic shaping, moreover as a necessary evil or an as in-between rather than in its quality of urban development. Nevertheless, the public space is a conflict space for various groups of interest:

By planning the buildings, the architect defines what will be around the space; the space in-between, then is the tentillate of the built space.

The arts set accents who reflect the freedom of expression and invite for interpretation.

Various public services from traffic to the department for sewage construction toil up and down the pedestrian and traffic ways.

The economy raises its demand for customer friendliness and conforms to the current concept of mobility that annihilates the space.

Public space is also a playground for administrative planning. Spatial planning determines specific kinds of usages and thereby builds the premises for a social living, for economic development, for shaping of free space or prescribes a spatial separation of the diverse functions in the city. Public and semi-public space - for instance the backyards of the founderageblocks (Gründerzeitwohnblocks) - is a realm for starting points of trans-magistrative activities, here the need for so-called horizontal approaches is especially evident. For the dwellers, the city space is a very much essential and materialised living world. Here social acting, interaction, disputation, conflict and communication is enabled. Here the social shaping competence of the dwellers can concretize: It is the place for playing, working, chatting, shopping and demonstrating, for upcoming mobility and dynamics or else for peace and composury idleness. In the interviews, different categories of space showed up, which came along with social standardization and aesthetic assignments. We can sort out large-scale and small-scalle city maps in the mind: The district, the city and the periphery.

The neighbourhood, the space surrounding your living space, is sensed in a similar way as your own flat or house: you know which furniture to expect at which place. Our interviewpartners know their urban space in a similar way:

In contrast with the very common feeling for the neighbourhood, for the trusted and the functioning, there stand some few but nevertheless distinctfully described built elements: The Franz Josephs-Station and the Friedensbridge. In these buildings social functionality and professional architectonic shaping are linked together. It's not free of accidence that these buildings equipped with own names are standing in contrast with the day-to-day-network of buildings.

The buildings sorted out by name do have - aside from their function in the district - a relation to the city as whole: The railwaystation, the undeground stop, the bridge, set the district within its relation to its urban connection as a whole. These buildings also constitute a historical context, these buildings in their functionality are the built-in presence of historical events and give a historical background to the "today".

The third dimension of the spatial map in the mind, the periphery, is described by negative attributions. The periphery seems to be the counterpart of the district on the one hand and of the vivid city on the other hand. Among other reasons this area becomes a „non-space", because there is no continuous space from the neighbourhood to the periphery. There is no trespassing by public transport. City is felt just as a distance, which is hard to overcome. In addition, there is no entertainment reason that would make you eager to take upon the burden of getting over this in between-space. There is neither a jazz bar nor a Schönbrunn castle waiting for you, just the unattractive "Schrebergarden".

A discussion of the centre-periphery-problem in this study would lead too far, at least it can be said that the city edge as the borderline between city and countryside is also a borderline between nature- and culture-society: The city stands as a "place of tidyness and order", the periphery becomes a place of "the repressed, infective and dirt." (Hainzel 1995)

Does someone who lives in a street that was formerly part of a village and is now part of the city area, live on the land or in the town? (Feldtkeller 1994)

Out of these city-edge areas, the intermediate town („Zwischenstadt) with its own understandings of city and non-city, interior and exterior, is emerging. (Sieverts, 1997). In their fragmentarity these „non-places" are on the other hand gaining new interest. The Viennese Gürtel with its reputation of pure traffic hell is apparently on its way to become an attraction for the night flaneur: Desolate underground arches mutate into attractive in-places (this, of course, doesn't mean that the authors ignore the problem of waste gas and noise). Old industry-ruins like the Gasometer in Vienna Simmering has recently become a centre of computer based urbanity and brings new shiny lifestyle to the intermediate city. The cement deserts along the Danube river have become an attraction for the skateboarders and even for people from the far distant lower-Austrian villages. The periphery will move to the centre of interests for the city planners, if the insight succeeds that building upon a green meadow and the permanent enlargement of the town will cause nothing but social, economic and ecological problems. The periphery forms a counterweight to the civilisation, sterilisation, temptation and petit-bourgeoisification of the moloch town. (Bourdieu 1974)

References

Dumreicher, Heidi, Levine, Richard S. (1996): Stadthügel Wien Westbahnhof, Zweiter Teil: Die Dreidimensionale Stadt, Projektbericht, Wien.

Dumreicher, Heidi (1999): Neue Territorien, ORF Ö1 feature Nova, 2./3. 2.99

Dumreicher, Heidi (1999): Information, Wissen Weisheit Nova, ORF Ö1 feature Nova, 18.5.99

Dumreicher, Heidi; Levine, Richard. S., Yanarella, Ernest J., Radmard, Taghi: (2000) Generating Models od Urban Sustainability: Vienna's Westbahnhof Sustainable Hill Town in Williams, Katie; Burton, Elizabeth; Jenks, Mike: (2000) Achieving Sustainable Urban Form, London, New York: E&FN Spon

Dumreicher, Heidi et al.: The appropriate scale for "Low Energy": Theory and practice at the Westbahnhof, in "Architecture, City, Environment", Ed. Koen Steemers, London 2000, James and James

Dumreicher, Heidi, Levine, Richard. S (1996): Tragbare Stadt, in Politische Ökologie 14. Jahrgang, Heft 44, München: ökom

Dumreicher, Heidi (1995): Bericht über die "European Conference of Sustainable Cities and Towns" vom 24.-27. Mai 1994 in Aalborg, Dänemark, Wien: Magistrat der Stadt Wien

Dumreicher, Heidi (1999): Ein urbanes Nachhaltigkeitsprojekt, Wien: edition dumreicher

Dumreicher, Heidi; Kolb. Bettina (2000): Multi or Polycultural Cities - Seven Theses on the Quality of Town A 4- 003 in "Metropolitan Ethnic Cultures: Maintainance and Interaction, The International Union of Anthropological and Ethnological Science, Interkongress, July 24-28 2000, Bejing, China

Dumreicher, Heidi; Kolb, Bettina (2000): Sieben Thesen zur Qualität von Stadt, paper at 9. Arbeitstagung der Arbeitsgemeinschaft objektive Hermeneutik e.V. 16./17.9.2000, Frankfurt

Dumreicher, Heidi; Kolb. Bettina (2000): Sieben Thesen zur Qualität von Stadt, paper at Jubiläumskongress der österreichischen Gesellschaft f. Soziologie: In welcher Gesellschaft leben wir?, 22./23.9.2000, Wien

Dumreicher, Heidi; Kolb, Bettina (2001): Sieben Thesen zur Qualität der Stadt, in:stadtplaene 24 (1/2001). pp7-44: Wien, edition dumreicher

Froschauer Ulrike, Lueger Manfred (1992): Das qualitative Interview, Zur Analyse sozialer Systeme, Wien

Garz, Detlef; Kraimer, Klaus (1994): Die Welt als Text, Theorie, Kritik und Praxis der objektiven Hermeneutik, Frankfurt

Glaser Barney G., Strauss Anselm (1967): The Discovery of Grounded Theory, New York.

Hainzel, Joachim. (1995): Über die Verdrängung der Scheisse aus Graz, in: Stadtplaene2/95:edition dumreicher, Wien

Jung, Thomas; Müller-Doohm, Stefan (1995^2): „Wirklichkeit" im Deutungsprozess, Verstehen und Methoden in den Kultur- und Sozialwissenschaften, Frankfurt

Knorr-Cetina, Karin (1991): Die Fabrikation von Erkenntnis, Zur Anthropologie der Naturwissenschaft, Frankfurt

Krämer-Badoni, Thomas (1998): Zeiten und Qualität der Stadt- Ein neues Thema erobert die Hitliste, Seite 94, in Ulrich Mückenberger (Hg.), Zeiten der Stadt. Reflexionen und Materialien zu einem neuen gesellschaftlichen Gestaltungsfeld, Bremen.

Kraus, Karl: Aphorismen, Schriften, Band 8, Hg. Christian Wagenknecht, Frankfurt

Lamnek, Siegfried (1988): Qualitative Sozialforschung, Band 1 Methodologie, München

Levine, Richard S. et al (1998) Sustainable Hilltown Vienna: A Comprehensive Approach to the Future of the European City in Rebuild the European City of Tomorrow, Proceedings of the Conference, Florence, Italy 1.-3.4.1998: ETA-Florence

Levine, R.S., Dumreicher Heidi, Radmard, Taghi, Yanarella, Ernest Y. (1999): The Sustainable City of the 21st Century: Westbahnhof, Vienna – Theory and Practice, in: Architecure of the 21st Century, XX UIA Congress, Beijing

Luhmann, Niklas (1997): Die Gesellschaft der Gesellschaft, Frankfurt

Mückenberger, Ulrich (1998): Zeiten der Stadt, Reflexionen und Materialien zu einem neuen gesellschaftlichen Gestaltungsfeld, Bremen

Novy, Katharina (1993): Straßenleben, Zur Geschichte und Gegenwart der Strasse als sozialer und öffentlicher Raum, Diplomarbeit an der Grund- und Integrativwissenschaftlichen Fakultät der Universität Wien, Wien Seite 55 in Anlehnung an Hans Paul Bahrdt, Die moderne Großstadt, Soziologische Überlegungen zum Städtebau, 1961 Reinbeck bei Hamburg,

Reichertz, Jo (1995): Abduktives Schlußfolgern und Typen(re)konstruktion, Abgesang auf eine liebgewonnene Hoffnung, in: Thomas Jung, Stefan Müller-Doohm, „Wirklichkeit" im Deutungsprozess. Verstehen und Methoden in den Kultur- und Sozialwissenschaften, Frankfurt

Reiterer, Albert F. (1998): Moderne Gesellschaften. Sozialstruktur und Sozialer Wandel in Österreich, Wien

Ritzer, Georg (2000): Die Gesellschaft als organisierte Erwartungs-Enttäuschungs-Spirale in: Schimanek, Uwe Volkmann, Ute: Soziologische Gegenwartsdiagnose I, Stuttgart: UTB

Schütz, Alfred (1981): Der sinnhafte Aufbau der sozialen Welt. Eine Einleitung in die verstehende Soziologie. Suhrkamp

Schütze, Jochen K. (2000): Vom Fremden, Wien: Passagen

Senett, Richard (1995): Fleisch und Stein, Der Körper und die Stadt in der westlichen Zivilisation, Berlin: Fischer

Sieverts, Thomas (1997): Zwischenstadt: Zwischen Ort und Welt, Raum und Zeit, Stadt und Land, Braunschweig, Wiesbaden: Vieweg

Simmel, Georg (1988): Soziologie des Raumes (1903), Gesamtausgabe, Frankfurt

Soeffner, Hans Georg (Hg.) (1979): Interpretative Verfahren in den Sozial- und Textwissenschaften, Stuttgart.

Steiner, Dieter (Hrsg.) (1997): Mensch und Lebensraum, Fragen zu Identität und Wissen, Opladen.

Thum, Karl (1979): Die soziale Bedeutung des Raumes, Dissertation an der Philosophischen Fakultät der Universität Wien.

Verkehrskonzept Wien, Generelles Maßnahmenprogramm, Heft 9 der Sonderreihe zum neuen Wiener Verkehrskonzept, Beiträge zur Stadtforschung, Stadtentwicklung und Stadtgestaltung Band 52, Wien 1994.

Winning, Hans- Henning von: Nachhaltigkeit und Urbanität, ttp://www.lpb.bwue.de/publikat/forum6/-forum6.htm, 3.3.99.

Media-Articles cited in the essay:

12.000 Bewohner, ein verschwundenes Kind, Die Presse, 20. 2. 99, Rennbahnweg 27: Seite 12

Millionenverluste durch Demonstrationen, Die Presse, 27. 2. 1999, Seite 12

Soziales Wohnen und archetypische Muster, Der Standard, 5. 3. 99, Seite 10.

Wang Wei

Cultural Performance and Ethnicized Space in Japan's China Towns

Abstract

Throughout history, Chinese Communities have been showing a certain degree of adaptation within Japan; socialization in response to the generation shift, and "assimilation" in daily life. However, as we can witness from the reformed spring festivals based on the old calendar that has begun in the mid-1980s, a revival of tradition and reorganization of ethnicity among the communities is evident. I have been conducting several research projects in Nagasaki, Kobe, Yokohama, and the home of Overseas Chinese, Fukken province, focusing on festivals and traditional performances, by discussing its characters and changes through time. In fact, festivals and performances are vital elements for maintenance of ethnic identity in several ways; while their 'localization' within the modernizing host society is inevitable, relatively 'unusual' customs such as festivals, tend to be a recognizable asset to the sustenance of ethnicity. Moreover, not only do they show 'differences' to other ordinary cultures but also serve as an occasion for communal activities.

In this paper, I will discuss the society in Nagasaki known for its longest history, and that of Kobe and Yokohama being representative of current Chinese Societies. By aiming to grasp the general view of ethnicity-reformation and focusing on festivals and performances, I'd wish to illustrate and overview Chinese society from a macro perspective and the differences pertaining to each area from a micro oriented view, in hope of revealing some of the features unique within.

I have divided the festivals currently practiced in the Chinese societies in Japan into 3 types:

1) 'Mingled Festivals': The Overseas Chinese's festivals and manners have been taken in, and fused in those festivals or rituals belonging to Japanese societies throughout the period. This is particularly the case in Nagasaki, best known as Nagasaki Kunchi.

2) 'Traditional Festivals': These represent the types developed by a group of people from the same town/district, mostly taught and practiced on a ceremonial occasions in a temple. They are 'Pudu' (Nagasaki, Kobe) and 'Guandiji' (Yokohama).

3) 'Renewed Traditional Festivals': These include part of the traditional aspect of Chinese customs, lately re-established in China Towns that serve not only as a means for vitalizing the town but also as a mark of tradition communicated through areas with other Japanese. These (new) cultures were formed in conjunction with those of Japan, under the State level normalization of Japan-China relations.

As for performance/entertainment, both 'mingled festivals' and 'performances' exist only in Nagasaki. Among them, the Dragon Dance and Lion Dance have been treated and handed down as 'Mingled performances' by Japanese. On the other hand, 'traditional performances' as in Lion and Dragon dance came to be revived shortly after World War II in Yokohama and thereafter until today, despite the split experienced by the Chinese Community. In the case of Kobe and Nagasaki, however, traditions, along with musical instruments, disappeared without sign of reform due to the shortage of successors.

After the restoration of relations between Japan and China, Lion and Dragon Dance were revived in Kobe, and the Lion Dance was reformed in Nagasaki as a 'Renewed Traditional Performance. In recent years, there are performances that have been newly incorporated from China and others that were introduced and played in China, also known as the 'Newly developed Performance of China' and 'Invited Performance.' Festivals recently established in China town are constituted of many of the above mentioned performances that contribute to the making of Chinese moods and experiences.

Each of the three areas showed recognition of the traditional calendar and began to hold the spring festivals according to it around a similar period of time as to activate the life in China town, typically seen in 'YuanxiaoJie', the Lantern Festival in Nagasaki. Such 'shift' among the overseas Chinese community is largely due to the effort of the restaurant owners of second generation. In doing so, they planned a new type of organization for promotional purposes as well as for the town's consolidation, intended for a kind of ethnicity symbol. The group has less in common with those traditional types formed by persons from similar backgrounds; notably in Nagasaki and Kobe, the organization is set up in collaboration with Japanese owners. Therefore, the new organization sought to generate a town with 'Chinese Taste' that resulted in the recognition of 'Renewed Traditional Festivals.'

Lately, Overseas Chinese Communities have been showing a sign of adaptation to the Japanese society. However, owing to the recovery of the relations between Japan and China, the improvement of the image reflecting China, and the need for town or touristic environment, they have also been consistent in selecting cultural elements from homeland China, thereby creating some symbols of ethnic identity, and further vitalizing their ethnicity. It could be said that these identities arose in part from practical ends and intentions. Nonetheless, given the people's underlying attachment to tradition, these processes may then have led to a further intimacy toward it.

While on a macro level, reformation of traditional culture and revitalization of ethnicity among the three areas have much in common, differences become apparent when looked from a micro perspective. For instance, the population of Overseas Chinese in Kobe-Yokohama area outnumbers 20,30 times that of Nagasaki. Also, Chinese schools in Nagasaki came to be closed from the decrease of Chinese population and the tendency to 'assimilation,' but those schools in Kobe played a promising role in bringing up traditional performances till today.

In Kobe, the effect of ideological conflict between mainland China and Taiwan, together with China-Taiwan's appeal prior to the restored relation of Japan and China not only made possible the introduction of Chinese customs in their own ways but also the reflection upon tradition. Thus, 'travelling' of culture eventually became frequent after the relations had restored, and owing to those Chinese Schools' effort, the situation entailed a reformation of tradition. While only those who were under Government relation had strongest access to tradition in Nagasaki, Yokohama faced problems related to Chinese schools that led to a certain split the in community as well as difficulties in the sustenance of traditional festivals and performances.

Yokohama's case is a little different. Communities in the area were capable of reviving immediately the tradition as well as the residential towns that suffered some damages from the war, which can be attributed to the relatively tight concentration of the Chinese's residential area in-and-around the city. In other words, whereas communities in Nagasaki and Kobe 'loosely' spread their living space (and forms) out to the suburbs, Yokohama tends to show a relative concentration upon areas, resulting in a certain stability of a closely bounded local community. But even so, such strong tie and autonomy of a local ethnic community were not only an asset to the passing on of traditional custom, but also became an obstacle to its transmission; the rise of the People's Republic of China caused an ideological rupture in the Overseas Chinese society. So the practice of Spring Festivals based on the old calendar meant a conscious effort by Overseas Chinese to overcome the ramification of ideologies.

Meanwhile, we can see some differences in the management base in Spring Festivals among the three areas. Festivals in Yokohama are primarily managed and conducted by Chinese. Although this is done by a collaborative effort of Chinese and Japanese in case of Kobe and Nagasaki, the festival in the latter has become virtually Japanese based rather than Chinese, after the city's offer of assisting in the Lantern Festival as an event for the whole city. In examining the Spring Festivals in the three areas, therefore, we may say that there are apparent differences in terms of management besides the similarity by means of 'events.'

In Nagasaki, we see a situation where the city (or an area) itself has embraced the Chinese Festival as a city endorsed festival. In Nagasaki, the following factors can be listed as the background for the formation of the Promotion Association, the subsequent furnishing of Chinatown, and the establishment of the Lantern Festival.

1) The fixing, socialization, and assimilation of the second generation of Chinese in Japan

The second and third generation Chinese who were born and raised in the Japanese society settled and were socialized within this society, thus developing a multi-dimensional identity.

Within this environment, the Overseas Chinese who operate businesses in Chinatown selected Chinese culture as "cultural capital" beneficial to themselves.

2) Changing relationships with the homeland: Restoration of Japan-China national relations and focus on the importance of Japanese-Chinese international exchange.

   The changes in Japan-China relations became an extremely important external factor for restoration and reorganization of the Overseas Chinese traditional culture. This chain of events clearly had a major influence on the Overseas Chinese activities to restore traditional culture.

3) Increased international influence capacity of the homeland, and the improvement of the Chinese reputation:
   Related to the point above, Chinese recovery and internationalization after the war led to improvements in the international influence capacity of the homeland, and the sense of Chinese presence. This boosted the confidence of the Overseas Chinese, and became the driving force for reestablishing their traditional culture.

4) Community reactivation and tourism development

   Tourism development regarding a Chinatown community event became the trigger for revitalization of "reorganized" traditional culture. Chinatown was not an area monopolized by Overseas Chinese, but was shared with Japanese. Therefore, the driving force, behind the community events were not just Overseas Chinese, but was a promotion association including Japanese.

5) Chinese history and Nagasaki culture mingles

   The arrival of Chinese in Nagasaki can be traced back to the Edo era, and most of them were either merchants who came in with trade boats from various areas, or refugees escaping the war in the end of Ming. Many stayed and naturalized, later becoming Chinese interpreters, who played a crucial role in shaping the culture of the Overseas Chinese.

Since the population and bond of Chinese in Yokohama is high and close, the Spring Festival held in China town tends to be governed by them, whereas participation of Japanese in Chinese performance groups is customary in Kobe and Nagasaki. In the case of Kobe, the Chinese population, despite its large number, is rather diffused within the Hyogo prefecture, with the result that their residence in Nang-Jing represents only a portion of the population. Moreover, almost half of the owners of Chinese restaurants are Japanese. Therefore, just as in Nagasaki, the Spring Festival in Kobe holds a meaning of 'vitalization' of the town that is made effective by both Chinese and Japanese engagement. Not only is the Festival meaningful in terms of reformation-activation of ethnicity for those Chinese residing in China town, but is also significant for trade and business. However, the festival will not be a direct economic asset to the Chinese outside the town.

As we have seen here, the management forms of the 'Spring Festival', which have been selected and reconstructed from the older Chinese Festival Customs by the Overseas Chinese in Japan, reflect the distinct characteristics of Overseas Chinese Society typically found in the representative cities of Japan.

References

Wang, Wei. 1998: Festivals and Traditional Entertainment of the Chinese Community in Nagasaki – Their typology and newly created traditions, in: Minzokugaku-Kenkyu (Japanese Journal of Ethnology). Vol. 63 No.2: 209-231.

Wang, Wei. 2000: Transmission and Ethnicity: Folk Performance among the Chinese Community in Yokohama, in: Chubu University-Journal of the College of Humanities. No.3: 109-136. Jan. 2000.

Wang, Wei. 2001: Newly Created Tradition and Ethnicity among the Chinese Community in Japan – On Festivals and Traditional Entertainment. Ph.D. Diss. Fukyo Company.

Myron J. Aronoff

Temporal and Spatial Dimensions of Contested Israeli Nationhood

Abstract

There are multiple ways of imagining the collective "we" that produce competing models of membership in every political community. Important aspects of such political cultural divisions can be understood in terms of divergent temporal and spatial perceptions. Contested interpretations of myths of origin and aspects of history selectively forgotten and remembered reveal contrasting imaginings of political community. Analysis of the relationship between the cultural construction of past, present, and future and political ideology reveals the link between contested collective memories and competing visions of nationhood.

Temporal and spatial perceptions are linked. Social and political boundaries are related to, but not always isomorphic with, actual geographic frontiers of the state. Alterations of the physical borders of a state, filtered through temporal cultural frames, shape citizens senses of personal and collective security which in turn influence their political sentiments and positions. I relate differing perceptions of history (time) and the land (space) to the analysis of competing models of Jewish and Israeli nationhood in the context of uncertain and changing state borders.

The process of nation formation involves a *tension* between ethnic loyalties and attachments to the state manifest in contestation over the definition of the nation and criteria for citizenship in the state. Analysis of the problematic nature of the inherent tensions in this *dual attachment* is necessary to understand competing models of more inclusive forms of civic nationalism, more exclusive forms of ethnic nationalism, and various combinations of the two. The dominant model in Israel has been a mixed form identified as ethno-republican nationalism.

Cultural conceptions of time frame the perceived relationship between past, present, and future. Unlike for Biblical Hebrews, the spatially anchored and measurable Hellenistic time is the basis for our contemporary conception of time in the West which is conceptualized as *linear*. The sequences in linear time connecting before and after facilitate the creation of modern narrative history. The secular form of Zionism that became dominant during the establishment of the state of Israel was profoundly influenced by the modern narrative of progress.

Linear notions of time contrasted with more traditional, religiously inspired, *cyclical* time. Continuity of action is the distinguishing feature of Hebrew verbs. The eschatological perspective of Israelis whose understanding of the past is dominated by a mythical notions of time has been characterized as *totemic* (a variant of cyclical time). Tension between linear and cyclical perceptions of history underlies the construction of Israeli collective memory and has been related to important divisions in Israeli political culture.[1] A third heuristic type, *mixed* time, combines *linear* and *cyclical* elements. Linear time is selectively *historical*. Cyclical time is predominantly *mythical*. Mixed time combines elements of both and predominates in most nationalist discourse.

Territorialization of historical memory in which the land becomes perceived to be unique and indispensable to the members of a community, having influence over their development, witness to their survival, and as the resting place of their ancestors is called by Smith *ethnoscape*.[2] Nature becomes historicized and history becomes naturalized through poetic spaces and sites of memory which invest a sacred quality to specific places which generates a powerful feeling of antiquity, reverence, and belonging. Territory is further made sacred through the holy deeds of heroic ancestors. Hegemonic Zionism exemplifies successful production of such an ethnoscape.

The meaning of the Land (of Israel) and the return to it are perceived differently by secular and religious Zionists. The differences in meaning between them and the ultra-Orthodox, on one hand, and Israel's Arab citizens, on the other – both of whom have traditionally been either non-Zionists or anti-Zionist – is even greater. Within each of these categories there are significant differences in understandings of the appropriate geographic borders of the Land and what should constitute the modern state, flexibility over the ability or willingness to make compromises regarding these borders, and the type and intensity of meanings attributed to them. Except for the Druze, the indigenous Arab population of Palestine was vehemently and even violently opposed to the Zionist project. The current dilemma of Arab citizens of Israel derives from the tension between their loyalties as citizens and their sense of belonging to the wider Palestinian, Arab, and Islamic worlds which are in varying degrees in conflict with their state.

The tension created by the dual attachment to ethnicity and state is manifest and seeks resolution in Israel through competing civic, ethno-republican, and ethno-nationalist forms of collective identity. The temporal perspective most closely associated with civic nationalism is linear and is grounded in selective narrative history. It's proponents favor the liberal democratic over the Jewish character of the state. Israeli ethno-nationalism is associated with mystical notions of cyclical messianic time and those who support it privilege Jewishness over democracy. The intermediary mixed time perspective combines linear historicity and totemic mythology. Its adherents oscillate between the two, favoring one over the other in different contexts. Those who operate on the mixed time perspective tend to support ethno-republicanism. Different ideological versions of

---

[1]Myron J. Aronoff, *Israeli Visions and Divisions*. New Brunswick: Transaction (1989); Yael Zerubavel, *Recovered Roots*. Chicago: University of Chicago Press (1995).

[2]Anthony D. Smith, "Sacred Territories and National Conflict," *Israel Affairs*, 5, 4 (Summer 1999): 13-31.

ethno-republican Zionism have been politically ascendent at different stages of Israeli history as they attempted to balance the tension between Israel as a democratic and a Jewish state.

While the Land constitutes an ethnoscape of emotive poetic space and a site of salient collective memory for most Jews and all Zionists, conflicting interpretations of its meaning divides them among themselves as well as from their fellow Arab citizens of Israel. Supporters of civic nationalism tend to be the most pragmatic about the borders of the state seeing them primarily in legal/rational terms. Therefore they are the most willing to bargain territory for peace with Israel's neighbors. Their sense of history leads them to perceive an urgency to find a political compromise while it is possible to do so. They conclude that time is running out for such compromises.

Adherents of ethno-republicanism are much more convinced that time is on Israel's side. They occupy a middle position in which the historic heritage is primary, but greater flexibility is shown than for the ethno-nationalists for whom the biblical Land is a religious fetish and indivisible. Whereas the former have compromised under pressure and withdrawn from previous borders, the latter are militant opponents of such compromise. Like the ethno-republicans, the ethno-nationalists perceive that time is on Israel's side – particularly those who are convinced it is part of a divinely ordained plan.

The majority of supporters of civic nationalism are secular. Among the minority of religious supporters of this liberal form, most are intellectuals. Most traditional Jews are ethno-republicans. Orthodox Jews are divided between the ultra-Orthodox for whom Israel is Exile and for whom messianic Redemption is deferred until the deeds of pious Jews bring it about in the future, and those for whom settlement of the Land by Jews is imperative for the continuation of the Redemptive process which they believe is underway. The latter are overwhelmingly ethno-nationalists. Gush Emunim's conviction that time can be conquered through space (settlement of the Land of Israel facilitates Redemption) makes territorial compromise virtually impossible.

Summary of the Relationship Between Nationalism, Time, Space, and Religion

Nationalism	**Civic**	**Ethno-republican**	**Ethno-nationalist**
Time	Linear	Mixed	Cyclical
	Historical	Mixed	Mythical
Space	Borders	Ethnoscape (Homeland)	Fetish
Religiosity	Secular	Traditional	Religious

The relationship between temporal and spatial perspectives and competing visions of nationhood can by summarized as follows: The more messianic nationalists with the strongest religious identification with the Land as a sacred ethnoscape are ethno-nationalists. The stronger the messianism, the more xenophobic the nationalism. Those most clearly identified with historic linear time, who have more pragmatic and flexible attitudes toward the boundaries of the state, are most supportive of civic liberal forms of nationalism. The middle position of ethno-republicanism, identified with more mixed temporal and spatial perceptions (oscillating between the two in different contexts) who have historically constituted the dominant majority, is challenged by the competing alternatives.

The confrontation over defining the national "we" is at the heart of many of the current political struggles taking place in the world today. This is particularly the case in the so-called Third Wave democratizing states, especially those which emerged after the disintegration of the Soviet Union and its empire. Therefore, it is hoped that this analysis of the cultural temporal and spatial dimensions of contested Israeli nationhood may provide a paradigm for broader comparative analysis.

Soheila Shahshahani

The Differential Use of Emotional Space in the Iranian Culture
A Study in Anthropology of Emotions

Abstract

In order to have a holistic view of human space, environmental or cultural, public and private, it is absolutely necessary to comprehend the building of that space, and the acting in that space; the mind and the culture which builds or arranges that space, in so doing, expects certain reactions, implicitly or explicitly. In anthropological literature no exploration has yet approached the study of space in Iran, which is extremely rich and complicated. In this paper, I work with Pierre Bourdieu's concept "habitus" which I have found helpful in defining space.

Introduction

Bourdieu, writing in French, has used the term "habitus" from Latin which refers to habitual or typical condition, state or appearance, particularly of the body, and the Greek term "hexis" meaning manner and style in which actors "carry themselves" (stance, gait, gesture). Habillement (clothing) habitat (housing) and habitude (ways and manners) come distinctly to mind with the use of this term in French. Trying to transcend the opposition between subjectivism and objectivism, Bourdieu uses it to go beyond the meaning of culture and social life as a compilation of individual behavior or supra-individual structures. His "habitus" approaches E.T. Hall's "informal" domain as distinct from the learned "formal" and "technical" domains (1959).

Bourdieu also uses the term "disposition" which is illuminating, if understood in its French meaning as configuration and readiness to create order and thus meaning. Habitus continues in time, so we have cultural continuity in history, and it can be displaced, so we have cultural continuity in space. "Stylistic coherence and thematic unity" are thus found in one culture across time and in a cultural diaspora. In short our topic in Bourdieu's term is "habitus ....the site of the internalization of reality and the externalization of internality ..... [It] is adjusted to objective conditions and there is a reciprocal or dialectical relationship between them" (Jenkins 1992:79). Lutz and White (1986) confirm this view when they say, "The core of the attempt to understand the relation between emotion and culture lies in the ethnographic description of the emotional lives of persons in their social contexts (427) ...Incorporating emotion into ethnography will entail presenting a fuller view of what is at stake for people in everyday life. In reintroducing pain and pleasure in all their complex forms into our picture of people's daily life in other societies, we might further humanize these others for the Western audience. That audience finds emotion at the core of being for reasons both cultural and political economic in origin, reasons that should simultaneously come under anthropological scrutiny. At issue is not only the humanity of our images, but the adequacy of our understanding of cultural social forms" (431).

As an Iranian anthropologist living in Iran for the past ten years, I wrote my daily observations, for this research over a period of one year. Reading anthropological literature on the topic simultaneously, made the process of objectification easier. Observations have all been "in situation" (Lutz 1988) adding to the validity of descriptions. "The anthropologist must simply be in attentive and intensive proximity to the everyday lives of others in order to apprehend their emotions" (Lutz and White 1986:415).

It is common practice to start such endeavours with an analysis of the meaning of "self" in the culture under scrutiny. Rosaldo says hierarchical societies appear much more concerned than others with the problem of how society controls an inner emotional self (Lutz & White 1986:422). Lutz & White consider "culturally constituted self" to be a key theoretical concept in anthropology of emotion, as it is "positioned at the nexux of social worlds. Concepts of emotion emerge as a kind of language of the self – a code for statements about intentions, actions and social relations... Emotions are a primary idiom for defining and negotiating social relations of the self in a moral order." (ibid: 417) Is the the Iranian self bounded self in the sense of Geertz's much quoted definition of the individual?

"The Western conception of the person as a bounded, unique, a dynamic center of awareness. emotion, judgment and action organized into a distinctive whole and set contrastively both against other such wholes and against its social and natural background, is, however incorrigible it may seem to us, a rather peculiar idea within the context of the world cultures" (1983:59). Is the Iranian self divided into the duality of body and mind or body and soul as it is in Western philosophy'?

Where are the boundaries in terms of relations with others, and in terms of the self-cosmos relations?

Looking for primal definition of self we refer to the term "I" ["man"] in a Persian encyclopaedia called Dehxodâ, and get certain indications for how to proceed. "I" is first defined grammatically and then four synonyms are given for it which will illuminate our way into this difficult topic. First is ["man bandeh"], I as a slave, or server; it describes the self in a very modest state, and this is in relationship to another person or to God. One is a servitor of a lord, a king or the Almighty, one is at the mercy of the other. This term is currently used in written or spoken language, in poetry, prose and irony.

The second term is "man man zadan" referring to narcissism and self-glorification. The term "we" [mâ] may be used instead of "I" [man] by persons such as lords and kings. Graham E. Fuller (1991) in his book: The Center of the Universe, The Geopolitics of Iran, succinctly portrays these opposing definitions of self when he speaks of "an innate sense of superiority stemming from a magnificent imperial past and rich culture, and a nagging sense of inferiority and even insecurity derived from Iran's experience of abject conquest and foreign domination" (p.8).

What gives life to living things is their "nafs" and there can be plant, animal or human "nafs" or "jân." "Nafs" or life or soul of a person is also a topic of great philosophical and religious importance. "Nal-e amâre" are the earthly needs of human body. The body itself is divided into two parts, the lower and the higher. The higher contains the brain, and the "del" to which we shall refer shortly, the faculties of reflection and wisdom. This upper part is separated from the lower part at the waiste line by a belt as the Zoroastrians puberty rite demonstrates beautifully through offering a belt called "kosti" to boys and girls passing the rite (Duchesne- Guillemin, J. 1966:50-52)

The fourth important term we encounter in this definition of self, is "del" and this is a very significant term, very common in daily usage, but also of central importance in mystical literature. "Del" (which is literally the heart, but also means the stomach) is the mirror of cosmic truth. It is the domain of the space where a reflection of the reality can be seen. Knowledge is the work of mind, it is acquired through thoughtful reflection, but getting to the truth is the work of love. After passing many stages of learning with a master arrives to see the truth within his/her own "del". This love befalls his/her "del" and makes abode within it, and burns the self into purity. From then on he no longer sees himself but the loved one, the truth. His "del" becomes overwhelmed by this love, and he gains freedom and contentment. Once this state is achieved, one does not speak about it (borrowing from Mithraic religious tradition), he keeps it and continues on his way to the promised world of truth at the end of which is paradise. (Nasafi, Azizoddin 1983) Thus "del" is the most important part of the self from this mystical perspective which has permeated daily life.

"Del" is susceptible to outer truth, God and the Cosmos. The compound terminology of "del" are also is very significant. One expresses many physical and emotional states with this terminology. "Del" meaning the middle it can be used in compound terms with the following natural phenomenon:

The earth ("del-e xâk"), with the sky ("del âsemân), with the day ("del-e ruz"), with night ("del šab"). meaning respectively the centre of the earth, middle of the sky, middle of the day and midnight.

"Del" may also mean the stomach and stomach ache ["del dard"] and nausea ["del beham xordegi"] and refers to physical problems of the gastric organs. A number of pleasant compounds use "del" such as "del pazir" meaning pleasant, "del garmi" meaning encouragement or appreciation. Conversely we have quite a number of terms referring to worry, "del âšub" and "del sureh", nostalgia "del tang", hurt and offended "delxor" ad "del zadeh", hesitant "del del konân". bereaved "del suxteh". and compassionate "del suz", empathy "hamdeli". To speak out one's heart "dardo der', and to engage in "dardo del" and to do "del suzi" are daily practices. A person without pain is non-existent, and everyone has his/her own pain and it is pain, sorrow and poverty which according to Shi'ite Islam make human beings realize their shortcomings. Pain could make one aware of previous wrong-doing, thus it is accompanied with a sense of guilt, or it could herald a future fortune after purification. Another line of reasoning is that it could be worse than what it actually is, therefore it is accepted complacently ("rezâ") and in surrender ("taslim"). Relating one's pain to another person, ("Dardo del") and compassion become mechanisms of joining people together in mutual pain (consider "gham" in Pakistan, see Grima: 1992)

Falling in love "del dâdan", or "del bâxtan", or becoming attached "del basteh", and the charming one, "delbar" are all very common. Courage also evokes "del" ("del beh daryâ zadan"). and finally cruelty is shown by "del sang" (stone-hearted).

We have dwelled enough on the definition of the self. Now we can move on to the relationship to others, starting from the centre of the self. The closest and most sublime of all relationships, besides that of self to God, is that of self to one's child. The child is first and foremost his/her mother's light of eyes ("nur-e česm") and part of the body (pâreye tan"), and corner of liver ("jegar guŝe"). "May I be sacrificed for you" ("qorbunet beram" or "fadât beŝam") is used profusedly by mothers addressing their children. referring to their quality of "gozašt" or devotion of their whole life to their children. It also refers to their responsibility to the whole family. No wonder we hear the expression "The paradise is under mothers' feet repeatedly. This way, a counter poise to the mother's devotion is expressed in everyday language.

Lutz and White (1986: 426) claim that "ethnographical studies demonstrate that cultural views of the child overlap in crucial ways, giving meaning and motivation to the relations between children and adults."

The Iranian family is emotionally heavily charged. Bateson's term "ethos", or emotional environment of a whole culture, is applicable here as the extended family is quite strong in Iran. We see its traces in the politico-economic structure of the country. We see its presence in traditional architecture of urban centres (Shahshahani 1995). The rural and pastoral nomadic environment in Iran can all be defined in terms of kinship relations (Shahshahani 1990). Units of all nomadic settlements ("mâl"), and units of agricultural work ("boneh") are all kinship units in which single families gather. In this "ethos", rules and regulations of behavior are strong and self-restraint and courteous speech ("tâârof) are prevalent. This brings us to the topic of communicating emotions, or sensitivity to emotional environment in relation with others. The trajectory of relationship goes from self-restraint, expression through the curteous veil of "tâârof, expression within bounded rules, through language, gesture, deepest self-expression through the eyes and tears, and finally through composite act, dance.

Self-restraint

Self-restraint and self-containment, reservation and reticence are qualities which are respected due to various reasons. Above, we mentioned self-restraint being practiced by the mystic who has seen the truth in his "del" and, should he talk about it, might loose the wisdom. This secretiveness can socially be understood as a mechanism to preserve and hide the identity of believers. "Taqiyeh" in shi'ite doctrine implies abstaining from declaring one's religion or belief lest it causes human, social or economic loss. Keeping the family secrets is a prerogative. "Keeping a broken arm in one's sleeve" is a saying. These secrets could concern economic, social or emotional matters. Boasting about extraordinary acquisitions is frowned upon because it could attract jealousy and ominous evil eyes. Walls surrounding houses in traditional urban setting hide the houses' inside. From outside one cannot perceive the riches of the dwellers.

Speaking one's mind is also not prudent as there is suspicion about listeners' identity. Long history of oppression has deeply engrained reticence and abstention from speaking one's mind. Political circumstances have changed numerous times and the proverb "An apple which is thrown up, turns many times before it comes down" shows that uncertainty reigns. Therefore, one should keep one's opinion and one's emotions well guarded. Spies could be lurking everywhere: "The walls have mice, and the mice have ears" portrays fear of being listened to. Not trusting even one's own eyes is also mentioned in this atmosphere of lack of trust, and suspicion, even great fear, of witchcraft exists. Paranoia is experienced within the family, in the work place and obviously in the political arena. In the past 100 years, fear of foreign powers has also occupied an active place in this space of suspicion. Fear of jealousy, evil eye, spying agents is always in the air. The inner fear for the self is fear of shame, humiliation ("tahqir"), social and economic loss. As Lutz and White say: "The fact that emotions are in many societies, a critical link in cultural interpretations of action implies that emotion concepts are likely to be actively used in the negotiation of social reality. Taussig describes one of the most pernicious forms this takes in demonstrating how historical and contemporary forms of torture thrive in a "culture of terror" or an emotional and ideological matrix in which the victim is both experienced and continually recreated in discourse as a terrifying and contemptible being" (1986:420).

Thus one finds ways of remaining silent. One passes time passing worry beads, eating seeds ("toxmeh"), playing backgammon, gardening, weaving and other time consuming activities which demand neither speech nor creativity while the mind moves on its own.

A first outward movement is the finding of oneself within the others' words and acts. Going to religious gatherings, either mourning ceremonies or annual religious gatherings, is "distancing of emotion in ritual" (Scheff 1977). Four distressful emotions: grief, fear, embarrassment or anger are released when one participates in catharsis. In listening to a sermon, one hears many life situations alluded to solutions and advices given. One hears one's own problem as the speaker is aware of daily stresses in people's lives, and tries to find solutions, stemming from religious teachings. Those listening get answers to their problems without themselves having talked about them. Since this is done in a congenial setting where people sit on the floor with their relatives, neighbours or acquaintances, where they share in simple food or drinks, a communal atmosphere surrounds the person. They might speak to others about their deep difficulties in life, but even if they don't, in group participations they get a sense of relief. They think in relative terms about their own problems as they hear about the problems of others. Through participating in such ritual, in the words of Scheff (1977) the following occurs: "Distress which is unbearable is repressed. How can one bear unbearable pain? – by experiencing it within a dinnatic frame, that is, by feeling assured that one can escape from it, if necessary. At aesthetic distance, there is a balance of thought and feeling. There is deep emotional resonance, but the person is in control. If a repressed emotion such as grief is restimulated at aesthetic distance. the crying that results is not unpleasant, it is not draining or tiring – the person feels refreshed when it is over"(p.486).

Weeping is encouraged in religious ceremonies. and is part of life in small closely knit communities (Lucas 1986). During the two months of Ramadan and Moharran and on other specific religious dates, lamentations are broadcast on radio and television, inviting observers and listeners to participate in mass catharsis in individual households.

A second outward movement is exercising some of the many arts of Iran: calligraphy, painting and music. In all of these arts one uses poetry (which is mystical) or imagery from traditional texts and some improvisation. Therefore, one recreates and through an erudit's text or imagery redefines his/her own experience. This is more committal than what is done in participating in rituals, but is less committal as we shall see later, in creating works of art or irony oneself.

Courteous behavior

'The ceremony of greeting, perhaps, is the ritual which coheres around the fear and embarrassment of making contact with others, particularly strangers" (Scheff 1977:488). Greetings and farewells are traditionally very time consuming in Iran. When one calls or meets a relative or an acquaintance, one has to ask how are the close kin of that person one by one. This takes a while, and if the silence after such exchange of news is heavy, again it is asked how they are, and what each of them is doing. Each side tries to put the other on a pedestal with flattering expressions and amiable manners. One becomes at the service of the other, flowery short speeches about the other follows. This is mostly exercised by men in relation to each other. Men who are powerful in vocabulary, prose, and poetry develop a style in narration, and exercise it utmost in group gatherings. G. Fuller finds this quality in Iranian relational approaches in other emanations when he says: "One look at a Persian rug and many qualities of the Persian mind spring out. This is a culture given to extravagance. Intervining arabesque, crowded floral motifs, lush prose, sensuous and evocative verse – all suggest the floweriness inherent in Persian mode of expression. Persians highly appreciate such richness and hyperbole" (1991:13).

Use of courteous language allows people to speak without being precise, it allows people to express nuances and go into detail without being self-committed, without being conclusive. Being precise might be against another person's opinion. Since one does not want to cause opposition but wants to have everyone's accord, one remains in an ambiguous position. Imagination is very helpful in such situations as one can recall poetry or anecdotes which help fill the narrative space.

This trend is observed in the political domain and is confirmed about the Shah (Mohammad Reza Shah who reigned 1941-1979) "Without a doubt, the shah leads most of his countrymen in the art of Persian politics [...] refusing to crystallize issues to the point where definite choices are made, thus disappointing or offending someone; never allowing any individual to become too powerful or too popular; never being so publicly identified with events that it is impossible to shift the blame onto others; and cultivating an ambiguity in political life that softens critics by pretending to espouse their hopes while reassuring vested interests by rarely carrying out promised reforms" (Baldwin). Using vague language can create an atmosphere of apprehension, unease and guilt if mistakes and problems are pointed out. It is left to individual guess about whom the notification is being made. Everyone tries to shove off responsibility unto others: "It wasn't me, it was my hand, no it was my sleeve's fault," proverbially dodges off responsibility unto others. Not accepting responsibility, being non-committed are qualities of courteous narratives. William M. Reddy (1977) in a very interesting discussion on French "delicatesse" of early 19th century, shows how this language helps to protect honor, "the more intense the feelings, the more imperative the need for restraint. Delicatesse was, therefore, an idiom for handling nodal points of intense ambivalence" (p.336). Reddy attributes this style of speech to early 19th century France to a shift made in the socio-political structure of the country. He says:

"Within the context of Western history, this was a moment when 'delicatesse' in language responded to a heightened sense of exposure to gossip and scrutiny in the newly founded laissez faire social order. The power of shame as a regulatory 'metasentiment' was reinforced. Delicatesse provided a buffer zone that for the continuation of a sense of family honor ill-suited to the realm of free speech and free contract that the Revolution had opened up" (p.338). This buffer time has lasted a very long in Iran. There has been a century long struggle to build up a civil society in Iran, but the family structure is still too strong and has not yet released the bridle. Gossip is a controlling mechanism, law is lingering behind.

Expressive modes

This brings us to the third domain, that of expression. We can start where we ended the last part, with gossip. "One crow, forty crows" is an expression showing how gossip can change on its way, to make forty out of one! Despite suspicion about its validity, yet it is practiced, sought, used and believed in extensively. "Unless there is something, people would not say a whole lot of things" is another proverb.

This informal way of getting information and communicating with others is prevalent in family settings, in work place and in the political arena. People try not to become object of negative gossip ["qeibat"]. In religious gatherings, the clerics speak against it. During the heyday of Iranian press (1997-99), when newspapers were highly informative. people depended much less on it, and exchanged much less gossip. Even the frequency of telling jokes had decrease. Ironic press had gained power and certain newspapers were purchased because of political satire. The humor of a particular columnist, Ebranirn Nabavi. had replaced telling jokes in everyday gatherings. It sufficed to say. "Did you read what he wrote last night?" or about such and such an event. Eulogies of his genius were then given, on his capacity to encapsulate the essence of political events and report it in a humorous way in such a short period of time: only one day after the events.

As Planap says, "A very common strategy for managing uncomfortable situations is to find humor in them. It is almost impossible to laugh and be angry at the same time. Humor tends to make situations seem less important by virtue of their absurdity or our detachment and humor reframes the situation as less threatening or anxiety producing" (1999:80).

Telling jokes is pane of almost every gathering. To break the ice in a gathering, or after serious discussions, or after depressive situations, this brings down tension. Even from the time children go to school, they exchange jokes, each child trying to remember a funnier one to relate to others. Certain jokes last for decades. Freud calls humor "The most self-sufficient of the comic forms; its process consumates itself in one single person (1938:798) [...] Humor is a means to gain pleasure despite the painful affects which disturb it; it acts as a substitute for this affective development, and takes its place, if we are in a situation which tempts us to liberate painful affects according to our habits, and motives then urge us to suppress these affects in statu nascendi, we have the conditions for humor [...] the person affected by misfortune, pain, etc. [...] could obtain humoristic pleasure [...] the pleasure of humor results at the cost of this discontinued liberation of affect..." (p.797).

An other example of the positive and expressive side is the outgoing personality who has always "success" stories to relate. In these stories such persons show how they have surpassed others in intelligence, cunning, and rapidity of reaction. Whatever they hear, is less than what they can offer. If the discussion is on clothing, they have the latest information on the best clothing, if it is about food, they know the best restaurants, if it is about health services, they know the best doctors and surgeons, if it is about connection to political personalities, they have the best and most powerful connections, and if it is about a specific situation, they show that they were the most intelligent. They are proud of being Iranian, they have a nationalistic stance, yet have an international awareness and attempt to incorporate what they like from other cultures in their own. Graham Fuller says, "An interesting counterpoint to Iran's xenophobia lies in its historical ability to absorb foreign invading cultures and incorporate them in the new social order" (ibid: 28).

Use of theatrical elements in such narrations is common place. The eyes are excellent means of attracting attention and influencing listeners, the hands can gesticulate and indicate the meaning, and the whole body might be used to re-enact events. When such pseudo-theatrical scenes are offered, if they are humorous, they might be imitation of various people known to the group. Men are most often actors of such scenes, and women are generally observers or listeners. But in the most expressive and space-occupying activity, it is women who are more active. This is the solo dance which is performed in friendly or family reunions. In different provinces group dance is common. In Kurdistan men and women may dance together, shoulder to shoulder. In central and southern Zagros (Western Iran) women and men engage separately in group dances. In Persian-speaking shi'ite regions where dancing is a private matter, solo dance is the practice. Women occupy much more space when they dance, and they are the experts in this art, to counter men in other realms. "...Male dancers tend to move from position to position more slowly than females. The males also tend to employ fewer varieties of movement than female performers"(Shay 1999:31). Anothony Shay gives the main tide to his book Choreophobia, Solo Improvised Dance in the Iranian World, to show the forbidden quality of this dance mode. Moneza Vaziri (1986:8) very justly says that all women "love dance and song. But although some of them are good at these performing arts, customarily they deny their skill, or even their knowledge of these things. They must be pushed into performance. But soon, they would get carried away with the dance music, and it would be difficult to stop them. At this stage everybody, skilful or clumsy. would be dragged into the dancing. This dancing would help them to release the emotional tension built up by the music" and I would add by everyday life. At a wedding in the holy city of Qom, women became very angry when they could not dance because of the death of a close relative of the bride some two months before the wedding. They had brought trays to play on for dancing. Anthony Shay relates solo dance to everyday life. and to other artistic manifestations such as calligraphy. He writes of the "aesthetic spell" this dance has had for him and describes it as a "surreal world of geometry; and movement, design and pattern: a world of lines and curves, webs and interesting points, jewelled and brilliant, beckoning the dancer to stretch, reach, and touch the sources of jewelled light at their points of insection" (p. 16). He then comments on the "freedom of expression" which "seems endless, at first frightening and then liberating in the vast possibilities the dance offers" and then "the sense of ambiguity. because one never knows what is coming next" (p.17). Finally he formulates three principles of "alternation, opposition and simultaneity" to show how the dancer alternates her movements from one foot to the other and whatever is done by one hand, is then done by the other in opposition. Knowing the principles. then it depends upon the individual's "self-confidence, grace and elegance" (p.135), forcefulness, energy and focus (p.128) how to perform simultaneously and improvise while controlling every movement, keeping in view the social context in which she is performing. Women's dance not only finds a balance in itself, it creates a balance with the public. Formal behavior, in dance, as well as and in women's informal theatrical performances (Safa Isfahani 1980) women act out the moral prerogatives of their society. They project on the informally created scene the moral and the immoral dictums and behaviors.

The most extreme form of "trickster"' style representation is the "siyâh bâzi" where the black slave becomes powerful and "satirizes ... to operate as a safety valve for expression of political and social discontent and frustration" (Shay ibid:. 155).

Conclusion

In conclusion, trying to find the differential use of the emotional space, that which gives stylistic coherence to Iranian culture, we can refer to the "habitus" of Bourdieu or the "informal domain" of E T. Hall. We have observed extremes and have witnessed a sense of balance. The positive side is the paradise and being with the Saints, the negative is hell, torture and loneliness. In the middle lies everyday life in an extended family, in a house with a garden (see Shashahani 1998) or in an enclosed space around a Persian carpet. In everyday life harmony and balance, reticence and courteous behavior are normative. Lots of negotiations take place here. In the various arts, harmony and balance are respected, be it on a carpet, in music or dance.

Freedom and creativity belong to the erudite, to the one who knows the rules and after having mastered such knowledge, because of his/her fluffier contact with the source of truth ("del" being the mirror of this truth), creativity and movement can be his/her emanations. A final test of truth, a test that a new creativity is truthful (has come from "del", and does not have any falsehood or cheating in it) is its having found a way to the "del" of the observer or listener allowing for the intersubjective world to exist. Proverbially "That which arises from del, is apprehended by the del". A new and perfect production causes tears to flow. The height of truth is felt deeply and its physical emanation comes from the human window to the world, the eyes. This causes tears in others. Thus truth is not a matter of reflection, it is a matter of revelation, and its faculty is the "del" and the test of its being the truth is its acceptance which occurs in sharing tears.

Here we have tried to show the axis of habitus, only the skeletal structure of it. What remains to be done is filling all the intricate spaces in between. Here we can see the differential use of imaginative space by men and women, children, adults and elderly, by rich and poor, by pastoral nomads, peasants and urban dwellers, and today by the global Iranian citizen.

References

Bourdieu, Pierre. 1980. Le Sens Pratique. Paris: Les Editions de Minuit.

Duchesne-Guillemin, Jacques. 1966. Symbols and Values in Zoroastrianism, Their Survival and Renewal. New York: Harper and Row, Publishers.

Freud, Sigmund. 1938. The Basic Writings of Sigmund Freud. New York: The Modern Library.

Fuller, Graham E. 1991. The Center of the Universe, The Geopolitics of Iran. Westview Press. A Rand Corporation Research Study.

Geertz, Clifford. 1983. Local Knowledge. New York: Basic Books.

Grima, Benedicte. 1978. The Performance of Emotion Among Paxtun Women. Austin: University of Texas Press.

Hall, Edward T. 1959. The Silent Language, Fawcett Premier.

Jenkins, Richard 1992. Pierre Bourdieu. Routledge.

Lazarus, Richard S. 1999. Hope: An Emotion and a Vital Coping Resource Against Despair, in: Social Research, Vol. 66. No.2.

Lutz, Catherine, Geoffrey M. White. 1986. The Anthropology of Emotions, in: Annual Review of Anthropology.

Lutz, Catherine 1988. Ethnographic Perspectives on the Emotion Lexicon, in: V. Handiton et al. (eds.). Cognitive Perspectives on Emotion and Motivation. Kluwer Academic Publishers.

Nasafi, Azizoddin. 1983. Le Livre de l'Homme Parfait, Tehran: Institut Français d' lranologie de Teheran.

Planalp, Sally 1999. Communicating Emotion, Social, Moral and Cultural Processes. Cambridge: University Pr.

Reddy, William M. 1997. Against Constructionism, The Historical Ethnography of Emotions, in: Current Anthropology, Vol. 38, No. 3.

Scheff, Thomas J. 1977. The Distancing of Emotion in Ritual. In: Current Anthropology, Vol. 18, No. 3.

Safa-Isfahani, Kaveh 1980. Female-centered World Views in Iranian Culture: Symbolic Representations of Sexuality in Dramatic Games, in: Signs. Journal of Women in Culture and Society, Vol. 6, No.11.

Shay, Anthony 1999. Choreophobia, Solo Improvised Dance in the Iranian World, Mazda Publishers.

Shahshahani, Soheila. 1990. Women in the Kinship Structure of Iran, in: Dube, Leela, Rajni Pairiwala (eds.). Structures and Strategies, Women, Work and Family. New Dehli / London: Sage Publications.

Shahshahani, Soheila.1995. Tensions Between Popular, Elite and Industrial Culture in the Iranian City of Kashan, in: Grazyna Ewa Karpinska (ed.). The City: Today, Yesterday, and the Day Before, Lodz: University of Poland.

Shahshahani, Soheila.1998. Esfahan's Gardens and Mosques, in: International Journal of Urban and Regional Research. Oxford: Blackwell Publishers.

Damaris Lüthi

Concepts of Space and Pollution in a South Indian Town Neighbourhood

Abstract

Environmental squalor is a salient feature of Indian cities and towns, and the specific odour of decay has become a typical characteristic to visitors of the Indian subcontinent, puzzling many of them because it is in striking contrast to orthodox upper caste purity requirements. The few studies on Indian habits of cleanliness which have been made, have attempted to explain this contrast using one or a combination of the following arguments. Pollution is, for example, seen as the consequence of the perpetuation of caste discrimination, with high castes refusing to allow technological improvements because they do not want to lose their underdogs, personified by the lowest-caste sweepers (Milner 1987). These are held responsible for environmental pollution since their cleaning performance is considered insufficient. Yet, according to Prashad (2001), the persistence of the role of the sweepers and their inadequate efforts was due to colonial reluctance to invest funds in the sanitary infrastructure, in combination with the insufficient adaptation of modern technology to the Indian context, justified by an orientalist ignorance of the hygienic needs of the Indian lower classes. In contrast, Kaviraj (1997) maintains that in Calcutta, habits related to the environment in the past were determined by the orthodox conceptual distinction 'home inside '/' world outside', with the idea of the inhospitable outside being uncontrollable; while today the Calcuttan middle class has adapted the Western idea of public space worthy of protection, environmental pollution there, according to the author, is now an expression of class protest by the lower orders. Harriss-White (1998: 16), on the other hand, suggests that the paradox of meticulous private cleanliness in combination with public squalor is the result of gendered space - the domestic precincts being female and clean, whereas the public spaces are male and filthy.

As my research among middle and lower middle castes and classes in Kottar, a neighbourhood in a South Indian town has shown, the environment there is polluted by everyone, irrespective of caste or class[1]*. In contrast to Calcutta, orthodox Brahmin ideas apparently still dominate, conflicting with the "modern ideas" promoted by the public authorities. According to traditional concepts, space is determined by the dichotomies of divine order and worldly chaos, home in- and world outside, with the outside irrelevant to well-being. Yet, there is an additional fact: in spite of awareness in the Indian administration since the end of the 19*th *century of the necessity of improving the sanitary infrastructure, the Kottar authorities – similar to the situation in most other Indian cities and towns (Arnold 1993; Prashad 2001) – have so far avoided making any*

[1] Lüthi 1999. Research took place over 16 months in 1995-96. Inspired by Mauss (1936; 1938) and Bourdieu (1972), it concentrated on the observation of physical habits and local concepts related to cleanliness in Kottar, part of the town of Nagercoil.

changes. The present desolate environmental situation in Kottar is hence neither the responsibility of the Sweeper caste and any attempts of their traditionalist masters to preserve the social system, nor due to gendered space or lower class protest, but is the result of the persistent validity of orthodox Brahmin concepts in combination with the conscious reluctance of the authorities to invest funds into improving the sanitary infrastructure.
In order to illustrate this, this paper is concerned with the concepts and habits of ordinary Kottar inhabitants relating to private and public spaces, linked to insights in the colonial politics of public sanitation.

The structure and concept of private space

The traditional Kottar home of a wealthy higher-caste family is an almost square structure surrounding an open courtyard (*see Fig. 1, p. 287*). In the past, buildings for wealthy joint families could be rather large structures with several courtyards (*Fig. 2, p. 287*, *Mayamata* 1985: 230; Moore 1989: 171). The house is, moreover, divided into front and back, with entrance doors on both sides. The main door, normally in the middle of the front, opens onto a small veranda or entrance room. From there one reaches the main room, which is next to, or includes the courtyard. Further in are a *puja* room, a store-room, a kitchen and a dining-room. The *puja* room is separated from the kitchen by at least one room. At the periphery there is a latrine, somewhat distant from the house at the end of the backyard, near the back door. A semi-traditional house is a long, narrow chain of connected small rooms extending from the front street to a backyard area (*Fig. 3, p. 288*). Apart from the reduced size of the structure, the arrangement of the rooms is more or less the same as in the full-sized traditional house. The tube-shape is a result of subdividing the traditional house between siblings. The houses of poor families emulate those of the higher castes and classes (cf. Moore 1989), though on a considerably smaller scale (*Fig. 4, p. 289*). A new house has a similar composition of rooms, with slight but typical alterations (*Fig. 5, p. 289*). There is no interior courtyard and there is often an inside toilet with a septic tank.

A decorative pattern drawn with chalk onto the street in front of the entrance steps, called *kōlam,* slightly extends the boundary of the house (*Plate 1, p. 297*). Other boundaries are the veranda, courtyard and backyard. Visitors are received on the veranda, or, in orthodox households, menstruating women are banished there. The backyard accommodates the hygienic facilities, pets, refuse and low-caste visitors.

The front door is on the clean side of the house with its auspicious facade, and is the representative sign of the house. The auspiciousness of this door is visible from its material, which is precious wood, and from the elaborateness of its wood carvings, which indicates the status of the house owner. When leaving the house, one should always use the front door, both for auspicious or inauspicious purposes. Yet on coming home, the front entrance is only used after auspicious events, for example after visiting a woman who has given birth. In contrast, after returning from an inauspicious visit to a death-house or the barber, one should enter by the back door.

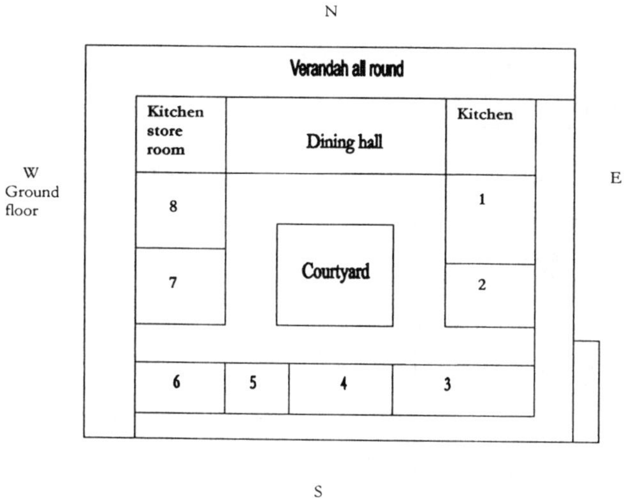

Fig. 1
Traditional upper caste house

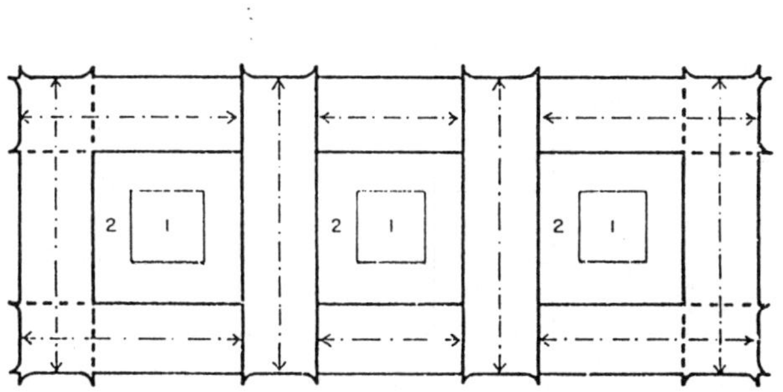

Fig. 2 Traditional house with several courtyards

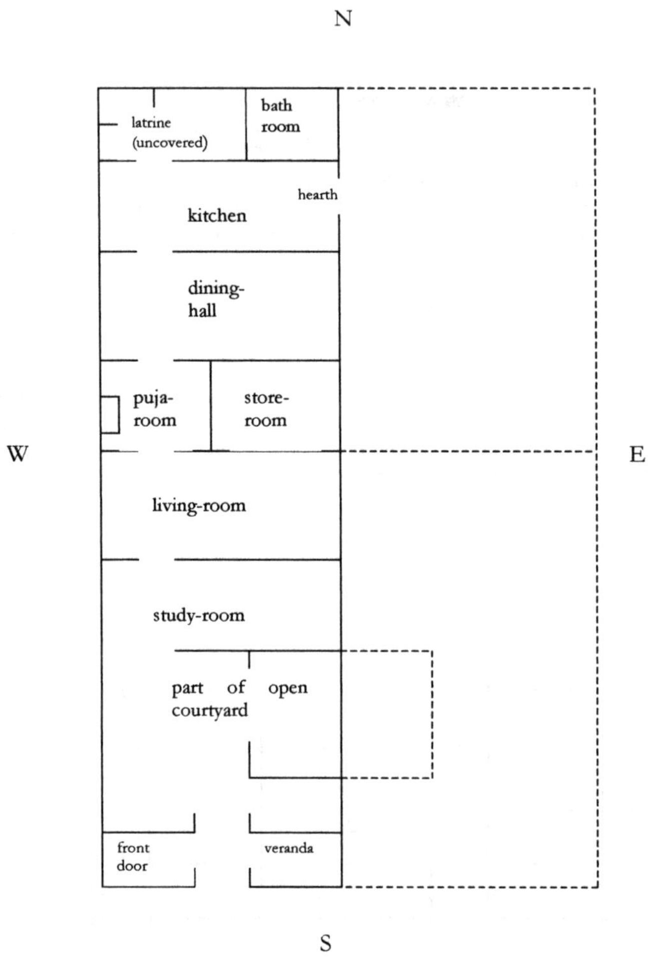

Fig 3: Traditional upper caste house divided up

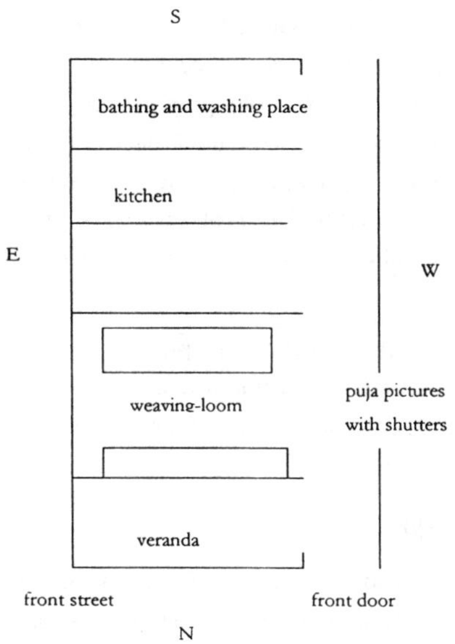

Fig. 4: Poor house

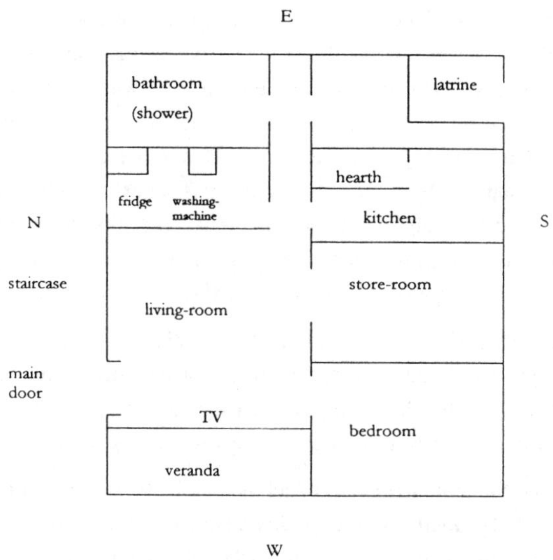

Fig. 5: Modern apartment

The inhabitants try to separate, and thereby protect, pure and clean from impure places in the house. It is important that the *puja* room is not next to the kitchen, so that the representations of the deities are not close to the hearth. Otherwise the deities could become polluted, for example during fish preparation, or if a menstruating woman did the cooking. In the past, the *kakkūs* ("latrine") was not tolerated inside the house, because people found that it made the whole place too polluted (cf. Vatuk 1972; Searle-Chatterjee 1981: 93). Even today the toilet should ideally be outside. Moreover, during menstruation, childbirth and the death of occupants, the whole house or parts of it are considered seriously polluted, called *thīṭṭu,* due to the biological waste occurring.

As the above data show, important concepts for the structuring of private space are hence the dichotomies of in/outside, clean/unclean, pure/impure, sacred/profane, front/rear, and auspicious/inauspicious. High and low caste approaches are more or less identical.

The structure and concept of the outside world

Similar dichotomies that pertain to the house are also valid outside. The fronts of the houses give on to respectable mud and sometimes paved streets, bound by narrow gutters. In contrast, the lanes at the back of the houses are unpaved, narrow and polluted, often looking like mere extensions of the sewers flowing there. Formerly, each Kottar caste used to live in a specific street or area. Nowadays such strict spatial separation between castes has been abandoned. Wealthy people and those with "decent jobs", hence the "respectable", irrespective of caste, have rented or bought houses in higher-caste streets. Hence the domiciles of families belonging to various castes, though often of similar caste or class status, are intermingled in the neighbourhoods. The traditional caste neighbourhoods are thus gradually converting into representations of class, though in most neighbourhoods there is still a majority of one specific caste, and most caste temples with a *manḏapam* and head office are surrounded by the houses of their caste members.

The "sacredness" of sites is an important spatial consideration. Temples and also most rivers and ponds are sacred and should, therefore, not be defiled, though in practice the waters are often considerably polluted. Bathing in such sacred waters is considered beneficial, because of the divine, purifying forces they embody, irrespective of scientific standards of cleanliness.

Moreover, the term *girāmam,* which is used in the sense of both "village" or town neighbourhood is relevant. *Girāmam* is an orthodox abstraction for a specific way of occupying and organising space. According to Zimmermann (1987: 101), throughout Sanskrit literature the term *gramya* ("domesticated") is the opposite of *aranya* ("wild"). In Vedic and Brahmin India the term *grama* described a social concentration of people, in contrast to *arayana*, the forest beyond them (Malamoud 1976: 4; Zimmermann 1987: 102). In later texts the expression was used besides other terms for the description of an artificial environment, in contrast to the earth as a primary site (*Mayamata* 1985: viii, 26; Lewandowski 1977: 185). According to old architectural treatises (*Mayamata* 1985 [9th-12th century]: xiii, 27; Kramrisch 1976: 42), *grama*s were divided into concentric zones. A temple or altar had to be placed at its centre, with a sanctum (*garbhagrha*) i.e. "womb" room[2]. The caste (varna) as well as the economic hierarchy were incorporated in the architectural plan, with the highest and wealthiest communities near the centre, and the lowest orders at the periphery[3]. The cremation site was also relegated to the outskirts, and the more inferior cemetery was even further outside (*Mayamata* 1985: 31-34). Similar town structures have been noted in more recent times (cf. Hofmeister 1980; Lewandowski 1977: 194).

The idea of an opposition between sacred and profane, inner social order and outer chaos, therefore, seems to be a central Hindu metaphor. In Kottar this was evident, according to high-caste informants, in *girāmams* with a temple and the high caste streets in the centre and the lower-caste neighbourhoods and *cheris*, situated further outside[4]. Today, temples and the Brahmin streets in front of them, as well as higher-caste and class neighbourhoods in the town centre, are considered "good", while the peripheries are considered "bad". People belonging to lower castes had no access to higher caste streets until recently.

There is, in addition, the Western concept of "public space", signifying spaces to which all castes and classes have the right of access and which came into being in the West in the eighteenth century (Kaviraj 1997). In colonial India this led to the creation of parks and other open spaces in bigger cities (ibid.: 87; Lewandowski 1977), for example in Calcutta, where this new idea was superimposed on the traditional dichotomies (Kaviraj 1997). In Nagercoil-Kottar the idea of "public space" is professed only by the municipal authorities and a small educated elite, manifest for example in the eight parks which are meant by the authorities for "passive recreation", but which are mainly used by the public as waste dumps and toilets.

Polluting and cleaning the home

The house should be *suttham* ("clean") and if possible even *pu̱nitham* ("holy, divine, sacred"). This concept applies not only to upper castes and classes but is also shared by the lower orders. Cleanliness is thought to be required by the deities, who feel invited if the house is clean. In particular Lakshmi, the goddess of wealth, comes at the twilight times of dawn or dusk. Tidiness is rewarded by the deities with physical health and wealth. In contrast, impurity angers the deities,

[2] *Mayamata* (1985: 28); Kramrisch (1976: 27); Beck (1976: 238); O'Flaherty (1980: 20); Malamoud (1989: 84).
[3] *Mayamata* (1985: xliii); Hofmeister (1980: 105); Lewandoswki (1977: 189, 192); Guilmoto et al. (1990: 195).
[4] Cf. Srinivas (1952: 27); Béteille (1965); Moffatt (1979); Deliège (1992: 170).

who punish the house with disease and poverty. Therefore, in the sacred space with the representations of deities and ancestors, no impurity is tolerated, and also the kitchen must be protected from specific impurities. Impure house inhabitants (menstruating women), lower castes and objects such as shoes do not belong in the house. Fish is cleaned in the backyard, since this is considered too polluting to be done inside. Only light dirt is tolerated within most of the house, including babies' excreta, which are often not immediately cleaned since the waste products of little children are not considered impure.

The house is regularly cleaned in tune with sacred schedules and spaces to please the deities, - analogous to efforts focused on the human body (cf. Lüthi 1999). Since Lakshmi mostly visits the house at twilight, specifically on the sacred days of Tuesday and Friday, most people clean their front entrance daily at dusk and dawn and draw a *kōlam*. The cleaning is normally done by female household members. Apart from sweeping before twilight, they sweep the main part of the house several times daily, but neglect the impure backyard. Washing the floors takes place in most households once a week before sacred Friday, but many women scrub the floors of the purest places of the house, the kitchen and *puja*-hall, daily. The floors are, moreover, washed on new and full moon days before ancestor worship, on the first day of the Tamil month, and before functions and festivities. After *thīṭṭu* pollution due to the biological waste of a girl's first menstruation, a childbirth, or a death, the house must be more thoroughly cleansed by a Brahmin priest. It must then, in addition, be whitewashed.

While sweeping is done with a broom made from fine grass, and washing with a strong palm-leaf fibre broom and soapy water, only washing with cowdung water is deemed adequate for mud floors (cf. Dubois 1906: 153; Leslie 1989: 59). Also, the spot on which a menstruating woman has slept, or where a lower caste person has eaten, is, in very orthodox households, cleansed with cowdung water. Nowadays, mud floors have largely disappeared, so that this practice is becoming obsolete. Cleanliness after more thorough *thīṭṭu* pollution is considered achievable by purifying with stronger agents such as *pañjakavviyam*, a mixture of products from the sacred cow, including cowdung, urine, milk and curd. This cleansing is performed by a Brahmin priest, who spells manthras and sprays the mixture all over the polluted spaces, and also gives some to the most polluted persons to drink.

Thus, the schedule as well as cleansing techniques and agents manifest Brahmin concepts of sacredness and classification of matter, which are incongruous with a Western germ theory of hygiene.

Polluting and cleaning the outside

Polluting and cleaning habits outside private homes define the outside as a negligible waste dump, except for sacred sites such as temples or rivers, for which similar rules apply as for private homes: the deities demand purity. These sites are, therefore, protected from visits by polluted persons such as menstruating women and formerly also low-caste persons. Impure bodily covers such as shirts and shoes are also not allowed inside, as the deities would become angry and inflict disease or poverty (Lüthi 1999). The pure-impure, in-outside dichotomies are hence also applied in practices relating to the outside. It is a spatial treatment that corresponds with the orthodox distinction 'inside order' and 'outside chaos', *grama* and *arayana.* Waste is moved to the periphery, rendering the centre clean and the outer areas unclean and thereby acting on space in terms of the concentrical concept of the *girāmam.*

Every piece of waste is simply thrown out of the house. Those whose compounds are surrounded by walls tend to throw the garbage over the wall. The waste, which is dropped on the floor since there are no waste bins inside the house, is swept outside. Larger pieces are either thrown into the gutter or put on an open garbage heap in the front or rear street (*Plate 2, p. 297*). Waste deposited outside is expected to be openly visible, so that people cannot hide very impure things such as sanitary towels in bags and thereby severely pollute passers-by without their knowledge. Some people have a container in their back garden, where they deposit the kitchen waste. When people walk or drive outside their houses they normally discard waste directly on the way. People without access to private toilets use the gutters, public toilets, parks or peripheral fields for relieving themselves.

The open gutter (*chākkaḏai*) at the rear of the house transports the faecal and bathwater to the open sewer in the rear street; the kitchen gutter with liquid kitchen refuse is either linked to it or transports its waste to the sewer passing in front of the house (*Plate 3, p. 298*). The open sewage system channels the dirty water from the open drains bordering the streets to the bigger *Parakkai* collecting sewer (*Plate 4, p. 298*), which proceeds to the *Pazhayar* river at the periphery. From there it flows untreated into a pond outside the town, from where the water is taken for irrigating the fields. During the monsoon the sewers overflow, and everyone has to wade through the lethal sauce.

The cleaning of the outside is the task of the lowest-caste scavengers and municipal Sweepers (*Plate 3, p. 298*). The men sweep the streets and remove the waste heaps, while the women clean the public latrines. The municipal cleaning takes place only irregularly, so that garbage heaps abound, toilets stink, and people complain. According to the municipal authorities, one of the reasons for the bad sanitary situation in the town is the inadequate number of Sweepers.

Spatio-social segregation

The effort to keep certain spaces clean is replicated in the access certain "impure" groups of people have to these spaces. Since the inside of the house is considered pure and auspicious, many landlords do not like to give access to lower-caste persons, a well-known fact in Indian sociology (e.g. Srinivas 1952: 74; Moore 1989: 178; Reiniche 1981: 24). As noted above, castes who are thought to be persistently polluted are, moreover, segregated outside the settlement[5], as are also the uneducated and poor nowadays. Nor are higher ranking people very enthusiastic about visiting the homes of people who are lower-caste. The homes of lower ranking people are thought to be "naturally" unclean, as are also those of the poor today, including impoverished high-caste families. Conversely, if the people are classified as educated and wealthy, their houses are thought to be automatically clean. Hence today the low-caste, uneducated and poor all tend to be considered unclean, which means that the Brahmin concept of purity/impurity, which was traditionally used to discriminate against lower castes, is nowadays also used against lower *classes*. Orthodox caste values are being applied to class.

Perceptions and reactions

In spite of participating actively in environmental pollution themselves, many Kottar residents complain about the filth and stench in their neighbourhood, though rather because of the inconvenience and for aesthetic reasons than for fear of health hazards: Kottarians do not see a connection between pollution and diseases such as dysentery, cholera, or tuberculosis, but favour explanations such as thermal imbalance of the body, the evil eye or divine wrath for these and other sufferings.

A few persons from the educated middle class seemed to be more conscious of the dangers of environmental pollution, but in consequence merely launched private initiatives in specific streets instead of pressing for a more systematic improvement of the whole infrastructure. The only bigger protest during the period of my fieldwork was conducted by a local branch of a fanatic Hindu party, directed against the placement of a sub-depot close to a dwelling site. The aim was, however, not to eradicate the sub-depot, but to move it away from the rear side of the Hindu temple to the rear side of the mosque.

In addition, the municipal authorities also seemed to be aware of the hazards of environmental pollution. The municipal health officer explained that among the main health problems in Nagercoil-Kottar were sicknesses that were clearly caused by pollution, such as various types of gastroenteritis and respiratory problems. Information campaigns and public rallies on topics such as

---

[5] Cf. Moffatt (1979: 64 ff.); Dumont (1966: 173); Lynch (1969: 169); Searle-Chatterjee (1981); Deliège (1995: 304; 1992: 169).

cleanliness and health are organised, and immunisation campaigns conducted. Yet the hazard is obviously not held to be big enough to find it necessary to improve the sanitary infrastructure and, for example, cover the open sewers. The authorities said that they did not have the funds for such an investment. "It would cost twenty crores, and it would damage the entire road system", lamented the Health Officer. He argued that open gutters had the big advantage that they could easily be de-blocked from solid materials.

Colonial heritage

Funds are not only lacking today, but the problems date back more than a hundred years. Unlike in urban Europe in the nineteenth century, where the danger of lethal epidemics was so acute that the authorities were forced to take all possible measures to improve the public sanitation and, for example, provided and enlarged water sewage systems, improved potable water supplies and prohibited the use of wells (Illi and Steiner 1987: 64; Williams 1991; Vigarello 1985), in India, political, class and practical obstacles prevented the execution of reforms (Arnold 1989: 273-4; Prashad 2001). The desirability of the improvement of public sanitation was already being discussed in South Indian medical circles in the 1850s, followed by the appointment of sanitary commissioners. But owing to shortage of funds and disrespect for the "natives", sanitary interventions were mostly restricted to major cities and military camps, and only to the more affluent wards and suburbs (Arnold 1989: 276, 279; Prashad 2001: 117; Silva Gracias 1994: 65).

In the few places where modern sanitary systems *were* implemented, they had a dramatic effect on the reduction of mortality (Arnold 1989: 277), as had the new inoculations and vaccinations (ibid.; Crook 1989: 292). Fatally, I assume, the availability of medical treatment for pollution-related disease has impeded in many places further pressure to improve the sanitary infrastructure. This has ultimately had important consequences. The permanent stress of expensive modern medication on the purses of the poor, who live in the most polluted neighbourhoods, worsens their living standard, especially their diet, which maintains their bad health. A bad public sanitary infrastructure, then, ultimately not only ruins health but also perpetuates poverty.

Summary

The perceptions and habits of cleanliness in relation to private and public spaces in Kottar show a pattern which is much closer to traditional Brahmin purity concepts than to the modern Western and Indian elitist distinction between private and public space. While negligence of the cleanliness of the private house is thought to have fatal consequences for the health and wealth of its inhabitants, because angered deities may punish the family, polluting the outside is deemed to have no such consequences and is thus considered unimportant. Not only do the orthodox concepts have an ongoing significance, but they are now, in addition to degrading impure castes, also used to discriminate against the poor and uneducated, and thus are applied to class. Ultimately, the financial concerns of the authorities in combination with orthodox Brahmin concepts which deny value to the "outside" and to "impure" social orders, are the background to the persistent environmental squalor and bad health of the poor in Kottar.

Source of illustrations

By the author (Figs. 3-5).
Ueli Grossenbacher (Plates 1-4).
Mayamata 1985, p. 231 (Fig. 2).
Thurston 1909, V, p. 362-3 (Fig. 1).

Plate 1/ Plate 2

Plate 3/ Plate 4

References

Arnold, David. *Colonizing the Body. State Medicine and Epidemic Disease in Nineteenth Century India.* University of California Press, 1993.

Beck, Brenda E.F. "The symbolic merger of body, space and cosmos in Hindu Tamil Nadu". *Contributions to Indian Sociology* (N.S.), Vol. 10, 1976: 213-243.

Béteille, André. *Caste, Class and Power.* University of California Press, 1965.

Bourdieu, Pierre. *Outline of a Theory of Practice.* Cambridge University Press, 1985 (1972).

Crook, Nigel. "On the Comparative Historical Perspective: India, Europe, the Far East". In Dyson, Tim (ed.). *India's Historical Demography. Studies in Famine, Disease and Society.* London 1989.

Deliège, Robert. "Replication and consensus: untouchability, caste and ideology in India". *Man* (N.S.) 27, 1992: 155-73.

Deliège, Robert. *Les intouchables en Inde. Des castes d'exclus.* Paris: Imago, 1995.

Dubois, Abbe J.A. *Hindu Manners, Customs and Ceremonies.* Oxford University Press, 1985 (1906).

Dumont, Louis. *homo hierarchicus. Le système des castes et ses implications.* Editions Gallimard, 1966.

Guilmoto, Christophe, M.-L. Reiniche and P. Pichard. *Tiruvannamalai: Un Lieu Saint Sivaite du Sud de l' Inde 5: La ville.* Paris: Ecole Française d'Extrême Orient, 1990.

Harriss-White, Barbara. "Rural infrastructure, urban civic services and the micro politics of governance". Workshop paper: *The Anthropology of the Indian State.* London: London School of Economics, 9 May, 1998.

Hofmeister, Burkhard. *Die Stadtstruktur.* Darmstadt: Wissenschaftliche Buchgesellschaft, 1980.

Illi, M. and Steiner, H.-R. *Von der Schissgruob zur modernen Stadtentwässerung.* Zürich: Verlag NZZ, 1987.

Kaviraj, Sudipta. "Filth and the Public Sphere: Concepts and Practices about Space in Calcutta". *Public Culture* 10 (1), 1997: 83-113.

Kramrisch, Stella. *The Hindu Temple.* 2 vols. Delhi: Motilal Banarsidass, 1976 (1946).

Leslie, Julia I. The Perfect Wife. *The Orthodox Hindu Woman according to the Stridharmapaddhati of Tryambakayajvan.* Delhi: Oxford University Press, 1989.

Lewandowski, Susan J. "Changing Form and Function in the Ceremonial and the Colonial Port City in India: An Historical Analysis of Madurai and Madras". *Modern Asian Studies*, 11, 2, 1977: 183-212.

Lüthi, Damaris. *Washing Off Sin. Cleanliness in Kottar, South India.* Inauguraldissertation, Bern: Selbstverlag, 1999.

Lynch, Owen M. *The Politics of Untouchability. Social Mobility and Social Change in a City of India.* Columbia University Press 1969.

Malamoud, Charles. "Village et forêt dans l'idéologie de l'Inde brâhmanique". *Archives Européennes de Sociologie*, xvii, 1976: 3-20.

Mauss, Marcel. "Les techniques du corps". *Journal de Psychologie*, xxxii, n°s 3-4, 1936.

Mauss, Marcel. "Une catégorie de l'esprit humain: la notion de personne, celle de 'moi'". *Journal of the Royal Anthropological Institute*, Vol. LXVIII, 1938.

Mayamata. An Indian treatise on housing, architecture and iconography. Translated by Bruno Dagens. New Delhi: Sitaram Bhartia Institute of Scientific Research, 1985.

Milner, Murray Jr. "Dirt and Development in India". *Virginia Quarterly* Review 63, 1987: 54-71.

Moffatt, Michael. *An Untouchable Community in South India. Structure and Consensus.* Princeton University Press, 1979.

Moore, Melinda A. "The Kerala house as a Hindu cosmos". *Contributions to Indian sociology* (n.s.) 23, 1, 1989: 169-202.

O'Flaherty, Wendy Doniger. *Women, Androgynes and other Mythical Beasts.* Chicago University Press, 1980.

Prashad, Vijay. "The Technology of Sanitation in Colonial Delhi". *Modern Asian Studies* 35, 1, 2001: 113-155.

Reiniche, Marie-Louise. "La maison au Tirunelveli". *Bulletin de l'Ecole Française d'Extrême Orient* 70, 1981: 21-57.

Searle-Chatterjee, Mary. *Reversible Sex Roles. The Special Case of Benares Sweepers.* Pergamon Press, 1981.

Silva Gracias, Fatima da. *Health and Hygiene in Colonial Goa 1510-1961.* New Delhi: Concept, 1994.

Srinivas, M.N. *Religion and Society among the Coorgs of South India.* Clarendon Press, 1952.

Thurston, Edgar. *Castes and Tribes of Southern India.* 1909.

Vatuk, Sylvia. *Kinship and Urbanization. White Collar Migrants in North India.* University of California Press, 1972.

Vigarello, Georges. *Le propre et le sale. L'hygiène du corps depuis le Moyen Age.* Paris: Editions du Seuil, 1985.

Williams, Marilyn Thornton. *Washing "The Great Unwashed". Public Baths in Urban America, 1840-1920.* Ohio State University Press, 1991.

Zimmermann, F. *The Jungle and the Aroma of Meats.* University of California Press, 1987 (1982).

Peter J.M. Nas
Rivke Jaffe

Working With Waste

Abstract

This paper will give an overview of scavenging systems in various developing countries, including Indonesia and Jamaica.

Introduction

At present in the town of Oegstgeest, the Netherlands, solid waste disposal is a highly diversified and sophisticated process. Inhabitants carry paper, glass in different colors, and textiles to fixed collection points. They keep dangerous waste and old medicaments in special boxes - which cannot be opened by children - and which may be emptied once a month when the itinerant chemical collector truck passes by. Composables and solid waste are collected in small, wheeled containers - made of decomposable materials - in front of the houses once in a fortnight. Large pieces, such as old chairs, beds, bicycles and so on, are collected separately. Solid waste collection has become a clean and highly mechanized activity.

This was very different in the 1980s in the city of Bandung, Indonesia, where scavengers dominated the solid waste disposal system (Versnel, 1986). There were various categories: cigarette-but collectors, wet scavengers, and scavengers roaming household waste at different stages in the collection process, namely the concrete household containers, the transfer point and the dump site. These scavengers complemented the municipal refuse collectors, who transported the refuse from the household bins with handcarts to the transfer points where it was loaded on trucks heading for the city dump. The scavengers basically applied a recycling system of their own selecting cardboard, plastic, bottles, tins, repairable items and so on, and cutting and cleaning the materials when apposite.

In this article we will present a picture of the great variety of solid waste and scavenging systems in the world on the basis of existing research results. In doing so we will isolate the important factors that characterize these systems as well as the trends that characterize their developments. Furthermore, we will pay attention to the experiments that have been conducted to improve solid waste and scavenger systems, with particular stress on those systems in developing countries.

Kingston

Kingston, Jamaica is another example of a Third World city coping with Solid Waste Management problems. As in other countries, one of the main problems is that the amount of waste being produced exceeds the municipality's capacity to process it. Collection, transport and disposal services are underfunded and suffer from a lack of managerial and technological expertise.

Scavenging in Kingston occurs primarily at the city's main waste disposal site, Riverton City. This dumpsite, which is currently being transformed into a sanitary landfill, is located on the periphery of the city. It has an area of 12 hectares, and is the designated destination of Kingston Metropolitan Area's (KMA) residential, commercial and industrial waste. Approximately five hundred tons of waste are deposited at the site daily. The garbage contains enough valuable resources to provide a livelihood to hundreds of scavengers. Many of these scavengers live around the dump, in the Riverton City community, but some travel to their place of work each day by bus, as they would to a job.

The scavengers are exposed to health risks and their socio-economic status is very low. They feel that they are seen as animals; because they work amidst trash, people regard them as trash themselves.

Actually, many scavenger systems, including this one in Kingston, are highly developed social systems. They effect a resource recovery system that is flexible, efficient and thorough; they constitute an organized, yet informal work force. Unlike in several other developing countries, the Jamaican government accepts the reality of scavenging and, instead of ignoring or harassing scavengers, seeks to integrate them into the formal waste management scheme. The Riverton City scavengers are included in the national solid waste management reorganization scheme, as the government tries to pursue economic and health security for those working in 'community-based recycling activities', while promoting a certain level of environmentalism at the same time (Jaffe 2000).

San Francisco

Stewart E. Perry (1978) has elaborately studied the San Francisco Scavengers. The solid waste management system evolved from fierce competition between individuals who with wagon and horse picked up refuse in the early days to a co-operative with equal partners under the name 'Sunset' which later turned into the conglomerate 'Envirocal Inc'. Perry using participant observation in the 1960s and 1970s lively relates the views of the mainly Italian-American scavengers on their work, their company and the clients they had to deal with. The historical perspective of his study is very illuminating, showing the interplay of four important factors, namely managerial developments in the scavenging system, technical improvements, the socio-cultural background of the scavengers, and the local and general socio-political context.

Technical aspects of waste management and scavenging

Following the 'life' of waste, different techniques and technological innovations can be observed along the way. After waste has been produced, there are basically three stages: collection, transport and disposal.

Gage (1995) has demonstrated the importance of the method of household containment on solid waste management; the method of storage and pre-collection handling influences the method, speed and efficiency of collection. Especially in lower-income areas, such as in Kingston, the nature of the community (layout or narrow roads) and improper practices at the household level influence collection services. In many cities, a large proportion of the waste management budget goes towards collection.

A tendency seen in many developing countries is to adopt technology from Northern countries; this often goes for all three stages mentioned above. Modern collection trucks cannot service irregularly laid out neighborhoods without wide, paved roads, such as slums or squatter communities. More 'old-fashioned' collection vehicles or a communal garbage collection point on the periphery of a neighborhood would be more appropriate in cases like these. Another drawback in using modern waste technology in developing countries is that the composition of waste differs. Refuse in poorer countries usually has a much higher proportion of organic matter, and is denser and moister than 'rich' garbage. These differences have consequences for the applied technology and management of solid waste systems, with the result that highly sophisticated solutions are unsuitable.

Transportation of waste or scavenged materials relates to collection methods in that modern equipment such as trucks is often inappropriate to local circumstances. On the other hand, manually pushed or animal-drawn transportation has limited range. This means that informal waste collectors often dump their loads illegally, as the distance to official waste disposal sites is prohibitive. A potential solution is the establishment of transfer and storage sites, where waste can be stored until it is taken to its final destination. These sites can also function as a location for (further) resource recovery activities.

When it comes to waste disposal, there are essentially three options: landfilling, incineration, and recycling. Some authors list export of waste as an option, but ethically and financially (especially for developing countries) this is not really a viable alternative. Recycling is generally the most environmentally conscious as well as cost-effective method of waste disposal. However, large-scale formal recycling schemes require a high level of public participation, one that is not always present or possible in the context of developing countries.

Socio-cultural aspects

In many, though certainly not all, developing countries, scavengers have a different socio-cultural background than the majority of the population. It can be stated that their socio-economic status is generally very low; the general population as well as the authorities often view and treat them as 'part of the rubbish they work with' (ASMARE, 1998). But a UNESCO report shows that this attitude has been adopted by scavengers themselves. 'Comparative research and experiences have shown that the scavengers consider themselves as a sort of social category associated with 'sub-human characteristics.'' Low education levels and unhealthy working conditions in combination with their popular status lead to a negative self-perception and a lack of self-confidence (UNESCO, 2001).

Organization

In formal and informal waste management systems one can find a great variety of organizational forms. The following list of instances found in the literature as well as our own research gives an example of the diversity: individual scavengers, informal scavenger systems, semi-formal waste recovery companies, cooperative organizations of scavengers, municipal waste collection organizations tied to community-based organizations, and formal municipal waste collection companies.

In trying to classify this heterogeneity, we find a series of contrasting aspects; the organizational forms range from formal to informal; small-scale to large-scale; private to public; individual to cooperative; and assisted to non-assisted (with or without external NGO or governmental facilitation). The scope of organization can range from the local urban level to a regional, national or international level. Of course the organizational forms do not always conform to one or the other extreme but often assume gradual or mixed forms.

Socio-political context

Large amounts of solid waste from mega-cities like New York and Tokyo can be disposed of in several ways. They can be exported, burned in incinerators and dumped in landfills. One way to diminish the quantity of waste material consists of decreasing consumption in general and the use of all sorts of throwaways, such as plastic bottles and package material, in particular. Another way is recycling and construction of products in such away that recycling becomes more easy. In his comparison of the solid waste systems of New York and Tokyo, Jerry Eades (1998) concludes that the cultural and administrative context in both cities is very different. Tokyo's local administration is much more centralized with limited political participation and more possibilities for urban planners to change administrative boundaries which often are a bottleneck for solving wage disposal problems. In New York the idea to export waste to other states led to protests from the local communities against the shift of the pollution problem to their area. This is most clearly shown by the garbage barge and the garbage train in respectively 1987 and 1992, which both headed from New York to other US states but under influence of the environmental movement had to return to the place where they started. Notwithstanding the sharp contextual differences in political and administrative culture between New York and Tokyo, in Tokyo local communities have begun to protest against waste disposal in their territory too. As landfills become difficult by these protests and the opening of more burning plants is a bad option because of air pollution, the only way to go seems to be recycling. This pushes for technological improvement in waste disposal and new invention in waste uses.

Historically New York practiced dumping and Tokyo incineration as the main solution for waste disposal. In comparison to Tokyo, local political mobilization has strongly limited the options for waste disposal in New York. In the long run both cities, however, will have to expand recycling and reduction strategies.

The relationship between scavengers or scavenging systems and the authorities vary strongly from country to country. We find Medina's categorization of the main responses to be apposite. He sees four main categories, namely: (1) repression; (2) neglect; (3) collusion, and (4) stimulation. In many developing countries, the government sees scavenging -whether on the streets, at dumpsites, or elsewhere- as a sign of failure to modernize and as an undesirable phenomenon. This attitude can lead to harassment and physical aggression towards scavenger communities though to our knowledge this has never led to 'solving the problem'. Neglect occurs when a government views neither the benefits nor the hazards associated with scavenging as a priority. Collusion is found in situations resembling clientelist systems, with hierarchy 'tying' lower level informal actors to higher-level formal government actors. In some countries, such as Jamaica or Indonesia the authorities promote a more progressive policy, trying to find safer and more equitable win-win situations rather than exploit or abolish the community and its activities.

Scavengers in context

The sections above have described scavenger systems within their own local context; but if we want to compare these systems, what generalizations can be made?

Martin Medina (1997) has compiled an overview of general characteristics applicable to scavenger systems; we believe that his list does not represent the great variety of scavenger systems throughout the world. Medina himself states the estimate that up to two percent of the population of developing countries survives through informal waste-recovery activities. This would imply that millions of people are involved in some kind of scavenging. It seems unlikely to us that one can typify such numbers and range of scavengers in such a list (Medina, 1997:2, 7-12). We tend to agree with DiGregorio's statement that scavenging (whether speaking of the occupation, the labor process, or the industry) has only two common characteristics: 'a recognition of waste as a resource and a varying degree of social opprobrium' (DiGregorio, 1994:1). This 'definition' seems more apt.

Academic trends

Refuse workers are made up by two categories, namely those who aim at the cleaning of the environment by collecting, transporting and disposing of waste, and those who use waste as a resource for the collection of items to be sold for profit. The latter category consists of the scavengers often working informally, and the former are the generally formally employed municipal or community refuse workers. This distinction is more or less theoretical as in practice scavengers also engage in transport, while municipal worker also pursue recycling activities. Sigular (1992) distinguishes the two types in relation to their use of refuse, namely waste-as-waste by refuse officials and waste-as-ore by scavengers. In the Bandung setting these two types of refuse workers were strongly intertwined, as municipal workers functioned as middlemen who bought the 'ore' from the scavengers to sell it further to industrial companies.

The labor relations of the scavengers have been annualized by Birkbeck (1979) in his study of Cali in Colombia in terms of self-employed informal sector workers who like factory labor engage in piece work of which the surplus is roamed by middlemen. The title of one of Birkbeck's articles expresses this view adequately: 'Self-employed proletarians in an informal factory' (Birkbeck, 1978). The work relations in the solid waste system between scavengers, municipal refuse workers, small middlemen, big middlemen and factories can, however, be characterized as patron-client relationships mainly based on mutual trust and cemented by rather stable product delivery and money lending patterns. These stable patron-client relations reduce the vulnerability of the scavengers by guaranteeing a certain security of living, albeit at a low standard, as the middlemen use the dependence to fix prizes at very low levels. Because of this basic survival strategy Sigular prefers to describe the scavenger systems in terms of gather and hunter societies, who survive under condition of common source exploitation. They gather 'ores' and hunt for 'valuables' in the same way as hunters and gatherers use the woods and plains. In Sigular's view the exploitation of scavengers by middlemen is occurring through market relations and not by means of employment relations in a capitalist industrial setting.

From this discussion we derive that scavengers maintain a special system of production relations that differs from that of the municipal or community employed refuse workers. The informal production relations of the scavengers are, however, completely intertwined with the formal municipal refuse work. Under the sway of existing perceptions about scavengers, as doing dirty, unhealthy work and being a criminal outcast, the larger society and local authorities generally aim for increased integration and formalization of the solid waste system.

Intervention

In attempting to 'solve' problems associated with scavengers and formal or informal systems of solid waste management, various levels of intervention can be discerned. Using our own case studies and those found in the literature, we have distinguished the following four levels:

- The level of the factories/industry that produce waste and use salvaged goods as raw materials.
- The level of the middlemen who mediate between the scavengers and industry or other buyers of scavenger materials.
- The levels of the scavengers themselves.
- The level of interventions realized by international or local government.

Conclusion

As we have demonstrated above, there is great variety in scavenging and waste management systems, in socio-cultural, technological, organizational and socio-political aspects. This variety extends to scientific analyses of (informal) waste management systems and forms of interventions in these systems. It is injudicious to view scavengers or scavenging as separate from waste management as a whole, as it is to try to compile a standard list of generalizations. Neither the neo-Marxist 'political economy models' of the likes of Birkbeck nor neo-liberal development approaches will succeed in forming foolproof universal models for such a wide range of locally formed and adapted activities and social systems. These are 'specific contextualized forms of organization that require dynamic, contextualized, and holistic modeling' (DiGregorio, 1994: 23).

On the whole, research done on scavening and informal waste mangement systems is very limited, with only a scattering of true fieldwork done throughout the world, mainly in Indonesia, Egypt, Colombia, the Philippines, and Brazil. One reason for the scarcity of the research data and grounded insights on scavengers is that this subject has only quite recently become an academic focus. Another reason is that it is difficult and sometimes dangerous to perform research among these often shunned communities. However, the research that has been done has had as a main effect that it put scavengers on the political agenda. To be able to form more empirically established 'dynamic models', we advocate research to expand and to work without inflexible or outdated paradigms and focus on the interaction of contextual conditions.

References

ASMARE Street Scavenger's Association, *Street Scavengers: Partners of the Selective Waste Collection of Belo Horizonte*, Belo Horizonte, Brazil: pamphlet, 1998.

Birkbeck, Chris, Self-employed Proletarians in an Informal Factory: The Case of Cali's Garbage Dump. *World Development* 6-9/10: 1173-1185, 1978.

Birkbeck, Chris, Garbage, Industry, and the 'Vultures' of Cali, Colombia. In: Ray Bromley and Chris Gerry (eds), *Casual Work and Poverty in Third World Cities*, pp. 161-183. New York: John Wiley and Sons, 1979.

Digregorio, Michael, *Urban Harvest: Recycling as a Peasant Industry in Northern Vietnam.* East west center occasional paper no. 17. Honolulu: east west center, 1994.

Eades, Jerry, The politics of waste disposal in New York and Tokyo. In: Kiyotaka Aoyagi, Peter J.M. Nas and John W. Traphagan (eds), *Toward Sustainable Cities: Readings in the Anthropology of Urban Environments*, pp. 85-106. Leiden Development Studies 15. Leiden: Institute of Cultural and Social Studies.

Gage, Ian, The Effect of the Method of Household Containment on Solid Waste Management. In: Elizabeth Thomas-Hope (ed.), *Solid Waste Management: Critical Issues for Developing Countries,* pp. 159-167. Kingston: Canoe Press, 1998.

Jaffe, Rivke, *Nice Up Your City, Nice Up Your Self: Solid Waste Management in Kingston, Jamaica.*. Leiden 2001. [Leiden University Master's Thesis]

Medina, Martin, *Informal Recycling and Collection of Solid Wastes in Developing Countries: Issues and Opportunities.* UNU/IAS Working Paper No. 24. Tokyo: United Nations University/ Institute of Advanced Studies, July 1997

Perry, Stewart E., *San Francisco Scavengers: Dirty Work and the Pride of Ownership.* Berkeley/Los Angeles/London: University of California Press, 1978.

Sigular, Daniel T., *Scavengers, Recyclers, and Solutions for Solid Waste Management in Indonesia.* Center for Southeast Asia Studies Monograph No. 32. Berkeley: University of California, 1992.

UNESCO, http://www.unesco.org/most/southam4.htm, May 11, 2001.

Versnel, Hans, Scavenging in Indonesian cities. In: Peter J.M. Nas (ed.), *The Indonesian City*, pp. 206-219. Verhandelingen van het Koninklijk Instituut voor Taal-, Land- en Volkenkunde 117. Dordrecht, Cinnaminson: Foris Publications, 1986.

6. Environmental Sociology

Bernhard Streck

Does Nature Strike Back?
Reflections on a Passion Anthropology

Abstract

Shortly before Christmas 2000, the Polish artist Maurizio Cattelan imposed an 'installation' on the Warsaw public showing the Pope being hit by a meteorite while officiating at a ritual. It was not just the otherwise tortured face of the Polish-descended spiritual leader that brought the church hierarchy, led by Cardinal Klemp, out against Cattelan, but the fact, not foreseen in Catholic dogma, that, despite the demonstrated remorse of souls, the via triumphalis of the Church, which alone can bless, ends merely in the rawness of nature. Certainly if required this anxiety-creating relationship between cultural orthodoxy or orthopraxis on the one hand and uncontrollable nature on the other may still be brought under control by the teaching of God's impenetrable wisdom, but then the meteorite would not be something ejected from chaotic space, but a divine projectile. This would have made sense in the Protestant milieu of the sixteenth and seventeenth centuries, when the Bishop of Rome was exposed as the anti-Christ and the road to salvation appeared to lead straight over his body. This idea is hardly sustainable in the Catholic situation of today, although, as one defender of this work of art asks us to remember, in the attitude he is shown in the Pontifex Maximus is imitating the redeemer on the via dolorosa.

A conference on 'Exploitation and Over-exploitation' cannot be able to solve questions of this kind. Nonetheless, the offending installation can nudge us directly into the theme of my contribution, which deals with contexts of explanation in which nature jumps out of the role of unending tolerance that we are familiar with and strikes us back. We are dealing with an exchange of roles: humans, active and re-working nature, must take over the passive role of nature, which re-works them in its turn. In the ideologically neutral and modern presentation of Cattelan's installation, this represents an unfortunate accident. The Pope sinks into prayer and holds fast to his ritual path to the crucified Christ. At precisely that moment, a meteorite, a fragment from a cosmic cloud of dust, rains down on earth and by chance hits the holy man. Only the superstitious would make a causal connection out of this.

The animal epidemics that were raging across Europe in the beginning of the year 2001 might have provided another way into our theme. For the Mexican farmers whom G. M. Forster questioned in the 1960s, this temporary halt to the expansion of agrobusiness is no surprise, but the inevitable consequence of a system of crimes, which together have trampled underfoot the laws of balance that are inherent in nature. These farmers, who could still be found in Germany in the

1950s, never needed a sinister, avenging power of nature for their understanding, such as – to refer to ethnographic material – the mistress of the cows who brings to an end the manifold misery of the stalls and the feeding troughs, the trucks and the slaughterhouses, by rapidly calling the animals to her. In accordance with the old ideas of reciprocity in the countryside, it was simply nature's law that the accumulations which were produced on the one hand caused symptoms of deficiency on the other, and that the massing together of live cattle, milk and meat also set free the corresponding viruses and destruction.

So-called superstition, which does not tolerate accidents but assumes unseen powers behind every event that is not immediately explicable, and the belief in the balancing righteousness of nature, which automatically avenges unconsidered attacks upon it, stands in the way of the modern understanding of the possible, as well as scientific experience: unseen powers cannot be verified, and nature allows almost anything, so long as its laws are respected. However, these laws belong to mechanics, optics, chemistry, electricity, atomic physics or biology, not to law, let alone sociology. It is natural scientists who have discovered how to deal successfully with nature. Nature itself has no voice, since it is object, not subject. The autonomous subject is the human being, who holds nature in his or her hands as an object. This idea has grown up with modern knowledge and has been confirmed thousands of times by technology and economics; as anthropology knows, it is alien to other cultures.

At the beginning of the modern period, nature still counted as a superior power faced by inquiring humans, who made great sacrifices in order to reveal its secrets. Since then, understanding has been turned upside down: humans, with their great apparatuses, which permit them to travel into space as well as experiment with the invisible building blocks of life, have become a threat to nature. In 1995, Hubert Markl called on us to take nature into our care, lest it die out. Talk of striking back has long ceased in the light of this triumph of the human mind. Nature has deteriorated into a case for treatment, and one fears that it will die out, not strike back.

In her article on the 'holy' cow as the popular and commercial symbol of a 'healthy homeland', the Swiss folklorist Kathrin Oester describes the connection between the mastery of nature and its celebration. The less say nature has in modern society, the more it is romanticised. Doubtless a connection that is also important for our theme becomes clear here: nor, in the modern period, can we speak ultimately of a nature that is autonomous from culture. Neither dependence on nature nor its total mastery allows it an autonomous existence. It is always a part of culture, whether as a superior power or as a case for treatment with romantic compensations. Nonetheless John W. Bennett has seen a development here, which he calls an 'ecological transition': with increasing success, humans are integrating themselves with their technology into nature and making it a part of their own culture. This started already with the hunter, who obviously uses 'his' nature as a resource, i.e. makes use of it culturally. Nature is thus always both cultivated and cultured.

Anthropology has not always been aware of the pan-cultural aspect. Thus Durkheim's dogmatic distinction between the sacred and the profane long hindered the anthropology of religion, just as Lévi-Strauss's dichotomy between culture and nature hampered the comparative anthropology of environmental awareness. In an article published in 1996, Eduard Viveiros de Castro separates the materialistic conception of nature of a Steward, White or Harris from the mentalistic approach of the structuralists and symbolists. However, both streams, which dominated the anthropology of the second half of the twentieth century, see nature as an object, either of re-working or of thought. And the subject authority in both cases is culture, as either technology or a mode of thought. Only with Descola's so-called 'animic model' (1985, 1992) has a path been carved out towards overcoming this traditional separation between nature and culture.

In what follows, I would like to show that in fact there have always been traditions of thought that have either been sceptical of this neat distinction or have sketched out an opposite model. In particular, I must point out that the dichotomy between nature and culture is almost routinely refuted in the more recent anthropology. I shall then sketch out the opposite model of the *passio*, as used by Lienhardt, and later by Fritz W. Kramer and others. Following this, and using the perspective of a passion anthropology, I shall attempt to make nature as 'striking back' plausible by using material on possession cults, since these illustrate precisely the unequal yet converging struggle between striking and being struck in the intensive interaction between nature and culture. Here, nature appears especially clearly as that part of culture that removes it from control. This does not mean postulating the total absence of *homo faber* re-working nature in societies lacking machines, even though he may find himself allied with other *homines*, who may possess shares in one and the same 'individual' and may, even in modern humans, contradict the ideologically and rationally demanded autonomy, responsibility and unanimity of the subject.

Nature 'with a soul'

Anthropology began its career as a university discipline with the discovery that nature had a soul, which in the heyday of ideas of progress meant a revolution. For the materialists of evolutionary anthropology, nature was always the same quantity: humans only tackled it with their bare hands or rough tools at the start, so that only later could they become its proper master. To this modern understanding of nature as a dead and thus limitlessly exploitable material, Edward B. Tylor opposed the concept of animism, which he developed for the first time in 1867 in a lecture to the Royal Society and then later in his *magnum opus*, *„Primitive Culture"* of 1871. As well as the many sources from the anthropology of Europe and outside Europe, his own experience of spiritualism, which became popular in the nineteenth century, also stimulated him to this revolution in thought.

By his idea of 'animism', to begin with Tylor mainly meant 'the animation of all nature', i.e. what for modern thought was dead nature was thought to be alive. Only later did he develop out of this the idea of a soul released or releasable from the body, thereby entering into controversy with theologians, religious scholars and psychologists. The anthropology of the twentieth century could not remove these uncertainties between living nature and ideas of the soul, because neither could be described in exact terms or canonically. However, connections between the powers active in the human breast and those in living nature were repeatedly established, and, because of their variety and pleasure in metamorphosis, references to the 'soul' that had already been defined in the Christian West were singularly unfortunate.

Other founding fathers of anthropology sought to support Tylor by correcting him. Andrew Lang called animism 'all-alivism', i.e. the teaching of the livingness of everything. Soederblom and others rendered Tylor's ubiquitous 'soul' more precisely as 'power' or 'force', a widespread view at the start of the twentieth century, which worked especially with the word '*mana*', derived from Melanesian languages, and was also called 'dynamism'. Interestingly, *mana* and its innumerable correspondences in almost all languages is often defined as 'supernatural force'. Here the modern understanding of nature, which accords it just the power that the laws of mechanics or chemistry allow it, is again brought to bear. In this case, a nature that strikes back would only be thought of as a punch bag that responds to a blow with the fist with a calculated return blow. However, 'supernatural' means overcoming the laws of a materialistically conceived nature and implies unpredictability, or even a subjectivity of its own.

Animism and dynamism are thus the concepts with which early anthropology summarised its findings concerning the non-modern conception of nature, and opposed the materialism that predominated in science and the economy. Materialist and agnostic anthropologists sought to trace these unsettling indications of a living nature back to the technological deficit of societies without machines. The more dependent humans are on nature, the greater the anxiety it causes them. With technological development, nature and humans moved apart, until finally the paternalistic treatment of nature, discovered by Hubert Markl as mentioned earlier, became possible. However, in this interpretation of nature, which is simultaneously paternalistic and materialistic, early primitive humans were only granted affective relationships with a nature that was experienced as a superior power. Reports in which nature may emerge as a 'dialogue partner' must be excluded – such as the 'call of the tree' or the 'call of the mountain', which find a remarkable correspondence in the romantic experience of nature, as well as in the animistic understanding of nature (Jensen 1951) – or else they stimulate psychopathological theory formation.

Understanding a nature that strikes back, i.e. an environment in which powers are active and which counts as uncontrollable if not entirely unapproachable, offers anthropology – aside from its rationalist, materialist and agnostic traditions of thought – a series of approaches building on the earlier animism and dynamism, though also linking up partly with the mythological schools of the early nineteenth century. Myths contain traditional concepts of a relationship between nature and culture that are neither conceived as opposed in structuralist fashion, nor grasped as being within clear structures of dominance. In particular, however, the livingness of nature in myth is beyond question with regard to the theme of a nature that strikes back, and myth precisely possesses an apparently inexhaustible fantasy.

Present-day environmental studies describe, for example, the death of the soil with which nature responds to over-population and over-exploitation in Africa. Revelatory religions, medical advances and agro-technical innovations have taken the fear of nature, the acceptance of early death and conceptual scruples about exploitation from tribal societies. In this many-sided process of emancipation, the earth first became dead ideationally, then actually. Humans now flee from their desertified and eroded homelands into the cities, to the drip-feed of industrial society. It is probably no longer possible to prevent this massive, apocalyptic process, and certainly not through anthropological studies. However, what anthropology can contribute to understanding here it must create from its mythological and animistic specialist tradition. Not even the refugee who is fleeing from a destroyed nature to the aid offered by civilisation is pursuing 'resource management strategies' alone. Perhaps, using this economic-ecological definition, much in the behaviour of those affected can be explained. However, a large remnant belongs to the anthropology of religion, which also looks at humans in interaction with the environment, but has come to see this as something alive and in a sense active, lying beyond the measurements of climatology, botany or soil science.

The human who is struck down

The myth of the origin and transformation of the world knows no separation between *res cogitans* and *res extensa*, with which Descartes founded the modern world. Even when there is separation in myth – e.g. the forcible separation of heaven and earth is a popular theme – it seldom occurs between the living and the non-living. After this separation of above and below, the two halves of the cosmos are equally consumed with desire for one another, and the anthropology of religion has discovered many rituals that promise, at least in part, to lift or alleviate this separation. Whatever happens in myth – and however incomprehensible individual actions, which in addition often appear without a context, may seem – the actors are all alive and endowed with a soul, and they suffer and act with heart and understanding, even when they represent nothing other than the powers of nature, or heavenly bodies that the modern natural sciences have long since discovered to be cold spheres.

However, in Cattelan's installation, such a body has now struck the Pope, the representative of Christ on earth. Cattelan did not have a direct model for his bold provocative work. He was also attacked for his apparent popularity. On the other hand, however, he was also defended mythologically: the prelate Wieslaw Niewglowski, who is in charge of artists in the Polish church, refers to the fact that Jesus also fell over on the *via dolorosa*. These scenes are represented on countless wayside shrines all over the Catholic world, and every year believers strive to imitate being struck down and falling over in the Good Friday procession in Jerusalem. The exemplary human being appears in many cultures as one who has fallen over or fallen down. In the Christian meaning, however, he was not struck by 'unreasoning' nature, but by sins, in the case of Jesus by the sins of others, in the case of the Pope and other representatives of Jesus by their own sins. We see how deeply the modern artist Cattelan is rooted in mythology. Artists relate myths, and the relating of myths is art.

If we now clarify further this picture of the human who is struck down, in fact we also encounter nature as the cause of the fall, because in the Christian understanding nature at its core is sinful, even the source of sin. In this respect, Christ and his apostles really were struck down by nature on the *via dolorosa*, and it tripped them up. But is this a nature that strikes back? Who has challenged it? Is it not rather God who strikes here, who punishes even his own son, 'who knew sin not', for sinfulness? Here we are probably encountering the boundary of the particular Christian mythology that indeed does not want to be a mythology but a redemptive religion, and as such wants to redeem itself from both mythology and nature. Beyond this boundary, however, we encounter the general mythology in which human laws count, e.g. the principle of reciprocity, according to which in particular he who is struck strikes back. In the understanding of the anthropology of religion, it is only this condition that is interested in a nature that strikes back.

Myth, which anthropology and archaeology have come to know in thousands of variants outside the revelatory religions, always deals with nature, but never as a source of sinfulness, let alone as modern environmental awareness, in which nature is released from the damnation of eternal exploitation and has turned into an object of protection or a case for care. The nature of the myth is neither good nor evil, but it suffers and strikes, gives birth and devours. Above all, it is not an abstract principle, but appears as a form – monster, animal, tree or human. Adolf Ellegard Jensen has reconstructed the type of the *dema* divinity from data from New Guinea as supposedly the oldest type of deity. These *dema* are all linked with the powers of nature and, for all their monstrosity, are great sufferers, and marvellous sufferers in silence. The world is created out of their wounds, tears and death, as humans know them and can use them.

The *dema* gods are deities of nature who have fought out their struggles amongst themselves. Dead since the original time, they nonetheless return regularly and tirelessly repeat their principle, the change between day and night, or the waning, dying and waxing moon. According to Jensen, the *dema* as divine sufferers in silence are the models for the later sun gods that the states of antiquity called upon, or gods of vegetation who turned into Osiris, Attis, Tamuz, Baal and

Jesus, of consequence for the martyrs of all lands combined. Here are the mythical models for the fallen human: death as the 'pay-off for sin' is fundamentally a later ingredient. Humans fall under the blows of nature because they are themselves nature, because falling and getting up again signify nature, which fundamentally consists of conditions of change.

However, why does such a nature, which neither knows nor is sin, strike back? Nature conceived mythologically consists of blow and counterblow – it is rhythmical, as perhaps Ludwig Klages among twentieth-century philosophers was able to express most clearly. According to him a rhythmic nature is the model for every culture – indeed culture is a part of nature through its efforts to achieve rhythm. In 'Vom Wesen des Rhythmus' (On the Nature of Rhythm' 1934) we read:

'How, according to our information, nothing else was to be expected, we see more or less the whole lives of primitives moving to some extent in a permanent rhythm. It is no exaggeration to say that they dance their divine services, dance their festivals, deal with their disputes while dancing through songs of mutual mockery, go to war dancing and carry out the most arduous work by dancing to the rhythm of collective songs!' (1934: 49)

When humans within or outside redemptive religions are possessed by deities or spirits, they begin to dance, often until they fall over. 'Living' nature has struck them and tripped them up, not because they have sinned, but because they have contributed to it. They have been included in the natural rhythm, understood as the exchange of blow and counter-blow, and may represent it. This is the deeper meaning of the notion of a 'nature religion', which knows no separation between nature and culture, but their identity. Culture depicts, represents or intensifies nature. This conception has been developed most consistently in the cultural morphology of Frobenius and Jensen, which also gave rise to the idea of an avenging nature. In the stories of ogres that are found world wide, mostly female demons who demand human flesh (cf. Geider 1990), the thanatological aspect has acquired the remaining expression of an *imitatio naturae*, which, however, also contains a systematic significance in the devouring nature of initiation rites: nature strikes life back, in order to be able to greet it on a new level. In African hunting societies Hermann Baumann found the avenging principle called *nyama*, which finds its expression in the fear of the sickening gaze of the killed game and causes the most varied protective measures. Here we seem to have arrived at the boundaries of the *dema* idea, because the *nyama* complex, however much it conceives nature as living and as having a soul, leads directly into professional magic, which is no longer dominated by motives of imitation, but by purposeful thoughts.

Passion anthropology

When, at the beginning of the 1950s, criticism of applied anthropology as social engineering began to build in America, Sol Tax called the attempts of the administered to stand together against administrators 'action anthropology'. In their actions, people whom one wanted to help through research or to research by being helpful were simply subordinated to their own motives, whether these had been anarchically, primordially or ecologically oriented. Anthropologists who have been active in this context, one that is associated with great moral expenditure, certainly stress that in each and every case they are the learners and that they only adopted the role of an advocate for indigenous peoples fighting for their rights, but in fact they subordinated their own self-understanding, stemming from pariah sociology, and their own functioning view of humanity, according to Descartes, to their 'clients'. In 1988, accordingly, with a German sense of consistency, Peter Stüben demanded restricting action research to groups that were interested in the maintenance of their environment.

We have seen that, while mythically directed cosmologies certainly concern themselves with nature – in fact with nothing else – they lack a modern understanding of nature, especially in respect of Oester's Janus-faced aspect of both mastering and glorifying nature. A nature that strikes back need be neither protected nor maintained. One fears it and is impressed by it to the extent that one seeks to copy it. No one who cultivates contact with nature spirits can have any enthusiasm for nature, since the *natura animata* is a much too serious, indeed existential question in archaic societies. Besides, fugitives in the city seldom understand fugitives in the countryside, since their original experiences and goals are exactly opposed to one another: like those in the youth movements of a hundred years ago, ecologists flee „aus grauer Städte Mauern"('from the walls of grey cities') to find uncorrupted rural life, while after the third drought country dwellers flee a nature that has become unreliable and join city queues.

Ultimately, the ecologists, with their academic backgrounds, distinguish their own belief in the possible from the many people for whom a nature that strikes back is simply closer than it is for the authors of the Kyoto protocol, in which now even the earth's carbon dioxide balance is to be rationed according to rational criteria and using the methods of stock exchange capitalism (Maxeiner 2000). Certainly these are not action anthropologists, but belief in an ability to be the master of nature and of fate, merely by arranging it sufficiently skilfully, unites the technocrats with the action researchers. To both of them is opposed a view of the world and of humanity with which anthropology has systematically concerned itself for over a hundred years, and in which the role of the suffering, as we learn of it in the shape of the fallen Pope or the crucified Jesus, is more important than the role, doubtless also world-renowned if not also absolute, of the activist.

Thus there are evaluations which divide modern from archaic views of the world and of nature. While, in the technocratic understanding, suffering is concentrated on to a narrow path of christian redemption, in order to be able to subject the rest of the world all the more objectively, ethnic groups that are in retreat world wide, like unwritten cosmologies, situate the figure of the *homo faber* in the realm of absolute necessity, in order to be able to manage the ample 'free time' better with a nature that strikes back and its *mimesis*. For this model of a humanity that is exposed to powerful forces without a hope of ever becoming their master, which predominates in almost all archaic cultures, the notion of *passio* has entered anthropology. With its double meaning as suffering and passion, it has been able to stimulate research in the proper direction, even though it has not achieved any greater distribution in the discipline than the previous, similarly conceived idea of „Ergriffenheit" (,seizure' or ,commitment') in the work of Frobenius and Jensen.

In his programmatic article „Notizen zu einer Ethnologie der Passiones"('Notes on an anthropology of the *passiones'* 1984), Fritz W. Kramer opposes the nature-culture dualism of Lévi-Strauss to the ethnographic significance of the wilderness as the location of powers that make people possessed. Here nature is no longer a non-place but a place of origin, which, however, humans do not approach with a joyful feeling that they are returning home, and certainly not as nature-seekers, but which seizes them with trembling and compels them to imitation long before rational mastery takes over. Mimesis and exorcism are thus rooted in the archaic nature cult; humans submit to a nature that strikes back by striking back themselves, e.g. with living victims – a chicken, a pig, a sheep, a cow – or, as the Rosaldos have clearly described for head-hunting, a defenceless human.

The first ethnography to contain the concept of *passiones* was that written by Godfrey Lienhardt in 1961, on the Dinka of the southern Sudan. Although it dealt with quite active and warlike pastoralists, it demonstrated the strikingly passive self-awareness of their religious conceptions. In many respects, the Dinka viewed themselves as the objects of powers that were located outside the controlled and controllable world of their villages, fields and herds, but incessantly lead them astray at their own discretion. On the other hand, these powers and images, which represent the actual subjects in Dinkaland, even appear to take up residence within humans themselves. The conclusion that Kramer draws from this evidence, which has also been confirmed in many other ethnographies since, is

'that the human subject is not, as in European thought, an integrated self, but a multiplicity of heterogeneous subjects, which dissociate themselves under particular ritual conditions' (1984: 308).

Among the Dinka and other societies with similar *passio* concepts, anyone struck by 'nature', i.e. with an uncontrollable power, is addressed using the name of this power. He is no longer the usual tribal confederate; rather, he embodies that alien power that has knocked him down. His own old „individuality" or „identity" – these notions, so popular with us, completely fail in a comparative ethno-anthropology – retire, at least for a time, until the person who has been struck has recovered from the blow. Here is the beginning of the possession cults, which are rapidly expanding in the tropical world, catching hold of people and teaching them to dance to the rhythm of the force of the nature that is striking them.

Fritz W. Kramer has reviewed this world of the possessed in Africa, concentrating on in doing so possession by alien spirits. Other alien cultures can put people under their spell like the forces of nature, which they do to an increasing extent in the newly mixed conditions of colonial and post-colonial Africa, even though Kramer represented the view that possession by alien spirits was a reaction to first contact that later gave way to more rational confrontations with the alien culture, which was experienced as superior. Research that has been stimulated in part by Kramer's book „Der rote Fes"('The red fez' 1987, engl. transl. 1993) has not uncovered any dying out of these elementary forms of contact with superior powers, but instead their dynamic spreading. From a series of new investigations, I would merely like to mention those by Tobias Wendl in Togo, Thomas Krings in Nigeria and Gabriele Boehringer-Thäringen in the Sudan.

Wendl sees the metamorphoses of the Mami Wata cult as processes of convalescence. Whoever is struck by Mami Wata, an exemplary force of nature that strikes back, only recovers from this blow by adopting a ritual role in the cult of the same name. Only then, as Wendl expresses it, using the concepts of research into shamanism, are „Plaggeister"('pests') turned into „Hilfsgeister"('spirits who aid'). Earlier, such appearances – the best known being the Hauka ritual of the Songhai filmed by Jean Rouch in 1954 – were explained with reference to satirical theatre or colonial drama. Wendl, however, sees possession by an alien spirit the other way round, as a flight from post-colonial reality into a ritual identification with a European world that is experienced as superior.

Kramer and Wendl speak of alternative ritual plans in one's own culture with which those who have been struck down react to their being such. The uncontrollable external world of wildness or strangeness provokes wild and strange behaviour. Kramer therefore also recognises in the possession cult „die Geburt des Tanzes im Schrecken"('the birth of the dance out of terror' 1987: 123), because dance seems to be the adequate control of the overpowering. Ludwig Klages was cited earlier regarding the rhythmically dancing culture, a theme that has been confirmed in the present-day ethnography of cult groups. Here we are no longer dealing with tribes and their cultures, but with the coming together of those who have been similarly struck down. 'Those similarly possessed come together at the festival of their spirits', writes Kramer (1987: 219). In the metaphors that Thomas Krings uses in translating the Bori cult of the Hausa, these are festivals of horsemen. Those struck down by uncontrollable powers are turned into horses on which the spirits sit as riders. Alfred Métraux already made this comparison in describing the *voodoo* ceremonies on Haiti (1958), where it corresponded to the local terminology. In particular, the horse evades all responsibility, since it is controlled by its rider, i.e. the superior power. Certainly in this stabilised stage the horse is no longer struck down. Humans and nature have come to an equilibrium; they have found the same rhythm.

Thomas Krings was able to put together a pantheon of 32 European spirits who were known in the Hausa Bori cult and had found horses for riding. In part, these turn up in fantasy uniforms, for besides Christianity, the military is always the most prominent image of the superior alien culture. In the 'ethnic displays' of the Zâr, however, which Gabriele Böringer-Thäringen experienced in Omdurman, there were also sufficient indications to reveal the identity of the authority causing the possession, such as cowry shells for black African spirits, coffee for Ethiopians or cigarettes for Europeans. On the other hand, in this cult, which is mainly contested by women, the violent encounter with the spirit was compared with sexual and marital contact. The cult followers are the brides of the Zâr spirits; when they come upon them, they look skywards, laugh as if transfigured, and begin to dance.

It is images of the 'wilderness', as the foreign is frequently called in the Sudan, that violently take over the festively decorated brides. The latter consent and play these powers, who want to possess them and therefore make them possessed. Yet they also want to go on living and therefore provide a sacrificial animal as a substitute for themselves. Bones and blood are brought to the spirits of the Nile. Sacrificers and victims merge when those struck down return the blows and the boundary between subject and object disappears. The Zâr brides themselves count as part of the wilderness that threatens the indigenous and already long Islamicised civilisation of the Nile valley. In the Zâr cult, suffering from external dangers – nature, alienness, fate – is turned into a passionate participation in them.

Yet is it really all the alien powers that pester the culture of women in the Sudanese Nile that are exorcised in this way? As an outsider, one might count fundamentalist Islam or unstoppable desertification among the greatest dangers to local survival. In China, the Gobi desert has now advanced to within 100 kilometres of the capital, Beijing; in the Sudan, the desert has already been in the metropolis for a long time. However, the women of Omdurman and other Nile towns do not seem to attach any particular anxiety to this: they are superior enough to make their own choices out of the repertoire of the alien environment and their historical torments. Not all blows are avenged with equivalent counter-blows. Islam thus cannot present itself as a Zâr spirit because it is placed above belief in spirits, and the trusting husbands of the Zâr brides only tolerate their pursuit with a bad grace. Other forms are used in the Sudan for contact with male, dominant Islam, since the religions of the book have only contempt for animism – which is how we must view the Zâr cult. Conversely the belief in spirits simply excludes the moralistic teaching of monotheism: it moves on another level of reality, which does not seem to touch prophetic orthodoxy.

Many inhabitants of the rural Sahel belt in the Sudan sweep the sand from their door every morning. When they can no longer do so, they move further south, and the sand of the Sahara, which is incessantly blown down from the north for six months of the year, successively covers the deserted houses and places. These are, individually, quite gentle blows from this awesome nature: it is only their relentless continuity that turns them into a violent threat, which every year eats up several square kilometres of dwelling and living space. Why does the local culture not confront this desertification? Why is this gradual devouring of the land not seen as a blow from the wilderness, to which one adjusts with one's own blows? Humans have always engaged quite pragmatically with pressures like the expanding desert, namely by withdrawing – this makes a ritual confrontation with superior powers superfluous. Yet there is also a thousand-year-old habit in it: in the Sudan and Egypt the desert represents absolute hostility to life, yet the dead are carried there, and out of it come the prophets.

Conclusions

In an article of 1991, Fritz W. Kramer reminds us that nature literally means 'place of birth'. Dying and becoming are the most powerful bonds uniting the two spheres of nature and culture that are separated by structuralism. While an action anthropology certainly grasps the goal-oriented relationship between working humans and the resources offered by nature, it disguises the spiritual interconnections between cultural nature and natural culture dealt with here. For this one requires a passion anthropology, whose perspective has been sketched out above. This seeks to exclude the conception, strongly rooted in the Western scientific tradition, of a passive matter without a soul, in order to free up one's view for other ideas of nature. That nature always describes the cultural other is thus not in question; it is simply that technical culture contests the privilege of providing the measure for varying conceptions.

With this picture of a nature that strikes back, this authority should be given back its subjectivity, which it certainly possesses in almost all societies lacking machines. This dimension of nature, which we have lost, may embrace being alive, being endowed individually with a soul, or a type of judicial office, i.e. its striking back may be involuntary, intended, or even directed and balanced. This is a matter of historical experience and of discourse on the theme of which form is ultimately re-worked out of an initially diffuse, unpredictable and superior nature. The excursus on possession has shown that the boundaries of experience of the alien are fluid. Kramer himself sees possession by alien spirits in modern Africa in the continuity of the mimesis of animals, which probably shaped pre-colonial Africa.

In the culture morphology tradition, one saw not only animals but also plants, and in the context of the state also stars, which have moved humans and forced them to imitate. Here, we have brought together all these moments of an uncontrollable external culture under the comprehensive and elusive concept of nature. The discovery of its being alive and possessing a soul can be described as the great moment in the history of anthropology. The main source for an anthropology based on the theory of animism is the myth of the human being who has been struck down, who recognises his or her own objective role in each case and reacts mimetically to it. This self-awareness, which is not envisaged in the modern picture of humanity, compels anthropology for its part to alter the objective. Instead of an action anthropology, what is required here is a passion anthropology, which studies not active solutions to problems, but the passive victim of an active nature.

In his retrospective on his life as a „Weltvagant", published in 1953, Paul Wirz, one of the most fruitful ethnographers of Southeast Asia, expressed the recognition that in the field an 'animistic view of nature and of the world' forces itself upon the fieldworker 'almost violently'. Clearly one must supply a certain readiness and sensibility to this, but perhaps this is precisely the ethnographer's virtue, even when the repeated change in objective – namely to find one's way back to a quantitative perception of the environment, of the sort required by modern humans – proves difficult. Paul Wirz suffered much from this, and ultimately felt himself to be properly at home in none of these world views.

Thomas Michel, another New Guinea researcher, had the actual misfortune, but good luck as a researcher, to experience two earthquakes in the Eipomek highlands in 1976. Such events – Stefan Seitz (1998) describes an other case on the Philipines - make it clear all over the world, including modern societies, that nature does strike back and that humans are helplessly subject to it. Almost every year, fearsome earthquakes, especially when they strike highly populated areas, throw up the absurd-sounding question, should one not have waited until the earth's crust had finally quietened down and cooled to a fixed mass before settling the earth. The Eipomek share their high-lying settlements with a large number of spirits, who are by no means pleasant neighbours, since they are seen as unpredictable and require great expenditure in terms of preventative and defensive measures. In the spirits of these mountain dwellers, nature and culture become mixed up into a confused tangle. The earthquakes shook this up; many settlements and gardens disappeared under masses of debris, and even the most sacred thing, the grave of the original pig, was destroyed.

Michel regards the world view of the highlanders as simultaneously pessimistic and pragmatic. In the victims' view, the spirits of the ancestors obviously struck again in the fearsome earthquakes. Nothing else was to be expected. The mountain farmers dig among the rock debris for any crops that can still be used and then set to, laying out new houses and gardens. If the Eipomek possess anything like a cultural soul, as Herder postulated for all peoples and which Frobenius reformulated with his notion of *paideuma*, then a 'soul of nature' also belongs here, equipped with an unpredictable potential for destruction. Perhaps their culture corresponds to the constructive principle, with nature containing that which is destructive. However, together the two produce a rhythm which the Eipomek endure and appropriate according to the powers, in order to be able to live and survive. In this sense, they show themselves as exemplary „Naturvölker"(‚nature people'), who, after falling down, get up again and continue. Their nature, whose return blows must be taken into account at all times, is not suitable as something owned; for this, nature can possess people. And there is no enthusiasm for such a nature, because it is simply the spirit, namely superior power, heteronomy and mystery. ‚Nature people' may define their nature, even construct it, but they cannot handle it, because they feel themselves handled by nature and that experience makes them passionate. This is the special relation between man and nature anthropology has to cope with.

References

Amborn, Hermann, 1993: Handlungsfähiger Diskurs: Reflexionen zur Aktionsethnologie. In: Schmied-Kowarzik, Wolfdietrich/Stagl, Justin (Hg.) *Grundfragen der Ethnologie*. 2. Aufl. S. 129-150. Berlin: Dietrich Reimer

Baumann, Hermann, 1950: Nyama, die Rachemacht. Über einige manaartige Vorstellungen in Afrika. *Paideuma* 4: 191-230

Bennett, John W. 1976: *The Ecological Transition*. Cultural Anthropology and Human Adaptation. Oxford: Pergamon Press

Böhringer-Thärigen, Gabriele, 1996: *Besessene Frauen*. Der zâr-Kult von Omdurman. Wuppertal: Edition Trickster im Peter Hammer Verlag

Castro, Eduardo Viveiros de, 1996: Images of Nature and Society in Amazonian Ethnology. *Annual Review of Anthropology* 25: 179-200

Descola, P. 1992: Societies of nature and the nature of society. In: Kuper, Adam (ed.) *Conceptualizing Society*. Pp. 107-26. London: Routledge

Foster, Georg M. 1965: Peasant Society and the Image of Limited Goods. *American Anthropologist* 67: 293-315

Frobenius, Leo. 1921: *Paideuma*. Umrisse einer Kultur- und Seelenlehre. München: C.H.Beck

Geider, Thomas, 1900: *Die Figur des Oger in der traditionellen Literatur und Lebenswelt der Pokomo in Ost-Kenya*. 2 Bde. Köln: Rüdiger Köppe

Jensen, Adolf E. 1951: *Mythos und Kult bei Naturvölkern*. Religionswissenschaftliche Betrachtungen. Wiesbaden: Franz Steiner

Klages, Ludwig, 1934: *Vom Wesen des Rhythmus*. Kampen: Niels Kampmann Verlag

Kramer, Fritz W. 1984: Notizen zur Ethnologie der Passiones. In: Müller, E.W. et al.: *Ethnologie als Sozialwissenschaft*. (Sonderheft 26 der Kölner Zeitschrift für Soziologie und Sozialpsychologie.) S.297-313. Opladen: Westdeutscher Verlag

Kramer, Fritz W. 1987: *Der rote Fes*. Über Besessenheit und Kunst in Afrika. Frankfurt/M.: Athenäum

Kramer, Fritz W. 1991: Masala – Vom Genus Gottes. In: Berg, E. et al.: *Ethnologie im Widerstreit*. Kontroversen über Macht, Geschäft, Geschlecht in fremden Kulturen. Festschrift für Lorenz G. Löffler. S. 63-74. München: Trickster

Krings, Matthias, 1997: *Geister des Feuers*. Zur Imagination des Fremden im Bori-Kult der Hausa. Hamburg: Lit

Lang, Andrew, 1887: *Myth, ritual, and religion*. London: Longmans, Green.

Lienhardt, Godfrey, 1961: *Divinity and Experience*. The Religion of the Dinka. Oxford: Clarendon Press

Markl, Hubert, 1995: Pflicht zur Widernatürlichkeit. *Der Spiegel* 48: 206-7

Maxeiner, Dirk, 2000: Basar der Bürokraten. *Der Spiegel* 45: 310-312

Métraux, Alfred. 1958 *Voodoo in Haiti*. (orig. frz.) Gifkendorf: Merlin 1994

Michel, Thomas, 1983: *Interdependenz von Wirtschaft und Umwelt in der Eipo-Kultur von Moknerkon. Bedingungen für Produktion und Reproduktion bei einer Dorfschaft im zentralen Bergland von Irian Jaya (West-Neuguinea), Indonesien*. Berlin: Dietrich Reimer

Münzel, Mark, 1991: Indianisches Umweltverständnis im Amazonasgebiet – und europäische Begeisterung dafür. *Gießener Beiträge zur Entwicklungsforschung* I, 19: 111-114

Oester, Kathrin, 1989: Mythos „Natürlichkeit“: Die Kuh als Metapher für Weiblichkeit und Landleben im technologischen Zeitalter. In: Sosoe, Lukas K. (Hg.) *Identität: Evolution oder Differenz*? Festgabe für Professor Hugo Huber. S. 167-194. Freiburg/Schweiz: Universitätsverlag

Rosaldo, Michelle, 1980: *Knowledge and Passion*. Ilongat Nations of Self and Social Life. Cambridge: Cambridge UP

Rosaldo, Renato, 1980: *Ilongot Headhunting, 1883-1974*. A Study in Society and History. Stanford: Stanford UP

Seitz, Stefan, 1998: *Die Aeta am Vulkan Pinatubo*. Katastrophenbewältigung in einer marginalen Gesellschaft auf den Philippinen. Pfaffenweiler: Centaurus

Soederblom, Nathan, 1916: Der Animismus. Belebung und Beseelung. In: Schmitz, C.A. (Hg.) *Religionsethnologie*. S. 9-29. Frankfurt am Main: Akademische Verlagsanstalt 1964

Stüben, Peter E. 1988: Earth first! Ethno-Ökologie: Von der Aktionsethnologie zur Aktionsökologie. In: Ders. (ed.) *Die neuen Wilden* (Ökozid 4) S. 98-130. Gießen: Focus

Tax, Sol. 1952: Action Anthropology. *América Indígena* 12: 103-106

Tylor, Edward B. 1871: *Primitive Culture*. Researches into the development of mythology, philosophy, religion, art, and custom. London: J. Murray

Wendl, Tobias. 1990: Kamm und Spiegel. Notizen zum Europäerbild in einem westafrikanischen Besessenheitskult. *KEA* Nr. 1:57-76

Gerd Spittler

Work – Transformation of Objects or Interaction Between Subjects?

One of the essential features of every definition of work is utility, the purpose external to the work (Spittler 2001). But how is this purpose achieved? Work can be basically conceived of in two different ways:

- as transformation of an object
- as interaction with a subject.

The first paradigm – I call it the technical paradigm – implies the transformation of a passive object. The process is controllable and can be planned. When one has the appropriate knowledge, skill, and power, one can form an object according to one's ideas. The means for this are tools or machines. The second paradigm, which I call the interactive paradigm, assumes an object that is not fully controllable. An element of unpredictability is involved. One devotes great attention to the object. One interprets the messages that this object emits and reacts to them. The object possesses a subject character.

The first paradigm is constitutive of the modern position. We "work over" a piece of wood in order to make a spoon. We work on a piece of raw stone and produce a club or a blade. We transform the soil in order to make it agriculturally useful. Production means for us making a product through the transformation of material, of things. This is most obvious in our ideas on transforming dead materials. But we pro-duce not only clubs, spoons and cars, but also wheat, grapes, milk, and pork by "working on" plants and animals. Treating animals as things is not without controversy, but it has been accepted within the technical paradigm at least ever since Descartes.

Habermas assumes the existence of this technical paradigm. In both of his essays "Arbeit und Interaktion" (Work and Interaction) (1968) and "Technik und Wissenschaft als Ideologie" (Technique and Knowledge as Ideology) (1968) he makes a distinction -- based on an interpretation of Hegel and Marx -- between two types of action, "work" and "interaction". Work is "instrumental action" and follows technical rules. Inter-action is "communicative" action and follows its own norms. Both types of action have to be kept strictly separated. Work is absolutely essential, but as Habermas observes -- critically of Marx – interaction cannot derive from work. Conversely, and here Habermas directs himself against Herbert Marcuse, work cannot be organized as an interaction. If we want to be technically successful, we cannot communicate with nature; we have to work on it. Work belongs to the area of technique and economy. The task of the cultural sciences is to examine interaction. Habermas consistently held this approach and worked it out in his "Theorie des kommunikativen Handelns" (Theory of Communicative Action) (1981).

Can work and interaction really be so clearly divided? Is interaction free of instrumentality? The foremost question in my discussion is: Is work indeed purely instrumental? Is it only a matter of working on objects or is it not also a matter of interaction between subjects? The idea that not only humans possess their own sense of self-will / selfdetermination (Eigensinn, Eigenwillen), but also animals, plants, and even things, which we regard as dead material, is widespread in non-industrial, non-capitalist societies. The objects, or rather subjects, not only have their own peculiar characteristics (Eigenarten), which one must know and take into account, but have also a self-will, which is not fully controllable. This self-will can be so strong that these subjects are as powerful as humans or even may dominate them. Work becomes a game, a fight, a service, a care, an exchange.

I shall treat these questions first in relation to hunters and gatherers (I), then herders (II) and peasants (III), and finally in relation to capitalist industrial work (IV).

1. Work Among Hunters and Gatherers

I am not starting with ethnographic examples, but rather with Ortega y Gasset's "Prólogo a un Tratado de Montería" (1944; english "About the Hunt") because the specific nature of hunting is better analyzed here than in most anthropological studies. Regardless of whether hunting is for subsistence as in the case with the Paleolithic hunters or for purposes of sport as among the aristocracy, wild game has a chance to escape. The hunted animal is an autonomous actor, a subject. Its behavior is not exactly calculated. In hunting there is no guarantee of success. That might be a cause of frustration. But, this is precisely what makes it attractive. Thus, hunting is a happy experience and so differs from arduous work. Happiness does not mean simply pleasure, for the effort involved in hunting is the same whether for sport or for work. But one freely undertakes this effort and with full freedom and for the sake of joy, "while work is an effort which one undertakes with a view to its result". Here Ortega y Gasset contradicts his comments about the Paleolithic hunters, who did not hunt for purposes of sport but to secure their subsistence. Thus, hunting can be just as much work, but it is a work of a specific sort, which cannot be interpreted as domination of an object, but rather as an interaction between subjects.

Ortega analyzed this better than social anthropologists taking the approach of "Cultural Materialism" and "Ecological Anthropology" where the idea of instrumental work dominates. What is hunted and gathered is explained by the "theory of optimal search for food" (Harris 1987). Hunters and gatherers optimize their returns in that they optimize the relation between work effort and return on calories obtained from different animals and plants. This theory has its merits but it can offer only a limited explanation. Hunting is a notoriously insecure activity. Hunters differ greatly in their knowledge, skill, and luck. Among the !Kung San studied by Lee (1979) the men spend more time hunting than the women gathering, but the returns are less. More than half of the food (when calculated in calories) comes from the women. However, meat is valued over plant food. While gathering has a constant return, the individual differences in hunting are enormous. That begins with the fact that not all men go hunting. During a study of a period of one month, 7 out of 11 men from one camp went hunting. Only every fourth day was successful and the individual differences again were great. The good hunters went hunting every second day and were disproportionally successful. One hunter, who went hunting only for four days did not bag one wild animal.

Descola (1986) in a study on the Achuar in Ecuador found that the hunting returns are small because the hunters often return home without success. While 80 minutes of planting a garden can attain 2500 calories, the same amount of time in hunting brings only 600 calories. In respect to protein supply, fishing is the most productive. From a purely utilitarian point of view one could do completely without hunting; the protein requirements can be met with less work effort by planting gardens and catching fish. But here one sees the limitation of input-output calculations and the principle of minimal expenditure of effort. Hunting is fun. The men are out 8 to 10 hours hunting. This activity is not, however, seen as work. When one goes hunting, one speaks of "going to the forest" or "going for a walk".

The interactive character of hunting is evidenced not only in the hunter's behavior. The hunters are conscious of the interaction (Ingold 1994). While we tend to exclude technical aspects as instrumental from social relations, Ingold thinks that this is an unjustified imposition of our culture on the culture of hunters. For them tools are not instruments for ruling nature, but rather are mediums for creating a social relation-ship. Arrows serve the interaction between humans and animals. When it does not reach its goal, then it is because the animal is not ready to enter into a relation. Ingold asserts a contrast between hunting and herding cultures. In contrast to herders, who dominate their animals and will break their self-will, hunters leave the animals to their own will.

Even when we do not accept the interpretation of the hunters for ourselves, everyone can understand that hunting is more like an uncertain interaction than a successful instrumental activity. For that reason it is argued not only by Ortega y Gasset that hunting is not to be designated as work. Eduard Hahn equates the "Origin of Economic Work ("Entstehung der wirtschaftlichen Arbeit", 1908) with the steady activities of the gatherers and the preparation of food by women. Men have fun with insecure hunting, but it is not work. This definitional typecasting of work associates it above all with toil, a position which often corresponds to emic ideas. But if we want to do comparative research, and if we stick to the analytical definition formulated at the start of this paper, then hunting within a subsistence economy is a matter of work.

Not only hunters, but also gatherers (men and women) interact with nature. The interaction is often seen as a gift or exchange relationship. Australian hunters and gatherers speak with the land on which they hunt and gather. Through their sweat and their talk they put the land in a favorable mood. The land is then ready to put at their disposal wild game and fruits. (Povinelli 1993). It is reported that the Mbuti, African hunters and gatherers, see themselves as children of the forest. They like to go to the forest in order to be together with their counterparts and "nature" and to gather at this time the fruits. They sing together with the spirits of the forest and the latter give them their food (Bird-David 1992).

2. The Work of Herders

That animals not only have their own distinctiveness (Eigenarten), but also their own self-will (Eigenwillen, Eigensinn) would be conceded by most of us. The question is whether this self-will is respected. Ingold disputed this in regard to herders (in contrast to hunters). My own studies on herders' work among the Tuareg (Spittler 1998) show other results. According to the Kel Ewey Tuareg, humans and animals, even things, have a well developed self-will. This self-will may turn into resistance as soon as others try to influence it. Consequently there are limits to feasibility and upbringing.

Not only humans have their own sense of self and self-will, animals do too. One tries partly to overcome this opposition, but one also respects it to a certain degree. Animals are no machines that can be ruled by the proper technique. They are rather living beings with their own will. According to one idea that was formerly widespread, but today is in retreat, the goats give, for example, less milk when the cheese produced from the milk is sold instead of being consumed in the household. Tugey, to refuse, is a word frequently used which emphasizes the sense of self and self-will of humans, animals, and things. Tugey puts a limit on the upbringing of humans and the domination of animals and things. The daughter who refuses to go to the goat sheds in the grazing area, the son, who refuses to work in the garden, the goats which re-fuse to come at the call of their women herders – these all encompass types of refusal that are familiar to us. It becomes more difficult when we hear that the goats refuse to give milk or indeed that the dates refuse to be sold, or a language refuses to cooperate. When my progress in learning the Tuareg language lagged behind my hopes, then I was often comforted by the Tuareg with the words: "The Tuareg language refuses", i.e. the reason was seen to be less my incapacity than the will of the language.

The idea of tugey limits the work principle in several aspects. The limits of what is feasible and what can be educated are narrowly drawn. This is not only because one sees opposition at work; that could be over-come in many cases. Important is that the refusal is often respected, even when it could be technically overcome. The woman herder could force the dog to go to the pastures with her, but she respects its refusal, without asking whether the dog is "justified" in refusing.

This respect is often shown in the handling of camels or goats. Goats are especially self-willed. Even we have, or have had, this view, for the word "capricious" comes from capra, goat. Goats have different characters, which are evidenced in the names which the Tuareg give them. There is inter alia the gazelle, which is shy towards the herder and behaves likes a gazelle; the quarrelsome, which is always fighting with the other goats; the strayer, who distances itself from the herd; the indifferent, which does not hear the calls of the goat herder; the coy, which has to be tempted with nice words to come to the water trough. These goats make the work of the herdswomen difficult. For example, the goats designated as gazelles do not allow themselves to be milked at all or several women herders have first to capture them. The milking, which normally can be done in a few minutes, lasts half an hour and requires the cooperation of several women.

Capricious goats exist everywhere. But we would sort them out by selling or slaughtering them so that the work becomes easier and these characteristics are not further reproduced in successive generations. Such considerations are not foreign to the herdswomen. But as a rule they dismiss these thoughts and say that one has to respect the goats' self-will just as of humans. They accept the extra work. But one can also imagine that this makes the work more fun. If the women were to see the goats as pure instruments for achieving their aims, then the lonely work in the wilderness would be intolerable. To watch a quarrelsome goat is fun. To capture a shy goat is a game that relieves the monotonous milking work.

Respect for the distinctive personality and self-will of animals can be developed into a specific service ethic. A conception of work as a service is common among nomads. Much more so than farmers or stationary cattle holders, nomads adapt their entire way of living to the needs of the animals in that they are as mobile as the animals. Kurt Beck has described this in detail in relation to the nomads in Kordofan (Beck 1994, 1996).The herders are to put their life at the service of the herd. That does not mean that they must always work, but they must always be ready for the herd.

3. Work Among Peasants

It is a widespread conception among peasants that work is care. Work alone cannot create a vegetable product but can only help in its growth. In the final analysis, the affluence of nature must be traced back to the will of God.

Anthropologists, like other people, often romanticize the work of peasants in pointing out its harmony with nature or its peaceful interaction with nature. But we should not forget that agricultural work always starts with the destruction of nature. Before sowing and planting can be done, the existing vegetation has to be destroyed. Clearing the field consists of cutting and burning down trees. To prepare fallow land for sowing means uprooting shrubs and grass. The destruction continues even after the sowing. Hoeing to make space for useful plants destroys the weeds. The soil is torn up with the hoe. Interaction with nature does not imply only peaceful exchange or care, but very often a battle. This fight may be dangerous. Tools like axes and hoes resemble weapons, with which the peasant can injure not only other people but himself as well.

In the following, I shall describe an extreme case of fighting found among the Bemba in Zambia. The basis of my description is Audrey Richards well known book "Land, Labour and Diet in Northern Rhodesia" (1939). Richards describes in great detail the agricultural work process, which is organized in a different way than in neighbouring societies. The martial tradition of the Bemba accounts for the difference. Whereas in many societies peaceful agriculture constitutes the opposite of war, the Bemba organize their most important agricultural work like war. This system has become known under its indigenous name citemene.

Clearing among the Bemba does not consist in destroying the trees completely, but in cutting the branches. To this end, the young men have to climb to the top of the trees. This work is seen as play, as pleasurable and exciting. But it is also very dangerous. Every year several young men fall to their death in this way. Richards gives a vivid description of the climbing: "At the top of the tree the work becomes more and more dangerous. A man may be left standing on a fork at the summit with one of the vertical stems as yet uncut. He has to clasp it with one hand to steady himself, while with the other he slashes at the trunk he is clinging to. He swings his axe till he hears the warning crack and feels the branch sway. Then he slides his body quick as a flash down the mutilated stump of the tree, yelling in triumph as he hears the bough fall". The Bemba particularly pride themselves on this citemene system. "Look at that man! He is an absolute monkey" is a high compliment to pay to a cultivator.

Audrey Richards was once asked whether Englishmen practised the citemene system in their own country. She gave a long and detailed description of the merits of English agriculture, but as she spoke she heard one of the young men behind her observe to his friend with a sort of derision: "Hm! Afraid to climb, I sup-pose."

4. Capitalist Industrial Work

Up to this point I have spoken about hunters and gatherers, peasants, and herders. They all have something to do with "nature", with plants and animals. At least when it comes to animals, most of us I suspect would be ready to accept their subject character. In regard to plants it is more difficult. But what about the craftsman who works with "raw materials", with dead wood, with stone and metals? Is there here an inter-action between subjects or is there only a working of objects? Social anthropology has long realized that things are not just dead objects for their owners. The argument in Marcel Mauss' famous "Essai sur le don (Mauss 1925) rests on the premise that "archaic societies" conceive of things having souls. Mauss studied what consequences this has for the gift, but he did not deal with the consequences for work.

The most important test for the question of interaction is not the handling of tools by a craftsman, but rather capitalist industrial work. This is the prototype of instrumental activity; it is the model for Marx's, Weber's, and Habermas' conceptions of work. As the technical or economic paradigms are dominating in research nearly all studies assume this framework. There, are, however, some noteworthy exceptions: sociologists and social anthropologists, using the method of participant observation, arrived at other views and were at least on the track of an interactive work.

"Manufacturing Consent. Changes in the Labor Process under Monopoly Capitalism" is the title of a book by Michael Burawoy (1979). The subject of the book is an old topic: How can it be explained that humans are ready to perform incessant and strenuous work? Burawoy's study is based on his own experiences. For a year he was a worker in a machine manufacturing factory. Burawoy found that supervision, salary attractions, and punishments could not sufficiently explain the achievements of the workers. It was not force or salary attractions which guaranteed a successful production, but rather the game. "Game" has nothing to do with "playing" in contrast to work. Rather it is an essential part of the work process. The playful-antagonistic character with which this work is done and conflicts settled with management and other workers gives a meaning to the work which would otherwise be absent under Tayloristic conditions. It simply drives away boredom. Time passes more quickly when "making out". One becomes less tired. The game makes the basic deprivations that work brings with it tolerable or renders it satisfactory.

Burawoy studied especially the game of "making out". In piecework one can either earn the basic salary without any further efforts, or one can play the game of salary raises by increasing output (making out). In the latter variation all turns on this game: one's own actions, contacts and talks with work colleagues, and supervisors. It is a game insofar as it promises a profit, has elements of insecurity, which arouses ambition, and stimulates competition and cooperation with other workers. It is less the higher salary as such than the forces aroused through the game which results in higher performance. Contrary to the assumption made by Marx and others that under capitalistic conditions the game or playful character of work is lost, and equally contrary to the assumption made by Ortega y Gasset, which postulates an absolute contrariness between hunting and work, play is an element of work even under the extreme conditions of capitalist factory work.

Nearly all of the studies on this, however, focus on the interaction between humans. Humans' self-determination ("Eigensinn") and games between them are examined. Working with objects is less discussed. Burawoy mentions playing with machines, but they are more an instrument in the game between coworkers than a partner or opponent. As a rule it is supposed that objects are worked on and transformed and that through work they are completely controlled. In reality this is not the case. Dealing with things is not the equivalent of dominating things. One of the few studies focusing on the interaction with machines is Julian E. Orr's "Talking about Machines. An Ethnography of a Modern Job" (1996). It examines the triangular relation between service technicians, customers, and copy machines. Orr worked many years as a service technician before he undertook his anthropological research.

Part of the technical service and repair work corresponds to the technical paradigm: "Technical service work is commonly perceived to be the fixing by rote procedure of uniform machines, and routine repair is indeed common." This applies, however, only to a part of the work. Orr continues after the above sentence: "However, individual machines are quite idiosyncratic, new failure modes appear continuously, and rote procedure cannot address unknown problems...Work in such circumstances is resistant to rationalization, since the expertise vital to such contingent and extemporaneous practice cannot easily be codified."

Machines are not objects, but rather subjects, in this case partner and opponent. "War stories" are told about the machines. These deal not only with heroic success, but also often with defeats in handling the machines. Even the heroic stories assume that the machines are difficult and incalculable. "These tales of the heroism required to service early machines seem balanced between celebrations of the perversity of the machines and celebrations of the technicians coping. It is not clear whether the technicians more admire the coping or the perversity." Each machine is an individual, even when many are of the same type. They are named individually by their users. A technician can differentiate between each machine in his herd. The machines are (like a livestock herd) in principle domesticated, but only in principle. When describing the negative characteristics of machines, one uses moral and value judgments. Machines can be "filthy", "per-verse", "crotchety", "odd". These characteristics are seen not only as negative. "The machines are both perverse and fascinating. Earlier models featured both fires and explosions, and the technicians speak with a fond pride of the labor involved in recovering from such disasters. Catastrophes resulting from oversight are described with the same pride as part of the process of becoming a real technician...Indeed, how could they resent the machines, for such a machine is a worthy opponent, partner, other."

Orr compares the way technicians deal with the machine with the description by Lévi-Strauss (1962) of the bricoleur, who works with what is momentarily available. This corresponds, however, only partially to the self-image of the technician. In practice the technician interacts with the machine as though it is an individual. Their stories are character descriptions and moral value judgments. On the other hand they have a technical world view insofar as they want to harness the chaos especially with orderly and systematic behavior, based on knowledge and skill.

5. Conclusion

Empirically we can establish that the interactive conception of work is widespread. This can be most easily seen in respect to hunters and gatherers, peasants and herders, first because of the living nature of the work objects and secondly because of the historical dimension. These forms of work dominate in a pre-modern world. Clearly, though, even in capitalist industrial work one finds a strong interactive element.

How can one explain, from the point of view of the technical paradigm, the wide extent of work with subjects?

Where interaction is indisputable (for example, in hunting), work proves to be inefficient. The hunters return often to the camp with nothing useful. The effort is high, the failure rate equally high. The average work productivity is thus low. As a consequence, the evolution is towards more efficient economic forms like agriculture and livestock raising.

Where the interaction rests on non-scientific world views, that is, they contradict our ideas, it is a matter of a magical world view and of superstition, which equally leads to inefficiency. This is also supplanted by an evolution in favor of a more efficient economic form. The demystifying of the world (Weber: "Entzauberung der Welt") leads to increasing rationality. Today the remains of such magical views merely show that the Enlightenment has not yet succeeded.

What the social anthropologists describe as an emic world view is often only a metaphor (e.g., wringing with nature), which does not correspond to reality.

There are several objections to these arguments:

Let us start with the latter argument (the interaction metaphor): This argument is indeed to be taken seriously. The protagonists of a culturalistic perspective in social anthropology limit themselves often to a se-mantic approach in studying work. It is simply supposed this is relevant for action. In my opinion that is anything but obvious. Work goes beyond talking, it has to be done. To my mind, the neglect of the action level and the limitation to the discourse level miss the object.

The technical paradigm assumes either the universality of its principles or an evolutionary perspective. The first assumption can be easily refuted. Work has never functioned alone according to the model of the technical paradigm. Rather it has always contained interactive elements. This is frequently overlooked, because of the dominance of the technical paradigm in the description and analysis of work. The evolutionary perspective too, which postulates an increasingly technical control of the world, cannot be sustained. Even when one is not a follower of the radical thesis of Latour ("We were never modern," 1995), then it is valid to say of the world of work today that interaction and communication, which evade a simple mechanistic perspective, are increasing, not decreasing. Here the technical paradigm is a poor adviser. This is possibly the case not only for the interaction among humans, but also with machines, e.g. computers.

The technical paradigm overlooks not only the subject in the object, but also in the actor, who works. It assumes a rational actor, in effect a machine (Rabinbach 1990), without thematizing the anthropological or cultural context of the actor. Work as interaction in any case is more fun than a successful domination of the object which excludes every surprise. Hunting is the best example of this. This is also valid for agricultural work, raising livestock, and industry as I have described above. Having fun at work is a value in itself. It also often increases work productivity as has been known since Fourier. Burawoy (1979) shows this persuasively for capitalist industrial work. Work can be not only a matter of fun, but also a fight. There are victories and defeats in interacting with other subjects. This is so not only for hunters, but also for herders, peasants, and industrial workers.

Persons (actors) and their actions have to be defined substantially in terms of culture. This applies as well to technical and interactive action. Anyone prepared to take risks will conduct work in a risky way (example: the Bemba). Whoever because of religious ideas finds that living in the wilderness is incompatible with human dignity will organize herding work differently from one who feels at home in the wilderness (Beck 1994; 1996; Spittler 1998). When modern persons define themselves as flexible individuals, then they will organize their work in a new way (Boltanski and Chiapello 1999). When the actor finds that the aim of work lies not only in practical utility, but also in playfulness and aesthetics, then he will perform the work in another way. The concepts of an actor mentioned here do not necessarily imply an interactive perspective; they do promote it.

(Translation by Chris Jones-Pauly)

References

Beck, Kurt. 1994. Die kulturelle Dimension der Arbeit in den nordkordofanischen Hirtengesellschaften, in: M.S.Laubscher und B. Turner (Hrsg.). Völkerkundetagung 1991, Bd.1, S.157-176. München: a-nacon

Beck, Kurt. 1996. Islam, Arbeitsethik, Lebensführung, in: Kurt Beck und Gerd Spittler (Hrsg.) Arbeit in Afrika, S.161-178. Hamburg: Lit

Bird-David, Nurit. 1992."Beyond "The Original Affluent Society". A Culturalist Reformulation, in: Current Anthropology, 33: 25-47

Boltanski, Luc und Ève Chiapello. 1999. Le nouvel esprit du capitalisme. Paris: Gallimard

Burawoy, Michael. 1979. Manufacturing Consent. Changes in the Labor Process under Monopoly Capital-ism. - Chicago: Univ. of Chicago Pr.

Descola, Philippe. 1986. La nature domestique. Symbolisme et praxis dans l'écologie des Achouar. - Paris: Ed. de la Maison des Sciences de l` Homme

Habermas, Jürgen. 1968. Arbeit und Interaktion, in: Technik und Wissenschaft als Ideologie, S.9-47. Frankfurt: Suhrkamp

Habermas, Jürgen. 1968.Technik und Wissenschaft als Ideologie. Frankfurt: Suhrkamp

Habermas, Jürgen. 1981. Theorie des kommunikativen Handeln. Frankfurt: Suhrkamp

Hahn, Eduard. 1908. Die Entstehung der wirtschaftlichen Arbeit. Heidelberg: Winter

Harris, Marvin. 1987. Cultural Anthropology. New York: Harpers & Row

Ingold, Tim. 1994. Tool-use, Sociality and Intelligence, in: Gibson, Kathleen und Tim Ingold, (Hrsg.), Tools, Language, and Cognition in Human Evolution, S. 429-445. Cambridge: Cambridge University Press

Latour, Bruno. 1995. Wir sind nie modern gewesen. Versuch einer symmetrischen Anthropologie. Berlin: Akademie

Lee, Richard B. 1979. The !Kung San. Men, Women, and Work in a Foraging Society. Cambridge: Cambridge University Pr.

Lévi-Strauss, Claude.1962. La pensée sauvage. Paris

Lüdtke, Alf. 1992. Practising Eigensinn: Workers Beyond Domination and Resistance, in: Focaal No.19: 16-35.

Mauss, Marcel. 1925. Essai sur le don. Paris

Orr, Julian E. 1996.Talking about Machines. An Ethnography of a Modern Job. Ithaca: Cornell University Press

Ortega y Gasset, José. 1944. Prólogo a un Tratado de Montería. Madrid

Povinelli, Elizabeth A. 1993. Labor's Lot. The Power, History, and Culture of Aboriginal Action. Chicago: University of Chicago Press

Rabinbach, Anson. 1990. The Human Motor. Energy, Fatigue, and the Origins of Modernity. New York: Basic Books

Richards, Audrey I. 1939. Land, Labour and Diet in Northern Rhodesia. London. International African Institute

Spittler, Gerd. 1998. Hirtenarbeit. Die Welt der Kamelhirten und Ziegenhirtinnen von Timia. Köln: Köppe

Spittler, Gerd. 2001. Work: Anthropological Aspects, in: International Encyclopedia of the Social and Behavioral Sciences (in press). Amsterdam: Pergamon

Werner Krauss

The Culture of Nature: Protected Landscapes as Sites of Conflict

Abstract

National Parks are intensively researched regions for various reasons: There is great demand on the part of the administration for knowledge as to what is actually being protected, and in an era of widely-heralded climate change and environmental crisis these areas serve as laboratories for scientific research. These scientific activities do not, however, always elicit equal affection amongst locals. The underlying question is the role played by the natural sciences in the specific "culture of nature", as it is represented by the national park.

This paper deals with a particular kind of landscape, namely 'protected landscapes', or national parks and nature reserves. The material I intend to present is derived from two research projects. In the 1990s I conducted fieldwork in a Nature Park in Portugal (Krauss 2001), and at present I am researching the 'Waddensea' (mud-flats) National Park in northern Germany in the framework of an interdisciplinary project entitled 'Nature in Conflict. Nature Protection, the Concept of Nature and Coastal Images' (http://www.pronik.de).

The starting point for both research projects can be located in conflicts between local populations and the nature protection lobby in national parks. In the Portuguese national park you can see graffiti such as 'Hang the greens'. On a visit to the 'Waddensea' National Park in Germany, one comes across protest flyers stuck up by fishermen or farmers, reading 'Down with Ecological Dictatorship', 'Freedom rather than Ecoism' and similar slogans. Talking to farmers, you hear things such as 'if one of those national park rangers ever crosses my path at night and I'm carrying my gun...'

Resistance to nature protection strategies is a world-wide phenomenon. How can one account for these protests, what are they all about? Are they merely a consequence of the fact that uneducated locals fail to understand the necessity of environmental protection, or that they are in favour of 'progress at any cost', even at the expense of nature? Seen from an anthropological, rather than an 'environmentalist' vantage point, the matter appears in a somewhat different light. The nature protection lobby's view of natural landscape is only one possible perspective amongst a large number of others, albeit a hegemonic one within the context of national parks. In contrast to this, and following Barbara Bender, I take the view that landscapes are of a 'polysemic nature:'

Landscapes are never passive. People engage with them, rework them, and contest them. They are part of the way in which identities are created and disputed, whether as individual, group or nation state. (Bender 1996:324)

And Barbara Bender further states:

Such an approach makes it clear that the separation of 'nature' from 'culture' and the passive role given to 'nature' forms a part of a quite specific 'western viewpoint'. (Bender 1996:323)

In this presentation, I shall defend the thesis according to which it is precisely this type of separation of nature and culture that characterises the western 'Culture of Nature', and that this has been enacted in national parks and placed on display as in a zoo or a museum. Protest by the local population, furthermore, indicates that a social order and a set of power relations are established whenever we go about protecting nature.

In the following, I shall present a number of points drawn from my research work that help to underpin this contention. In the first part, I shall present the national parks as ecologically endangered coastal landscapes. In the second part, I change the focus and illustrate 'political landscapes'. Following on from this, I illustrate the conflict between nature conservation and local populations using a concrete example, and then, in conclusion, tackle the specific role of modern natural sciences in the so-called 'schools of the nation'.

Endangered coastal landscapes

The future of the Earth has been seen as endangered ever since the Rio environmental summit of 1992. This has led to a global environmental discourse: Environment and development need to be conciliated, and this is what is being accomplished in an exemplary fashion by the extension of already-existing national parks to take account of this dimension, or the creation of wholly new ones.

New national parks of this kind that I have worked on in my research are located in Southwestern Portugal (founded in 1988) and in Northern Germany (1986). In both cases we are dealing with coastal landscapes. Coastal landscapes play a particular role in the global ecological discourse, and are considered as being particularly endangered through toxic discharges deriving from agriculture and industry; through tanker disasters and the pollution of seas around the globe, through coastal erosion, and, most recently, through climate change and the associated forecasts of rising sea levels. The latter threat is relevant especially to the Waddensea National Park and its hinterland, which is protected by dykes. In addition, there is the particular land-based threat of steadily-growing tourism, and as a result, that of mushrooming constructions and over-development in the countryside.

These processes endanger flora and fauna, such as storks, sea vultures or otters in Portugal, or seals, salt meadows and other rare patterns of vegetation in the Waddensea. On top of this, the landscape 'image', the aesthetic dimension of these secular cultural landscapes, is under threat. The rhetoric of environmental discourse thus presents these national parks as 'unique landscapes', as 'the last largely unspoilt steep coasts of southern Europe' (in Portugal), or as 'the last largely intact natural landscape of central Europe besides the upper Alps' (in Germany), containing especially rare species threatened by extinction in each of the respective cases.

Political landscapes

These ecologically threatened coastal landscapes are at the same time political landscapes. Both landscapes are geographically marginal and are to be found on the margins of the states in question, and in the case of Portugal at the very margins of Europe itself. But in economic terms too, they are marginal, with the difference of course being that Portugal is amongst the poorest and Germany amongst the richest nations in Europe. Both regions are essentially free of industry and marked by agriculture – agriculture for which there is little demand within the EU. Both regions are characterised by emigration of the local population, with tourism constituting a major option for the future.

In cultural terms, too, there exist many points in common: the Alentejanos in Portugal and the Friesians in Germany are subject to severe stereotyping both amongst and beyond the respective nations in question. They are seen as backward and as possessing a peasant cunning at one and the same time; they are the subject of numerous jokes, and precisely because of their peculiarities, they are seen as part and parcel of the mosaic of the respective national identity.

Both regions can, however, also be characterised as 'landscapes of resistance'. The struggle against the Moorish occupiers in Portugal and against the Danish and other foreign overlords in Northern Germany are components of these national identities. It was in the Alentejo that the agrarian reform was initiated following the Portuguese revolution of 1974, with the previously landless workers occupying the lands of the latifundists: 'The soil belongs to those who work it', ran the battle cry. A complimentary slogan, which is an integral part of Friesian folklore, runs 'rather dead than a slave'.

This somewhat cursory rendition of regional stereotypes nevertheless acts as a pointer to a specific type of relationship to nature, that is, a political and cultural relationship, an ownership mentality, and thus, a societal order. In the case of the Friesians in northern Germany there is the additional factor that the land was only to be made arable at all after a centuries-long struggle against nature, against the sea.

Nature protection

This general comparison of the ecological and political perception of the same stretches of landscape also gives an indication that what is at stake here are competing models of knowledge. Before going on to describe the actual conflict situations in question, I must first briefly discuss the special role played by nature conservation as a central societal force.

The history of nature conservation is older than today's 'environmental discourse'. Indeed, it stretches back into the previous century, when, first in the US, and then in the UK, the first nature conservation organisations, followed by the first national parks, were founded. Classical nature conservationists have tended to be highly committed individuals from an elite background and from within academia. They endeavoured to maintain largely unspoilt stretches of nature for the purposes of research, teaching and collective national memory and identity. In the UK, rurally-tinged cultural landscapes constituted the centrepiece of conservation efforts, although globally, it was the American model of virgin stretches of nature, or wilderness, which won the day.

Up to the present, the darker side of the project has rarely been recounted: Many of today's nature reserves were previously populated, and the memory of the existence of such populations and thus their connection to nature was obliterated. In respect of West-Africa, Fairhead and Leach have shown in their book 'Misreading Landscape' (1996) that many of the supposedly once primeval landscapes currently under nature protection regimes, were in fact once inhabited, and there exist examples of entire ethnic groups being deported from their regions in the name of nature conservation.

It was only in the 1980s that the principle of sustainable development was adopted by the umbrella organisation of the national parks, the International Union for the Conservation of Nature, with the result that local populations were also seen as components of the areas under the organisation's administration. The Portuguese national park thus has as its stated aim, 'the protection of natural and cultural values', and the German national park aims to protect the Waddensea in accordance with the interests of the locals.

Yet to the present day, the setting aside of 'untouched stretches of nature' continues to be the primary goal of nature conservation. In addition, the elitist background of the Portuguese nature conservationists continues to be conspicuous, as witnessed in numerous interviews in which they simply deny the local population any 'culture' whatsoever, considering them to be simple, uneducated or alternatively avaricious people in need of enlightenment – enlightenment as to the culture for which they are expected to act as bearers, and above all as to the value of nature *per se*. The scientific grounding of the national parks is, in turn, almost exclusively derived from the natural sciences; culture only plays a part as far as archaeology, historical monuments, and, at most, folklore are concerned.

The thus-postulated cultural distinction also manifests itself in social terms - the majority of nature conservationists being urban-dwellers and university graduates; they have come to the province from outside, and barely have any contacts with the locals at all.

Resistance

The national park administrations are responsible for establishing access to the land in question. They promulgate rules, statutes and restrictions, which necessarily touch the inhabitants of the protected areas and their economic activities in the first instance. During demonstrations and public hearings, vocal protests by peasants, fishermen, tourist operators and hunters, backed by local politicians, continue to be heard. One of the central slogans of the local resistance in both national parks runs, 'We don't want to live in a Red Indian reservation.'

The notion of an 'Indian reservation' is, of course, an allusion to restricted citizens' rights; rights which are supposedly, or in actual fact, denied to locals by enclosing them within a reservation. The term 'Indians' furthermore alludes to the discursive reduction of the locals to potential 'culture bearers', something which is experienced as discriminatory. At the same time, however, the notion of Red Indians is also seen positively in environmental discourse, insofar as the latter are often depicted as 'environmental saints', or as a positive role model for what is seen as the right sort of interaction with nature. Or, as one of the prominent opponents of nature conservationists in Portugal put it: 'It wasn't the Indians who wiped out the bison, but the whites.'

In this way, the term 'Indians' is imbued with a further positive dimension: The locals as 'Indians' are better nature conservationists, or at the very least necessary interlocutors for the elitist nature protection lobby. This positive self-appreciation amongst the locals allows the possibility for the creation of a stronger bargaining position in the unequal dialogue with nature conservationists.

The founding of national parks also implies the simultaneous creation of a discursive regime. All types of reasoning, whether political, economic, or cultural in nature, are henceforth subject to the primacy of environmental discourse. Even protest against nature protection can be interpreted in this way: As Indians, the previously administratively subjugated locals are able to get a hearing, and are thus able to formulate their demands. This is not without success, as the national park directors are now obliged to travel from one assembly to the next in order to sound out the local population, and the national parks are now subject to enormous pressure not only to protect nature, but also, above all, to promote tourism – and naturally enough, 'ecological tourism'.

The scientific landscape

It is not only conservationists who are seen as unwanted guests by the locals in the national parks, but also academics. A protest poster designed by local fishermen at Wattenmeer says:

'The Waddensea is the livelihood of fishermen and not a playground for researchers'.

What is meant by the expression 'a playground for researchers'? Researchers or academics often come on the heels of the conservationists. In both cases, in Portugal as in Germany, scientific undertakings to find out what exactly is being protected are only able to be pursued once the respective conservation areas have been established.

It is worth taking a closer look at the development of the natural sciences and their societal role, a role which becomes all the more apparent in their activities within national parks. In historical terms, conservationists as biologists or geologists, were also often so-called 'field, wood or countryside researchers'. They observed what they were investigating within a given cultural context, whether flowers, animals, or soils. They were often personally acquainted with local peasants on whose fields they pottered around, talked to them and had an overall sense of the landscape.

With today's biologists or geo-scientists it is often very different, with a strict division of labour between those responsible for collecting data, and those responsible for modelling them. In modern ecosystem research, models of systems are established and refined using masses of data. It is here a matter of 'total images' of ecosystems created by highly-specialised teams on the ground, and then with the aid of computers.

Hence, in a first step, nature is entirely removed from its cultural context and recorded in purely objective terms. In this way, of course, key knowledge is continually being derived, for instance on the climate, oceans and meteorology (weatherforecasts). However, in order for this to be possible at all, it is first necessary to purge nature of its cultural dimension.

It is only in the second stage that the thus-purged natural image is once more relocated within its corresponding 'cultural system' – to use the language of natural scientists – and then once more loaded with sets of values. In this regard, let me quote the director of Waddensea National Park:

"Knowledge of how nature functions is, of course, quite useless if it remains restricted to a small number of experts. For a predominantly urban society whose real contact with nature is often restricted to holidays, there's a need for topical objects of interest. In order to achieve this, people's love of their homeland needs to be awakened, as does a sense of awe at creation. The national parks have been given the task of transmitting values. In this sense, national parks ought thus to be seen as environmental schools of the nation." (Scherer 1998)

The creation which is supposed to reawaken our sense of awe is at the same time a total image of nature derived using hi-tech means – one of the most interesting paradoxes of modern nature conservation. Nature conservation reconnects scientific nature to older values such as nation, gender and identity. But just what does this environmental school of the nation really consist of?

Knowledge of nature is conveyed to the public using notice boards, information stands, ecological museums, guided tours, etc. Tourists, as well as fishermen or peasants, stand around agog, as external rangers explain to them 'the culture of nature' – or their own landscape.

'A livelihood for fishermen, not a playground for researchers' – it is above all fishermen who find their fishing rights restricted by nature conservation. Science has itself become the great competitor and driving force in the 'coastal market' – in an era of climate catastrophe, coastal research is experiencing a boom, and many a research establishment is reinventing itself as a specialist agency within such a field. At the same time, science and nature conservation together are creating a wholly new market: scientific tourism – thereby demoting locals, together with their image of landscape, to the status of cardboard cut-outs.

Conclusion

I have tried to bring to light a number of aspects and views of national parks in terms of 'multi-faceted' landscapes. They are seen as endangered coastal landscapes, political landscapes, protected landscapes, disputed landscapes, scientific landscapes and as schools of the nation at one and the same time.

The example of the national parks in their historical trajectory illustrates how the separation of culture and nature, the dogma of classical nature conservation, has managed to survive in times of a modern nature protection lobby allied to modern natural science. As I have indicated, the concept of 'landscape' permits an insight into the production of culture and nature. Protests by the local population act as a pointer to the political dimension of nature, to the questions of social welfare and power relations. The option of ecological tourism (dependent as it is on economic supply and demand trends), and hence the production of 'pure unspoilt stretches of nature' and presentable 'cultural identities', at best helps to turn the national parks into scientific 'Disney- or theme parks' or into 'temples' of our present 'Culture of Nature'.

Reference

Bender, Barbara (1996): Landscape. In: Barnard, Allen and Jonathan Spencer (eds.), Encyclopedia of Social and Cultural Anthropology; pp.323-324. London, New York

Fairhead, James and Melissa Leach (1996): Misreading the African Landscape. Society and Ecology in a Forest-Savanna Mosaic. Cambridge

Krauss, Werner (2001): 'Hängt die Grünen!' Umweltkonflikte, nachhaltige Entwicklung und ökologischer Diskurs. Ein ethnologisches Fallbeispiel (Portugal). Berlin

Landesamt für den Nationalpark Schleswig-Holsteinisches Wattenmeer (ed.) (1998): Umweltatlas Wattenmeer, Band 1, Nordfriesisches und Dithmarscher Wattenmeer. Stuttgart

Scherer, Bernd (1998): Der Nationalpark Schleswig-Holsteinisches Wattenmeer in: Landesamt für den Nationalpark Schleswig-Holsteinisches Wattenmeer (ed.) (1998) Umweltatlas Wattenmeer, Band 1, Nordfriesisches und Dithmarscher Wattenmeer, p.10. Stuttgart

Nikolaos D. Hasanagas

Forest Policy Reports and Environment-Sociological Reflections on North America and Europe in Comparison

Abstract

This paper presents in the most global and coherent possible view the multifaceted results of an extensive field research of politological and ethnographic character in British Columbia and seven US States (California, Oregon, Washington, Idaho, Utah, Arizona and Nevada) in comparison with the European reality supported by original visual material. The classic and recently developed policy analysis schools applied on studying policy change in Forest Policy and Nature Conservation fields are presented The environmental awareness policy is illustrated and the Indians' situation is also discussed. The north American forestry and nature conservation policies are characterized by similar content problems with Europe related to conflict between forest owners and environmental groups and socio-political priorities but also by different processes, politics and structures reflecting a particular socio-environmental zeitgeist. Emphasis is laid on the spatial planning, in which the mutual influence between nature and culture is illustrated, the role of peculiar natural phenomena in the formation of cultural identity is explored. The transferability of socio-cultural elements from America to Europe and vice versa is discussed. It is claimed that the European contribution to this issue can be quite important.

Introduction

It is self-evident to experts and laypeople that there is a rapid progress of natural sciences realising and signalising an effective technical-economic influence of society on nature[1]. However, the mental and structural influence of nature on society remains discernible only by particular experts and it is a challenge for the social sciences. The promising potential of the social sciences in this research terrain is mainly shared between two fields: a) the *modern societies* represented by the paradigm of the technologically developed western world which falls as a rule within the competence of Sociology, and b) *nature- societies*, which are more susceptible to the natural conditions and lay firstly on the empirical work of Anthropology[2]. This paper does not intend to work out a

[1] Nature is simply here defined as the not human-created environment

[2] In the face of this separation coming up for traditional or other reasons (Fischer 1998:10), there is an obvious empirical and theoretical gap, which makes the exploration of this influence of nature on society difficult.

complete analysis of these interactions or to achieve a bridgeover between the two fields. It raises eventually more questions than answers[3]. It is based on data collected in North America[4].

It aims at:

- relating certain *political structures* with the *socio-environmental zeitgeist*,
- suggesting eventual research points concerning *social-conditioning of spatial structures* (in contrast to spatial-conditioning social structures)
- posing hypotheses about *socio-historical* and *natural factors* building a rather *culture-* or *nature- identity* for a nation
- and occasionally scratching only the surface of the complex problematic about the *future of Sociology* in the light of the rapid progress of Political Science.

The North American society, in which culture and nature are mutually conformed or integrated into each other, is selected as an illuminating case study. The formulation of general hypotheses necessitates a comparison. The second case to compare is Europe. The manifest and the latent "Nature"!

The above-mentioned four topics can be analysed in sense of manifest and latent interaction between nature and society.

The manifest aspect consists in the nature-induced impacts, which are characterised as "relevant" for the people and count very often to the political agenda as specific issues. They derive from the intended use of natural resources (environmental decision-making). Normally, they are regarded as a socially relevant feedback of the human technical intervention in the nature (e.g. clear cutting- exhaustion of wood resources- unemployment). At the highest socio-political communcation level they can be aggregated to supply-induced, demand-induced and structural[5] environmental scarcity (Homer-Dixon 1999:133-135). In other words, manifest nature is the nature described by the natural sciences. A particular description presumes the observation of particular features. Must the description of coal include only the calories per kg while burning or also the

---

[3] As a case-oriented study, it is sensitive to complexity and historical specificity (Ragin 1989:viii-ix). It can point out eventually relevant categories especially through observation of extreme situations (e.g. hierarchical -horizontal networks/ common –peculiar nature). Then it can suggest casual linkages between them through deepening qualitative analysis of research units (e.g. visitors of national monument), which can prove from singular cases (e.g. a romantic-inspired person) to categorial representatives (Bude 2000:577) with a range of general properties (e.g. a group with nature-identity). Hopefully, we will have the chance to control the applicability of these case-based hypotheses through a variable-oriented study in future.

[4] Interviews, documents analysis and original visual material from California, Oregon, Washington, Idaho, Utah, Nevada and British Columbia in August 2000.

[5] Due to redistribution.

smoke emission in the atmosphere? The description norms and in the next step the research norms of the science and consequently the "reasonable" projects (namely which functions must be further described) are set through current politics and market economy conditions. Thus, the "nature" we know is a cognitive construction through natural sciences as well as through media (Daele 1996:420,422).

The latent aspect includes the influence of nature on society that is not recognised as feedback of any particular intended human intervention in nature. This is e.g. the adoption of natural elements as collective symbols over long socio-historical procedures (like the American eagle as a national symbol or the oak on German coin etc.). Therefore, it is obvious that the nature influences latently the identity building of a certain group as well as its way of life and perception of the social reality or even world outlook in procedures intangible and independent of the individuals.

Manifest social functions of nature

Political structures and socio-environmental zeitgeist

While in Europe nature and in particular the forest had - and has - mainly an economic value as a specific agricultural market sector, in North America and especially in Canada, it can – or at least could- open up potential fields of action even in the wider politics (not only in agricultural policy). The Canadian forestry had for several decades a noticeable value among the other environment-concerning policy areas meaning agriculture, water management, mining and health (Williston, Keller 1997). The forest is really meaningful for the Canadian politics and society, the more so as the forest production sector enabled a remarkable vertical social mobility (e.g. from logger to politician or to a millionaire) or even a brilliant political career (Minister that developed favour power relations in the political arena through forestry) (Gibson, Renison 2000).

The tension field between the pragmatism-oriented forestry (forest owners and industries seeking market profit) and the ideology-oriented nature conservation (environmental groups) appears not only in Europe but also in American political arena. It appeared in 1960s, became gradually more intensive and in 1990s it led to new policy initiatives (Hoberg 2001)[6].

However, it is worth mentioning that the strategic potential fields of action of the environmental activists are relatively restricted because of the policy-making process of British Columbia. The environmentalists have no big chance to follow a single strategy at the federal level because of

[6] Innovative consensus processes for land use policies in favour of conservation areas, more regulated wood harvesting, new forest planning providing compensation for the unemployment caused by nature conservation through more intensive investments on silviculture and ecological projects.

the dominance of the regional policies in the forest sector. In Europe, these policy networks are - even in federal systems like Germany- much more hierarchical than in Canada and USA. In this way, the European environmental groups have the chance to implement a co-ordinated strategy and to be integrated in the state decision-making, while the forestry groups have many difficulties from this point of view due to their heterogeneous clientele (from forest and land owners over hunters up to cork producers), and their not so popular orientation (rather pragmatism than ideology). In the face of this situation, the American environmentalists prefer rather market-related than lobbying tactics, e.g. boycotts in Europe and afterwards in the USA (Wapner 1996).

The enormous number of policy-analysis theories applied in studies of policy change in forestry and nature conservation is very characteristic of the intractable interplay of the horizontal policy networks in the USA and Canada. Various theoretical streams[7] have been identified in recent years, which pay more or less attention to each one of the three basic policy elements: *actors*, *processes*, *ideas* conditioning the policy-output. Most attention has been paid to the analysis of *actors* and *processes*. The *ideas*, namely the way of thinking, and consequently the discourse of social construction of "nature", do not pertain to the first research priorities of the applied social sciences in North America. Why? Because this particular policy field is characterized not only by complexity due to the above-mentioned horizontal structure but also by outside-control. In other word, forestry is a not self-regulated field (and this is also the status of forestry in Europe). It depends on many other multifarious, strongly institutionalised sectors varying from energy production up to cultural resources management (English 1999:6-8).

How can one explore networks including so many and heterogeneous actors? They are easier to contact because there – in contrast to Europe – the "lobbyist" constitutes rather a normal profession than a taboo. One could get the impression that in such complexity and variability, the thinking way is not considered to be so policy-relevant, because it has only a long-term cause of environmental issues without direct influence on the policy-outputs. Much more important for a concrete policy-output is the who and how of decision making. In Europe, which maintains a more "classical" character, a quite popular approach is that of the Advocacy Coalition Framework[8], paying more attention to the *ideas*. That is a certain difference in the socio-environmental zeitgeist:

The more horizontal and liberal the network, the more complex and uncertain it is, and the less the motive to explore the discourse, which constitutes the long-term and, general root of envi-

[7] Policy communities, Historical Institutionalism, Rational Choice, Discourse approach, Punctuated Equilibrium, Advocacy Coalition Framework, Policy Regime approach (Hoberg 2001).

[8] Policy Communities, dealing mainly with the actors, and the Institutionalism, studying processes and institutions are also not excluded of the European forest-nature conservation policy analysis.

ronmental issues. There exists much more a motive to examine the policy-relevant actors and processes so as to foresee the immediate and concrete policy-output.

Latent social functions of nature

Social-conditioning of natural structures?

The intervention of social structures in the nature is already well known and perceivable by everyone[9]. But what about the intervention of the nature in the human expansion?

There are fordistic cities with centralised functions and spatial-functional differentiation, which are on the way to postfordistic transformation. That means a diffusion of the centre into the periphery like a large part of Vancouver, where however the forested area remains still isolated from the outside-diffused urban area. There are also postfordistic global cities like Los Angeles with polycentric regions, based on the service sector and not on industrial or agricultural production. In this way, the forest is integrated in the suburbs. The question is, *if the forest favours or prevents the postfordistic transformation of the city*. In Europe, one can observe a certain isolation of the forest area from the urban environment. There are normally only parks in the residential areas. One can see only a few exceptional cases of remarkable integration of nature and city in Europe (e.g. Luxemburg).

At this point, it is worthy mentioning also the isolation impact of nature on Indian reservation areas in North America, which are desirable at least by the previous generations so that they preserve their own culture without adopting many mental or material elements from the western civilisation. It is however worthy of discussing to what extent this conservative attitude comes in accordance with the expectations of the new generations of Indians.

Nationalising nature

Reading classical literature works or cultural history, one can pose the question how each nation would be looking like now under completely different natural conditions. How their "typical behaviour", thinking way, traditions and institutions would be shaped? How can we imagine now Greeks without their sea, which inspired so many myths, literature works and also offered so much experience of distance and adventure, or Germans without the middle-European forests, which played not only a mental-cultural role over centuries as a real or imaginary scenery of so many tales and legends but also a political-historical role as pedagogic-ideological means in the

[9] Spatial planning theories claim that the market economy favors the proliferation of underdeveloped areas and the development of congested urban areas with ecological deficit (Krott 2001). This is the spatial expression of the capital accumulation in a liberal market.

National Socialism (Lehmann 1999)? And how should Americans look like now without their giant-trees as well as the other unprecedented natural monuments?

Many points have been discussed concerning the relation between environment and lifestyle but mostly focused on ecological issues and not so much on the cultural history (Brand 1997). Looking back on the culture building of various nations and comparing their civilisation, we can realise that every nation bases its identity on a material peculiarity situated in its "original" geographical area. *The older it becomes, the more it reconstructs its dominance region reflecting its mentality gradually more elaborately on domestic materials.* A classic example is the Greek nation which developed mental and social traditions over thousand years and through intensive acculturation between the near each other established city-states, "shaping" them on the marble statues and other monuments, which continue to be regarded as prototypes of artist elaboration until today. In some other European countries, there came about even special artists' movements setting place-related norms (e.g. in Swedish National Romantic, all raw materials for a work of art should be of national origin).

What could be the special localised *material peculiarity* of such a *young* and so widely *extended* nation like USA or Canada with such a social *heterogeneity*[10], which could be diffused and adopted as quickly and evenly as possible so as to "unify" it under a single characteristic identity? Nothing more effective than the above mentioned natural monuments, which were already relatively evenly spread. When I paid a visit to Yosemite Park and the giant-trees with the American friends, who put me up for some days, they said to me straightforwardly and simply: "this is our culture". A hypothesis on the factors conditioning the identity of a nation could be formulated as follows: *the shorter the history of the nation and the more its extensiveness and heterogeneity, the stronger the role of nature in identity shaping and subsequently the stronger the tendency to nature- identity* (fig. 1).

[10] Because of many multi-national immigrants.

Figure 1. Factors conditioning the natural or cultural character of the national identity

		Nature- identity
	Short	↑
History		
	Long	↓
	Short	↓
Extensiveness		
	Large	↑
	Short	↓
Heterogeneity		
	Large	↑
		Culture- identity

Which social features are conditioned through this natural or cultural character of the national identity? If we compare a developed culture with widely known socio-historical conditions, we see that the more developed a culture, the more developed the norms system, which is induced by this culture and consequently the more difficult to learn and adopt them. It is well known that USA and Canada are multi-cultural countries, where the immigrants get socialised and integrated more quickly[11] than in any European country. In this way, the largest part of the North-American population consists today of immigrants. The only "native" Americans are the Indians. In contrast to the culture-identity, the nature- identity allows a large scope for acceptance and assimilation of new cultural elements and individual perception of the world (cp. Cady 1999:13-17). In so far, *North America is characterized by more social accessibility than Europe* (social accessibility-inaccessibility).

The more elaborated and stabilised a culture over the time, the more the evolution and thus the differentiation of the value systems and the related ideologies, which cause segmentation of the whole population in groups of different interests and mentalities increasing the probability of polarization conflict between them. It is well known that the American history includes only a civil war, while the European history is characterized by numerous severe conflicts (wars and civil wars). In this sense, *North America is characterized by stronger group-coherence than Europe* (group coherence-segmentation). As a result of the two above-discussed factors but also through the nature- identity directly, the *individual freedom is emphasised in America while in Europe more collectivism is reserved* (individualism-collectivism). In America there is a remark-

[11] Except for racism cases in particular places of America.

able horizontal mobility. The American individualism, which is considered to be the base of the dynamic material development of America, means simultaneously an extremely high risk, in so far the institution of the "social network" is markedly restricted. In Europe, this social network is still maintained hierarchically either through the family or insurance institutions. While the European collectivism induces a quite extended group-differentiation according to nationalities and origins, ideologies, traditions etc., the American individualism leads to more class-differentiation, and a lot of severe conflicts appear on the individual level in form of criminality or isolation (homelessness, narcotics etc.). Perhaps, the existence of so many religious groups (small churches) in the USA is a reaction of social homeostasis aiming at strengthening a horizontal group consciousness and thus mitigating the vertical social gap. The three hypotheses are summarised in the figure 2.

Figure 2. Identity and social features

	Social accessibility (adoptability of social norms)	**Group coherence** (less probability of conflict between groups)	**Individualism** (horizontal network, vertical differentiation, more risk, criminality)
American Nature Identity	↑	↑	↑
European Culture Identity	↓	↓	↓
	Social inaccessibility	**Segmentation**	**Collectivism**

Is Sociology useless?

In the face of the rapid progress of the much-promising Political Science, which has gained a reputation as an applied as well as a basic and thus "autonomous" science, restlessness has emerged about the future of Sociology. Many believe – or feel – that Sociology is "threatened". We cannot analyze in a paragraph such a serious and complicated issue. We can however make some thoughts with reserve. As (almost) everything today, the production and marketing of knowledge is subject to the law of supply - demand, and, as discussed, it is not so interesting what the real cause of a problem is, as who decides how. This is exactly the power of the Political Science in comparison to Sociology. However, the competence of Political Science is restricted to fields which are markedly and formally influenced by public institutions (even when dealing with informal factors). Any other field, which is not conditioned directly through such institutions, can only remain within the competence of Sociology. The quantitative American Sociology seems to be mostly "endangered", because it is directly substitutable by the Rational Choice theory. Although Rational Choice originates from Sociology (by Homans in 1961), it is regarded today as a Trojan horse of the Political Science or as an autonomous toolbox tending to replace many classical theoretical instruments. Thus, American sociological departments in particular are looking back on the more "classical" European Sociology – a survival strategy?

References

Brand K-W. 1997: Environmental consciousness and behaviour: the greening of lifestyles. In: The international handbook of Environmental Sociology. M. Redclift, G. Woodgate. 204-217. Cheltenham, UK-Northampton, MA, USA

Bude, H. 2000: Die Kunst der Interpretation. In: Qualitative Forschung. U. Flick, E. Kardorff, I. Steinke (Edrs). 569-578. Hamburg.

Cady, J. 1999: The American writer. Shaping a Nations Mind. New York.

Daele v.d. W. 1996: Soziologische Beobachtung und ökologische Krise. In: Umweltsoziologie. A. Diekmann, C.C. Jäger (Eds), der Kölner Z.f.S.u.S.

English R.M. 1999: Overview. In: Tools to aid. Environmental decision-making. Dale H.V., English R.M. (Eds). 1-31. New York.

Fischer, H. 1998:Was ist Ethnologie?. In: Ethnologie. H. Fischer (Edrs). 3-20. Berlin-Hamburg

Gibson G. with Renison C. 2000: Bull of the woods. Vancouver

Hoberg, G. and others 2001: In Search of Sustainability. British Columbia Forest Policy in the 1990s. British Columbia

Homer-Dixon F.T. 1999: Environment, Scarcity, and Violence. Princeton, New Jersey

Krott M. 2001: Politikfeldanalyse Forstwirtschaft: eine Einführung für Studium und Praxis. Berlin

Lehmann A. 1999: Von Menschen und Bäumen. Hamburg

Ragin, C. 1989: The comparative method. Berkeley, Los Angeles, London

Wapner P. 1996: Environmental Activism and World Civic Politics. New York

Williston E., Keller B. 1997: Forests, Power and Policy. British Columbia

Mirjam de Bruijn

From Pastoralist to Peripatetic: The Fulbe and Environmental Stress in Central Mali

Abstract

The consequences of continuous environmental stress in the Sahel have led to deprivation and marginalisation. At the same time, new cultural forms have been created that do not demand a break with former lifestyles but are continuous, albeit different, with the Fulbe way of life. In Central Mali the Sahelian droughts of the 1970s and 1980s were followed by difficult years in the 1990s. The effects of this continuous stress are not the same for all the inhabitants of the region, which is explained by the different risk positions they occupy, related to social hierarchies and wealth. It appears that poorer pastoralists are the most deprived groups because they have few resources left and are being pushed to the margins of rural and urban societies where they depend on others. Their pastoral nomadism is changing into a peripatetic existence. However, the new identity this implies is still based on mobility, their pastoral background and on their identity as strangers.

Introduction

In the last few decades the Sahel has experienced regular periods of environmental stress due to recurring droughts and irregular rainfall combined with an expansion of agriculture. This paper considers the effects of this period of hardship on a group of semi-nomadic pastoralists of Fulbe in Central Mali.

Although this period has characteristics differentiating it from past times of hardship, stress is not a new phenomenon for the inhabitants of the Sahel. On the contrary, environmental stress is part of their lives and various strategies have been developed to cope with it (Bovin, Manger 1990, Bovin 2001, Spittler 1992). The 'experience of hardship is', especially in the Sahelian case, 'continuous with ordinary social life' (Hastrup 1993: 734). In this confrontation with environmental stress the disappearance of a certain group of pastoralists is considered part of the game (cf. Burnham 1999, Iliffe 1987). Often impoverished pastoralists continue a (semi-)nomadic lifestyle, but not as pastoralists *per se*. Their occupations may vary from the herding of animals to offering different services, and sometimes begging, i.e. they become peripatetic. 'Some peripatetics were originally pastoral nomads [...] but turned to a peripatetic way of life either because they lost their herds and pastures as an aftermath of war [...] or due to progressive impoverishment [...]'(Rao 1987: 21). 'As opposed to pastoral nomads and hunters and gatherers the ideal type of peripatetics obtains their food almost exclusively from and through other human populations and one important distinction between these different categories of nomads thus lies in the amount of control they exercise over food resources' (Rao 1987: 4). A few general characteristics of peripatetics are that they are a minority ethnic group and regarded as strangers; they are socially marginalised people; interaction between peripatetic people and their neighbours is characterised as a dependency chain with the peripatetic occupying the weaker end of this chain; they are endogamous; often they are ascribed magic powers; they have developed a certain specialisation; and they are a mobile people (Rao 1987, Bollig 1987, Berland 1992).

In this paper the change from a pastoral nomadic lifestyle to a peripatetic lifestyle as a consequence of environmental stress is analysed in the light of the continuity of life. The dynamics behind such a change can be best understood through individual stories and an analysis of the differences. Individual differences are related to a person's position in society (risk position, cf. Beck 1992), to his or her social, material and cultural capital, and to each individual's specific history. The reconstruction of individual pathways provides insight into how these processes evolve (cf. De Bruijn, Van Dijk 2001).

Environmental stress in Central Mali

The region with which this paper deals is part of the West African Sahel and is situated at the bend of the River Niger, south of the Gurma (see map). The region is ecologically divided into two sub-regions: the Bandiagara Plateau and the Hayre-Seeno area. The Plateau is densely populated in relation to the available cultivation area. It has always been a transhumance area for pastoralists from the Seeno who went over the Plateau to enter the Inner Delta of the Niger, but also served as a pasture area in the wet season. From the Gandamia mountains (Hayre) to the south is the Seeno, or sandy dunes that offer good pastures in the wet season. The water table is very deep and therefore the Seeno is not much frequented during the dry season. Today annual precipitation in this region is about 350 mm but rainfall is very irregular in time and space and is concentrated in 2-3 months of the year. The main crop is millet. Herds consist mainly of small ruminants and cattle, though over the last few decades there has been an increase in the number of camels kept. The two main ethnic groups are the Dogon (the cultivators) and the Fulbe (the herders). The Fulbe were politically dominant during the 19th century but in the course of the 20th century the power balance has shifted towards the Dogon.

Droughts are not new to the inhabitants of this region and the old people clearly remember the drought of 1914. They still talk of the slaves who escaped the droughts by moving to the West (the Gimmballa), the hunger food they had to eat, and the general starvation in the area. Droughts returned frequently during the first half of the 20th century until the 1950s when a wet period started that lasted until the 1960s. After this, the droughts began that are known today as the Sahelian droughts of the 1970s and 1980s. Put and de Vos (1999) have analysed the rainfall patterns over the past four decades. The pattern is one of extremely good rains to a very severe drought situation in the 1970s and 1980s and an upward trend in the 1990s. This improvement may already have been broken since the last couple of years have again been years of drought. In general the inhabitants of the area experience a short rainy season that starts late in the year and irregular rainfall at intervals during the rainy season. This change in their environment is perceived as a downward trend and runs parallel to changes in vegetation in the area (De Boer 2001, De Bruijn, Van Dijk 1995).

Recent trends in land use seem contradictory. Despite the desiccation of the environment, farmers are deciding to extend the areas cultivated as a result of innovations in cultivation technology whereby plough traction by camels makes it possible to work larger fields in a short period of time. The diminishing yields due to the climatic circumstances force people to cultivate larger fields to harvest sufficient millet (Maas 2001). Herders are now equally starting to work larger fields. They tend to be mainly the richer herdsmen who have decided to stay in the area and have started to breed camels. Wasteland is increasingly being turned into cropland leading to an ever decrease of available good pastures. Pastoralists are being forced to move to other areas because the areas where they used to settle during the dry season are no longer accessible. The pastoralists are considered as strangers, whereas the cultivators define themselves as the owners of the land and thus enjoy a position of power (De Bruijn, Van Dijk 2001).

The combination of a long period (30 years) of irregular and insufficient rainfall and the adaptive strategy of expansion of the cultivation area has led many herdsmen and cultivators to leave the area. Migration or mobility has been the main reaction to environmental stress.

Map: Central Mali

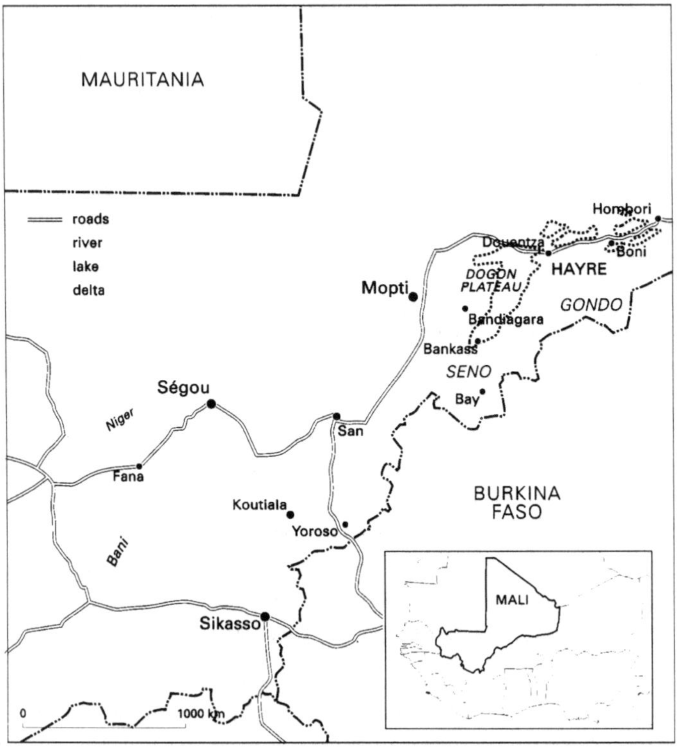

Stress migration

Migration as a result of drought or environmental stress is a historical phenomenon, and forms part of oral tradition in the region. It is difficult to estimate the importance of past and present migration because statistics are largely missing. Data from a Fulbe camp in the north of the area (near Boni) reveal that about 35-40 per cent of herders left their camps after the droughts of the 1980s due to impoverishment and a lack of good pasture and grazing for their animals (De Bruijn, Van Dijk 1995). For some, the lack of confidence in the future of the area was the main reason for moving to another region. Some stayed in the vicinity and tried their luck as salaried herdsmen near Duwari and Bandiagara while others went to the frontier area of Bay and further south. Many families left for Burkina Faso and others headed to the south of Mali and ended up in Côte d'Ivoire (Diallo 2001).

On a visit to the camp near Boni in 1997, it appeared that most of the people who had left the camp before 1992 had not returned. Only a few families had rejoined their kin, attracted by the improved weather conditions. Others had not returned and there were no news of many of those who had left. It is hard to trace moving families who disappear and start a new life elsewhere (see De Bruijn, Van Dijk 1999). It seems that the continuous environmental stress did not encourage them to return to the area, nor did it allow the rebuilding of their herds, which in general is assumed to be the main reason for herders to move to other areas after a drought. Did they join the rural proletariat? Did they become rich? How did their lives work out?[1]

Fulbe Doumanke on the plateau of Bandiagara

On the outskirts of the small town of Bandiagara two Fulbe families camped on fields owned by Dogon townspeople during the dry season. These families were not related but had set up a sort of camp together though they lived their own lives. It appeared that each family lived on their host's field and was responsible for bringing manure to the field with their hosts' or someone else's animals. Other families lived somewhat further from Bandiagara under similar circumstances, while more relatives lived in town. They had shared origins, all having come originally from Douma, a large and wealthy Fulbe cattle camp.

They lived off various 'jobs'. Two old ladies in town received charity from the Dogon, and another woman lived with her sons who took care of her. They herded Dogon cattle and took them to markets. Their wives sold the animals' milk in Bandiagara town. Most of the time, they said, it was difficult to survive because the milk did not bring in enough revenue. However with their income from the accompanying work of cattle to the markets, it appeared they were making a reasonable living. This family depended on the Dogon in difficult times and also for the care for their old people. The Dogon were willing to help because of the long relationship they had with the family: they served as a safety net for this specific Fulbe family.

All the sons of another family had left the Bandiagara area to try their luck elsewhere, except for one who was looking after his father and his family. Their income depended largely on the skills of the father, an Islamic diviner. This divination practice not only gave him an income but also ensured him a respected position in society. The herding of Dogon animals carries a certain risk,

[1] The discussion about the reasons why some people have to move and others do not cannot be included in this paper because of its limited length. This issue is discussed elsewhere, see De Bruijn 1999, 2000, De Bruijn *et al.* 1997. This paper is based on fieldwork done in 1997 by Mirjam de Bruijn and Han van Dijk.

as the story of another family reveals. The Dogon whose cattle they were looking after suddenly started to distrust them and withdrew all the animals from the family's care, leaving them with no means of earning a living.

Fulbe relations with the Dogon and local townspeople may best be characterised as exploitative from both sides. The relationships the Fulbe have built up with the Dogon depend on Dogon feelings of pity and are based on long-standing interethnic relations. The Dogon feel responsible for the Fulbe whose fathers and grandfathers experienced good relations with the same Dogon family. At the same time, the treatment of the herding families around Bandiagara indicates a relationship based on exploitation. The Dogon (who are also poor) use the Fulbe and pay them very little, even by local standards, but create a relationship in which they have power over the Fulbe herders because they are dependent on the crucial resource the Dogon offer the Pullo (pl. Fulbe): cattle. However this relationship of dependency only exists as long as the Pullo accepts it. The Fulbe always have the option of moving on and finding a better host.

There is an important religious aspect to the relationship between the Dogon and the Fulbe. The Dogon consider the Fulbe as good Muslims and learned men. The old diviner makes a living from this respect, and from the Dogon point of view it is their religious duty to help their poor Muslim brothers.

The Fulbe women create social relations by selling milk to gain a place in a 'hostile' world in which they are strangers. In town and in the villages they establish a network of relationships with the families to whom they sell their milk. If for whatever reason they have no milk they can go to the same families and ask for help, something those customers will not refuse. This network is extensive and important for the social sense of belonging of these Fulbe.

The Fulbe Doumanke are totally dependent for their survival on the goodwill of the Dogon and the townspeople. On the other hand, it could be reasoned that they have found a niche by providing services to the Dogon and to the townspeople, which in turn offers them a pertinent position in society. The relationship has an interdependent character.

All the separate families from this larger group of Doumanke live their own lives, but still feel connected. They regularly visit each other and maintain contacts. Although they all long to go back to Douma, it is unlikely to happen for several reasons. They simply cannot leave with their limited resources and possessions: they own very few animals. The other reason is ideologically: they cannot stay in Douma with rich families who will look down upon them as poor and inferior members of society. For the younger people, returning is simply not an option because they cannot go back to a place they hardly know. For them, Bandiagara and the Plateau is their world. Bandiagara town is attractive for the opportunities it offers them: trade, the mil market, etc.

In short, this group of impoverished herding families has indeed created a position for themselves, however marginal, near Bandiagara town. They can be considered as a group or even a community, though dispersed and loosely knit, with their mutual origins and shared social position on the Plateau.

Discussion

The persistent environmental stress in the Sahelian zone has resulted in the economic and social marginalisation of some pastoral nomadic groups, who have been forced to start a different nomadic life on the margins of society, as a peripatetic people.

The enduring environmental stress has forced some pastoralists (like the group discussed in this paper) to leave their 'original' camp and to leave the people with whom they shared a life before the droughts. Indeed it could be argued that their forced movement is a consequence of the pastoral ideology of a travelling culture with loose social bonds and a tradition of movement. Furthermore, these forced migrants accept the consequences of being poor and the feelings of shame it provokes: they maintain their dignity, and move. The decisions these forced migrants take are a logical consequence of the culture in which they live. The impoverished Fulbe seek opportunities in the urban economy as sedentary farmers, preferably in the domain of animal husbandry: trade, herding for others, etc. They have no other choice! These decisions may have been taken with the idea that they would return to the pastoral enterprise. It is clear, however, that returning is virtually impossible. They go through a contradictory development in which their dependency on natural resources decreases and their dependency on other non-pastoral people increases. In their new world they have specific relations with the other ethnic groups who, for instance, have become their patrons with regard to access to natural resources (cattle and land). Interethnic relations more than intra-ethnic relations form the social security relations. Social relations other than kin become of crucial importance to them. They no longer experience environmental stress directly through the loss of their animals or through the diminishing quality of pastures (they are not allowed to explore extensive pastures), but through the decisions of the Dogon. Some families have been forced to move on because they could not find cattle with the Dogon. The shift from being proud nomads controlling their own resources to being a peripatetic people dependent on their customers is complete. These people are indeed endogamous and do not recognise marriages with the Dogon or others. They relate to the other ethnic groups only through a dependency relationship. The Dogon and others regard them as having magic power, and they have become specialised in offering services related to animals. These are all characteristics of peripatetic people.

The shift from being nomad and pastoralist to being peripatetic influences the ideology of the people, though not as a rupture. The Doumanke near Bandiagara still keep to their specialisation as cattle keepers and are proud of it. They no longer control the resources but they control the skills. They are also ordering their life according to old ways of doing so: host-guest and kinship. They keep their mobility. In addition, their ideology may have shifted from livestock more to religion, which is regarded by their host as one of their strong points and which in the ideology of nobility may replace their pastoral side.

Nevertheless, the Fulbe near Bandiagara live in poverty. Their children die, they are ill, they have limited access to food for long periods of the year. Though child mortality and the amount of illness may be higher in this group of peripatetics, it is not a rupture with their former life. One of the continuities in their lives and the transformations they go through is the reality of fact. It cannot be denied that they have lost part of their autonomy. The people who now live around Bandiagara have accepted their situation and are trying to restructure their lives. The others, who it was not possible to talk to because they were no longer there, had fled the situation - it was reported that some had gone mad while others were trying their luck in the south, where they may or may not succeed.

A society's confrontation with environmental stress has created a new social group that is developing a peripatetic lifestyle. More groups will become involved in this process since the environmental stress is not expected to decrease.[2] For this specific group any possible return to a pastoral nomadic life appears unlikely. Pastoral groups in other areas in Mali and the Sahel share their plight. They have had to develop a new identity in which relations with other ethnic groups occupy a prominent place and force them to place a strong claim on their identity as strangers. These poor and marginalised people have carved out a new existence with their own rules and norms to allow themselves to live the best life possible in the circumstances they find themselves in.

References

Beck, Ulrich, 1992: *Risk Society, Towards a New Modernity*, Sage, London.

Berland, Joseph C. 1992: Territorial Activities among Peripatetic Peoples in Pakistan, in: Michael Casimir and Aparno Rao (eds) *Mobility and Territoriality, Social and Spatial Boundaries among Foragers, Fishers, Pastoralists and Peripatetics*, Berg, New York/Oxford, pp. 375-397.

Bollig, Michael, 1987: Ethnic relations and Spatial Mobility in Africa: A Review of the Peripatetic niche, in: Aparna rao (ed) *The Other Nomads, Peripatetic minorities in cross-Cultural Perspective*, Bohlau Verlag, Koln Wien, pp. 179-229.

Bovin, Mette, 2001: *Nomads who Cultivate Beauty*, Nordiska Afrika Institutet, Uppsala.

[2] Climate models predict further desiccation of this area.

Bovin, Mette; Leif Manger (eds), 1990: *Adaptive Strategies in African Arid Lands*, Proceedings from a Seminar at the Scandinavian Institute of African Studies, Uppsala Sweden, April 1989, Scandinavian Institute of African studies, Uppsala.

Burnham, Philip, 1999: Pastoralism under Pressure? – Understanding Social Change in Fulbe Society, in: Victor Azarya, A. Breedveld, M. de Bruijn, H. van Dijk (eds*) Pastoralists under Pressure? Fulbe Societies Confronting Change in West Africa*, Brill, Leiden, pp. 269-285.

De Boer, Yvonne 2001: On the Road to Timbouctou, Climatic, Ecological and Human Influences on the Vegetation of Semi-Arid Mali, ICCD/ASC Student Research Report.

De Bruijn, Mirjam, 1999: The Pastoral Poor: Hazard, Crisis and Insecurity in Fulbe Society in Central Mali, in: Victor Azarya, A. Breedveld, M. de Bruijn, H. van Dijk (eds) *Pastoralists under Pressure? Fulbe Societies Confronting Change in West Africa*, Brill, Leiden, pp. 285-312.

De Bruijn, Mirjam, 2000: Poverty and Mobility in Arid Lands: The Case of Sahelian Pastoralists, in: Wil Pansters *et al.* (eds), *Rethinking Poverty, Comparative Perspectives from Below*, Van Gorcum, Assen, pp. 136-149.

De Bruijn, Mirjam, Walter Van Beek, Han Van Dijk, 1997: 'Antagonimse et solidarité: Les relations entre Peuls et Dogons du Mali central', in: Mirjam De Bruijn & Han Van Dijk (éds), *Peuls et Mandingues: Dialectique des constructions identitaires*, Paris Karthala, pp. 243-265.

De Bruijn, Mirjam, Han van Dijk 1995: *Arid Ways, Cultural Understandings of Insecurity in Fulbe Society in Central Mali*, Amsterdam, Thela.

De Bruijn, Mirjam, Han van Dijk,1999: Fulbe Mobility: Migration and Travel into Mande, *Mande Studies* 1, pp. 41-62.

De Bruijn, Mirjam, Han van Dijk, 2001: Moving People: Pathways in the Hayre-Seeno Area, Central Mali, ASC/ICCD Working paper.

Diallo, Youssouf, 2001: Processes and Types of Pastoral Migration in Northern Côte d'Ivoire, *African Dynamics*, vol 1, (Mirjam de Bruijn, Rijk van Dijk, Dick Foeken (eds), *Mobile Africa, Changing patterns of Movement in Africa and Beyond*), Leiden, Brill, pp. 153-169.

Maas Pieter J.B. 2000: *'L'influence des changements climatologiques sur l'exploitation du mil à Wayre, un village Dogon,* Mali central', ASC/ICCD Working paper.

Hastrup, Kirsten, 1993: Hunger and the Hardness of Facts, *Man (N.S.)*, 28, pp. 727-739.

Iliffe, John, 1987: *The African Poor: A History*, Cambridge University Press, Cambridge.

Put, Marcel; S. de Vos 1999: Klimaatonderzoek in West Afrika, *Rooilijn*, AGIDS & AME, Amsterdam.

Rao, Aparno, 1987: The Concept of Peripatetics: An Introduction, in: Aparno Rao (ed), *The Other Nomads, Peripatetic Minorities in Cross-Cultural Perspective*, Bohlau Verlag, Koln, Wien, pp. 1-35.

Spittler, Gerd, 1992: *Les Touaregs face aux sécheresses et aux famines, les Kel Ewey de l'Air (Niger)*, Karthala, Paris.

On the Authors

Myron J. Aronoff

Professor of Political Science and Anthropology at Rutgers University where he has taught for 25 years. He received his Ph.D. in Political Science from U.C.L.A. and his Ph.D. in Social Anthropology from Manchester University. He held research appointments at Manchester University for four years, taught at Tel Aviv University for eight years, was twice a fellow in residence at the Netherlands Institute for Advanced Studies, and was a visiting professor at the University of Cape Town. He has published extensively on various aspects of Israeli society, culture, and politics and in the field of political anthropology – especially on the relationship between culture and politics. He is a former associate editor of *Transaction SOCIETY* and editor of *Political Anthropology*. Dr. Aronoff is a past president of the Association for Political and Legal Anthropology and was the founding president of the Association for Israel Studies in which he serves on the Board of Directors. He has been vice president of the International Union of Anthropological and Ethnological Sciences since 1993.

Brigitta Benzing

teaches Ethnology (Cultural/Social Anthropology) at the University of Göttingen since 1981. She studied Ethnology, African and Semitic Languages at Mainz University and obtained her Ph.D. in 1969, her thesis had the topic "The History and Political System of the Dagomba in Northern Ghana". After several years as assistant, later assistant professor at the same university, she lectured at the universities of Zürich, Marburg, Tübingen and Berlin. Since her appointment as full-time professor at Göttingen University, she teaches general ethnology (theories, methods) and regional ethnology (Islamic societies of West- and Central-Asia).
In the years 1985 – 87 and 1993 – 96, she was on leave from Göttingen University to work as visiting professor at Addis Ababa University, where she helped set up the course of study in social anthropology and taught in this programme.

Balázs Borsos

was born in Budapest in 1961
Ethnographer, Geologist, Film Director
Education: 1980-1988 ELTE University of Budapest, geologist 1987, ethnographer 1988, 1993-1996 Hungarian Academy of Drama and Film, Director for non-fiction films and multimedia, 1996; 1994 Ph.D. in Ethnography.

Grants: 1998-2000 Bolyai Scholarship, Hungary; 2000-2001 Humboldt Scholarship, University of Bonn.
Employment: Since 1987 at the Institute of Ethnography, Budapest, since 1999 senior research fellow, since 2002 deputy director, since 1993 at the University of Miskolc, Department of Cultural and Visual Anthropology (part time associate professor since 1998)
Fieldwork: 1984-1985 Tanzania, Kenya, Uganda, Rwanda, Burundi, Zaire; 1986 Canada, USA; 1990-1991 SU, Ukraine;
Some of his publications: Books: Matatuháton Afrikában. (Riding on Matatu in Africa., with János Móga, 1998) Szafari a pále, pále (Safari a pale, pale. 1998) Három folyó között. (Among Three Rivers. 2000) Vadészakról Vadnyugatra. (From Wild North to Wild West. 2000);
50 articles.
Films: Fel és le az Egyenlítõn (Up and Down along the Equator. 1996). A Nap fiainak földjén 1-2. (Land of the Sun's Sons. 1996-97)

Mirjam de Bruijn
Senior researcher at the African Studies Centre in Leiden. Her research concentrates largely on the Sahelian countries in Africa. She has done fieldwork in Mali, Niger, and Cameroon and started fieldwork in Chad in 2002. Her main interest is in how people manage to live in insecure environments (drought, war, ecological deterioration). So far, most fieldwork was conducted among and with pastoral people. A major research theme has been climate change and changes in people's livelihoods. She has written an ethnography on Fulbe pastoralists in Central Mali (Arid Ways, 1995, Amsterdam: Rozenberg). She has published articles in journals like Africa, Cahier d'études africaines, History in Africa, Development and Change and African Affairs. She is co-editor of several books like:
Peuls et Mandigues (1997, Paris: Karthala), Pastoralists under Pressure (1999, Leiden: Brill), and she is series editor of the journal 'African Dynamics'.

Heidi Dumreicher
studied Linguistics, Eastern European History, Sinology, History of Art and Sports at the University of Vienna and the Sorbonne in Paris. Dr. phil. 1968.
Project lead
Research grants:
Times of the city, MA18, Vienna 2000
7 Theses on Town and City Quality, 1999/2000
Von der Information zum Wissen (From information to knowledge), Ministry of Science and Art, Vienna, 2000/01/02
Symphonie einer Großstadt (Symphony of a big town), Vienna. 2001

Sustainability in Inner China, Grant from University of Zheng Zhou and Province of Henan, together with Lu Hongyi, 2000/2001

Publications

Editor of the quarterly journal Oikodrom Stadtpläne since 1994

Im Anfang war der Blick, Animation film in co-operation with Bady Minck. (In the beginning was the eye) 1998 – 2005

Urban Ethnic Encounters – Routledge Research in Population and Migration (A. Erdentug, F. Colombijn, editors) 2002

Marina Fischer-Kowalski

Ph.D. in Sociology, professor of Social Ecology at the University of Vienna. She is director of the Vienna base of the Institute for Interdisciplinary Studies of Austrian Universities (IFF), heading the Department of Social Ecology. She is, inter alia, member of the steering committee of the International Human Dimensions Program - Industrial Transformation (IHDP-IT) of the International Society for Industrial Ecology (ISIE) and member of board of the Research Committee "Environment and Society" of the International Sociological Association. She was chairperson of Greenpeace Austria and International Greenpeace Liaison person, 1994 – 1999. She published several books on social and environmental issues, and was co-author to the World Resources Institute publication "The Weight of Nations: Material Outflows from Industrial Economies" in 2000. Website: http://www.iff.ac.at/socec

Andrew S. Goudie

Professor of Geography in the University of Oxford and a former Pro-Vice-Chancellor. He is currently Vice-President of the International Association of Geomorphologists. He has worked extensively with archaeologists in India, Pakistan and Africa and has a major interest in environmental change. He has recently edited the Encyclopedia of Global Change (Oxford University Press, New York, 2002).

Nikolaos D. Hasanagas

was born in 1974 in Thessaloniki. He has obtained his M. Eng. eq. in Forest and Environmental Sciences at the Aristotle University of Thessaloniki. He is carrying out a Ph.D. thesis as well as M.A. studies in Social Sciences (Sociology, Political Science and Ethnology) since1998 at the University of Goettingen. Simultaneously, he is engaged in applied and basic research and teaching assistantship. He has published research results in various international and German scientific journals. His research interests are: EU environmental policy and politics, environmental sociology and anthropology, sustainable development, sociology of science, comparative studies (North America – Europe), power theory and network analysis. He is member of the Interdisciplinary Environmental Association (Massachussetts) as Environmental Policy Consultant, and of the Geotechnical Chamber of Greece. He has also worked in NGOs as a project manager and policy consultant regarding sustainable development, social and environmental issues.

Bernd Herrmann

Professional Preparation

Free University Berlin Diploma in Biology 1970, Free University Berlin Ph.D. in Biology (Physical Anthropology) 1973, Free University Berlin Habilitation for Anthropology, 1975

Present Appointments

Professor, Head of the Department of Anthropology, University of Goettingen.

Since 1978 Member of the Centre of Sustainable Development and the Centre of Biodiversity, Research and Ecology, University of Goettingen.

Founder and Speaker of the Task Group on Environmental History at the University of Goettingen and member of the Board of the Graduate School on Evaluating Sustainable Development.

Guest professorships in Halle, Florence, London, Vienna.

Publications

Some 160 papers and 8 books

Editor of Naturwissenschaften, Anthropologischer Anzeiger;

Co-Editor of two book series;

Board Member of: Human Biology, International Journal of Legal Medicine; Ancient Biomolecules.

Anke Höltermann

Ph.D. student at the Institute of Forest Economics and Management at the University of Freiburg. She mainly worked about sustainability in forestry, intergenerational equity and ecosystem management. Her thesis „Verantwortung für zukünftige Generationen in der Forstwirtschaft - Zur ethischen Rechtfertigung verschiedener Konzepte von forstlicher Nachhaltigkeit“ is available from the Institute of Forest Economics and Management at the University of Freiburg.

Huang Fengxiang

Vice President of the China Urban Anthropology Association

Rivke Jaffe

born in the United States, later moved to the Netherlands, where she completed her Master's degree in Environment and Development at Leiden University with a research project in Kingston, Jamaica, on Solid Waste Management. She is currently working as a Ph.D. candidate at Leiden University's CNWS Institute, with research on culture, nature and environment in Jamaica and Curaçaõ.

Bettina Kolb

Social scientist, born in Vienna1965, obtained her Ph.D. from the University of Vienna.

Researches

Sociology of health, evaluation of health promoting projects, qualitative methodology: Foto - interview , hermeneutic studies

Project Management WHO – Project: "Vienna Network of Health Promoting Schools"

Scientific projects:

„From Information to Knowledge" – A contribution to the development of a theory of sustainability, sponsored by the Department of Science, Cultural Landscapes, 2001-2002 (bmbwk/Kulturlandschaftsforschung)

Publications

Bettina Kolb, Karl Krajic, Jürgen M. Pelikan. Forschungsperspektiven zum 'Gesundheitsfördernden Krankenhaus', in: Hubert Lobnig, Jürgen M. Pelikan (Hg.) Gesundheitsförderung in Settings: Gemeinde, Betrieb, Schule, Krankenhaus. Wien 1996

Kolb, Bettina. „Sagen Sie „klick". Zum partizipativen Charakter der Fotobefragung", in: Oikodrom Stadtplaene 14, 1/98: Probehandeln, teilnehmen, mitgestalten – Partzipation 1.

Kolb, Bettina, Heidi Dumreicher. Multi- or Polycultural Cities – 7 Thesis on the Quality of Town, in: Tagungsband Inter-Congress, Metropolitan Ethnic Cultures: Maintenance and Interaction. Beijing 2000: 48; 180.

Werner Krauss

Dr. phil., is research fellow at the Institute of Social Anthropology, University of Hamburg. Main areas of interest are: Political ecology, anthropology of coastal landscapes, science- and gender studies and the anthropology of sports. Fieldwork on environmental conflicts in Portugal and currently in Northern Germany/Wadden Sea (interdisciplinary VW research project „Nature in Conflict: Nature Conservation, Nature Concepts and Coastal Images", www.pronik.de).

Recent publications include:

„Hängt die Grünen!" Umweltkonflikte, nachhaltige Entwicklung und ökologischer Diskurs. Berlin 2001: Reimer

Eine glückliche Liebe. Heteronormativität und Feldforschung, in: kea, 2001, Zeitschrift für Kulturwissenschaften 14

Der konstruierte Mann oder: Wie männlich ist die (deutsche) Ethnologie?, in: Schlehe, Judith (ed.) Interkulturelle Geschlechterforschung 2001

Leendert P. Louwe Kooijmans
studied Physical Geography (Utrecht) and Prehistory (Leiden). He was curator in the National Museum of Antiquities in Leiden from 1966 – 1982, when he was appointed to the Chair of Prehistory, Leiden University. He is founder and dean of the Faculty of Archaeology at Leiden since 1997. In his research he combines his interests in environment and human society. It concentrates on the Neolithic of the Lower Rhine Basin and on wetland archaeology in the Rhine/Meuse delta, where he was currently digging Late Mesolithic sites down to 10 m below sea level.

Damaris Lüthi
did her postgraduate studies at the London School of Economics and at the University of Berne, from where she has a Ph.D. in Social Anthropology. Her thesis with the title "Washing off Sin. Cleanliness in Kottar, South India" focuses on the relationship between everyday hygiene and so-called ritual concepts of im/purity and their relevance for the Indian caste system. It was based on fieldwork in a South Indian town neighbourhood for 16 months in 1995-96. After a few years of teaching Anthropology at the University of Berne, she is presently (2001-03) conducting research on social change among Sri Lankan Tamil refugees in Switzerland, supported by the Swiss National Science Foundation. She is also an ethnographic filmmaker (*1000° Celsius. Working in the Crematory*, 1993; *Silk, Muthappar and VHS*, 1998).

John R. McNeill
studied at Swarthmore College and Duke University, where he completed a Ph.D. in 1981. Since 1985 he has taught at Georgetown University's School of Foreign Service, where he has been Professor of History since 1993. His research interests lie in the environmental history of the Mediterranean world, the tropical Atlantic world, and Pacific islands. His books are *The Atlantic Empires of France and Spain, 1700-1765* (Chapel Hill: University of North Carolina Press 1985); *Atlantic American Societies from Columbus through Abolition* (co-edited, London: Routledge 1992); *The Mountains of the Mediterranean World* (New York: Cambridge University Press); *The Environmental History of the Pacific World* (edited London: Variorum 2001); and *Something New Under the Sun: An Environmental History of the Twentieth-century World* (New York: Norton 2000). He is currently working on a history of yellow fever.

Mou Benli
Advisor, China Urban Anthropology Association

Salomón Nahmad
Social Anthropologist .
Education
Universidad Nacional Autónoma de México: Ph.D 1971 in Ethnology and Social Anthropology.

Escuela Nacional de Antropología e Historia: M.A. 1963 in Ethnology. Universidad Nacional Autónoma de México: B.A. 1957 in Social Work.

Work Experience

University of Arizona Fulbrigh Visiting Professor 1985. Texas Technical University Fulbrigh Visiting Professor 1985. CECODES (Centro de Ecodesarrollo): Project Head (1984). INI (Instituto Nacional Indigenista): General Director (1982-83). Secretaria de Educacion Publica Direccion General de Educación Indigena (1978-1982). Centro de Investigaciones y Estudios Superiores en Antropologia. CIESAS: Research and Director of Projects (1987). Research of the Sistema Nacional de Investigadores (1987-1999). Consultant of the World Bank 1996-99. Consultant of BID for the project FONDO INDIGENA IBEROAMERICANO (1991).

Research Experience

Completed the following research projects: - Traditional Technology and its Effects on Ecology.- Centro de Ecodesarrollo. Mexico 1984 - 1985. Handicrafts from the Cora and Huichol Region. Consejo Nacional de Turismo. México 1969. Socio-economic situation of Mixtecos, Nahuas and Tlapaneco-Indians. INI. Mexico 1961-1969. Study of a Tzeltal Community in Zaragoza de la Montana, Chis. INI. Mexico 1962. Ethnological Study of an Otomi Community in Zitacuaro, Mich. INI. Mexico 1963. Regional Study of Mixe Indians in Oaxaca, INI. Mexico 1963.

Publications

Published books include seven titles as author, coauthor and editor. Author of 14 articles in different scientific journals as well as 7 technical reports.

Peter J.M. Nas

Associate Professor at the Department of Cultural Anthropology, Leiden University. He is specialized in urban and applied anthropology and has conducted extensive research in Indonesia, publishing on a wide variety of subjects including sustainable urban development, the Indonesian city and urban symbolism. He is secretary-general of the International Union of Anthropological and Ethnological Sciences (IUAES).

Keiichi Omoto

Prof. Dr., born in Tokyo in 1933. 1978 – 1993: Professor at the University of Tokyo. 1994 – 1999: Professor of the International Research Center for Japanese Studies, Kyoto. 1999 – Present: Professor of St. Andrew's University, Osaka. Member-at-Large of IUAES. President of IUAES Inter-Congress 2002 (Tokyo). Research interests: Molecular Anthropology, Humans in the Modern Civilization, Human Rights of Indigenous Peoples.

Lajos Rácz

Ph.D., environmental historian, Szeged University, Juhász Gyula College Historical Department, assistant professor; regional representative of the European Society for Environmental History

Main publications

Climate History of Hungary Since 16th Century: Past, Present and Future. Discussion Papers, Pécs 1999. 160 p.

Variations of climate in Hungary (1540-1779), in: B. Frenzel, C. Pfister (eds.): European climate reconstructed from documentary data: Methods and results, Stuttgart 1992: 82-93.

The Climate of Hungary during the Maunder Minimum Period, in: B. Frenzel, C. Pfister (eds.): Climatic Trends and Anomalies in Europe 1675-1715, Stuttgart 1994: 95-108.

Viatcheslav Roudnev

Senior Research Fellow in the Institute of Ethnology and Anthropology, Russian Academy of Sciences, and Co-chair of the Commission on Indigenous Knowledge and Sustainable Development of the International Union of Anthropological and Ethnological Sciences (IUAES).

Graduation

Moscow State University (1980); Institute of Ethnography of the USSR Academy of Sciences, Ph.D. (1986); Senior Visitor at Oxford University (1990).

Author of numerous articles, participant in International Conferences in Europe and America.

Fieldwork

North and Central Russia, Volga area, and the Caucasus.

Research interests

Theory of anthropology, ethnoscience, cognitive anthropology, ethnometeorology, folk experience in life-support activity and problems of sustainability.

Heinz Schandl

PhD in Sociology from the University of Vienna, since 1994 employed at the Institute for Interdisciplinary Studies of Austrian Universities, Department of Social Ecology, Lecturer for Environmental Sociology. Head of and contributor to several interdisciplinary research projects dealing with society's natural relations both with an historical or a policy oriented focus, among others: 'Southeast Asia in Transition' funded by the EU commission, and a historical case study on integrated environmental accounting for the UK funded by the Breuninger Stiftung and the Austrian Ministry of Science. Active in the fields of Environmental Accounting, Social Theory and the Environment and Ecological Economics.

Éva Sebestyén

born in Budapest 1950, degree in Spanish and English Studies in 1975 and Ethnography 1978 at Eötvös Loránd University in Budapest. Postgraduate dissertations defended in Ethnology in1991 (Doctor Univ.) and in 1995 (PhD.). In 1997: Post-doctorate grant with Professor Jan Vansina at the University of Wisconsin (Madison), between 1979 and 1985: Lecturer at the Portuguese Studies Department, 1986 – 89: Visiting lecturer at Agostinho Neto University in Luanda, An-

gola. 1989 – 2000: Teaching Anthropology at different Hungarian Universities. 2000 –2001: Visiting lecturer of Anthropology at the State University of Vale de Acaraú (Ceará State, Brazil). At present lecturer at the African Studies Program at Eötvös Loránd University in Budapest.
Research
1. Ambundu village chiefs' historical writings (18.-20. centuries). 2. An archivistic research about László Magyar, a Hungarian explorer in Angola 1848 – 1864. My Brazilian studies deal with a Russian archivistical material of H.H. Manizer's research among Botokuds in 1915. My recent Brazilian research is about the cure and use of medical plants in Afro-Brazilian cults.

Soheila Shahshahani
Ph.D. from the New School for Social Research, New York, is assistant professor of Anthropology at Shahid Beheshti University in Tehran. She is editor of the Journal of Anthropology in Persian. Her thesis focused on the Mamassani pastoral nomads of Iran, but ever since, joining the IUAES Urban Commission, she has turned her attention toward urban studies. Traditional urban spaces, public and private, women's issues, material culture (in particular clothing) have been some of her research topics. She has published The Four Seasons of the Sun (1987), A Pictorial History of Iranian Headdresses (1995), and A Bibliography of Iranian Women in Social Sciences, Humanities and Arts (1995), in Persian. She has been publishing her articles in English since 1984. "History of Anthropology in Iran" (1986) marks her interest in bringing Iranian Anthropology into the international arena, her publications in Persian show her attempts at introducing and establishing more and more the field of anthropology in Iran.

Shen Lin
Member of the China Anthropology Association

Rolf Peter Sieferle
born 1949 in Stuttgart, studied History, Political Science and Sociology in Heidelberg and Konstanz. His main fields of research are environmental history, history of ideas and world history. Since 2000 he is Professor of History at the University of St. Gallen, Switzerland.

Simron Jit Singh
currently living and working in Vienna as a Research Fellow with the Institute for Interdisciplinary Studies of Austrian Universities, Department of Social Ecology. His main scientific interests are: Empirical research on the patterns of society – nature interactions among non-industrialised and subsistence communities; understanding co-evolution of societal and natural systems; historical and current transitions among subsistence societies; energy and labour; environmental indicators; material and energy flow analysis; colonial history and world systems theory. He has worked extensively among the Van Gujjars, a forest dwelling nomadic ethnic group

of the north western Himalayas. Since early 1999, following a grant from the Government of India, he has been conducting extensive fieldwork among the Nicobarese of the Nicobar Islands. In September 2000, he was awarded an International Fellowship from the Austrian Ministry of Education, Science and Culture, and more recently, an IHDP-START Visiting Fellowship for his study in the context of global change research.

Gerd Spittler

born 1939 in Donaueschingen. Studies of Anthropology, Sociology and Economics in Heidelberg, Hamburg, Bordeaux, Basel, and Freiburg. Dr. phil. 1966, Habilitation 1978 at Freiburg University, 1980 – 1988 Professor of Sociology at Freiburg University, since 1988 Chairholder of Social Anthropology at Bayreuth University, 1990 - 1999 Director of the Graduate Programme (Graduiertenkolleg): "Interkulturelle Beziehungen in Afrika" (Intercultural Relations in Africa), since 2000 Director of the SFB/FK 560 (Humanities Collaborative Research Centre), both at Bayreuth University, 1999/2000: Fellow of the "Wissenschaftskolleg zu Berlin" (Institute for Advanced Studies). Many years of research in West Africa among Hausa und Tuareg about peasants and politics, drought and famines, the life of camelherdsmen and goatherdswomen, material culture and consumption. Publications include: "Verwaltung in einem afrikanischen Bauernstaat. Das koloniale Französisch-Westafrika 1919-1939" (Administration in an African Peasant State. Colonial French Westafrica between 1919-1939), Stuttgart 1981; "Les Touaregs face aux sécheresses et aux famines" (The Tuareg facing droughts and famines), Paris 1993; "Arbeit in Afrika" (Work in Africa), Hamburg 1996 (edited together with Kurt Beck); „Hirtenarbeit. Die Welt der Kamelhirten und Ziegenhirtinnen von Timia" (The Work of Herdsmen – The World of Camelherdsmen and Goatherdswomen of Timia), Köln 1998; "Work", in: The International Encyclopaedia of the Social and Behavioral Sciences, 2001.

Peter-M. Steinsiek

Department of Historical Anthropology and Human Ecology,
Institute for Zoology and Anthropology, University of Goettingen

Professional Preparation

University of Goettingen, Confederate Technological University of Zurich:
Forestry Diploma, 1985
University of Goettingen: Doctor of Forestry, 1999

Present Appointments

Researcher at the Environmental History Unit, University of Goettingen, since 2000.

Society Affiliations

European Society for Environmental History, Working Group for Applied Historical Geography within the Association of Genetic Settlement Research in Central Europe, German Dendrological Society.
Several Publications

Bernhard Streck
born 1945, studies in Ethnology, Sociology, Psychology and Anthropology at the universities of Bale and Frankfurt a.M., 1974 doctorate, 1992 habilitation, fieldworks in East and North-East-Africa, lecturerships for Cultural and Social Anthropology at the Universities of Giessen, Berlin, Mainz and Heidelberg, since 1994 director of the Institut für Ethnologie der Universität Leipzig.
Main research interests: History of anthropology, gypsiology, Sudan ethnography
Recent publications:
Translation and Ethnography (with Tullio Maranhao), in print
Wörterbuch der Ethnologie 2000
Ethnologie und Nationalsozialismus 2000
Fröhliche Wissenschaft Ethnologie 1997
Die Halab 1996

Wang Wei
University of Kagawa
Takamarsu – shi, Japan

Verena Winiwarter
Ph.D. in Environmental History at the University of Vienna after training in History and Chemistry. She currently holds a postdoctoral fellowship in Environmental History awarded by the Austrian Science Fund within the "Hertha Firnberg Program for Women" at the Institute for Anthropology, University of Vienna. Currently she is President of the European Society for Environmental History.

Kai W. Wirtz
born 1967. Studies in Physics and Theology at the Universities of Mainz and Pisa. Diploma thesis in Hydrodynamics and Ecosystem Modelling at the Institute for Chemistry and Biology of the Marine Environment (ICBM), University of Oldenburg, in 1993. In 1994 he worked with the Potsdam Institute of Climate Impact Research on ecosystem modelling. From 1995 to 1997 he developed new modelling techniques coping with adaptation phenomena in biosystems as scientific associate at the Center for Environmental Systems Research, University of Kassel. There, Kai Wirtz received his Ph.D. in 1998. A special focus of this work was laid on plant ecophysiol-

ogy and forest dynamics. Till 1999 he was a member of the interdisciplinary synthesis group "Ecosystem Research Waddensea" at the Terramare e.V., Wilhelmshaven, developing qualitative evaluation methods. From 1999 he has been a scientific associate at the ICBM, WG Mathematical Modelling, working on microbial adaptation, and the integrated assessment of marine and near-shore biogeochemistry. In doing so, he occupies a central position within the research group "Biogeochemistry of the Wadden Sea" funded by the Deutsche Forschungsgemeinschaft. Since 2001 he is developing mathematical models of human-biosphere interactions in early human societies, being a member of the transdisciplinary "Mappae Mundi" project led by H.J.M. de Vries and J. Goudsblom. Publications cover a wide range.

William I. Woods

Professor in the Department of Geography and Director of the Office of Contract Archaeology at Southern Illinois University Edwardsville. All three of his degrees are from the University of Wisconsin-Milwaukee. Since 1970 he has conducted field investigations in the Eastern United States, Latin America, and Europe and is the author or co-author of over 55 publications. His research interests focus on prehistoric settlement-subsistence systems, soils and sediments, and paleo-landscapes.